THE RIVERKEEPER'S GUIDE TO THE

Chattahoochee

THE RIVERKEEPER'S GUIDE TO THE

Chattahoochee River

FROM ITS ORIGIN AT CHATTAHOOCHEE GAP TO APALACHICOLA BAY

Fred Brown and Sherri M. L. Smith
with Richard Stenger

Illustrations By Garry Pound
Book Design By Vicki L. Rice

With technical support from Dick Rice and Meredith Anton

Published By CI Publishing, Atlanta

Funding Provided By Georgia Power Foundation
Graphics Funding Provided By The W. C. Bradley Company

CI Publishing
1401 Peachtree Street
Suite 100
Atlanta, Georgia 30309

Established in 1994, the Upper Chattahoochee Riverkeeper is a nonprofit environmental advocacy organization dedicated solely to protecting the Chattahoochee River, its tributaries and watershed.
For more information: Upper Chattahoochee Riverkeeper, 1900 Emery Street, Suite 450, Atlanta, Georgia 30318; 404/352-9828.

Cover photograph by Joe and Monica Cook
Riverkeeper Logo Design by Donahue Studios, Atlanta, Georgia

Every effort has been made to ensure the accuracy of information throughout this book. Bear in mind, however, that prices, schedules and routes are constantly changing. Readers should always verify information before making final plans.

This material is provided for information only and no recommendation or endorsement of the experience is implied. Neither CI Publishing, The Upper Chattahoochee Riverkeeper nor the writers of the material are responsible for the actions of readers taken with regard to the material presented here.

ISBN 1-58072-000-5

Manufactured in the United States of America

Second printing

DEDICATION

I n 1971, a small group of self-designated "river rats" took on the challenge of fighting a proposed sewer line which was to be blasted into the rock face of the Palisades cliffs, just a few feet above the surface of the Chattahoochee. Convinced that the river was a national treasure worth saving, these citizens demanded that the scenic integrity and water quality of the river be protected. Effectively using the media and gaining the attention of local politicians, the citizens won. The sewer line was moved, and the newly-formed group, "Friends of the River," became an influential force in charting the future of the Chattahoochee. At the State Capitol, they lobbied for a law to control growth along the river corridor, ultimately succeeding in the passage of the Metro River Protection Act, which regulates development along a 48-mile stretch of the Chattahoochee from Buford Dam to Peachtree Creek in Atlanta. In 1978, members of Friends of the River stood in the Rose Garden at the White House as President Jimmy Carter signed legislation creating the Chattahoochee River National Recreation Area.

An aggressive advocate of the Chattahoochee throughout the 1970s, Friends had faded into the river mists by the early 1980s as its leaders moved on to other issues. Much of the work of the Upper Chattahoochee Riverkeeper is possible because of the efforts of these early river advocates to preserve a national treasure.

For their foresight, courage and passion, this book is dedicated to these Friends of the River.

Roger Buerki, Jim Morrison, Lovell Greathouse, Liz Gilliam, Jane Yarn, Claude Terry, Lee Roach and Natalie, Roy Wood, Bob Milledge, Joe Nicholson, Henry Howell, Jody Smith, Jerry Hightower, Alistair Black, Marcia Bansley, Barbara Blum, Kay McKenzie, Bob Humphries, Bob Kerr, Ann Johnson, Chatty Wight, David Eldridge, Schild Grant, Furman Smith, Jr., Louise Franklin, Bob Walling, Al Burruss, John Pruitt, Ed Lynch, Bill Mankin, Alan Toney, Holcomb Green, Dave Wiltsee, Charlie Schreeder, Bob Schwind, Jo Jones, Bill Kroeck, Jamie Mackay, Elliott Levitas, Andy Young, Jack Spalding, Holly Miller, Glen Davis, Howard and Eve Hoffman, Dolph and Judy Orthwein, Nan and Britt Pendergrast, Bobby Rowan, Jimmy Carter, Wyche Fowler, George Warren, Pierre Howard, Sam Nunn, Jim Cone, Paul Coverdell, Dan Sweat, Lucy Smethurst, Alice McDonough, Linda Billingsley, Virginia Harbin, Rachel Frantz, George Busbee, Sam Rawls, Laura Mylrea, David Dillon, Preston Stevens, Jack Stout, Reinald Dersch, Merle Lefkoff, Jeff Nesmith, Carlton Neville, Richard Rudman and Briarcliff High School Ecology Club, John Hoyle, Carol Ruckdeschel, Betty Terry, Lou Regenstein, Tom Offenberger, Holly Miller, Glen Davis, Larry Patrick.

TABLE OF CONTENTS

ACKNOWLEDGEMENTS

Books like *The Riverkeeper's Guide to the Chattahoochee* are expensive to produce and the return on investment, if there is one, is small and spread over seven to ten years. Publishers tend to shy away from a big detailed guide like this. It contains a massive amount of detail and must be updated frequently, which in itself is an expensive process.

I have been involved with two guides of this type, this one and *The Georgia Conservancy's Guide to the North Georgia Mountains* published in 1991. Over the years the Conservancy book found a wide audience and was generally acknowledged as the standard guide to the mountains. We have similar aspirations for this *Riverkeeper's Guide to the Chattahoochee*—we hope it will become to the Chattahoochee Valley what the Conservancy's guide was to the North Georgia Mountains.

Georgia Power Company provided significant financial support for the Mountain Guide and provided the entire funding for the editorial development and production of this book. Georgia Power asked for and expected no editorial say so in the development of the books even though the editorial views may differ from its company policies. It realizes no profit from the sale of books. Profits go to the environmental organizations involved, in this case the Upper Chattahoochee Riverkeeper. Georgia Power has been consistently generous in providing support for the promotion and distribution of the book. In the coming years many thousands of people will have an opportunity to learn about the Chattahoochee River, to understand and enjoy its treasures and help protect it because of the vision and generosity of Georgia Power Company. It is corporate involvement with the arts, the nonprofit sector and the community at large at its highest level, and CI Publishing and Upper Chattahoochee Riverkeeper express a sincere thank you to Georgia Power for it.

The W. C. Bradley Company of Columbus, Georgia, provided additional funding for the development of maps and other graphic elements of the book. We were well into production when we realized that certain graphic enhancements would improve the book's readability and usefulness. The Bradley Company immediately recognized the opportunities that the graphics presented and provided the funds that allowed us to incorporate them into the book.

Gary Greenhut of Guides, Inc. unhesitatingly allowed us to reprint excerpts from a number of *Brown's Guide to Georgia* articles about the Chattahoochee River. These capture wonderful moments in time from canoeing and fishing experiences on the river by Claude Terry, Wilson Hall and Reece Turrentine. It is a privilege to share those experiences with a new generation of river lovers.

Likewise David Osier allowed us to reprint or adapt material from his fine publication, *Georgia Journal.* Our walking tour of Fort Gaines is reproduced almost word for word from *Georgia Journal,* and we have excerpted more Reece Turrentine Flint and Chestatee river experiences from the pages of that magazine.

Reece Turrentine has been canoeing and writing about Georgia and southern rivers for 50 (or more) years. An uncountable number of people have come to love and appreciate rivers because of him. For his "Song," Sidney Lanier is justly credited with being the Chattahoochee's poet, but Reece Turrentine is its prose writer.

We have used many books in the development of the text and a complete list of those is included in the Resources section, but one that I have relied on in particular is W. Kenneth Hamblin and Eric H. Christiansen's *Earth's Dynamic Systems.* It provides the best basic understanding of river systems I have ever read. The illustrations are unusual, by far the best I have seen in a book of this type. We have adapted two of them in these pages and drawn freely on the book's text. Anyone who is the slightest bit interested in rivers or any other physical aspects of our planet would do themselves a favor by obtaining a copy of this book.

Our appreciation to the Riverkeeper staff members who were always willing to go that extra mile for this project: Sally Bethea, of course, for her dedication to making this the best book possible; Harlan Trammell, a person who knows the river well and is dedicated to the Riverkeeper ideal, for countless river miles; Dana Poole and Mary Johnson for what we called "filling in the X's"–obtaining those details that were hard to pin down; Katherine Baer for her insights into the headwaters area.

Many thanks to Kim Blass for proofreading and Vera Siguel, a Riverkeeper legal intern, for indexing. Both jobs took many hours under stressful deadline conditions, and both Kim and Vera were completely dedicated to a task well done.

There are countless others who have answered questions, provided information, checked directions and given us tours of their facilities: Riverkeeper volunteers, whose names are found in the hiking sections with the trails they hiked, updating information; staff members of the Resource Manger's Office at Lakes Lanier, West Point, Walter F. George and Seminole; Tom Hawks and staff at the U.S. Forest Service, Chattooga Ranger District Office in Clarkesville; Doug Purcell at the Historic Chattahoochee Commission in Eufaula; staff members at the Chattahoochee National Recreation Center and the Chattahoochee Nature Center; Ben Harris, Bill Archer, Gandy Glover; Taylor Glover; Gary Gaines; Cecil Bray; O'Neill Williams; Bruce O'Connor; Tim LaTour; Alan Hope; Alfred Westbrook; David Coughlin; John Lupold; Ann Gale; James Sullivan; B. Elliott; Karen Plant; Margaret Zachry; our families and friends who encouraged and supported us –and of course, the Chattahoochee for providing us with a Great American River to learn about, care about and write about.

FB/SMLS

ALL IS BORN OF WATER;
ALL IS SUSTAINED BY WATER.
Goethe

RIVERKEEPER

PREFACE BY ROBERT F. KENNEDY JR.

The first Riverkeeper was hatched by the Hudson River Fishermen's Association, a coalition of commercial and recreational fishermen whose first public meeting was at the American Legion Hall in Crotonville, New York, in 1966. Crotonville was a blue-collar hamlet carved into the steep banks of the Croton River, a Hudson tributary 30 miles north of Manhattan. Members of the newly formed organization worked as factory workers, carpenters, lathers or commercial fishermen. Few of these people would ever see Yellowstone or Yosemite. None of them would vacation in the Rockies or Florida. The Hudson was everything to them, their employment, their property and recreational values, the centerpiece of their communities. "Our Riviera, our Monte Carlo," said Ritchie Garrett, the group's newly-elected president. A standing room crowd that flowed from the building, hung from the rafters and crowded against the rifle racks, applauded wildly when Garrett, an ex-marine and professional grave digger, promised his new followers, "I'll be the last to let you down."

When Garrett finished, men and women rose to take the microphone. Most of them spoke about the river and how much it meant to them. River men from Verplank and Claverack, some descended from generations of commercial fishermen, spoke of the great runs of striped bass, blue fish and shad, of giant sturgeon bursting with caviar, of herring and alewives so numerous they turned the tributaries to quick silver, the succulent blue crab and lucrative eel, and the carp, or gefilte fish, fishery that peaked during the Jewish holidays. Recreational fishermen boasted of the trout, black bass and perch they caught on plugs at the tributary mouth. They spoke about how youngsters would net shrimp, goldfish or herring for bait in the marsh at the mouth of the Croton and how most of Crotonville congregated on its beaches in the summer months for beer and barbecues. But each of them fretted about what was happening to the river–the polluters seemed to be stealing it from the public. New York City was dumping 1.5 billion gallons per day of raw sewage into the river. Indian Point Power Plant was killing a million fish a day, the National Guard was filling tidal wetlands at Camp Smith, and Penn Central Railroad was dumping oil from a four-foot pipe at the Croton rail yard. The oil floated up the Croton on the tide, blackening the beaches and making the shad taste of diesel. As a result of this abuse, the river was dying. Already a 20-mile stretch south of Albany was dead.

As these tales were recited, the mood grew black. Someone said they should plug the Penn Central pipe with a mattress or detonate it with a match. Someone else suggested floating a raft of dynamite into Indian Point's intake. Then Bob Boyle rose to speak. Boyle was an ornery angler and writer for *Sports Illustrated*. In the course of researching an article about the river two years earlier, he'd discovered two little known laws: the Rivers and Harbors Act of 1888 and the Refuse Act of 1899. Both Acts forbade pollution of American waters and provided high penalties for violators and bounties to those who reported them. The bounty provision had never been enforced but the Fishermen resolved that night that they would use these laws to go after every polluter on the Hudson River. They were good as their word. Two years later they collected their half of a $4,000 penalty paid by Penn Central and they were soon collecting even larger bounties against Standard Brands, Ciba Geigy, the National Guard, Westchester County and Anaconda Wire and Copper. They used winnings from these cases to build and launch the Riverkeeper boat, which today patrols the Hudson searching out environmental lawbreakers and bringing them to justice.

In his 1969 book about the Hudson, Boyle had called for a Riverkeeper "out on the river the length of the year, nailing polluters on the spot...giving a sense of time, place and purpose to people who live in or visit the valley...with idiosyncrasies, migrations and workings of the Hudson ingrained in his mind. We need someone like this on the Hudson and on every major river in the country." The Fishermen's Association started a Riverkeeper program in 1972. John Cronin began work as Hudson Riverkeeper in 1983. One year later, I joined Riverkeeper as legal adviser and became Chief Prosecuting Attorney in 1985. Since then we have brought over 100 polluters to justice and forced them to spend hundreds of millions of dollars bringing remedies to the Hudson.

The idea quickly caught on. By 1997, eighteen Keeper programs would criss-cross the country. The Riverkeeper's philosophy is based on the notion that the protection and enjoyment of a community's natural resources requires the daily vigilance of its citizens. The Riverkeeper movement is an environmental "neighborhood watch" program, a citizen's patrol to protect the nation's waters. Keeper's are found amongst the rank-and-file public, the owners of the waterbody. Keepers symbolize the ancient right of those owners to enforce the law and defend their home waters.

The Upper Chattahoochee Riverkeeper has been among the most aggressive and successful Keeper programs. Its mission, to reclaim the Chattahoochee from the polluters and encourage public sense of ownership, is advanced by this extraordinary book which will introduce Georgians to their river. From its headwaters in North Georgia to the Apalachicola estuary, the Chattahoochee River forms one of the most geologically and biologically diverse river systems in the world. *The Riverkeeper's Guide to the Chattahoochee* will introduce Chattahoochee River lovers to opportunities for fun and adventure that they never imagined. Hopefully, the book will also apprise Georgians of, and galvanize them against, the threats to the river from pollution and development—and make every river lover into a Riverkeeper.

INTRODUCTION by Fred Brown

Sherri and I had been working on this book for six months. I was reading the chapter "River Systems" in the stunningly insightful *Earth's Dynamic Systems* by Kenneth Hamblin and Eric Christiansen. I was fascinated and puzzled by one of the book's drawings that is shown here on a small scale and in a larger version on page 15. I spent weeks looking at this drawing and just didn't get it. I could understand the first part–how small creeks form larger creeks that eventually flow into the river. I was familiar with that pattern from my experience at the headwaters of the Chattahoochee. But the little detail in the inset? No, I had never seen that. I just didn't get it.

Then one day in February after a rain, I walked out into my backyard in Fayette County. The trees were bare and the sky was gray. A thick brown mat of pine straw, hickory and sweet gum leaves covered the ground. As I walked along I noticed slight indentations in the leaf mat made by the rain runoff. I raised my line of vision and saw a vast network of these indentations spread all across the three-acre lot. If the yard had been a leaf, these faint channels would have been its veins. The veins collected in a stem that pointed downhill to a suburban pond called Lake Kedron.

I went inside and looked at my topo maps. Lake Kedron drains into Flat Creek. Flat Creek flows into Line Creek. Line Creek

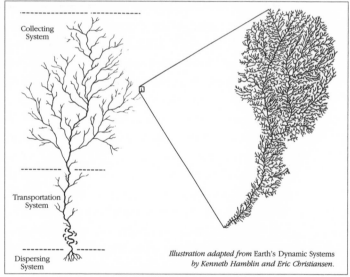

Illustration adapted from Earth's Dynamic Systems *by Kenneth Hamblin and Eric Christiansen.*

flows into the Flint River. The Flint River flows into the Chattahoochee at Bainbridge.

I got it. It took six months, but I finally got it.

Since that day I have stood on the US 27 bridge in Bainbridge and looked down at the Flint River as it flows south into Lake Seminole where it joins the Chattahoochee. Below Seminole's Jim Woodruff Dam, the two rivers become the Apalachicola and flow into the sea–carrying water from my back yard.

Whether it was exploring the beginning of the river in my own back yard or hiking to the headwaters at Chattahoochee Gap or discovering the moat of a 1689

Spanish fort built on the banks of the Chattahoochee, the actual physical experience of being on and around the river has been the way I have learned about and come to understand the Great Chattahoochee. And I recommend the same thing to you.

If someone asked me, " I have three days to explore the Chattahoochee. Can I do it in that period of time?" my answer would be an unhesitating and enthusiastic "Yes."

Here is a three-day exploration, distilled from 18 months of traveling and writing about the Chattahoochee, that will forever change your perception of that river or for that matter, any other river.

Start at Brasstown Bald, the highest point in Georgia. From the observation deck look southeast through Tesnatee Gap. If it is a clear day, you will see Lake Lanier, the Chattahoochee dammed by Buford Dam, shimmering in the distance. Look more to the south for Mount Yonah. Its oddly shaped granite profile will appear again and again as you explore the upper section of the river.

Drive south on FSR 44 beginning at Unicoi Gap on GA 75 and US 17. This winding mountain road follows the river's headwaters through some of north Georgia's most beautiful scenery. Explore Horse Trough Falls in the Chattahoochee River Recreation Area and stop at the FSR 44 bridge, the first stone bridge over the river.

Take the Nacoochee Valley driving tour, beginning on page 25, for a marvelous insight into the early settlement and gold mining era of this area.

Drive south to Sweetwater Creek State Park off I-20 west of Atlanta. Hike to the overlook with its remarkable view of rapids flowing over a geological formation called the Brevard Fault that drops 120 feet from Austell to the Chattahoochee. Not many scenes in north Georgia rival this for pure scenic beauty, a scant 12 miles from Atlanta's Five Points. The picturesque mill ruins here are just one of many such sites along the river.

The only dark cloud over this beautiful scene is the realization that just downstream Sweetwater Creek flows into the most disgustingly polluted section of the entire Chattahoochee River. A tour of this area may extend the three-day trip and is not recommended for everyone, but I believe anyone who is seriously interested in the Chattahoochee River should call Riverkeeper boat captain Harlan Trammell (404/816-9888) and spend about a $100 for a half-day boat ride from the GA 166 bridge upstream to Peachtree Creek. This experience will take you past Utoy Creek, Proctor Creek, Peachtree Creek, Sweetwater Creek, Nickajack Creek, Atlanta's R. M. Clayton Sewage Treatment Plant, the Cobb County discharge and under the shadow of other industrial plants and discharges along this section of the river. Chlorine fumes burn the eyes. The odor on any given day can be nauseating. Incredibly a few local residents fish from the banks. They are not using Orvis fly rods. You have the distinct impression they are going to eat what they catch. It is a sobering and frightening experience.

Go to the intersection of Marietta Boulevard and Bolton Road and drive south on the old Newnan Road, known as GA 70 for most if its length, passing through Bolton, Campbellton, Rico, and Rosco before reaching Newnan. The road, running parallel to the river on its right, still reflects the rural south despite the fact that it is entirely within the Atlanta Metropolitan area. Roads running perpendicular to it, with names like Bakers Ferry, Boat Rock, Jones Ferry, Capps Ferry, Hutcheson Ferry and Sewell Mill recall an era when gristmills and ferries were common sites along the river.

Drive south toward Columbus on GA 219, crossing creeks such as Flat Creek, Mountain Oak, Mulberry, Standing Boy, Hatchiatchee–all of which flow west into the Chattahoochee. Unless you take time to visit Kolomoki Indian Mounds or Rood Mounds, Indian named creeks and towns like Coweta, Centralhatchee, Wehadkee and Senoia are about the only reminders in the entire Chattahoochee Valley of its extensive Indian occupation from prehistoric times to the 1830s.

In Columbus follow 12th Street down to the red bricks of the Riverwalk. Upstream to Eagle and Phenix Mills and downstream to the Dillingham Street Bridge is the most dramatic and picturesque urban setting on the river. It is a reminder that this river has been a transportation corridor, a location for military forts, a source of power and a site for industry. It is, and during the entire history of this country has been, a working river.

This is also the location of the fall line where the river dramatically changes character. Upstream from Columbus the river flows from the mountains. Downstream it flows to the coast.

Continue south on US 431 and AL 165 to Eufaula. Go east (left) on Broad Street and follow it to where it merges with Riverside Drive. Being extremely watchful of traffic, walk out onto the Richard Russell Bridge which spans the original channel of the Chattahoochee before Lake Walter F. George was impounded. Looking up and down the river, imagine what this corridor looked like before the lake was here. Take particular note of the bluff where you parked your car and where the old jail is located.

Take GA 39 south to another bluff–the bluff at Fort Gaines. To me this is the most interesting physical location on the entire river. Rising high above the river is the kind of terrain that existed in Eufaula, Franklin and Bainbridge before the building of dams and the impoundment of lakes. Standing here you'll get a clear understanding of how one cannon atop this bluff could control boat transportation up and down the waterway.

Take the self-guided tour of Fort Gaines on page 215 that starts at this location and compare it to the driving tour of Nacoochee Valley earlier in the trip.

Continue south on GA 39 and US 84 to Bainbridge, crossing the Flint River on the US 27 Bridge. My backyard water flows under this bridge to Lake Seminole through the Jim Woodruff Dam and on to the Apalachicola.

Drive through downtown Bainbridge, stopping for a walk around the town square, one of the most interesting in all of Georgia. Go east on Waters Street to the Flint where a dirt road follows its east bank. This urban river scene is second only to the Columbus Riverwalk. But with its red clay road and Spanish moss laden oak trees, this is a more rural, traditional setting. Local residents congregate here–fishing, cooking out or just enjoying the atmosphere. On a summer evening at sunset this is a timeless southern scene.

Drive south on the wildflower lined FL 65. Dirt roads with names like Aspalaga Landing, Johnson Landing, Rock Bluff Landing and Dawson Landing cross the highway and lead to the Apalachicola. In the 1800s there were more than 200 riverboat landings along the river between Apalachicola and Columbus. Riverboats stopped at farms to pick up crops and drop off supplies. Compare these names to the road names that led to mill sites on the old Newnan Road. Mills, which required falling water to generate power, were not viable enterprises along this section of river because the terrain was too flat. Above Columbus the roads never bear the suffix "landing" and below Columbus you seldom see a road named after someone's mill.

Turn on FSR 129 and visit Fort Gadsden with its interesting outdoor display explaining the river's importance in the region's early military history. And here, as at the bluff at Fort Gaines, visiting the physical location of a river fort crystallizes the realization of what a strategic military advantage a well-positioned cannon on the river could be.

Continue on FL 65 to East Point. Explore US 98 and CR 30 between East Point and Port St. Joe, stopping to examine the great mounds of oyster shells and the starkly plain oyster boats. Eat at one of the seafood shacks along the route. The Indian Pass Trading Post at Indian Pass is a particularly good choice, but any one of a dozen will do.

Go out to St. George Island to the state park on the east end. Walk from the bay side of the island to the ocean side. Look out to the Gulf.

The Chattahoochee starts as a wet place in the leaves in the north Georgia mountains, flows through great cities and ends in the ocean. In the relatively short space of 540 miles, it displays all the characteristics of a Great American River. Understanding the Chattahoochee will give you an understanding of every river across the country.

I hope you will use this book to explore, enjoy and appreciate the Great Chattahoochee River. It–or some other river–starts in your own back yard.

Section 1
The Headwaters

"We all know that the water in the river goes to the ocean. But that ain't all. The whole mineral supply of the ocean–iodine, calcium, phosphorus and so forth–comes down the river. That's the only way the ocean can get its mineral supply.

Philip W. C. Greear

You go up on the bank of the Chattahoochee River on Blue Mountain. Go up there. Take a soil sample, and you'll find potassium and sodium, chlorine and phosphorus in the soil. It is being moved down the Chattahoochee River to the Gulf of Mexico. It *is* being moved. Not it *was* being moved.

Then there is the matter of the sediments, the silica sands, quartz sands that end up on the edge of the ocean transported there by the river. I used to know a man who was a specialist in the origin of sand. He could go down to the Gulf of Mexico and tell you where every one of those grains of sand came from.

The river is important in terms of the organic detritus or whatever you want to call the decomposing organic material that comes down the river and is deposited at the edge of the ocean to make up the extremely nutrient rich estuarine water. The salt marsh waters are the most productive ecosystem in the world per square foot or square acre.

Of course the water gets through the hydrologic cycle over and over again. But the minerals don't and the organic materials don't. So the Coastal Plain of the Chattahoochee down towards Apalachicola is built up of these materials that were extracted from the sides of the hills and the mountains up above.

Week before last my son Delbert took his family and one of our other granddaughters to Apalachicola to camp. When they got back I asked 'em why they didn't bring a gallon of water from the Apalachicola Bay up to Helen and start it over again."

Philip W. C. Greear chaired the Biology and Earth Sciences Department at Shorter College, Rome, Georgia, from 1961 to 1986. He grew up in Helen on the banks of the Chattahoochee.

THE RIVER

Thirty-five hundred feet high into the Blue Ridge Mountains at Chattahoochee Gap, where Jack's Knob Trail dead ends into the Appalachian Trail, is a simple sign, pointing downhill, with a blue "W" for water. Thus begins the Chattahoochee River, a small trickle which quickly picks up speed as it tumbles 1,580 feet to Helen. Numerous creeks like Smith, Low Gap, Henson, Dukes and Sautee pour into the river as it descends through the Helen Valley and makes an eastward swing across Nacoochee Valley before turning back to the west and heading for the slowdown of Lake Lanier.

Most of these 36 river miles from Chattahoochee Gap to Belton Bridge roll through land that was once home to the Cherokee Indians, who lived there from the 1500s until the early 1800s when miners rushed into the area in search of gold. The gold miners wrecked havoc on the land, mostly during the 1830s, before leaving for the gold fields of California. And in 1837 the federal government made sure the Cherokees left, too. Federal troops rounded up the last of the Indians in the area and forced them to move to the Indian Territory in present-day Oklahoma.

With the removal of the Indians, white settlers quickly cleared the former Indian land, furthering the deterioration the gold miners had begun with their constant burning, their failure to plant cover crops in winter and their practice of farming on steep slopes. By the 1880s the farmers, who could no longer make a living from the exhausted land, sold it to the large lumber companies. Within 30 years, the timber was gone; and the lumber companies left the land to erode.

Today, much of the area surrounding the headwaters lies in the Chattahoochee Wildlife Management Area, managed by the U.S. Forest Service and the state of Georgia. Tourists roam Helen and the Nacoochee Valley, and explorers hike the trails around the headwaters and canoe the river and creeks.

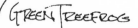

GREEN TREEFROG

The Riverkeeper

Established in 1994, the Upper Chattahoochee Riverkeeper is a nonprofit environmental advocacy organization dedicated solely to protecting the Chatta-hoochee River, its tributaries and watershed. For more information: Upper Chattahoochee Riverkeeper, 1900 Emery Street, Suite 450, Atlanta, Georgia 30318; 404/352-9828; fax: 404/352-8676; e-mail: rivrkeeper@mindspring.com.

"All of the rivers run to the sea, yet the sea is not full; unto the place from whence the rivers came thither they return again."

—Ecclesiastes 1:7

Ralph McGill at the Headwaters

"Up above Poplar Stump Gap, where the great rock rim of the Blue Ridge marks the southwestern border of the huge highland area, a small trickle of water spills from the rocks. It splashes down to form a small pool. Two small streams, not more than two or three inches wide, flow from it, splashing down into the laurel thickets.

Thus begins the Chattahoochee River. Once in the thickets it is joined by other streams, and soon there is what might be called a small mountain creek. Others hurry to merge with it. In Habersham, Rabun, White, Towns, Union, and Lumpkin counties, there are waters which flow into it."

Ralph McGill, "Chattahoochee," Georgia Rivers, *University of Georgia Press, Copyright 1962, Atlanta Newspapers, Inc.*

PARKS AND RECREATION

CHATTAHOOCHEE NATIONAL FOREST –The Chattahoochee National Forest (CNF) consists of about 750,000 acres which stretch from the wild waters of the Chattooga River on its northeastern boundaries, westward through the Blue Ridge Mountains and across the Cohutta Wilderness. Most of this land was once home to the Cherokee Indians who lived there from the 1500s until they were removed by the U.S. Government in 1837. Gold mining, poor farming practices and lumbering then exhausted the once-fertile land. When the government began to buy land in north Georgia in the 1920s, most people were eager to sell their burned-out and cut-over property. The Chattahoochee National Forest was officially established in 1936, and restoration of the land began. Today the area consists of developed recreation areas with hundreds of campsites, scenic areas, wilderness, thousands of acres of lakes and streams and several hundred miles of hiking trails. For management purposes, the forest is divided into seven ranger districts. The area surrounding the headwaters of the Chattahoochee River falls within the Brasstown and Chattooga ranger districts. *More Information:* Brasstown Ranger District, 1881 Highway 515, P.O. Box 9, Blairsville, GA 30514; 706/745-6928. Chattooga Ranger District, P.O. Box 196, Clarkesville, GA 30523; 706/754-6221.

CHATTAHOOCHEE WILDLIFE MANAGEMENT AREA –The Chattahoochee Wildlife Management Area lies within the Chattahoochee National Forest and takes in much of the forest land north and west of Helen, which encompasses the headwaters of the Chattahoochee River. It is one of 12 wildlife management areas within the Chattahoochee National Forest and is maintained by the U.S. Forest Service, in cooperation with the Georgia Wildlife Resource Division. These areas provide the habitat needs for more than 500 wildlife species and are open for hunting during special seasons and according to state regulations. There are more than 1,000 miles of primary trout and warm-water streams throughout these areas, and state fishing regulations, fees and seasons apply. *Facilities:* Year-round dispersed camping is allowed in much of the area, at no charge. No permit is needed. All camping guidelines are subject to change; check with the Forest Service before planning a trip. *More Information:* Department of Natural Resources, 2258 Northlake Parkway, Suite 100, Tucker, GA 30084; 770/493-5770. Chattooga Ranger District, P.O. Box 196, Clarkesville, GA 30523; 706/754-6221.

MARK TRAIL WILDERNESS –This recently developed wilderness area has been carved out of the Chattahoochee Wildlife Management Area and is part of the Chattahoochee National Forest. It consists of about 16,400 acres which cover northern portions of the Chattahoochee River and Tennessee River Valley watersheds. Nearly 13,000 acres can be found in the Chattahoochee watershed alone, encompassing the headwaters of the river. Hiking and primitive camping are allowed, as well as hunting and fishing in season. The wilderness area will not be indicated on CNF maps until 1999. *Facilities:* No facilities in a wilderness. *More Information:* Chattooga Ranger District, P.O. Box 196, Clarkesville, GA 30523; 706/754-6221.

CHATTAHOOCHEE RIVER RECREATION AREA –This developed campground, operated by the U.S. Forest Service, is located in the headwaters of the Chattahoochee, adjacent to the Mark Trail Wilderness Area. The trailhead to Horse Trough Falls (see page 20) is located here. Little Horse Trough Creek flows into the Chattahoochee River just below the falls and Henson Creek flows into the river just outside the recreation area entrance on FSR 44, heading south. *Facilities:* 34 camp sites, flush toilets, drinking water, hiking trail, fishing. *Days/Hrs.:* Closed mid-Dec. to last weekend in Mar. *Fees:* $8/single, $10/double. *Directions:* From Helen, take GA 75 north for 1.5 miles. Turn left on GA 356 (75 Alt), cross river and turn right on Poplar Stump Road, next to Chattahoochee Church. Pavement will end at FSR 44. Follow for 9 miles to campground. *More Information:* Chattooga Ranger District, P.O. Box 196, Clarkesville, GA 30523; 706/754-6221.

JASUS CREEK CAMPGROUND –This undeveloped campground lies near Jasus Creek in the Chattahoochee National Forest. It and Low Gap Creek Campground (see page 12) are both operated by the U.S. Forest Service and are due to become developed campgrounds in the near future. *Facilities:* Dispersed

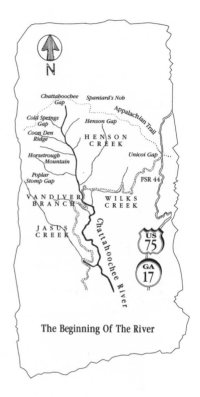

The Beginning Of The River

"Running water is part of Earth's hydrologic system and is the most important agent of erosion. Stream valleys are the most abundant and widespread landforms on the continents."

—Earth's Dynamic Systems

Reece and Dave on the Upper, Upper Hooch

"We gonna canoe that?" I asked in disbelief. Dave just smiled. The entire creek bed was scarcely 12 feet wide. The little ribbon of water in it raced around a large boulder and then disappeared completely into some underbrush below.

"That's fast, tight stuff," I commented skeptically.

"That's the point," Dave said, bounding from the truck. "It'll show us what kind of canoeists we are. Let's get to it."

We unloaded the canoes and slid them to the water's edge.

"You go first," I suggested. "This is your country."

"Well, give me plenty of room to get ahead," he instructed. "I don't want you bashing me from behind when I get stuck. And we'll get stuck."

With that observation he planted one foot solidly in the center of his canoe, and with hands on gunnels, used the other foot to push off from the bank and into the swift current. Dropping to his knees, he swung deftly around the boulder downstream, leaned over and disappeared into the underbrush and out of sight...

...Soon we emerged from the trees, and a series of bumpy cascades slid us out of Jasus Creek and into the Chattahoochee River. The scene we came upon stopped us cold.

"Not many folks ever see this," Dave said as I slid my canoe into the little eddy next to his. Dave's face was lifted upward, and he was gazing all around. The view we beheld was one that excited every sense. The whole scene was framed in autumn gold. Even the bottom of our little eddy pool was covered with golden leaves. Jasus Creek bounded in from the

camping. *Days/Hrs.:* Daily, year-round. *Fees:* None. *Directions:* From Helen, take GA 75 north for 1.5 miles. Turn left on GA 356 (75 Alt), cross river and turn right on Poplar Stump Road, next to Chattahoochee Church. Pavement will end at FSR 44. Follow for 6 miles to campground. *More Information:* Chattooga Ranger District, P.O. Box 196, Clarkesville, GA 30523; 706/754-6221.

LOW GAP CREEK CAMPGROUND –On a Saturday night in October, Low Gap Creek Campground is shoulder to shoulder with tents—family reunions, kids and big wheels, people sitting on lawn chars and seats out of vans around campfires with the sounds of a Braves ball game filling the air. *Facilities:* Dispersed camping. *Days/Hrs.:* Daily, year-round. *Fees:* None. *Directions:* From Helen, take GA 75 north for 1.5 miles. Turn left on GA 356 (75 Alt), cross river and turn right on Poplar Stump Road, next to Chattahoochee Church. Pavement will end at FSR 44. Follow for 5 miles to campground. *More Information:* Chattooga Ranger District, P.O. Box 196, Clarkesville, GA 30523; 706/754-6221.

ANDREWS COVE RECREATION AREA –Andrews Creek, a beautiful mountain stream, runs through this heavily wooded recreation area located between Helen and Unicoi Gap in the Chattahoochee National Forest. *Facilities:* 10 camp sites, flush toilets, drinking water pump, hiking trails (see page 16), fishing. *Fees:* Designated fee area. *Days/Hrs.:* Apr. 1-Nov. 1, 7am-10pm. *Directions:* From Helen, take GA 75 north about 5 miles. Andrews Cove Recreation Area is on the right at a hard left bend in the road. The sign is small and easy to miss. *More Information:* Chattooga Ranger District, P.O. Box 196, Clarkesville, GA 30523; 706/754-6221.

ANNA RUBY FALLS SCENIC AREA –The 1,600-acre Anna Ruby Falls Scenic Area lies in the heart of the Chattahoochee National Forest and features twin waterfalls cascading off of Tray Mountain which are collectively known as Anna Ruby Falls. Anna Ruby Falls marks the junction of Curtis and York creeks, two streams which begin on Tray Mountain and are fed by rain, snow and underground springs. Curtis Creek then drops 153 feet and York Creek drops 50 feet to form the two waterfalls which merge into Smith Creek, a tributary of the

Chattahoochee. Once Cherokee Indian territory, the land surrounding and including the falls was purchased in 1869 by John H. Nichols, who also owned property in the Nacoochee Valley (see page 27). He named the falls Anna Ruby after his adored daughter, who was his sole family after the death of his wife and two infant sons. Around the turn of the century, the Byrd-Matthews Lumber Company purchased and logged the land surrounding the falls. Mules pulled the felled trees along tarred log slides to the top of the falls. Lumbermen then loaded the logs onto a flume that looped around the face of the falls and ended on the opposite side of Smith Creek. Next a narrow-gauge railroad transported the logs to a mill in Helen. In 1925 the U.S. Government purchased the land, making it a part of the national forest and allowing it to regain its natural beauty. *Facilities:* Visitor Center selling original paintings, pottery and crafts; 11 picnic sites with tables and grills; hiking trails (see page 17), including the Lion's Eye Trail for the visually impaired; observation deck; fishing; drinking water; restrooms; vending machines; public phones. *Days/Hrs.:* Daily, year-round, 9am to dusk. *Fees:* Parking, cars/RVs $2, buses $10. *Directions:* From Helen, take GA 75 north for 1 mile. Turn right on GA 356 for 1.5 miles, then left at the sign to Anna Ruby Falls. Follow road for 3.6 miles to the parking area. *More Information:* Anna Ruby Falls Visitor Center, 706/878-3574. Chattooga Ranger District, P.O. Box 196, Clarkesville, GA 30523; 706/754-6221.

DUKES CREEK RECREATION AREA –Dukes Creek is a developed recreation area in the Chattooga Ranger District of the Chattahoochee National Forest which centers around the 300-foot Dukes Creek Falls. Camping is not allowed in the Recreation Area. *Facilities:* Flush toilets, hiking trails (see page 19), fishing. *Days/Hrs.:* Daily, year-round. *Directions:* From Helen, take GA 75 north for 1.5 miles and turn left on GA 356 (75 Alt). Go 2.3 miles to the Russell/Brasstown Scenic Byway and turn right. Go 2 miles to the Dukes Creek Recreation Area on the left. *More Information:* Chattooga Ranger District, P.O. Box 196, Clarkesville, GA 30523; 706/754-6221.

RAVEN CLIFFS WILDERNESS AREA –Dodd Creek, which eventually flows into the Chattahoochee, winds through this 9,600-

left, and from the right, high overhead, a silken waterfall sprayed down into the river. We were in the bright sun now and out of the tunneled creek. The river's descent looked like a giant staircase dropping into the distance. Its water danced with a silver lucency. This was not white water; it was silver water. It was wilderness at its peak, full of raw contrasts, full of design and pattern."

Reece Turrentine, canoeing with outfitter Dave Gale, Brown's Guide to Georgia, *January 1980*

WATER RELIGION:
BAPTISM

"Baptism" originates from the Greek "baptein," which means to plunge, immerse or wash. The ritual of baptism began in the belief that water is the source of life, rebirth and immortality.

acre wilderness west of Helen. This is one of the few areas in the state where the common raven can be found, hence the name; listen for its guttural croaking. A trail leads to the Raven Cliffs Falls (see page 22). *Facilities:* Hiking and primitive camping. *Directions:* From Helen, take GA 75 north 1.5 miles to GA 356 (75 Alt) and turn left. Go 2.3 miles to the Richard Russell Scenic Highway and turn right. Go 2.8 miles to a gravel, unmarked parking area along the side of the road. *More Information:* Chattooga Ranger District, P.O. Box 197, Clarkesville, GA 30523; 706/754-6221.

UNICOI STATE PARK –Unicoi State Park lies just two miles north of Helen and is adjacent to the southern side of Anna Ruby Falls Scenic Area. Its 1,081 acres made up of forest, field and lake is one of Georgia's most popular state parks. It offers programs throughout the year, including a music festival, art show, primitive skills demonstrations and nature programs. The 5-mile Smith Creek Hiking Trail (see page 23) links Unicoi with Anna Ruby Falls (see page 12). *Facilities:* 84 tent, trailer and RV sites; 30 cottages; 53-acre lake and beach; 4 lighted tennis courts; 100-room lodge and conference center; buffet-style restaurant; craft shop; hiking; picnicking; swimming and boating; and mountain bike trails. *Days/Hrs.:* Daily, year-round, 7am-10pm. Park office, 8am-4:30pm. *Directions:* From Helen, take GA 75 north for 1 mile. Turn right on GA 356 for 1.5 miles to entrance of park. *More Information:* Unicoi State Park and Lodge, P.O. Box 849, Helen, GA 30545; 706/878-2201. Georgia State Parks and Historic Sites, 205 Butler Street, Suite 1352 East, Atlanta, GA 30334; 404/656-3530; 770/389-7404 TDD. Reservations, 770/389-7275; 800/864-7275.

SMITHGALL WOODS-DUKES CREEK CONSERVATION AREA –For over 100 years, the area around Dukes Creek suffered from the same intrusions of man as the rest of the area around the Chattahoochee River headwaters. First came the miners in 1828. For decades they dug into the streams and cut into the land until every vein was depleted of its gold. Next came the lumbermen with their poor logging practices, carrying away the quality hardwoods and leaving the yellow pines and scrub.

In 1980, however, one man, Charles A. Smithgall, Jr., made it his goal to acquire this land which had been exhausted of its

Our paddles keen and bright,
flashing like silver!
Swift as the wild goose flight,
dip, dip and swing.

—Boy Scout song from The Official Boy Scout Handbook

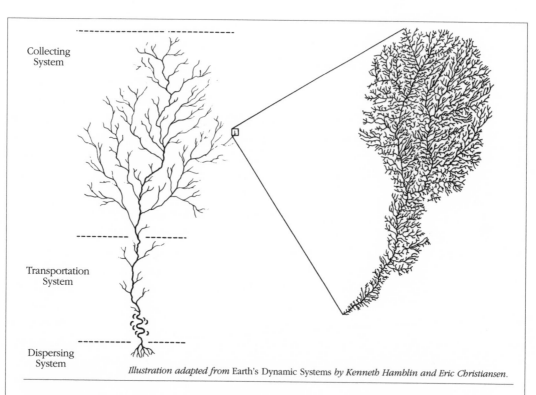

Collecting System

Transportation System

Dispersing System

Illustration adapted from Earth's Dynamic Systems *by Kenneth Hamblin and Eric Christiansen.*

The Watershed

More than 100 years ago, John Wesley Powell–scientist, geographer, explorer and Colorado River runner–understood the significance of watersheds and advocated that new western states organize themselves politically around drainages, or watersheds. Unfortunately, no one heeded his advice. In the past few years we have begun to act on Powell's vision, focusing river management and protection work in the larger watershed context.

What is a watershed? According to the National Park Service's Christopher Brown, it is "that area of land, a bounded hydrologic system, within which all living things are inextricably linked by their common water course–where simple logic demands that they become part of the community." ("The Watershed Approach," *River Voices,* Winter 1997.) In more graphic terms, a watershed can be viewed as a giant bathtub. The edges of the tub are the mountain ridge tops. Water falling on any part of the tub flows (downstream) to a single outlet–a river, a lake or the ocean. Every piece of land on earth is located within a watershed, and sub-watersheds are nested within one another, down to the land area which drains the smallest rivulet. What occurs on the land within a particular watershed can affect the water quality and quantity in its rivers, streams and lakes.

Increasingly, scientific data is being collected and analyzed at the watershed scale, and planning and management solutions are being based on this rational, geographic approach.

The future of the river will depend on the commitment of landowners, farmers, businesses and government agencies (at all levels) to focus protection and restoration efforts on the river's watershed–in other words, the entire land area which drains into this magnificent waterway. Everything is interconnected, including the solutions. It is only by recognizing that all stakeholders–even across jurisdictional lines–must be involved that solutions to environmental problems will be secured. Ultimately, the newly developing watershed movement can help people regain a sense of place, ownership and responsibility for their watershed and their community.

Sally Bethea, Upper Chattahoochee Riverkeeper

River Song

God cupped his hands and
scooped up some mountains;
Looked down upon them, said,
"My these are fine!
Now I think I'll add a few
fountains;
Nothing's too good for children
of mine;
Nothing's too good for children
of mine."

Then God with a finger drew in
the sand.
"Here's where their channels will
flow.
Wherever the water sweetens
the land
My children like flowers will
grow.
My children like flowers will
grow."

And God said, "I'll make them a
river!
Surely they'll look from the gift
to the giver;
When they see water sweeten
the land
They will say it has flowed from
my hand;
They will say it has flowed from
my hand."

Life itself is a stream of the years
Flowing from source to the sea.
Everyone borne on a river of
mercies
Even as you and as me;
Even as you and as me.

If we in our pride keep killing
God's river,
Scorning the wisdom of years;
Turning our backs on the grace
of the giver,
Who can make a river from
tears?
Who can make a river from
tears?

natural resources and restore it to a mature hardwood forest once again. He hired a horse logging expert to manage the restoration project. Because horses disturb the forest floor less than any other method, teams of Belgian draft horses hauled out logs and debris from the forest. Oaks, walnuts, hemlocks poplars and white pine were planted. Streams were cleaned of garbage and debris. Trees and shrubs were planted to shade the streams and gravel was added to the pools to cover excess silt. Sorghum and corn were planted for the benefit of white-tailed deer, bear, wild turkey, hawks and other wildlife.

Smithgall dedicated himself to restoring some 5,562 acres of woods around Dukes Creek and, through The Nature Conservancy of Georgia, sold his effort for half its appraised value to the state of Georgia. The land is now a Heritage Preserve and is under the management of the Georgia Department of Natural Resources.

The Conservation Area is open for quota hunts during the hunting season, which begins in autumn and ends in spring. Trout fishing is regulated to catch and release using artificial lures with barbless hooks. Reservations are required to fish. Hiking and biking permits are available at the Visitor Center. Several days a week there are shuttle tours available through the interior of the conservation area. The Smithgall Woods Conservation Center is a retreat center for groups of 8 to 25 people. *Facilities:* Smithgall Woods Conservation Center, Conservation Center Pavilion, 4 picnic shelters, stream fishing, 4 hiking trails, observation tower, beaver pond, youth fishing area. *Days/Hrs.:* Daily, year-round. Wed., Sat., Sun., 0.5 hour before sunrise to 0.5 hour after sunset; Mon.-Tues. and Thurs.-Fri., 8am-4:30pm. *Fees:* $2 per car. *Directions:* From Cleveland, go north on US 129 for approximately 3 miles. Turn right on GA 75 Alt. Go 5.6 miles to the entrance on the right. *More Information:* Smithgall Woods Conservation Area, 61 Tsalaki Trail, Helen, GA 30545; 706/878-3087.

HIKING TRAILS

ANDREWS COVE HIKE –This trail follows an old logging road from Andrews Cove Recreation Area to the intersections of the

Appalachian Trail and FSR 283 at Indian Grave Gap with its elevation of 3,100 feet. As one hiker put it, "If it's really only 2 miles, it's a long 2 miles." This well-marked trail gradually ascends from the parking lot, alternating between steeper and flatter grades. But the last .25 mile or so is very steep and strenuous—so be prepared. *Distance:* 4 miles round trip. *Trailhead Location:* Andrews Cove Recreation Area (see page 12). Stay right turning into the recreation area and there will be a small trail parking area. Trailhead sign labeled "Andrews Cove Trail Appalachian Trail - 2 miles." *Features:* The trail follows Andrews Creek for about 300 yards and then veers up to the right away from the stream. There are many easy spring crossings on the trail, more mud than water. A few small waterfalls can be seen in the distance, paralleling Andrews Creek. This mountain trail affords excellent opportunities to spot deer and small mammals. There are dogwoods and wildflowers for spring hikers, and a full canopy of hardwoods makes for beautiful fall colors. *Hiked by Riverkeeper member Michelle Hamel and Riverkeeper volunteer Todd Fedell.*

ANNA RUBY FALLS TRAIL –Walking is easy to moderate on this paved footpath which leads from the parking lot to an observation deck overlooking Anna Ruby Falls, but it can also be very busy as these twin waterfalls for York and Curtis creeks are said to be Georgia's most visited. *Distance:* 0.4 mile. *Trailhead Location:* Anna Ruby Falls Scenic Area parking lot (see page 12). *Fees:* Parking, cars/RVs $2, buses $10. *Features:* This short but rewarding hike follows Smith Creek upstream through a predominately hardwood forest to an observation deck at the base of the two waterfalls forming Anna Ruby Falls. To get a closer view of the smaller of the two falls, take the gravel path on the other side of Smith Creek to the upper observation deck.

APPALACHIAN TRAIL (SECTION 13, FROM UNICOI GAP TO TESNATEE GAP) –The Appalachian Trail (AT) is a 2,100-mile wilderness footpath which winds along the crest of the Appalachian Mountains. It runs through 14 states as it stretches from Springer Mountain in Georgia to Mount Katahdin in Maine. The Georgia portion of the AT winds about 75.6 miles through the Chattahoochee National Forest. At times elevations rise to

And God said, "I'll make them a river!
Surely they'll look from the gift to the giver.
When they see water sweeten the land
They will say it has flowed from my hand.
They will say it has flowed from my hand."

Mildred Greear, 1990

Unicoi Turnpike

Over 150 miles long in its early years, the Unicoi Turnpike was the first vehicular road to link eastern Tennessee, western North Carolina and north Georgia with the Savannah River and the coast. Twenty feet wide, except where digging or bridges were necessary and a minimum of 12 feet was allowed, the turnpike basically followed the route of the Unicoi Trail, an old Indian footpath. That footpath was preceded by an ancient animal trail which was part of a network of pathways crisscrossing the wilderness of the North American continent thousands of years before the white man. Completed in 1819, the turnpike passed through the Cherokee Nation by way of a treaty written in 1813. Beginning on the Tugalo River east of Toccoa, the wagon road followed the length of the Nacoochee and Helen valleys, fording the Chattahoochee River as well as numerous streams many times as it wound its way to Unicoi Gap. At Unicoi Gap, 10 miles north of the Helen Valley and at 3,000 feet the lowest spot for miles in any direction, the road crossed the Blue Ridge and via Murphy, North Carolina, headed for the settlements in Tennessee. As the toll was paid at the start of the road, a long pole or pike was typically turned aside, thus came the word turnpike. Since the average distance that a horse and wagon could travel in a day was 20 miles, roadhouses, which offered hot meals and dry beds, were located every 20 miles along the turnpike for weary travelers. The opening of the Unicoi Turnpike and the gradual forcing out of the Cherokees paved the way for white settlement in the Nacoochee Valley and north Georgia.

over 4,400 feet, but mostly the trail follows ridges at about 3,000 feet. This hike covers what is called Section 13 of the trail from Unicoi Gap to Tesnatee Gap, passing the source of the Chattahoochee River at Chattahoochee Gap and encompassing the headwater area. *Distance*: 14.5 miles one way. *Trail Access Location:* A shuttle can be set up at either end of the trail, Unicoi Gap or Tesnatee Gap. To Unicoi Gap: From Helen, take GA 75 north about 10 miles. Look for the Unicoi Gap parking area on right side of the road right before the AT crosses the highway. To Tesnatee Gap: From Helen, take GA 75 north about one mile to Robertstown and turn left across the Chattahoochee River bridge onto GA 356. Go 2.5 miles and turn right onto GA 348 to Tesnatee Gap parking area. *Features:* This portion of the AT comes within 200 feet of the headwaters of the Chattahoochee at Chattahoochee Gap. At an elevation of 3,500 feet, Chattahoochee Gap is about 5 miles south of Unicoi Gap and clearly marked. The only indication of the spring, however, is a sign marked with a "W" and pointing downhill. Hiking north from Unicoi Gap, the sign is on the left. A steep blue-blazed trail leads down to the spring which is down the slope on the other side of the gap.

Brasstown Bald Summit Trail –At 4,784 feet Brasstown Bald is the highest peak in the state of Georgia; and from the observation deck of its summit, visitors get a 360-degree panoramic view of mountain ranges in Georgia, Tennessee and North and South Carolina. But of all the views in this panorama, the one that is most important to the student of the Chattahoochee is the one that faces south. On a clear day the Atlanta skyline is visible, and Lake Lanier glistens on the horizon just beyond Tesnatee Gap. With their eyes, visitors can trace the silver ribbon that is Russell-Brasstown Scenic Highway (see page 30) as it winds diagonally up Tesnatee Gap and then cuts perpendicularly across Wildcat Mountain, heading toward Cleveland, the Gateway to the Mountains, then follows the left face of Jack's Knob downward to Chattahoochee Gap. The granite face of Mt. Yonah appears to the southeast, a distinct profile against the blue sky. This is the view of the Upper Chattahoochee headwaters from the highest peak in Georgia. *Distance:* 0.5 mile, moderate. *Trailhead Location:* From Blairsville, take US

19 and 129 south for 8 miles. Turn left on GA 180 for 9 miles. Turn left on GA 180 Spur for 3 miles. This leads to the Brasstown Bald visitor's parking lot. *Features:* This paved but steep trail leads to a visitor's center at the summit of Brasstown Bald. The rosebay rhododendron and the mountain laurel are just two of the mountain flora described by the interpretive markers which line the trail. A kudzu-like vine known as old man's beard covers many of the plants at the top of the bald. The mountain panorama is spectacular, but in the fall look to the northwest side of the observation deck at the clusters of flaming red berries peaking above the deck. This is the mountain ash in bloom and is worth the hike alone. *Facilities:* At the visitor's center there are interpretive exhibits which trace the natural and cultural history of the area, regularly shown video presentations, an observation deck, restrooms and drinking water. In the parking area, there is access to four hiking trails ranging from 0.5 to 6 miles, picnic tables, snack food concessions and a gift shop and book store. There is also a shuttle bus for a small fee which runs from the parking lot to the summit for those who do not care to hike. *Days/Hrs.:* The Visitor's Center is open weekends beginning in Apr.; open 7 days a week Memorial Day until Nov. Parking lot observation deck open year-round, weather permitting. It is very cold at the top of the summit in the winter, however, so dress warmly. *Fees:* Parking, $1. *Hiked by Riverkeeper member Michelle Hamel.*

DUKES CREEK FALLS –Known as Dukes Creek Falls, the 250-foot waterfall at the end of this trail is actually on Davis Creek close to its confluence with Dukes Creek. The water cascades down a wide, rocky course rather than dropping straight down. This dilutes the power of the fall but makes for a beautiful waterfall. Dukes Creek itself is a boulder strewn mountain stream where water splashes around foaming pools and riffles. *Distance:* About 1 mile each way, easy to moderate. *Trailhead Location:* Dukes Creek Recreation Area (see page 13). Trailhead starts on right side of parking lot. *Features:* This blue-blazed, easy-to-walk trail is graded and graveled and has steps to help smooth out the steep sections. Patches of rhododendron and mountain laurel adorn this west-facing slope. The upper, drier portion of the slope is a hardwood forest made up

*Crossing
the summer river,
sandals in my hand.*

—18th Century Japanese Haiku

of oaks, hickories and tulip poplars, while along Dukes Creek and the end of the trail a cove of hemlock and white pine is developing. There are several more small waterfalls upstream on Dukes Creek, but further rock-hopping exploration is up to the hiker. At the bottom of the trail, there's a wonderful observation deck system and nice rock vegetation. *Hiked by Robin Wyatt and Riverkeeper member Sherri Hand.*

HORSE TROUGH FALLS TRAIL –Said to be one of Georgia's best-kept scenic secrets, Horse Trough Falls is an impressive waterfall located on Little Horse Trough Creek right before its flows into the Chattahoochee River. The flow from the fall spreads out over its massive rock face, tumbling over numerous ledges until it reaches the pool 75 feet below. *Distance:* 0.4 mile, easy. *Trailhead Location:* Mark Trail Wilderness (see page 11). From Helen, take GA 75 north about 10 miles to the Chattahoochee River Road, FSR 44, and the entrance of Mark Trail Wilderness. Turn left and go 5 miles and turn right into the Chattahoochee River Recreation Area campground (see page 11). Cross the bridge over Henson Creek and drive about 0.5 mile through the campground, following the signs to Horse Trough Falls parking area. *Features:* This easy-to-walk gravel trail first crosses the Chattahoochee River via a wooden bridge (which just happens to be the first bridge over the Chattahoochee) then proceeds along the river bank before heading up Little Horse Trough Creek to an observation deck overlooking the falls.

JACK'S KNOB TRAIL –This is not a trail for waterfalls and expansive mountain views and overlooks. Beyond the initial rhododendron arcade, it winds through a typical south-facing slope pine forest. But of all the hikes presented in this section, this is the one that lovers of the Chattahoochee might find most rewarding. It leads to a spot where water drips from a few rocks, only to pick up volume quickly as it descends Jack's Knob to become the Chattahoochee River. *Distance:* 4.5 miles, one way. *Trailhead Location:* Brasstown Bald Visitor Center parking lot. Trail access is at the south end of the parking lot opposite from the concession and gift shop buildings. For a shorter hike, access trail at GA 180 and GA 180 Spur, which is the road to Brasstown Bald Visitor Center. There is a small parking area on the north side of the highway. Look for the trail access on the south side of the highway. *Features:* This blue-blazed trail, which begins at an elevation of about 4,440 feet, first winds through a dense, dark green rhododendron forest and then does a steep, switchbacking descent down Wolfpen Ridge for about 2 miles until it reaches its second access point at Jack's Gap, elevation 3,000 feet. Here the trail crosses GA 180 and begins a series of ups and downs as it follows Hiawassee Ridge past Jack's Knob at 3,805 feet to Chattahoochee Gap where it joins the Appalachian Trail at 3,500 feet. At this point, which is well-marked, there is a small sign to the left of the trail which is lettered with a "W" and points downhill. Follow this steep downhill trail for several yards to a spot where water runs over a few rocks. Look up to the right and there will be water dripping from a rock. This is the source of the Chattahoochee. Cup your hands and take a drink. *Hiked by Riverkeeper member Michelle Hamel and Riverkeeper volunteer Steve White.*

LOW GAP CREEK FALLS TRAIL –This trail leads to a 15-foot waterfall on Low Gap Creek, a mountain stream which runs through the Mark Trail Wilderness area and eventually flows into the Chattahoochee. *Distance:* About 0.5 mile, easy to moderate. *Trailhead Location:* Mark Trail Wilderness (see page 11). From Helen, take GA 75 north for 1.5 miles and turn left on GA 356 (75 Alt). Go 0.1 mile to FSR 44 (also known as the Chattahoochee River Road) and turn right. Go 4.4 miles to FSR 44A and turn left. Drive through the Low Gap Creek camping area (see page 12), fording Low Gap Creek twice. Water may be high so beware of conditions. Park right past the second ford. *Features:* This trail follows the banks of Low Gap Creek, passing through a steep rhododendron thicket at the beginning. Just below the confluence of Low Gap Creek and England Camp Branch, ford the stream and continue along the east side of Low Gap. This part of the hike is steep with thick vegetation all along the stream. The waterfall tumbles over a rocky ledge into a narrow chasm of boulders. There are several more small waterfalls further upstream, but the hiking is very strenuous over steep and overgrown terrain.

MT. YONAH –This 3,166-foot high granite outcrop stands out clearly against a blue northeast Georgia sky. The U.S. Forest

Mt. Yonah
The Nacoochee Valley

Yonah Mountain is Cherokee for bear from "yanu" meaning "bear."

—Marion Hemperley, Indian Heritage of Georgia

River Rapid Classifications

If river rapids generally fit into one of the following classifications, but the water temperature is below 50 degrees, or if the trip is an extended one in a wilderness area, the river should be considered one class more difficult than normal.

Class I–Moving water with a few riffles and small waves; few or no obstructions.

Class II–Easy rapids with waves up to three feet, and wide, clear channels that are obvious without scouting; some maneuvering is required.

Class III–Rapids with high, irregular waves often capable of swamping an open canoe; narrow passages that often require complex maneuvering; may require scouting from shore.

Class IV–Long, difficult rapids with constricted passages that often require precise maneuvering in very turbulent waters. Scouting from shore is often necessary, and conditions make rescue difficult. Generally not possible for open canoes: boaters in covered canoes and kayaks should be able to Eskimo roll.

Class V–Extremely difficult, long, and very violent rapids with highly congested routes that nearly always must be scouted from shore. Rescue conditions are difficult and there is significant hazard to life in event of mishap. Ability to Eskimo roll is essential for kayaks and canoes.

Class VI–Difficulties of Class V carried to the extreme of navigability. Nearly impossible and very dangerous. For teams of experts only, after close study and with precautions taken.

Service owns the rock face and 960 acres at the top of this prominent landmark. But the rest is private property, and as a result there is virtually no public access. Several years ago, before owners closed to vehicular traffic a private road leading to the top, as many as 30,000 visitors per year came to Mt. Yonah to hike, mountain climb and rappel. It's a tough, steep walk up the private road from the very small parking lot along the side of GA 75. But from the top, the vistas of Pink Mountain, the Nacoochee Valley and the Upper Chattahoochee River watershed are clear and expansive. *Distance:* 2.5 miles, moderate to strenuous. *Trailhead Location:* From Cleveland, take GA 75 north for 3.5 miles. On the right, directly past the Mt. Yonah RV Park, turn right onto the dirt road, Yonah Mountain Road. From Helen, take GA 75 south and from its intersection with GA 384, Yonah Mountain is 1.5 miles on the left. Take an immediate left into an ungraded parking area. Hikers cannot drive vehicles up the road. It is gated and locked. There are plenty of warning signs not to enter, but "hikers are welcome." *Features:* The real exploration of Mt. Yonah does not begin until after hiking the private, graded gravel road which leads to the old Mt. Yonah parking lot. Upon entering the parking area, a rocky path to the right leads up to the mountain's face. This is very steep. The path leads past several granite areas, eventually coming to a large grassy clearing where camping is evident. From here, there are a number of ways down to the granite ledges for views. Once again, this is a steep climb. People rock climb and rappel here, including the U.S. Army, which trains rangers on the mountain.

RAVEN CLIFFS TRAIL –The sound of rushing water is always a part of the landscape as Raven Cliffs Trail follows upstream the banks of Dodd Creek, passing numerous cascades and waterfalls until it dead ends into the most spectacular of all, Raven Cliffs Falls. This fall, with its massive cliff face of solid rock, rises vertically from the landscape about 80 to 90 feet. From the trail the cliffs look like large blocks with a narrow crevasse between. Dodd Creek falls straight through that crevice and into a dark pool at the bottom. The sound of the falling water is amplified by the cliff face, leaving a fast-motion picture of the powerful slow-motion forces which sculpt the mountain landscape. *Distance:* 2.5 miles one way. *Trailhead Location:* Raven Cliffs Wilderness Area (see page 13). From Helen, take GA 75 north 1.5 miles to GA 356 (75 Alt) and turn left. Go 2.3 miles to the Richard Russell Scenic Highway and turn right. Go 2.8 miles to a gravel, unmarked parking area along the side of the road which is often times full. *Features:* Expect to find a lot of traffic along this popular blue-blazed trail. Dodd Creek is a beautiful mountain stream which splashes and winds through the valley with lots of white water, ripples and pools. The 100-foot-or-so climb to the top of the cliffs is strenuous and very steep, with narrow pathways along the dropoffs. There is an abundance of moss, mushrooms, wildflowers and rhododen-dron and overhead tangles of laurel. Look for the deciduous Fraser magnolia with its 10-to-12-inch long and 6-to-7-inch wide leaves. *Hiked by Riverkeeper member Michelle Hamel and Riverkeeper volunteers Carol Horn and Kelli Coggins.*

SMITH CREEK TRAIL –When York and Curtis creeks merge at Anna Ruby Falls to form Smith Creek, Smith Creek then flows off of Smith Mountain and into the lake at Unicoi State Park. A hiker would expect Smith Creek Trail to follow that same path. But instead, this trail only comes close to the creek at its north end's first 0.5 mile. After that the trail travels along Hickory Nut Ridge between its two access points, Anna Ruby Falls at approximately 2,180 feet and Unicoi State Park at approxi-mately 1,760 feet. *Distance:* 5 miles one way, easy to moderate from Anna Ruby Falls to Unicoi State Park and moderate from Unicoi State Park to Anna Ruby Falls. *Trailhead Location:* From Helen, take GA 75 north for 1 mile. Turn right on GA 356. Go 1.5 miles to the entrance of Unicoi State Park (see page 14). Northern trail access: Turn left at the entrance of Unicoi State Park and follow the signs to the Anna Ruby Falls parking area. Hike the 0.4-mile trail to the falls (see page 17). Trailhead for Smith Creek Trail begins at the right of the lower observation deck. Southern trail access: Follow the signs to the Unicoi State Park Campground. Trailhead sign and blue blaze is adjacent to a small parking area at Little Brook Camping area. *Features:* If this blue-blazed trail is accessed from the Anna Ruby Falls end, about the first mile lies within the Anna Ruby Falls Scenic Area, traveling along the lower slopes of Smith Mountain through

Nacoochee is named for a Cherokee settlement located about the junction of the Soquee and Santee Rivers. The meaning is unknown and it is doubtful that it is of Cherokee origin. The word may be connected with the Uchee Indians.

—*Marion Hemperley,* Indian Heritage of Georgia

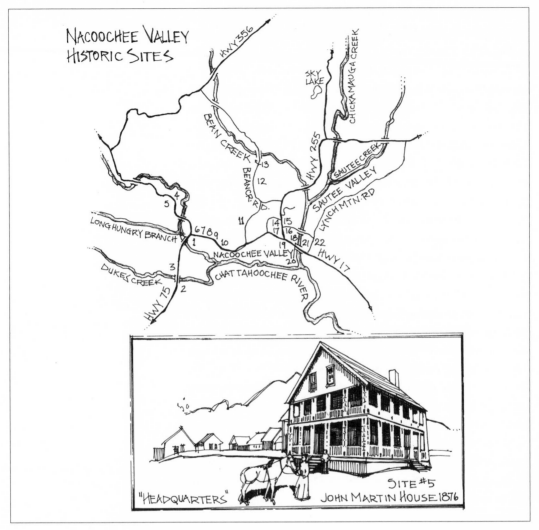

NACOOCHEE VALLEY
HISTORIC SITES

"HEADQUARTERS"   SITE #5
JOHN MARTIN HOUSE 1876

hardwood stands of maturing oaks and hickories. As the trail goes up and over Hickory Nut Ridge, it passes through dense areas of mountain laurel, hemlock rhododendron and ferns and crosses streams several times before it ends at the Unicoi State Park Campground. *Trail hiked by Riverkeeper members Michelle Hamel and David Diaz.*

DRIVING TOURS

FOREST SERVICE ROAD 44 –FSR 44, also known as the Chattahoochee River Road, covers about 15 miles as it winds its way through the Chattahoochee Wildlife Management Area (see page 10). There are plenty of views along this mountain road of the Chattahoochee River headwaters as well as Mt. Yonah and the piedmont. The road is narrow and full of curves. If it is raining or snowing, it would be best to drive the road in a 4-wheel drive vehicle. Most RVs are too big to maneuver around the curves. (A lot of RVs are parked to camp on the lower or southern end of the road, closer to Helen). Also, it is probably a good idea to drive the full length of the road before the sun goes down. *Directions to drive the route from north to south:* From Helen, go north on GA 75 for about 9 miles. FSR 44 and the entrance to the Mark Trail Wilderness Area are on the left, right before Unicoi Gap. Turn left and follow the road which heads south, back to Helen.

NACOOCHEE VALLEY DRIVING TOUR –Once the Chattahoochee River leaves Helen, it flows in an easterly direction through the Nacoochee Valley, an area dotted with historical markers. Ancient Indian villages, major travel routes pounded out first by animals and then by Indians and white settlers, gold mining, lumbering, depression — all have been a part of the valley's history. This driving tour points out the historical aspects of the property only. Some of the sites are open to the public, others are not. Please be respectful of private property.

The tour begins at the intersection of GA 75 and GA 17, just south of Helen, at Nacoochee Valley's oldest historical site.

NACOOCHEE INDIAN MOUND (1) - A white latticework gazebo sits atop this ancient Indian burial mound in the middle of flat pasture near the banks of the Chattahoochee. This mound gradually grew as burial after burial occurred. A partial excavation of the mound in 1915 identified several house sites and 75 burials. Clovis projectile points, clay vessels and bone and shell beads date human habitation in Nacoochee back some 12,000 to 14,000 years at the close of the last ice age. For centuries these migrant people moved through the Nacoochee Valley, building their simple homes with central fire pits. They lived off the fruits and berries of the land, hunted its forests and fished the waters of the nearby river and creeks. They buried their dead in mounds like this and eventually moved on. Captain John Nichols (see page 27), who owned the property

Nora Mill Dam

The first dam constructed on the Chattahoochee was on this site just south of Helen. Built in 1824, it powered John Brown's grist and lumber mill. In 1876, Englishman John Martin built the present Nora Mill (see this page) and then replaced Brown's original dam in 1893. Today, this log dam, which is the northernmost dam on the river, is one of only 50 or 60 in the U.S. still operating a water-powered mill. The dam is presently being restored with new logs. The current owners had thought about using concrete but have decided to stay with log construction, at least for now. *Directions:* From Helen, take GA 75 south about 1 mile. The dam and mill are on the left.

during the late 1800s, built the gazebo on top of the mound. Some sources say it was built as a place of entertainment. Others say it was erected as a tribute to the vanquished natives.

Continue south on GA 75, crossing the Chattahoochee River and then Dukes Creek. Historical marker is on the left.

DUKES CREEK GOLD (2) - In 1834 the uncovering of a village site on Dukes Creek, as well as the finding of hewn pitch pine deep in Bean Creek, suggested that the first discoverers of gold in the Nacoochee Valley were mid-sixteenth century Spanish explorers. The second gold discovery came about 1828. This time it is believed that it was the result of a slave, belonging to Major Frank Logan, who had seen the gold fields in North Carolina and thought they looked similar to the gravel and creek beds in Nacoochee. Once a trace of gold was found, the rush was on. Within 10 years, the Indians had been driven out of the Nacoochee Valley. Mining developed from crude ground sluices to wooden sluice boxes, rockers and crude stamp mills to hydraulics. Once the stream beds were exhausted, the miners began tunneling into the hills.

Continue south on GA 75. Signs for Dukes Creek Mines will be on the right after crossing the Chattahoochee.

RICHARDSON-LUMSDEN HOUSE (3) - A brick in the west chimney of the Richardson-Lumsden House bears the inscription "1830s" making this the oldest house standing in White County. The Reverend J. L. Richardson, an ordained Methodist minister and circuit rider, built it along the banks of Dukes Creek after gold was discovered on the creek in 1828. The two-story house was constructed of lumber cut by a sash sawmill operated on Dukes Creek by John G. Lumsden. The house, which is in ill-repair, can be toured. It stands next to the Dukes Creek Mines, a gold and gem mining tourist operation. *More Information:* Dukes Creek Mines, Box 207, Helen, GA 30545, 706/878-2625.

Turn back north on GA 75 toward Helen. After crossing intersection with GA 17, look for Nora Mill on the right.

NORA GRIST MILL (4) - On this site in 1824 Daniel Brown harnessed the power of the Chattahoochee River and built the first grist and sawmill in Nacoochee near the Unicoi Turnpike. Local farmers brought their grain to be ground into meal, flour and grits. Brown used the same water power to saw lumber for their homes. The present Nora Mill was established in 1876 and has been grinding locally grown corn and wheat on the same stones for more than 120 years. In 1893, John Martin replaced the original dam built by Brown. Today Nora Mill grinds cornmeal, grits and whole wheat, rye and buckwheat flours as well as a line of grain mixes. Purchases can be made on the premises or through mail order. *More Information:* Nora Mill Granary, P.O. Box 41, Sautee-Nacoochee, GA 30571; 706/878-2375.

The next stop is across the road from Nora Mill.

JOHN MARTIN HOUSE (5) - John Martin, a Scotsman who came to Nacoochee to mine gold, ended up with one of the largest holdings of gold mining property in White County. He built this house in 1876. After he moved to Clarkesville in 1905, the house was used as a hotel.

Head back south on GA 75 to GA 17 intersection. Turn left. House sits on left side of the road as do the next few stops.

WEST END (6) - The Nichols-Hunnicutt-Hardman House, also known as West End because it anchors the west end of the Nacoochee Valley, was built in 1870 by retired Confederate soldier John Nichols. Conflicting information on Nichols has designated him a colonel, a major and a captain. Whatever his rank, he apparently was quite wealthy. He built this impressive Italianate Victorian house on the site formerly occupied by the home of Daniel Brown, who had built the nearby Nora Mill. The home had a horse barn, deer park, bear pens, a swan pond, a green house, cast iron fountains and a recreation building with card room and billiard parlor. He also built the gazebo on top of the Indian burial mound (see page 25). After Nichols died, Calvin Hunnicutt of Atlanta purchased the property. Later it was sold to Lamartine Griffin Hardman, who was governor of Georgia from 1927 to 1931.

CRESCENT HILL BAPTIST CHURCH (7) - John Nichols built this church in 1871 for the Presbyterian congregation. The Presbyterians held services here until 1898, shortly after Nichols' death. In 1902 Dr. Hardman purchased Nichols' property and organized the Baptist Church in the building. The Presbyterians moved their services to the chapel of the Nacoochee Institute in 1903.

NACOOCHEE POST OFFICE (8) - On this site Charles Williams

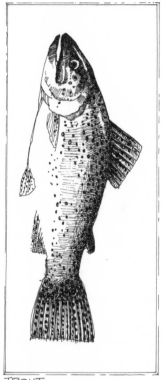

TROUT

Fish Consumption Guidelines
Headwaters to Lanier–No restrictions. As a general rule, eat smaller fish to be safe.

Source: Georgia Department of Natural Resources, 1997.

Chattahoochee Trout

Three salmonids (members of the family *Salmonidae)* live in a number of streams in the Chattahoochee watershed. Brook trout *(Salvelinus fontinalis)*, brown trout *(Salmo trutta)* and rainbow trout *(Oncorhynchus mykiss)* all inhabit waters of the Chattahoochee basin. These fish require clean, cold water to survive. Many streams in the headwaters area are designated as primary (supporting self-sustaining populations) and secondary (supporting stocked populations) trout streams. These stream designations provide added protection related to maintenance of stream buffers and restrictions on allowable increase of water temperature. Brook trout are the only trout native to this area; rainbow trout are native to the western U. S. and brown trout were introduced from Europe. The native brook trout are outcompeted by the aggressive rainbow trout and live mostly in first and second-order streams, often above barriers such as waterfalls that prevent upstream travel of the rainbow and brown trout.

Katherine Baer, Upper Chattahoochee Riverkeeper Staff

once operated the local post office from his country store. Mail was delivered weekly from Augusta by a carrier on horseback.

CHARLES WILLIAMS-PAT DYER HOME (9) - Charles Williams, Nacoochee's first postmaster, built this home in 1828 as a two-story home with brick chimneys at both ends. Since then, the upper story has been removed.

STARLIGHT (10) - Major Edward Williams built this home in the 1830s using lumber sawed at the sash sawmill of his father-in-law, Daniel Brown. Williams entertained statesmen, mining engineers and authors in this two-story, white-columned home. The home was named Starlight when Williams's daughter, Hannah, lived here with her husband, Dr. Elijah Starr.

Turn left on Henry Hunter Road.

RABUN ROAD (11) - The first road that went along this route connecting Nacoochee to the Rabun County area was an Indian footpath. White settlement in the area saw the footpath evolve into a horse trail and then into a wagon road.

Turn left on Bean Creek Road.

BEAN CREEK COMMUNITY (12) - At the end of the Civil War, freed slaves in the Helen-Nacoochee area faced the prospect of no work and no money. Although now free to leave the area, some of them chose to stay, taking on the name of their former owners and continuing to work the same fields their ancestors had worked. The Bean Creek Community, just north of Sautee and east of Helen, is a black community which is home to a number of these slave descendants. It centers around the Bean Creek Baptist Church, which was built on land donated by Captain Nichols, a Confederate veteran.

Continue on Bean Creek Road to its crossing of Bean Creek.

BEAN CREEK (13) - North of the community is Bean Creek itself, which flows into nearby Sautee Creek before that creek flows into the Chattahoochee River. The creek was the site of much gold mining activity beginning about 1832. It holds a significance to many of the community residents as the mines located here were worked by slave labor.

Turn back south on Bean Creek Road and stay on it until it intersects with GA 255. Turn right, heading into the center of the town of Sautee.

NACOOCHEE SCHOOL COMPLEX (14) - The Nacoochee Institute,

a Presbyterian school founded in 1903, once occupied part of this site. The present building was built in 1928 to replace the main building of the school which burned in 1926. However, to the dismay of local residents, the Nacoochee faculty was consolidated with that of another Presbyterian school in adjacent Rabun County. Today, the Sautee-Nacoochee Community Association has restored the old Nacoochee school building as an arts and community center that houses gallery space, a dance studio and a history museum. *More Information:* Sautee-Nacoochee Community Association, P.O. Box 460, Sautee-Nacoochee, GA 30571; 706/878-3300.

The next stop is directly across GA 255 from the school.

NACOOCHEE PRESBYTERIAN CHURCH (15) - Until the fire at the school, Presbyterian church services were held in the school auditorium. After the fire, this white frame church was built.

OLD SAUTEE STORE (16) - This building dates back to 1873 when it was built as a U.S. Post Office, operating until about 1962. Mail was distributed to the community six days a week in individual pigeon-hole boxes. Today, the 120-year-old building is a country store museum and gift shop. *More Information:* Old Sautee Store, Sautee-Nacoochee, GA 30571; 706/878-2281.

SAUTEE INN (17) - Known as the Alley House when it was built about 1900, it replaced the Greene Hotel which had been built in 1872 and burned in 1898. Earlier, the site was the residence of E. P. Williams, who supposedly owned one of the biggest tracts of land in Nacoochee.

Go to the intersection where GA 255 merges with GA 17. Turn left, heading south.

JOHNSTON HOUSE (18) - This house was built in 1914 on the site of another home which had burned down. The Nacoochee Institute apparently built the house for the J. Lamb Johnston family in exchange for property traded to the school.

THE "CABIN" (19) - This small house between the Johnston home and the Old Sautee Store is the only surviving building in Nacoochee which is known to have been a slave cabin.

Continue on GA 17/255 to the bridge at Sautee Creek.

SAUTEE CREEK (20) - Sautee Creek runs into the Chattahoochee River just below Sautee. The word "Sautee" is derived

Legacy of Gold

The Dahlonega gold rush sent people scurrying to make their fortune and left a legacy of contaminated floodplain sediments. Gold mining, common from 1829 to around 1940, occurred in several areas of the upper Chattahoochee watershed. Extensively mined areas include Dukes and Bean creeks, the Chattahoochee in the Sautee-Nacoochee Valley area and Yahoola Creek and the Chestatee River in Lumpkin County. Remnants of this mining are still visible today. Placer mining was used initially, but around 1868 miners began to use hydraulic methods whereby weathered bedrock was "washed" from hills into sluices and then into streams and rivers. Mercury was used to separate the gold from other materials. University of Georgia scientists sampled floodplain sediments near mines in the Chestatee and Yahoola areas and found that these sediments were still contaminated with mercury; mercury levels were 10 to 100 times greater than natural background levels. Although the contamination has not travelled far from the mining sites, mercury can pose a toxic threat to organisms living in the water and on the land. Tissue from mussels collected from the Chestatee River indicates that mercury is indeed bioaccummulating and may threaten certain organisms.

Katherine Baer, Upper Chattahoochee Riverkeeper Staff

The Soquee River

Sitting on the rock outcrop along the trail to the Tray Mountain Appalachian Trail shelter, a spectacular view of a steep, wild watershed unfolds to the east. This is the headwaters of the left fork of the Soquee River, which is a 29-mile long major tributary of the Chattahoochee River in the headwaters area. Most of the left fork of the Soquee is in the Tray Mountain Wilderness Area, providing a wonderful opportunity for adventurous folks to explore a wild headwaters area. The area has no marked or maintained trails, but there are many trails and old road beds to use. You will feel more confident with a USGS topographical map and compass to find your way to the waterfalls and beautiful campsites on the north and south prongs of the Soquee and Wolfpen Branch. There are only two reasonable ways to access the Soquee headwaters area. Hiking from FSR 79 north of Chimney Mountain Road, you can climb over the ridge to the South Prong. Chimney Mountain Road does a loop north of GA 356 in White County northeast of Unicoi State Park. Hiking from the end of FSR 166 gets you into Wolfpen Branch and the north prong. Take GA 197 0.1 mile north from GA 356, turn left onto Goshen Creek Road, go 1.2 miles then left on Goshen Mountain Road, go 0.5 mile to end of pavement, bear right on gravel 2 miles to FSR 166 on left, another 0.5 mile brings you to a parking area. Following the trail to the southwest from the parking area will take you into Tray Mountain Wilderness Area and the headwaters of the Soquee River. The Lake Burton and Tray Mountain USGS maps are a necessity.

from the Cherokee word, "Echota" or "Itsati." On old maps of the area, the river is called Chota River. The Cherokee Indian village which was located in the Nacoochee Valley also was called Chota.

Continue on GA 17/255 to the other side of the bridge.

WILLIAMS MILL (21) - On this site Edwin P. Williams operated a grist and sawmill, blacksmith shop and tan-yard. The mill's dam is located about 150 yards upstream from the GA 17 bridge over Sautee Creek. What looks like a small waterfall extending across the creek is what is left of the dam's heart pine mudsill. The foundation ruins of the mill house are located downstream from the dam site between Lynch Mountain Road and the creek. The blacksmith shop was where Joe Brown's pikes were manufactured during the Civil War. These were daggers on long poles which Georgia Governor Joseph E. Brown ordered to arm the Home Guard for "close fighting."

Go a little further on GA 17/255, just past where Lynch Mountain Road used to intersect the highway on the left.

WYLY-ROGERS HOUSE (22) - This house sits on the site of the Nacoochee Hotel, the first hotel built in Nacoochee. The hotel belonged to J. R. Wyly, a builder of the Unicoi Turnpike. Wyly owned two other hotels along the turnpike, Traveller's Rest in Toccoa, which is a state historic site, and the Wyly-Brown House near the Hiawassee River in Towns County.

RUSSELL-BRASSTOWN SCENIC BYWAY —Nationally designated by the U.S. Forest Service, this 38-mile, well-marked loop winds its way through the area of the Chattahoochee National Forest which surrounds the headwaters of the Chattahoochee River. The loop, which begins and ends outside of Helen, has good views of Raven Cliffs Wilderness to the south and Mark Trail Wilderness to the north. It passes Jack's Gap where Jack's Gap Trail leads to Chattahoochee Gap and the source of the river. The drive also passes through Unicoi Gap where the Unicoi Turnpike crossed the Blue Ridge. The vegetation along the route is beautiful at any time of the year, but on a clear, fall weekend, the colors can be spectacular. Banks of purple asters cover the highway and glowing red maples and oaks mix among the white pine. *Directions to drive the loop clockwise from Helen:* From Helen, take GA 75 north for 1.5 miles to GA

356/75 Alt. Turn left and go 2.3 miles to Richard Russell Scenic Highway. Turn right. This will eventually dead end into GA 180. Turn right and follow to where GA 180 dead ends into GA 75. Turn right (south), heading back to Helen.

SIGNIFICANT URBAN EXPERIENCES

HELEN –At 2:45 on a sky-blue Saturday afternoon in October, traffic heading north into Helen is backed up for several miles, all the way to Duncan Bridge Road. A mixture of rock and umpa band music blares out from restaurants and shops along Main Street. The crowd is diverse. Dads in polo shirts carry toddlers while moms push baby buggies loaded with shopping bags. Groups of senior citizens in brightly colored polyester jumpsuits and warm-up jackets saunter along. The college crowd is out in front of the Wurst House—a favorite hangout—eating bratwurst and drinking Bitburger and Becks. Preteens on skateboards with ice cream cones in hand whip around the throngs of people. Gigantic pumpkins are piled up around the picnic tables and benches in front of Betty's Country Store. Kids sit on the pumpkins while smiling moms click cameras. Inside people are sampling hot, hot jalapeno relish, browsing through regional books and crafts, picking up pasta salad, sandwiches and drinks and trying to check out in lines backed up to the deli counter. Cars and sightseeing buses line streets and fill parking lots. Every imaginable combination of hiking boots, shorts and sweatshirt walks past. It's a typical Oktoberfest weekend in Helen.

Helen sits in the headwaters of the Chattahoochee River, about 14 river miles below the river's source at Chattahoochee Gap. Two ridges run along either side of the town, and a narrow gap on Helen's north and south ends separates the town from the communities of Robertstown and Nacoochee, respectively.

The Helen Valley saw its first white settlers come about 100 years before the town of Helen was founded. The cutting of the Unicoi Turnpike in 1819 through the valley and what is now Helen's main street led the way for the first pioneer families who settled in the area. The discovery of gold on Dukes

Access to the river for fishing downstream of the wilderness area is limited by private ownership of the river. There are two access areas on national forest land for fishing. These are at 3.5 and 3.8 miles south of GA 255 on GA 197. There is no canoeing access and landowners are unfriendly to paddlers.

Stops at several local business are very worthwhile. At Batesville (GA 197/GA 255), the Wood Duck Gallery has a variety of local art, especially wildlife carvings. Nearby is the famous Batesville Store featuring wonderful food from the grill and oven as well as basic groceries. Traveling south down GA 197, 1 mile from Batesville is the Serendipity Shop featuring stained glass. Mark of the Potter occupies an old mill on the Soquee River on GA 197, 2 miles south of Batesville. Mark of the Potter features a remarkable selection of local arts and crafts and a back porch above the river from which you can view and feed the giant trout in the pool below.

James Sullivan, Georgia Forest Watch

Soque is a Cherokee word, the exact meaning of which is unknown, but may have been from "soquo" meaning "first." There was an old Cherokee town of Soque in present-day White County.

—*Marion Hemperley,* Indian Heritage of Georgia

Riparian Buffers

The word riparian comes from a Latin word meaning "belonging to a river or a shore" and refers to the vegetated environments bordering streams, rivers, lakes and wetlands. Riparian zones, the crucial interface between land and water, play many roles that are valuable to people and wildlife.

Although riparian buffers cannot absorb unlimited pollution runoff, they are effective at removing, transforming and/or storing a large amount of pollution such as nutrients and sediment. Riparian zones in agricultural areas are known to be extremely effective at reducing the amount of nutrients that reach local streams. Sediment from upland erosion can be trapped and retained in the riparian zone, preventing it from reaching local waterways where it is detrimental to stream habitat, fish and drinking water supplies.

Riparian zones are able to hold water during a flood when the water rises out and over the banks of the stream. This prevents further flooding downstream, traps sediments and nutrients and slows water velocities to reduce erosion.

The root mass of trees, grasses and shrubs in the riparian zone helps to stabilize stream banks and prevent them from eroding. Riparian areas are often more diverse than the adjacent upland areas because this unique environment represents a gradient in vegetation, moisture and soils that create a number of habitats. Twigs, branches and leaves falling from riparian vegetation into the water also provide important instream habitat for aquatic organisms such as insects and fish. Additionally, this vegetation provides a food

Creek in 1828 brought an increase in activity. Some miners came and left, but others brought their families, mining in the fall and winter and farming in the spring and summer. They cut ditches through the ridges around Helen, diverting the streams into the valley and washing the gold out of the beds. By the 1900s gold fever was in remission, but another new and maybe more devastating era was to begin. Timbering came to the Helen Valley and a railroad was built to haul the lumber away from the mountains. The town of Helen developed around the Byrd-Matthews Sawmill, which was built in 1913. The town was named for the daughter of John McCombs, a prominent citizen of that era, who was part-owner of the mill and of the newly built railroad. The sawmill operated continuously until 1928, depleting the area of its once plentiful virgin pines and hardwoods. When the last of the trees was run through its blades, the mill was demolished and the fortune of Helen languished for the next 40 years. In the early 1960s a man named Jim Wilkins opened a women's apparel plant, Orbit Manufacturing, and hired a few people. But for the most part Helen was nearly a ghost town until 1968 when a new idea brought change.

Three men were prime movers behind born-again Helen. One was Jim Wilkins, the founder of Orbit Manufacturing, who owned most of the west side of the business district. Another was Pete Hodkinson, who lived in nearby Clarkesville, worked with Wilkins in the management of Orbit and also owned land in Helen. Both men stood to gain if Helen were to become a major tourist attraction, which is what they had in mind. In late 1968, they added their ideas and resources to those of the third member of the triumvirate, John Kollock, an artist living nearby who had a passion for the architecture and landscape of the Bavarian Alps. Within a week of their first meeting, these men drew up the initial plan for putting a new face on Helen, one calculated to be alluring to mountain tourists. Kollock drew a series of sketches depicting his vision of what the town would look like after its projected transformation, and the other two wasted no time in convincing their fellow businessmen and property owners in town to cooperate with the effort.

Today, Helen is an Alpine village with overhanging roofs,

carefully cluttered shop windows and colorful shutters and balconies, and a simulated Bavarian bell tower watching over it all. It is one of the top tourist draws in the state. And the Chattahoochee River runs right through its heart.

Directions: From Cleveland, go north on GA 75 for 13 miles. *More Information:* Alpine Helen/White County Convention and Visitors Center, P.O. Box 730, Helen, GA 30545; 706/878-2181.

FISHING

BEST ADVICE –Fish spots in this upper section of the Chattahoochee that offer the trout a hiding or feeding place. These spots are usually found near the bottom of pools or in slower pockets of water near boulders and submerged logs. Stand downstream of the spot to fish and cast the bait or lure several feet upstream of the target area. Let the bait drift through the target area while slowly taking up the slack in the line. A stop in the downstream drift of the line along with a sharp "tap-tap-tap" signals a bite. Give the fish a moment to take the bait then pull back and set the hook.

TACKLE AND BAIT –A light rod with an ultralight spinning or spincast reel filled with 4-or-6-pound test line is best suited for this section of the river. Rods should be no longer than six feet to keep the line out of trees while casting. Use a short shank size 10 hook with one or two BB-size split shot weights secured about 10-to-12 inches above the hook to weight the line. Another alternative is fly-fishing. However, fly-fishing is for advanced anglers and advice on rod lengths, line weight, fly patterns and other aspects of the sport will vary depending on the person asked. Consult a knowledgeable salesperson at a fly-fishing shop or sporting goods store for advice.

Common trout baits include worms, crickets, salmon eggs, spinning lures and corn. Take two types of bait in case the trout are finicky that day. Use just enough bait to cover the hook. These lures work well: Rooster Tail (1/8 oz. or less), Panther Martin, Rapala (size 5) or less and Little Cleos.

GUIDES –For professional guides who specialize in fishing the Upper Chattahoochee, contact Unicoi Outfitters (706/878-

or energy source that is important to the entire aquatic food web.

While the state requires that a minimum 25-foot vegetated buffer be preserved along warm water streams in Georgia, a much wider buffer of 50 to 100 feet is recommended in areas with steep slopes and/or cold water fisheries, such as the trout streams of the Chattahoochee's headwaters region above Lake Lanier.

Katherine Baer, Upper Chattahoochee Riverkeeper Staff

Trout shun warm water, but largely because it contains insufficient oxygen. Wherever vigorous aeration beefs up oxygen content, browns and rainbows will tolerate temperatures of 80 degrees and more. Look for them below dams, natural falls, and at the base of whitewater rapids. Any spring fed tributary will draw trout to its mouth, and they'll congregate at underwater springs. Bass are not nearly as sensitive, but they do become sluggish during the heat of the day.

The Chattahoochee in Winter

"Contrary to the opinion of many, winter canoeing is fantastic. The water is generally high and southern temperatures are mild. We wear wet suit pants (scuba diver's neoprene rubber suits) and wet suit vests or woolen sweaters under a coated nylon jacket.

About four years ago Payson and Aurelia Kennedy, Ross Wilson, Frank Hatfield and I went to this stretch of the upper Chattahoochee and found it frozen over except for one small channel down the center. We decided to go anyway since the water was high. At Buck Shoals I knocked a two-inch hole in my new kayak, which rapidly began to swamp. We discovered then that it is very difficult to get out of the current across ice. Finally, after floundering down a couple of rapids, I was able to reach the side. It had begun snowing. We built a fire to dry the boat for taping; and opening several cans of chili, we placed them in the edge of the fire. As we sat on logs watching the chili bubble, drinking hot chocolate and bouillon from thermos bottles, there was a moment when we all stopped talking and just grinned at each other through the snowflakes. I finally broke the spell by saying, 'Most people would consider this insanity, yet it's a totally beautiful, exciting day.' There was instant agreement; I still recall that day as one of my great canoeing adventures."

Claude Terry, Brown's Guide to Georgia, *Winter 1973-74.*

3083). They are located 2 miles north of Helen on US 75. Also, Phil Sharp (770/319-7012) teaches basic through advanced fly-fishing on the Chattahoochee below Buford Dam, and the techniques he uses are applicable to the Upper 'Hooch.

BEST BOOKS AND MAPS – "Trout Streams of Georgia," a free map, published by the Georgia Department of Natural Resources, includes the Chattahoochee and shows access roads. (To order see page 326.)

"Chattahoochee River Trout Fishing, Canoeing and Rafting Guide," produced by Atlantic Mapping, Inc., shows the Chattahoochee River from Helen in northeast Georgia to Peachtree Creek (with the exception of Lane Lanier, which is covered on a separate map). The map shows access roads, boat ramps, canoe and raft put-ins and take-outs and includes significant historical sites, state parks, historical and natural features and campgrounds. Available only at outdoor stores, bait and tackle shops and marinas. (To order see page 325.)

U.S. Geological Survey 1:24,000 scale topographical maps covering this section of the river are Jack's Gap, Cow Rock, Helen, Leaf, Clarkesville and Lula. (To order see page 326.)

BOATING

There has been a metamorphosis of the upper Chattahoochee River from the isolated crystalline mountain stream of a few decades ago to the overcrowded and often abused stream of today. Increased construction of riverbank homes and businesses, lumbering scars, hordes of weekend paddlers and increasingly turbid waters have begun to take their toll on the Chattahoochee. Despite that, the canoe trip from Sautee Creek downstream to Lake Lanier is one of the most rewarding, varied and beautiful water routes in the region. It is a rite of passage for all Georgia canoeists. This section of the river can be canoed as a whole, or divided up into the smaller trips listed below.

THE UPPER, UPPER 'HOOCH –This section above Helen beginning in the Chattahoochee National Forest is a tight, difficult and rapidly descending mountain stream. Only experts should run it. Water levels vary almost hourly, and this section should

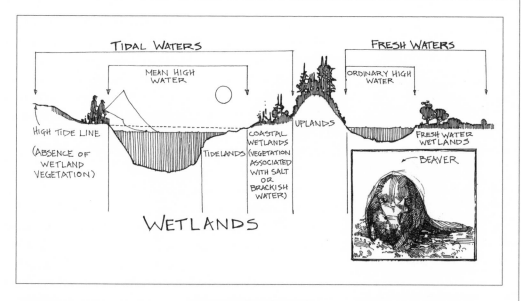

TIDAL WATERS

FRESH WATERS

MEAN HIGH WATER

ORDINARY HIGH WATER

HIGH TIDE LINE

(ABSENCE OF WETLAND VEGETATION)

TIDELANDS

COASTAL WETLANDS (VEGETATION ASSOCIATED WITH SALT OR BRACKISH WATER)

UPLANDS

FRESH WATER WETLANDS

BEAVER

WETLANDS

Wetlands

A wetland is an area of land where the water level remains near or above the surface of the ground for most of the year. Considerable debate has gone on between regulators and developers over what constitutes a wetland. Dr. Eugene Odum, a renowned ecologist at the University of Georgia, quips that the plot in question should pass the squish test. "If you put a foot in and you hear a squish, it's a wetland." A compromise definition among biologists, regulators and others is that wetlands mean areas with enough surface or groundwater to support vegetation adapted to life in saturated soil conditions. Some wetlands are wetter than others. They may hold water permanently, or only a few days each year.

Wetlands support a variety of plant and animal life and occur throughout the world. The major types of wetlands include bogs, fens, marshes and swamps. Bogs and fens are found primarily in northern climates. Acidic soils and the heavy growth of mosses, particularly sphagnum moss, characterize bogs while grasses and sedges characterize fens, where the soil is neither highly acidic nor basic. Both bogs and fens contain a large amount of partially decayed plant life called peat. Some bogs and fens have trees and shrubs, but woody plants are absent from others. Marshes and swamps generally occur in warmer climates. Marshes are dominated by grasses, reeds, rushes, sedges and other non-woody plants. Swamps, on the other hand, include trees and shrubs.

Critical to the survival of countless plants and animals, wetlands provide refuge to one-third of America's endangered or threatened species. Wetlands help control floods because they hold back water, and they store large amounts of water for long periods. The rich aquatic ecosystems also filter pollutants from human activities better than any water treatment plant. The cost of replacing 30 million acres of wetlands with equivalent pollution control for agricultural wastes has been estimated in excess of $100 billion.

Despite their value, wetlands have become as threatened as the wildlife they protect. Conservationists estimate that the continental United States has lost half of its 200 million acres of original wetlands. An additional 1,000 acres are lost each day to development.

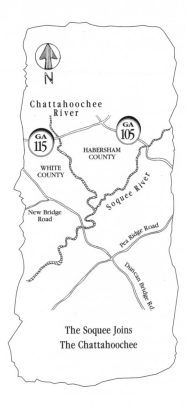

Chattahoochee
River

GA
115

GA
105

HABERSHAM
COUNTY

WHITE
COUNTY

Soquee River

New Bridge
Road

Pea Ridge Road

Duncan Bridge Rd.

N

**The Soquee Joins
The Chattahoochee**

*"It is difficult to find in life any event
which so effectually condenses intense
nervous sensation into the shortest possible
space of time as does the work of shooting,
or running an immense rapid. There is no
toil, no heart breaking labor about it, but as
much coolness, dexterity, and skill as a man
can throw into the work of hand, eye, and
head; knowledge of when to strike and how
to do it; knowledge of water and rock, and
of one hundred combinations which rock
and water can assume..."*

—Sir William Francis Butler, 1872

probably only be run after a night's rain. Canoeing through
Helen is not recommended. Most canoeists prefer to begin the
ride at Sautee Creek (see below). *Put-In:* From Helen, go north
on GA 75 about 1.5 miles to GA 356 and turn left. Cross the
bridge, then immediately turn back right on the dirt road on
the west side of the river. Follow this road past the ranger station (3.5 miles) and on to where the road crosses Jasus Creek.
Put in there. *Take-Out:* At Robertstown picnic area by the
Chattahoochee Barbeque. *Distance:* 7 miles, approximately 6
hours. From put-in on Jasus Creek to junction with
Chattahoochee River is 1 mile, (about 2 hours). From this point
to take-out is about 6 miles (about 4 hours). *Hazards:* This
upper stretch is extremely rocky and tight. Prepare for much
scraping and many bumpy drops. Overhanging bushes on
Jasus Creek can be treacherous in high water. Dead falls on
blind turns completely block some portions of the river. Drops
and ledges are so numerous that scouting is all but impossible.
Experienced canoeists can run them if water level is safe.
Otherwise, don't even try it. *Gauges:* A water-level gauge is on
the northwest corner of bridge in downtown Helen. Water
level of 1.2 to 1.5 feet is runable. Under 1.2 feet would result
in being grounded. Over 1.5 feet conditions could become
dangerous. *USGS Topos:* Jack's Gap, Cow Rock and Helen.

SAUTEE CREEK TO THE 255 BRIDGE –Sautee Creek enters the
Chattahoochee River from the left on the east end of the
Nacoochee Valley. From this junction down to GA 255 is one
of the longest undisturbed stretches of the river. The terrain is
heavily forested with large white pines and frequent rock outcroppings. Rapids are fairly frequent but never go beyond a
mild Class II category. The float down the creek is only 100
yards to the main stream of the Chattahoochee River. *Put-In:*
Sautee Creek. From Helen, take GA 75 south to its intersection
with GA 17 and turn left. In Sautee, turn left on GA 255 then
turn right on Lovers Lane. Cross bridge over Sautee Creek and
turn right on Lynch Mountain Road and parking. *Take-Out:* GA
255 Bridge. From Helen, take GA 75 south to its intersection
with GA 17. Turn left onto GA 17, past Sautee Creek to where
255 departs from 17 and turn right on 255. This is also called
Blue Creek Road. Go to where the highway crosses the

Who Owns the River

In boating on the Chattahoochee and its tributaries, please keep in mind some legalities and common sense niceties. You will find that your trip is much more pleasant if controversy and confrontation are avoided.

Although the Chattahoochee and its major tributaries are generally considered public waters, remember that the land surrounding them is not. To park, put-in or take-out, you need to be using public right-of-way or local, state or national park property. If not, you need permission from the landowner. Please be courteous and considerate.

Once you are on the river, so long as you are floating peacefully down the stream, you should be within your rights. Nevertheless, what most take for granted as an age-old public right has been the subject of some dispute in recent years. In the mid-1980s, one landowner adjacent to Smith Island on the upper section of the Chattahoochee between Highways 255 and 115 claimed to "own" the river, too. This was a vacation home owner whose idea of weekend fun was to sit in a lawn chair on the riverbank with his German shepherd and 45 Magnum and shout at boaters to "go back" as they came onto "his" stretch of the river. On occasion, the sheriff, dog and the gun got involved, too. Fortunately, that landowner moved on. Other landowners on portions of the Chestatee and Soquee Rivers, both Chattahoochee tributaries, have attempted to restrict boating, as well. Most recently, the Douglas County government tried to keep paddlers from boating on the Dog River, a tributary of the Chattahoochee near Six Flags, just downstream of Atlanta. A federal court judge ruled that since the Dog River was capable of supporting commercially assisted recreation in the nature of kayak clinics, it was a public stream that could not be closed to public use.

The question of public rights on Georgia streams is fraught with confusing, conflicting and complicated legal issues. Many different standards and arguments apply. River rights proponents see it this way: the adjacent landowner owns the riverbank and the riverbed, but a public easement or "navigational servitude" exists to travel on the water by boat, whether or not some form of commerce is involved. The landowner can use the stream and its bed for any purpose desired, so long as that use is not inconsistent with the public's right of travel. Those uses can include agricultural or industrial uses and may even include the right to fence or dam the stream if necessary. But if fencing or damming is necessary, the landowner should provide an alternate route for boaters.

Some, but blessedly few, landowners feel that their ownership of the bed and banks of a boatable stream also constitutes the right to prohibit boaters from paddling the stream altogether. They look to an 1863 Georgia statute that they claim gives them absolute ownership without any public boating easement, unless the stream can support "boats loaded with freight in the ordinary course of trade." To invoke such claim, these landowners typically post "no boating signs" or the like.

Most of the relevant legal history derives from Roman and British ancient law and from state and federal law dating back to the 19th century. Historically, and in modern times, most state and federal courts throughout the country have held that a stream's capability to support travel by canoes is sufficient to establish public or commercial boating rights on that stream. Nevertheless, some courts have taken a narrower view and insisted that only major rivers capable of supporting deep-draft watercraft are "navigable" so as to result in public boating rights.

The right to fish is a different issue altogether. Even though it is generally considered a public right to boat on the Chattahoochee and its tributaries, that does not mean that there is a general public right to fish wherever one chooses, even from a boat. The right of fishery belongs to the owner of the bed and banks, even though the fish themselves are considered to be owned by the state, not the landowner. Does that mean that you can't fish from a boat, except on stretches owned by the government? Probably not. The main thing to watch out for are posted signs saying "no fishing." If you see those signs, don't fish. If the landowner asks you not to fish, don't fish. Otherwise, it would appear that the landowner has not chosen to exercise his or her rights to keep you from fishing, and you are probably okay doing so.

Even with public boating rights, as more and more people paddle, and more and more homes are built on Georgia's streams, the potential for annoyance and conflict mounts. So, be careful and be nice. Do not assume that there is an automatic right to hike, portage, scout, or camp on riverbank land. Take only pictures: leave only paddle strokes. If you run into problems, call the Riverkeeper or the Georgia Canoeing Association after the trip, and maybe they can help.

Craig Pendergrast, attorney and canoeist

Delbert Greear

Canoeing with Delbert Greear

"Soon after we broke camp, we came to the famed Horseshoe rapids, an intense area which funnels most of the Chattahoochee River simultaneously though a fast chute and over a high waterfall, causing canoeists to have to make a U-turn as they traverse the rapids. It is a thrilling and awesome sight. But what I saw Delbert do in a canoe impressed me even more. All during the trip I had watched Delbert to learn canoeing, and as I watched, my appreciation for his skills increased again and again. But even so, I was unprepared for what I saw at the Horseshoe. Or maybe by then I had learned enough to appreciate what I was seeing.

As I watched him position his canoe in the slack water above the falls and, then, with a deft stroke, move the canoe into the part of the current that was going exactly where he wanted to go, I was witnessing a white-water ballet. With the slightest touch of the paddle, he kept the

Chattahoochee River. Access is before the bridge on the Habersham County side of the river only. *Distance:* About 6 miles. *Gauges:* The only gauge for this stretch of river is located 150 yards upstream of the GA 115 Bridge (see gauges below). *USGS Topos:* Helen.

GA 255 BRIDGE TO GA 115 BRIDGE –This section of the river enters a long, slow area nicknamed the "Dead Sea" because its stillness offers a marked contrast to the rapids above and below. The Smith Island rapid, which follows the Dead Sea, is the first of the significant rapids on the upper Chattahoochee. It should be scouted by first timers or by anyone running the river at extreme water levels. *Put-In:* GA 255 Bridge (see directions above). *Take-Out:* GA 115 Bridge. From the GA 255 Bridge, continue on 255 until it intersects with GA 115. Turn left and follow to the 115 Bridge. Cross the bridge. Take-out is on the downstream side of the bridge where the Wildewood Outfitters Outpost is located. *Distance:* About 5 miles. *Gauges:* A U.S. Geological Survey gauge is located 150 yards upstream of the GA 115 Bridge on the east side. A reading of 0.8 to 1.4 feet indicates low water; 1.8 to 2.5 feet medium water; 2.8 to 3.5 feet high water and 4 feet and up very high water. *USGS Topos:* Helen and Leaf.

GA 115 BRIDGE TO DUNCAN BRIDGE –White water buffs will find the section from the GA 115 Bridge to Duncan Bridge (GA 384) a pleasant and rewarding experience. The gradient for this section averages 20 feet per mile with the Buck Island Shoals area averaging 36 feet per mile. None of the rapids is intimidating at normal water levels, but altogether they are frequent enough and challenging enough to keep you occupied. The Soquee River, which drains much of Habersham County, enters the Chattahoochee on the left, right below the Horseshoe Rapid. *Put-In:* GA 115 Bridge (see directions above). Put-in or take-out on the east (left) side of the river near the Wildewood Outfitters Outpost. *Take-Out:* Duncan Bridge. From the 115 Bridge, go west on GA 115 to its intersection with GA 254 and turn left. Go to the intersection of GA 254 and GA 384 (Duncan Bridge Road) and turn left. Go to the Wildewood Outfitters next to the bridge. *Distance:* About 5 miles. *High Points:* All of the following rapids should be scouted: Buck Island Shoals is a fairly continuous 0.25 mile section of Class II water. Three Ledges are three ledges that many consider to be the most fun and challenging rapid on the river. Horseshoe Rapids is Class II plus. A long, low ledge of rocks that the river hooks around give Horseshoe its name. Enter on the left and be ready to cut back hard to the right. *Gauges:* The only gauge for this stretch of river is located 150 yards upstream of the GA 115 Bridge (see page 38). *USGS Topos:* Leaf and Clarkesville. *Note:* Wildewood Outfitters (see page 334), located at Duncan Bridge (GA 384), has parking, rents canoes and operates a shuttle service to put-ins and take-outs on the above section of river.

DUNCAN BRIDGE TO BELTON BRIDGE –This 10-mile section offers a serene, wilderness canoeing experience. The river flow is moderate and includes a few Class I and Class II rapids. The decreasing current flow signals the backwater of Lake Lanier and the approach of Belton Bridge Park, the first public access along this section of river (see page 48). *Put-In:* Duncan Bridge. About 65 miles from Atlanta. From Atlanta, take I-85 north to I-985 then north on GA 365. Turn left on GA 384 (Duncan Bridge Road) at the traffic light. Go 5 miles to Duncan Bridge. Parking, shuttle and canoe rental are available at the Wildewood Outfitters next to the bridge. *Take-Out:* Belton Bridge. This ramp is in poor condition and sometimes closed. Scout before using. About 59 miles from Atlanta. From Atlanta, take I-85 north to I-985 then north on GA 365. Turn left on Belton Bridge Road. Follow signs. The Corps of Engineers park here has no public facilities, and due to its remoteness it is not a good location to leave a car unattended. Camping is not officially permitted in the park, but in the past the Corps has been lenient enforcing that rule for one-night campers canoeing the river. The best camping sites are on the east bank between the bridge and the boat ramp. The park is beautiful, but unfortunately can be trashy. *Distance:* About 10 miles. *USGS Topos:* Clarkesville, Leaf and Lula.

BELTON BRIDGE TO LULA BRIDGE –This is essentially a lake canoeing experience on a portion of the river backed up to form Lake Lanier. *Put-In:* Belton Bridge. As mentioned above, this ramp is in poor condition and sometimes closed. Scout before using (see directions above). *Take-Out:* Lula Park (see

canoe where he wanted it. As he moved in the water, picking his way deliberately and with delicate control, he was a paradox of slowness in a world of fast fluid motion. He made the canoe traverse the very brink of the waterfall, letting the current carry him along at its own speed. At the intersection of the falls and the chute, he seemed to hesitate for a moment, to come to a complete stop. Then, with a dig of the paddle, he made a hard right turn into the chute and went speeding through the aquatic chaos below.

Watching him, I thought of a hawk I had watched once riding the thermals coming up from the base of Whiteside Mountain near Highlands, North Carolina. Both Delbert and the hawk had the same delicate–serene even–control of their element, a control that allowed them to be where they wanted to be and do what they wanted to do, cooperating with instead of competing against forces and currents around them."

Wilson Hall canoeing and fishing with Delbert Greear, Brown's Guide to Georgia, *July/Aug 1976*

The Chestatee in Winter

"I remember one frigid day, canoeing alone, I rounded a tight bend in a river that normally was active with a small waterfall on the left bank and a large room-size circling eddy near the right bank. It was wet suit temperature, and I didn't want to take any risks in that cold. But the sight I saw was too astounding not to examine closer. The waterfall was frozen into countless icicles. The large eddy had frozen into a circle of solid ice. Leaves and sticks were embedded deep into the ice mound. It was still circular, but only because little waves from the still flowing body of the river washed into it, to be frozen before they could exit. Through the clear ice, you could see how layer after layer had frozen, one on top of the other, building to a thickness of over half a foot at the center. The weather was warming; and by afternoon, it would all be gone. I would be the only person to see this marvel."

Reece Turrentine, "Winter Solitude on the Chestatee," Georgia Journal, *November/December 1996*

Chestatee River means "Firelight Place" from the Cherokee word "atsilsunti" referring to the fire hunting method of killing deer in the river at night.

–Marion Hemperley, Indian Heritage of Georgia

page 48). About 56 miles from Atlanta. From Atlanta, take I-85 north to I-985 to GA 365. Turn left on GA 52 and follow signs. This park, a good place to leave a car, has a large, paved parking area next to the bridge. It is a popular launching place for fishermen, particularly in the spring when crappie and white bass fishing are good. No camping permitted. *Distance:* About 3 miles. *USGS Topos:* Lula.

LULA BRIDGE TO CLARK'S BRIDGE OLYMPIC PARK –This section is all pleasant, scenic lake paddling. The narrow waterway follows the original river channel. The 1,322-acre Chattahoochee River Park begins approximately 3 miles from Clark's Bridge. Purchased in 1994 by the state of Georgia and the Preservation 2000 program, its permanent use has yet to be decided. About one mile from Olympic Park (or Clark's Bridge), the glassed Olympic Finish Tower used in the canoe and kayak competition of the 1996 Olympic Games comes into view. *Put-In:* Lula Bridge (see directions above). *Take-Out:* Olympic Park. From Atlanta, take I-85 north to I-985, exit 7, and turn left on Jesse Jewell Parkway. Go to the second traffic light and turn right on Limestone Parkway. Go to the second traffic light and turn right on Clark's Bridge Road and follow it across Clark's Bridge. The Olympic boathouses are on the left. *Distance:* About 10 miles. *USGS Topos:* Lula, Clermont and Gainesville.

DAY TRIPS FROM CLARK'S BRIDGE OLYMPIC PARK –This is a good put-in for day trips of 3 to 5 miles or longer up river along the Chattahoochee River Park.

CHESTATEE RIVER –North Georgia's Chestatee River lies within the Chattahoochee watershed and was a tributary of the Chattahoochee before Lake Lanier was formed. Born in the rock faces of Blood Mountain, the Chestatee cascades out of the Chattahoochee National Forest as one of Georgia's best trout streams. From Turner's Corner to GA 52, the river is one of the best canoeing streams in the state. Its small watershed limits its use to winter, spring and rainy periods in the summer. Azaleas and dogwoods bloom along its banks in April, laurel in May and rhododendron in early June–all against a backdrop of white pine and hemlocks. Below Grindle Bridge is Chestatee Falls which cascades about 40 feet in a series of leaps. Wildlife along the river include beavers, deer, hawks, osprey, kingfishers, wood ducks and green heron. As on other mountain rivers, woods and sandbanks can suddenly turn into high rock out-croppings. The Chestatee once flowed into the Chattahoochee just west of Gainesville. Now the last 19 miles of its length is part of Lake Lanier.

A popular canoe trip on the Chestatee begins at the Appalachian Outfitters on GA 60 near Dahlonega and goes downriver 6.3 miles to the GA 400 bridge. For a longer trip, put-in on Tesnatee Creek, 10 miles above the outpost and canoe down to the outpost or continue to the GA 400 bridge. For detailed information on canoeing the Chestatee or guided trips, contact Ben or Dana LaChance at Appalachian Outfitters (see page 333). The outpost is open seven days a week, April through September.

Lanier power boaters can go up the Chestatee as far as the GA 400 bridge. Use extreme care here. There is a no wake zone about 2 miles below the bridge; strictly observe this zone to preserve the delicate riverbank environment.

www.chattahoochee.org

We welcome your comments, suggestions, recommendations and input regarding this book and the river, via the Internet at the Riverkeeper's website: www.chattahoochee.org.

You can also access the website for additional information regarding the Chattahoochee and the many issues that affect the river.

ALL IS BORN OF WATER;
ALL IS SUSTAINED BY WATER.

A COMMON SIGHT! TURTLES BASKING ON A ROCK IN THE CHATTAHOOCHEE.

Section 2
Lanier

Jack Beachem

"The lake has meant a great deal to Atlanta and that's proven by the number of people moving in this direction. The growth in Atlanta is north towards the lake, and the land on the lake has quadrupled in the last ten years. We're running out of lake lots and the average lot was $126,000, just for the lot. And then the houses were around $500,000 for the builder that's building most of them. The closer people get to the lake the more opportunity there is for them to use it. The more Atlanta grows the more customers you have for the facilities and services on the lake.

They talk about the lake being too crowded...The only place that Lanier is crowded even on the Fourth of July weekend is in the vicinity of the marinas. You can get away from here and get out into the boonies so to speak in about ten minutes. There's literally no use during the week and in the wintertime. So utilization of the lake is maybe ten percent of what it could be if you used it on a daily basis year 'round. The big problem we had, and everybody else in the marina-type business has, is you make your living in two days a week. We don't have the sale of gas and oil and other things during the week that you do on weekends. And, of course, if you get a bad weekend weatherwise, why that can cut your income 75 percent for that weekend.

Wintertime there's nobody here. But even today, we can get in the boat and you can ride and you might see 15 boats that's out in the lake. I mean that's deserted. And we don't have the activity that a lot of lakes have during the week. Now Lake of the Ozarks, for example, they have a jillion different cottages and hotels and motels and so forth on the lake and it's developed much greater than here. I spent some time at Lake of the Ozarks when we were building to see what they offered and what would induce the public to use the facilities on weekdays. And, of course, what it boiled down to was all of the hotels and the tourists. Now we've got two hotels here. But they're in their infancy. If this became a good tourist area other than a local recreation area, why you'd find the use of the lake would be much greater."

Jack Beachem, owner of Beachem Motor-Yachts, started Holiday Marina on Lake Lanier in 1957.

THE LAKE

Lake Lanier is an area in transition. The landscape is a crazy mixture of trailer parks, subdivisions, single houses, dry boat storage, farmland and farmhouses. The lake is continually going upscale. Houses along the lake are getting grander, and the boats are getting increasingly larger. It is a landscape that reflects the South itself — new replacing old, urban areas gobbling up rural and, in this case, tourism supplanting an agricultural economy.

It is estimated that there are 23,000 boats in the area, 10,000 houses on the lake and 7,200 private docks. The lake has its own radio station, Lake 102-FM, which plays oldies and gives lake news, and its own lakeside newspaper. It is one of the most visited Corps of Engineers lakes in the nation. There are campgrounds, day use parks, marinas and an island resort with everything from championship golf to a waterslide park. During the summer when the ski boats, houseboats and jet skis control the south end of the lake, the fishermen head to the north end. But in the winter, the anglers fish the entire lake. In the summer, Atlanta consumes Lanier; but in the winter it feels like the north Georgia mountain terrain it once was.

Sidney Clopton Lanier, the 19th-century poet who wrote about the free and tumbling waters of the Chattahoochee, would possibly be amazed that this huge and bustling impoundment of his river is his namesake. Lake Sidney Lanier touches five Georgia counties: Forsyth, Dawson, Lumpkin, Hall and Gwinnett. Impounded by Buford Dam in 1956, it encompasses 38,000 surface acres of water with 540 miles of shoreline at full capacity. The lake extends 44 miles up the Chattahoochee River and 19 miles up the Chestatee River. It is operated under the direction of the Mobile District, U.S. Army Corps of Engineers, Mobile, Alabama.

However, this man-made lake, sometimes called Georgia's freshwater ocean, sits over an area as rich in history as it is in the bottom land soil which once lined the banks of the Chattahoochee. Around 8,000 BC small bands of Indians settled the area, finding it an ideal place because of its plentiful game, excellent fishing and abundance of fruit and vegetables.

Sidney Lanier

The poet Sidney Lanier considered his primary passion, music, perhaps a talent inherited from ancestor Charles Lanier, court composer to Britain's James I and Huguenot refugee from whom many Laniers scattered along the Chattahoochee River trace their lineage. During the Civil War, Sidney survived a deathly illness in a Union prison by making up melodies on a song flute, his only possession. After the War, the Macon, Georgia, native moved to Baltimore where, renowned for conjuring up haunting violin effects on his instrument, he played in the orchestra.

An English lecturer at Johns Hopkins University, Lanier was as capable with the pen as the flute. His gripping anti-war message in "Tiger Lilies" and mysterious natural images in "The Marshes of Glynn" earned him a national literary reputation as a poet.

In 1877 Lanier wrote "The Song of the Chattahoochee," a poetic defense of the call of duty over the pleasures of life. The critics panned it as simple, monotonous and awkwardly constructed. But the public embraced it, making the poem Lanier's most popular work.

A geographical ride down the river, the poem begins at the headwaters, mentioning the rocks and waterfalls, laurel and ferns, quartz and gem. It continues along the main part of the river, mentioning chestnut trees, which have since disappeared in North America because of blight. The poem then refers to mills, probably those on the fall line, including that of West Point Manufacturing, a company started by a distant relation of the poet. A descendant of this part of the clan, Bruce Lanier, today runs the Wehaddekee Yarn

Recurrent flooding of the river carried rich topsoil to the bottom lands. Here, the Indians began to grow corn, beans and squash. By 900 AD the Indians had developed an agricultural economy. Much later the Cherokees settled the area. They eventually developed strong ties with the white man. But by the turn of the century the white man had removed the Cherokees, and roads, rail lines and covered bridges began to span the river throughout Hall County. Rivers were an important link in the county's economic growth, providing the power for mills that processed the area's cotton, lumber and grain.

Throughout the 20th century growth continued. This growth emphasized the need to harness the area's water resources. Periodic flooding continued as it had for thousands of years, but now it threatened residential areas and crops. Also, there was no dependable water supply for a growing population just south in Atlanta.

The idea for Lake Lanier goes back to 1946 when Congress authorized a development program to put the Chattahoochee River to work for the benefit of man. As a part of the Apalachicola-Chattahoochee-Flint River System (ACF), the U.S. Army Corps of Engineers was directed to design and build a series of dams and lakes along the river. The main purposes for building the lakes and dams at that time were hydroelectric power, water quality and supply, navigation and flood control. The Corps planned for the construction of five dams of which Buford Dam would be the farthest upstream in the Chattahoochee headwaters area, making it the headwater installation of the ACF River System. As the Chattahoochee flowed southward toward Columbus, it would be dredged so boats could navigate from there to the ocean. Along the way a series of locks, dams and lakes would be constructed so boats could move freely up and down the river.

The Corps acquired more than 58,000 acres of land for the Lake Lanier project. Most of this was rural farmland. Families who had farmed the land for years were offered about $40 per acre for their land. Fourteen thousand rolling acres of North Georgia forest were cleared for the shoreline. During the process houses along the shoreline were removed and in some cases even grave sites were relocated away from the lake.

Buildings, trees and other structures that would be covered with many feet of water were usually left standing and remain submerged today.

PARKS AND RECREATION

There are more than 60 recreational areas around Lake Lanier. These include campgrounds, day use parks and Lake Lanier Islands Resort. The Corps of Engineers manages most of these, while others are leased to county and city governments.

Although parking is plentiful at most of the recreation areas, it cannot be guaranteed. The areas on the southern end of the lake–nearest to Atlanta–fill up first and are usually crowded. Most any area below, or south of, Brown's Bridge is heavily trafficked. Arrival is recommended before 11am on a summer day to insure a place to park. However, if driving a couple of extra miles to the north end of the lake isn't a problem, the same well-maintained parks can be found there but with less people.

Brown Corps of Engineers signs clearly mark the entrances of recreational areas and are also located at the boat ramps, facing the lake, for the boat traveler. Generally, boat ramps are never closed and can be used 24 hours a day, year-round. However, at times when the lake is low, some ramps may be better to use than others. Restrooms on the north end of the lake are usually closed during the winter months. Whether other facilities are open in the winter in an area varies. For the most part, facilities open the first weekend in April and close sometime in September. During the season, most Corps campgrounds have park attendants on duty to assist visitors, and uniformed park rangers patrol the parks year-round. Hours for all day use areas are 7am-10pm. Except for Toto Creek and War Hill, which remain unlocked at night, all Corps campground gates are locked from 10:30pm-7am. Campground fees depend upon the type of campsite—primitive campsite, $10 per night; campsite without hookups, $12 per night; campsite with electricity and water, $18 per night; group campsites, $80 - 120 per night. Day use fees are charged at several park areas which have boat ramps or beach areas—boat launching, $2; swim-

Company on an Alabama tributary of the Chattahoochee.

Older Southerners, able to recite the poem by rote from grammar school memories, say its rhymes, alliterations and onomatopoeias, or words that sound like what they mean, are best enjoyed aloud.

Song of the Chattahoochee

Out of the Hills of Habersham,
Down the valleys of Hall,
I hurry amain to reach the plain,
Run the rapid and leap the fall,
Split at the rock and together
again,
Accept my bed, or narrow or
wide,
And flee from folly on every side
With a lover's pain to attain the
plain
Far from the hills of Habersham,
Far from the valleys of Hall.

All down the hills of Habersham,
All through the valleys of Hall,
The rushes cried *Abide, abide,*
The willful waterweeds held me
thrall,
The laving laurel turned my tide,
The ferns and the fondling grass
said Stay,
The dewberry dipped for work
delay,
And the little reeds sighed
Abide, abide,
Here in the hills of Habersham,
Here in the valleys of Hall.

High o'er the hills of
Habersham,
Veiling the valleys of Hall,
The hickory told me manifold
Fair tales of shade, the poplar
tall
Wrought me her shadowy self to
hold,
The chestnut, the oak, the wal-
nut, the pine,
Overleaning, with flickering
meaning and sign,
Said, *Pass not, so cold, these
manifold*
*Deep shades of the hills of
Habersham,*
*These glades in the valleys of
Hall.*

And oft in the hills of
Habersham,
And oft in the valleys of Hall,
The White quartz shone, and the

ming beach, $1 per person with a maximum of $3 per vehicle. Annual passes are $25 and senior citizens with Golden Age and Golden Access Passports will receive a 50 percent discount on day user fees. Contact the Resource Manager's Office for more information concerning Corps parks. For county and city parks, call the individual park. A free locator map of all parks is distributed by the Corps. *More Information:* Resource Manager's Office, Lake Sidney Lanier, P.O. Box 567, Buford, GA 30518; 770/945-9531.

The following list of recreational areas begins at Belton Bridge, the Corps of Engineers' northernmost park on Lanier, and goes clockwise around the lake.

BELTON BRIDGE –In poor condition, this northernmost boat ramp on Lanier is sometimes closed. It lies right below Belton Bridge which crosses the Chattahoochee River as it comes tumbling "down the valleys of Hall" County. Shortly after this, the river becomes a lake. *Facilities:* Boat ramp. *Directions:* From I-985 north, turn left on Belton Bridge Road and watch for signs.

LULA PARK –This park is on the northern section of Lanier where the Chattahoochee is still somewhat of a river. It lies next to Lula Bridge, the second northernmost bridge on Lanier. *Facilities:* Boat ramp, restrooms. *Directions*: From I-985, take GA 52 (Lula Road) north to Lula Bridge.

CLARK'S BRIDGE –Clark's Bridge Park is a City of Gainesville recreation area located on the extreme northern end of Lanier, along the original bed of the Chattahoochee River. It is named after Clark's Bridge which crosses the Chattahoochee at the park location. The bridge is named for Miss Elizabeth Clark, the only woman to build a bridge across the Chattahoochee, who operated a toll bridge here. Clark's Bridge Park, sometimes referred to as Olympic Park, was the venue for the 1996 Olympic Rowing, Sprint Canoe/Kayak Competition and is now the top facility in the United States for these Olympic sports, serving as the site for training and competitions. It is also home to the Lanier Canoe and Kayak Club and the Lake Lanier Rowing Club, which operates the rowing part of the facility. Included in this facility and left as an Olympic legacy is a multimillion dollar boathouse where members of the Lanier Canoe and Kayak Club offer a variety of programs from sprint racing to storage of boats for lake use. *Facilities:* Rowing facility, boat ramp, picnic tables, swimming area, restrooms, water. *Days/Hrs.:* Daily, year-round. *Fees:* None for day use. *Directions:* From I-985, take Exit 7, turning north on Jesse Jewell Parkway. Go to the second traffic light and turn right on Limestone Parkway. Go to the second traffic light and turn right on Clark's Bridge Road and follow it across Clark's Bridge. The park is on the left. *More Information:* 770/535-8280.

LAUREL PARK –This 136-acre Hall County park is located between Clark's Bridge and Longstreet Bridge in the Gainesville area. *Facilities:* Boat ramp, picnic tables, grills, picnic shelters, concessions, swimming area, fishing, playground, ball fields, tennis courts, archery range, restrooms, water. *Days/Hrs.:* Daily, 8am until dark. *Fees:* User fees for picnic shelters and ball fields. *Directions:* From I-985, take Exit 6, US 129, turn west and follow to the park. *More Information:* 770/535-8280.

LITTLE RIVER –This park is on the Little River in the Gainesville area of Lake Lanier. *Facilities:* Boat ramp, handicap access, picnic tables, water, restrooms. *Directions:* From I-985, take Exit 6, US 129, turn west and follow to the park.

HOLLY PARK –This City of Gainesville park is located right below Thompson Bridge. *Facilities:* Boat ramp, picnic shelters, picnic tables, fishing, swimming area, concessions, restrooms, water. *Days/Hrs.:* Daily, year-round. *Directions:* From I-985, take Exit 6, US 129, turn west and follow to GA 60. Stay on GA 60 to the park. *More Information:* 770/531-2680.

LONGWOOD PARK –This city-operated park sits at the end of Woods Mill Bay in Gainesville. *Facilities:* Picnic tables, picnic shelters, fishing, walking and nature trails, bike trails, restrooms, water. *Days/Hrs.:* Daily, year-round. *Fees:* Picnic shelter, $50, $25 to reserve. *Directions:* From I-985, take Exit 6, GA 129, and turn west. Go to GA 53, turn left and watch for signs. *More Information:* 770/531-2680.

LANIER POINT PARK –This community park, with softball and baseball fields, sits on the lake near Lanier Bridge and is operated by the City of Gainesville. *Facilities:* Boat ramp, group picnic shelter, picnic tables, ball fields, fishing, bike trails, hiking trails, restrooms, water. *Days/Hrs.:* Daily, year-round, 7am until

smooth brook-stone
Did bar me of passage with friendly brawl,
And many luminous jewel lone
-Crystals clear or a cloud with mist,
Ruby, garnet and amethyst-
Made lures with the lights of streaming stone
In the clefts of the hills of Habersham,
In the beds of the valleys of Hall.

But oh, not the hills of Habersham,
And of, not the valleys of Hall
Avail: I am fain for to water the plain.
Downward the voices of Duty call-
Downward, to toil and be mixed with the main,
The dry fields burn, and the mills are to turn,
And a myriad flowers mortally yearn,
And the lordly main from beyond the plain
Calls o'er the hills of Habersham,
Calls through the valleys of Hall.

Sidney Lanier, 1877

Corps of Engineers

Although the U. S. Army Corps of Engineers may work closely with other federal, state and local agencies, the Corps is the major agency in charge of managing the lake and lakeshore. Its duties include managing most of the park areas and campgrounds around the lake and ensuring public safety and protection of the lake environment by enforcing the rules and regulations that govern how the public can use the lake. In conjunction with the Department of Natural Resources (DNR), the Corps monitors water quality by routinely testing the lake's waters. The Corps also works with the DNR and the U.S. Fish and Wildlife Service to protect and enhance fish, wildlife and plant populations around the lake. The Corps also presents water safety and environmental awareness programs to thousands of schoolchildren.

COVE IN SUMMER

Days dart by like startled salamanders,
Lingering long enough
To satisfy a need.

And with their passing, the cove is littered
With remnants of summer
While lake waters recede.

—Marne H. Finfrock

dark. *Directions:* From I-985, take Exit 6, US 129, and turn west. Go to GA 53, turn left and watch for signs. *More Infor-mation:* 770/535-8280.

RIVER FORKS PARK –This 118-acre Hall County park has numerous amenities and is very well-maintained. Just west of Gainesville, it is located on the portion of Lake Lanier where the Chestatee River flows into the Chattahoochee. *Facilities*: Boat ramp, boat docks, beach bathhouse with covered pavilion and tables, 3 pavilions with large grill and tables, meeting hall with fireplace, 50 picnic tables with grills, 4 playgrounds, dump station, handicapped fishing pier, white sand volleyball court, snack area, telephone, 24-hour "live-in" security. *Days/Hrs.:* Mar. 1-Dec. 31. *Fees:* Parking, $2; user fees for various amenities. *Directions:* From I-985, take Exit 5, GA 60 and turn west. Go to GA 369, turn left and watch for signs. *More Information:* River Forks Park, 3500 Keith Bridge Road, Gainesville, GA 30504; 770/531-3952.

MOUNTAIN VIEW –Mountain View is the first day use area south of Brown's Bridge, which is said to be the cutoff point for the most lake activity. Everything south of Brown's Bridge is extremely crowded; north of Brown's Bridge is less congested. This is a particularly nice setting for a park: a hilly, winding road along the lake with nice vistas—probably a true mountain view before the dam was built. *Facilities:* Boat ramp, picnic tables, water, restrooms. *Directions:* From I-985, take Exit 4, GA 53, and turn west. Go to McEver Road and turn right. Go to GA 369, turn left and watch for signs.

BALUS CREEK –This small recreation area is near Brown's Bridge, tucked between Balus and Flat creeks. *Facilities:* Boat ramp, handicap access, water, restrooms. *Fees:* User fee. *Directions:* From I-985, take Exit 4, GA 53, and turn west. Go to McEver Road, turn right and watch for signs.

OLD FEDERAL DAY USE –This day use facility, south of Brown's Bridge, looks out at the waters of Mud Creek as they merge into the Chattahoochee and Lake Lanier. *Facilities:* Boat ramp, handicap access, water, swimming area, restrooms, telephone, no pets. *Directions:* From I-985, take Exit 3, Lights Ferry Road, and turn west. Go to McEver Road and turn right. Go to Jim Crow Road, turn left and watch for signs.

OLD FEDERAL –The south side of this campground lies on the Chattahoochee Bay portion of Lake Lanier, site of the 1996 Paralympic Yachting Competition. *Facilities:* Campsites with hookups, campsites without hookups, showers, dump station, laundry, restrooms, picnic tables, picnic shelter, boat ramp, swimming area, playground, handicap access, water, telephone. *Fees:* User fees. *Directions:* From I-985, take Exit 3, Lights Ferry Road, and turn west. Go to McEver Road and turn right. Go to Jim Crow Road, turn left and watch for signs. *More Information:* 770/967-6757.

CHESTNUT RIDGE –This finger of land points into the Flowery Branch Bay area of Lanier. *Facilities:* Campsites with hookups, campsites without hookups, showers, dump station, laundry, restrooms, picnic tables, boat ramp, swimming area, playground, handicap access, water, telephone. *Fees:* User fees. *Directions:* From I-985, take Exit 2 and turn west. Go to GA 13 and turn right. Go to Gaines Ferry Road and turn left, then right on Chestnut Ridge Road which ends at the campground. *More Information:* 770/967-6710.

VAN PUGH NORTH DAY USE –This large day use park has more facilities than its sister park, Van Pugh South. There is a nice sand beach and a well-landscaped, wooded picnic area with good views of the lake. *Facilities:* 70-person picnic shelter, boat ramp, playground, handicap access, picnic tables, water, swimming area, restrooms, telephone, no pets. *Fees:* User fee; picnic shelter, $75. *Directions:* From I-985, take Exit 2 and turn west. Go to GA 13 and turn right. Go to Gaines Ferry Road, turn left and watch for signs.

VAN PUGH SOUTH DAY USE –This day use park is located south of Brown's Bridge at the mouth of Big Creek. *Facilities:* Boat ramp, handicap access, picnic tables, water, restrooms, telephone. *Fees:* User fee. *Directions:* From I-985, take Exit 2 and turn west. Go to GA 13 and turn right. Go to Gaines Ferry Road, turn left and watch for signs.

BURTON MILL –This boat ramp and picnic area are located on Big Creek near the high activity area surrounding Lake Lanier Islands. *Facilities:* Boat ramp, picnic tables, swimming area, restrooms. *Directions:* From I-985, take Exit 2 and turn west. Go to GA 13 and turn right. Go to Gaines Ferry Road,

MOUNTAIN
LAUREL

Buford Dam

Construction on Buford Dam and its three smaller adjacent dams, called saddle dikes, began in 1953. To keep costs low, they were built of raw earth instead of concrete. The main dam is 192 feet high and 2,360 feet long. The total length of the saddle dike system is 6,600 feet. On the west side of the main dam a large concrete building called the Powerhouse was constructed in a depression excavated from solid rock. Completed in 1956, the Powerhouse contains the machinery necessary to produce electricity and to regulate the flow of water released from the lake back into the Chattahoochee River. Although construction of Buford Dam was essentially completed in 1956, it took two more years for the lake to fill. All total, the cost to construct Lake Lanier, Buford Dam and the lake's recreation areas was about $45 million.

WATER RITES:
SOUTHEASTERN NATIVE
AMERICAN INDIANS

Believing fire and water to symbolize the opposing upper and under worlds, they forbade extinguishing fire with water, save when someone died. Even in winter, they were supposed to immerse themselves in running water every morning. In reality, it seems only young warriors practiced the ritual strictly. Before a newborn suckled, it was dipped into a creek or stream.

turn left and watch for signs.

BIG CREEK –This park is located in a high activity area. It's just off Holiday Road which leads to Lake Lanier Islands and several marinas, all of which are facing the confluence of Big Creek and the Chattahoochee. *Facilities:* Boat ramp, handicap access, picnic tables, water, restrooms, telephone. *Fees:* User fees. *Directions:* From I-985, take Exit 2 and turn west. Go to GA 13 and turn left. Go to Holiday Road and watch for signs.

LAKE LANIER ISLANDS –Once four mountain tops which looked out over the Chattahoochee River, these "islands" are now the major resort area on Lake Lanier. Developed by the state of Georgia and the Corps of Engineers, the 1,100-acre islands are managed by KSL Recreation Corporation. The Islands host special events all year, including concerts, arts and crafts festivals, cardboard boat races, a bluegrass festival, fireworks shows and a holiday light show. *Facilities:* Lake Lanier Islands Hilton Resort; Renaissance Pine Isle Resort; two championship golf courses; over 300 campsites with a fishing pier, outdoor pavilion, laundry facilities, boat ramp, dump station; RV sites with water and electricity hookups, some with sewer hookups; water park with 1.5 miles of beach, miniature golf and paddle boats; canoes, sailboats, powerboat, houseboat and pontoon rentals; bike rentals; horseback riding. *Days/Hrs.:* Daily, year-round with some activities closed during the winter months. *Fees:* Parking, $4. Various fees for different activities. *Directions:* From I-985 go to either Exit 1 or 2. Then follow signs. *More Information:* Lake Lanier Islands, 6950 Holiday Road, Lake Lanier Islands, GA 30518; 770/932-7200.

SHOAL CREEK DAY USE –This boat ramp, adjacent to Shoal Creek Campground, is in a very popular section of Lanier, the southern end near Lake Lanier Islands. *Facilities:* Boat ramp, restrooms. *Fees:* User fee. *Directions:* From I-985, take Exit 1 and turn left onto GA 20, turn right on Peachtree Industrial Boulevard, turn left on Shadburn Ferry Road. After Buford Dam Road intersection, park is 1.5 miles on right.

SHOAL CREEK –This campground sits in the midst of Lake Lanier activity. It is on the southern side of the lake, directly across from Lake Lanier Islands and surrounded by large marinas. Shadburn Ferry Road which leads to Shoal Creek picks up again on the other side of Lanier at Shady Grove Campground. *Facilities:* Campsites with hookups, campsites without hookups, group camping, showers, dump station, laundry, restrooms, picnic tables, picnic shelter, boat ramp, swimming area, playground, handicap access, water, telephone. *Fees:* User fee. *Directions:* From I-985, take Exit 1 and turn left onto GA 20, turn right on Peachtree Industrial Boulevard, turn left on Shadburn Ferry Road which ends at the campground. *More Information:* 770/945-9541.

EAST BANK –This large recreation area, which Gwinnett County recently turned back over to the Corps, is at the southern end of Lake Lanier near Buford Dam. *Facilities:* Boat ramp, picnic tables, restrooms, water. *Fees:* User fee. *Directions:* From I-985, take Exit 1 and turn left onto GA 20, turn right on Peachtree Industrial Boulevard, turn left on Shadburn Ferry Road, turn left on Buford Dam Road and watch for signs.

BUFORD DAM PARK –Located on the east side of Buford Dam, this is a very popular section of Lake Lanier. There is no boat ramp here, but there are three large capacity picnic shelters and a nice swimming area. The Resource Manager's Office, which has a vast amount of lake literature and interesting displays concerning the history of the lake, is also located in this area and open to the public. *Facilities:* 3 90-person picnic shelters, playground, handicap access, water, swimming area, restrooms, telephone, no pets. *Fees:* User fee; picnic shelter, $75. *Directions:* From I-985, take Exit 1 and turn left onto GA 20, turn right on Peachtree Industrial Boulevard, turn left on Shadburn Ferry Road, turn left on Buford Dam Road. The park is on an access road to the right of the Resource Manager's Office.

LOWER OVERLOOK –This viewing area is on the east bank of Buford Dam and looks out over Lake Lanier. *Facilities:* Handicap access, picnic tables, water, restrooms, no pets. *Directions:* From I-985, take Exit 1 and turn left onto GA 20, turn right on Peachtree Industrial Boulevard, turn left on Shadburn Ferry Road, turn left on Buford Dam Road. Overlook is to the right, just before the dam.

UPPER OVERLOOK –This nicely landscaped area looks out over the Chattahoochee River right below Buford Dam. The

shoals along the river here are a great place to trout fish, but beware of water releases. When the horn sounds, get to higher ground. *Facilities:* 80 and 90-person picnic shelters, playground, handicap access, picnic tables, water, restrooms, no pets. *Fees:* Picnic shelter, $75. *Directions:* From I-985, take Exit 1 and turn left onto GA 20, turn right on Peachtree Industrial Boulevard, turn left on Shadburn Ferry Road, turn left on Buford Dam Road. Overlook is to the left, just before the dam.

POWERHOUSE –The powerhouse sits next to Buford Dam, built into a granite ridge. Water flows out of the south side of the powerhouse through a canyon of granite into the river and over the shoals on its way to Atlanta. *Facilities:* Handicap access, restrooms, telephone, no pets. *Directions:* From I-985, take Exit 1 and turn left onto GA 20, turn right on Peachtree Industrial Boulevard, turn left on Shadburn Ferry Road, turn left on Buford Dam Road. Cross the dam. Powerhouse is to the left. Visitors can also walk to the Powerhouse from the Upper Overlook area.

LOWER POOL –This facility sits on the south side of Buford Dam where the Chattahoochee returns to being a mountain river. The boat launch provides access into the Chattahoochee River, not Lake Lanier. This is the first access to the river below the dam. *Facilities:* Boat ramp, handicap access, picnic tables, water, restrooms. *Days/Hrs.:* Daily, from the first weekend in Apr. to sometime in Sept., 7am-10pm. *Directions:* From I-985, take Exit 1 and turn left on GA 20, turn right on Peachtree Industrial Boulevard, turn left on Shadburn Ferry Road, turn left on Buford Dam Road. Cross the dam. Park is on the left, just past the Powerhouse.

WEST BANK OVERLOOK –This Lake Lanier viewing area is located to the left of the Buford Dam Powerhouse. *Facilities:* Handicap access, no pets. *Directions:* From GA 400, go to Exit

Canada Goose

Of the 13 kinds of wild geese that live in the United States and Canada, the Canada goose is the best-known. It has a broad white band across its throat and cheeks. Geese are migratory birds, flying north in the summer and south in the winter. But by the late 1970s the geese had gradually stopped flying as far south as Georgia, so the Department of Natural Resources decided to release Canada geese in the state for two reasons: to merely reintroduce a bird that had disappeared in the state and to provide a valued migratory species for hunting. From 1978 to 1982, the DNR released 500 Canada geese in northeast Georgia, 200 of those on Lake Lanier. Today there are about 2,500 on Lake Lanier alone, and the birds range along the Chattahoochee from the Helen area all the way down to the gulf.

14, turn east on GA 20, turn left on Sanders Road, at first stop sign turn right on Buford Dam Road. Cross the dam. Overlook is to the right.

WEST BANK –This heavily used recreation area lies to the left, or on the west bank, of Buford Dam. There is no boat ramp here, but a paved path winds along the edge of the beach area. *Facilities*: 2 70-person picnic shelters, playground, handicap access, tables, water, swimming area, restrooms, telephone, no pets. *Fees:* User fee; picnic shelter, $75. *Directions:* From GA 400, go to Exit 14, turn east on GA 20, turn left on Sanders Road, at first stop sign turn right on Buford Dam Road and watch for signs. Park is on the left.

SAWNEE –This campground is located in a popular area of Lake Lanier, the southernmost portion and close to Buford Dam. *Facilities:* Campsites with hookups, campsites without hookups, showers, dump station, laundry, restrooms, picnic tables, boat ramp, swimming area, playground, handicap access, water, restrooms, telephone. *Fees:* User fees. *Directions:* From GA 400, go to Exit 14, turn east on GA 20, turn left on Sanders Road, at first stop sign turn right on Buford Dam Road. Campground is on the left. *More Information:* 770/887-0592.

LITTLE RIDGE –This boat ramp is in the Cumming area of Lake Lanier where Little Ridge Creek merges with Bald Ridge Creek. *Facilities:* Boat ramp. *Directions:* From GA 400, go to Exit 14, turn east on GA 20, turn left on Sanders Road, at first stop sign turn right on Buford Dam Road and watch for signs.

MARY ALICE –This day use park, with its picnic shelter and swimming beach, is in the Cumming area of Lake Lanier where Little Ridge Creek merges with Bald Ridge Creek. *Facilities:* 70-person picnic shelter, boat ramp, playground, handicap access, water, swimming area, restrooms, telephone, no pets. *Fees:* User fee; picnic shelter, $75. *Directions:* From GA 400, go to Exit 14, turn east on GA 20, turn left on Sanders Road, turn right on Mary Alice Park Road.

BALD RIDGE CREEK –This campground sits at the confluence of Little Ridge Creek and Bald Ridge Creek in the Cumming area of Lake Lanier. *Facilities:* Campsites with hookups, campsites without hookups, showers, dump station, laundry, restrooms, picnic tables, boat ramp, swimming area, playground, handicap access, water, telephone. *Fees:* User fee. *Directions:* From GA 400 north, go to Exit 16, turn right on Pilgrim Mill Road, turn right on Sinclair Shoals Road, turn left on Bald Ridge Road, which ends at the campground. *More Information:* Bald Ridge Creek, 770/889-1591.

THE MIGHTY BULLFROG

TIDWELL –This small day use area is located south of Brown's Bridge near Young Deer Creek. *Facilities:* Boat ramp, handicap access, water, restrooms, telephone. *Fees:* User fee. *Directions:* From GA 400 north, go to Exit 16, turn right on Pilgrim Mill Road and watch for signs.

YOUNG DEER –This small, but well-equipped park is south of Brown's Bridge on Young Deer Creek. *Facilities:* 70-person picnic shelter, boat ramp, playground, handicap access, picnic tables, water, swimming area, restrooms, telephone. *Fees:* Picnic shelter, $50. *Directions:* From GA 400 north, go to Exit 17 and turn right on GA 306. Turn right on Shady Grove Road and watch for signs.

SHADY GROVE –Before Lake Lanier, this area would have looked out over Six Mile, Four Mile and Two Mile creeks merging to flow into the Chattahoochee. Today it looks out over a broad expanse of Lake Lanier and a lot of submerged roads and house foundations. Except for its lack of picnic shelters, this campground has all the amenities that a Corps of Engineers park can offer. *Facilities:* Campsites with hookups, campsites without hookups, walk-in campsites, group camping, showers, dump station, laundry, restrooms, picnic tables, boat ramp, swimming area, playground, handicap access, water, telephone. *Fees:* User fees. *Directions:* From GA 400 north, go to Exit 17, turn right on GA 306, turn right on Shady Grove Road which ends at campground. *More Information:* 770/887-2067.

CHARLESTON –Charleston day use area lies below the bridge which crosses Six Mile Creek on Brown's Bridge Road. It is directly across the creek from the Six Mile day use area which just has a boat ramp. *Facilities:* Boat ramp, playground, handicap access, picnic tables, water, restrooms, telephone. *Directions:* From GA 400 north, go to Exit 17, turn right on GA 306, turn right on GA 369 (Brown's Bridge Road) and watch for signs.

SIX MILE CREEK –This boat ramp lies directly below the Six

Mile Creek Bridge. *Facilities:* Boat ramp. *Directions:* From GA 400 north, go to Exit 17, turn right on GA 306, turn right on GA 369 (Brown's Bridge Road) and watch for signs.

TWO MILE –Just below Brown's Bridge, three creeks–Two Mile, Four Mile and Six Mile–feed into Lake Lanier. Two Mile Park sits along Lanier at the mouth of Two Mile Creek. The road leading to Two Mile Park as well as the park itself recall the mountain terrain that these creeks once flowed through when they flowed into the Chattahoochee River rather than Lake Lanier. Riding the dirt-and-gravel road which winds to and through this park is reminiscent of a ride through a North Georgia mountain town, like Blairsville or Ellijay. In the fall, red and golden leaves of maple, hickory and sumac line the way. Pumpkins sit around the small farmhouses, and a Baptist church stands white against the clear, blue sky. *Facilities:* Boat ramp, picnic tables, water, restrooms. *Directions:* From GA 400 north, go to Exit 17, turn right on GA 306, turn right on GA 369 (Brown's Bridge Road) and watch for signs.

BETHEL –Bethel shares the same mountain atmosphere as Vann's Tavern and Two Mile, the two recreation areas it lies between. It sits on the higher elevations of Two Mile Creek where it begins to meet Lanier. Many of the park areas around Lanier are named after places that once were where the water is now. Bethel park is located off Bethel Road which leads to Bethel Church, a white, clapboard church with leaded windows and a white painted tin roof, which was first organized in 1836. *Facilities:* Boat ramp, picnic tables, handicap access, restrooms. *Directions:* From GA 400 north, go to Exit 17, turn right on GA 306, turn right on GA 369 (Brown's Bridge Road) and watch for signs.

VANN'S TAVERN –Vann's Tavern sits below Two Mile Creek Bridge and like other parks in this area, it has a distinct North Georgia mountain feel. On a fall evening, sumac is glowing red on the hilly terrain. But instead of leaf lookers, the parking lot is filled with fishermen and bass boats. There's a striper tournament going on. As one expert explains, "The shad are moving to the north end of the lake, and the stripers are following the shad." *Facilities:* Boat ramp, handicap access, water, restrooms, telephones. *Directions:* From GA 400 north, go to

"The Georgia Conservancy has been in business for 30 years, and we have come to realize that water is the unifying common denominator of all we are doing."

—Carolyn Boyd Hatcher, President and CEO 1990-1998, The Georgia Conservancy

Exit 17, turn right on GA 306, turn right on GA 369 (Brown's Bridge Road) and watch for signs.

LONG HOLLOW –This park area is tucked away on Chestatee Bay just north of Brown's Bridge. *Facilities:* Boat ramp, playground, handicap access, picnic tables, water, swimming area, restrooms. *Directions:* From GA 400 north, go to Exit 17, turn right on GA 306 and watch for signs.

KEITH'S BRIDGE –This park sits where the Chestatee River and Chestatee Bay areas meet the Chattahoochee. *Facilities:* Boat ramp, playground, handicap access, picnic tables, water, swimming area, restrooms. *Directions:* From GA 400 north, go to Exit 17, turn right on GA 306 and watch for signs.

WAR HILL –In the area of Lanier north of Brown's Bridge, this day use area is adjacent to the War Hill Campground. It is located where Julian Creek flows into the Chestatee River. *Facilities:* Boat ramp, handicap access, picnic tables, water, swimming area, restrooms. *Directions:* From GA 400 north, take Exit 17, turn right on GA 306, turn left on GA 53 and watch for signs.

WAR HILL CAMPGROUND –This campground is located on the Chestatee where Julian and Latham creeks meet the river. This is one of two undeveloped Corps campgrounds. Camping is designated as primitive, with no electrical hookups. *Facilities:* Campsites without hookups, restrooms, picnic tables, boat ramp, swimming area, handicap access, water. *Fees:* User fee. *Directions:* From GA 400 north, take Exit 17, turn right on GA 306, turn left on GA 53 and watch for signs. *More Information:* Resource Manager's Office, Lake Sidney Lanier, P.O. Box 567, Buford, GA 30518; 770/945-9531.

THOMPSON CREEK –This day use area is located on Thompson Creek where it feeds into the Chestatee River. *Facilities:* 70-person picnic shelter, boat ramp, handicap access, water, restrooms. *Days/Hrs.:* Daily, from the first weekend in Apr. to sometime in Sept., 7am to 10pm. *Fees:* Picnic shelter, $50. *Directions:* From GA 400 north, take Exit 17, turn right on GA 306, turn left on GA 53 and watch for signs.

NIX BRIDGE –This is a small day use area located where Thompson Creek and the Chestatee River meet as they make their way into Lanier. *Facilities:* Boat ramp, handicap access, picnic tables, water, restrooms. *Directions:* From GA 400 north, take Exit 17, turn right on GA 306, turn left on GA 53, turn right on GA 9E, turn right on GA 226 (Nix Bridge Road) and watch for signs.

TOTO CREEK –This day use area is adjacent to the Toto Creek Campground on the Chestatee River portion of Lake Lanier. *Facilities:* Boat ramp, picnic tables, swimming area, handicap access, water, restrooms. *Directions:* From GA 400 north, take Exit 17, turn right on GA 306, turn left on GA 53, turn right on GA 9E and watch for signs.

TOTO CREEK CAMPGROUND –This campground is located next to Toto Creek Bridge and the Chestatee River. This is one of two Corps undeveloped campgrounds. Camping is designated as primitive, with no electrical hookups. *Facilities:* Campsites without hookups, restrooms, picnic tables, boat ramp, swimming area, handicap access, water. *Fees:* User fee. *Directions:* From GA 400 north, take Exit 17, turn right on GA 306, turn left on GA 53, turn right on GA 9E. This will merge with GA 136. Campground is on the left just past the bridge over Toto Creek. *More Information:* Resource Manager's Office, Lake Sidney Lanier, P.O. Box 567, Buford, GA 30518; 770/945-9531.

LUMPKIN COUNTY PARK –This is the northernmost Lanier boat ramp on the Chestatee River. *Facilities:* Boat ramp. *Directions:* Take GA 400 north to Lumpkin County Parkway. Turn right and watch for the signs.

BOLDING MILL DAY USE –This day use area is adjacent to Bolding Mill Campgrounds. It is located up the Chestatee River section of Lanier right above the Chestatee's confluence with Latham Creek. The park has the two largest picnic shelters on Lanier, each with 14 tables and a capacity of 100 people. *Facilities:* 2 100-person picnic shelters, boat ramp, playground, handicap access, picnic tables, water, swimming area, restrooms, telephone. *Fees:* Picnic shelter, $50. *Directions:* From GA 400 north, take Exit 17, turn right on GA 306, turn right on GA 53, turn left on Chestatee Road and follow signs.

BOLDING MILL –This campground sits on the Chestatee River portion of Lake Lanier in an area where Latham and Julian creeks flow into the Chestatee. *Facilities:* Campsites with hookups, campsites without hookups, walk-in campsites, showers, dump station, laundry, restrooms, picnic tables, boat

"Anyone who can solve the problem of water will be worthy of two Nobel Prizes—one for peace and one for science."

—John F. Kennedy

ramp, swimming area, playground, handicap access, telephone. *Fees:* User fee. *Directions:* From GA 400 north, take Exit 17, turn right on GA 306, turn right on GA 53, turn left on Chestatee Road, which ends at the campground. *More Information:* Bolding Mill, 770/532-3650.

LITTLE HALL –This park, with its nice swimming area and large picnic shelter, lies on the Chestatee River portion of Lanier where Bolling Bridge crosses the river. *Facilities:* 80-person picnic shelter, boat ramp, playground, handicap access, picnic tables, water, swimming area, restrooms. *Fees:* User fees; picnic shelter, $50. *Directions:* From GA 400 north, take Exit 17, turn right on GA 306, turn right on GA 53. The park is just past the bridge.

DUCKETT MILL DAY USE –This boat ramp lies adjacent to the Duckett Mill Campground on the Chestatee River. *Facilities:* Boat ramp, handicap access. *Directions:* From GA 400 north, take Exit 17, turn right on GA 306, turn right on GA 53, turn right on Duckett Mill Road and watch for signs.

DUCKETT MILL –The waters around Duckett Mill are those of the Chestatee River right before it merges into the Chattahoochee. *Facilities:* Campsites with hookups, campsites without hookups, walk-in campsites, showers, dump station, laundry, restrooms, picnic tables, boat ramp, swimming area, playground, handicap access, water, telephone. *Fees:* User fee. *Directions:* From GA 400 north, take Exit 17, turn right on GA 306, turn right on GA 53, turn right on Duckett Mill Road and follow to campground. *More Information:* 770/532-9802.

ROBINSON –This facility is in the Gainesville area of Lake Lanier just south of the Lanier Bridge. *Facilities:* Boat ramp, handicap access, picnic tables, water, restrooms. *Directions:* From GA 400 north, take Exit 17, turn right on GA 306, turn right on GA 53 and watch for signs.

SIMPSON PARK –This small park is in the Gainesville area of the lake, just below Lanier Bridge. *Facilities:* Boat ramp, picnic tables, restrooms. *Directions:* From GA 400 north, take Exit 17, turn right on GA 306, turn right on GA 53 and watch for signs.

SARDIS CREEK –This park is located on Sardis Creek just north of the Lanier Bridge in the Gainesville area of Lake Lanier. *Facilities:* Boat ramp, handicap access, picnic tables, water,

The length of the anchor rope or chain is called SCOPE. Six to one scope means that the length of the anchor rope from the boat to the anchor is six times the depth of the water.

restrooms. *Directions:* From GA 400 north, take Exit 17, turn right on GA 306, turn right on GA 53, turn left on Chestatee Road and watch for signs to the right.

THOMPSON BRIDGE –This boat ramp sits along the northern side of Thompson Bridge and looks out over Little River merging with the Chattahoochee. *Facilities:* Boat ramp. *Directions:* From I-985, take Exit 5, GA 60, turn west. Watch for signs just past Thompson Bridge.

WAHOO CREEK –Wahoo Creek flows into Little River on the northern end of Lanier. This day use area lies well up the creek next to Wahoo Creek Bridge. *Facilities:* Boat ramp, picnic tables, restrooms. *Directions:* From I-985, take Exit 5, GA 60, turn west. Turn right on GA 283 and follow to bridge.

MARINAS

GAINESVILLE MARINA –"Escape the Traffic" is the motto of this marina which is the northernmost commercial marina on Lanier. In fact, it is the only marina north of Brown's Bridge— a selling point for those who want to deal with less water volume, less wave action and fewer boats. Besides being a full-service marina, Gainesville Marina also sells boats and has an in-water display of runabouts, ski boats, cruisers and pontoons. *Facilities:* 500 slips, 60 percent wet and 40 percent dry, covered and uncovered to 62 feet; cruiser and houseboat slips with water and electricity; smaller slips with courtesy water and electricity; dry stack storage to 21 feet, 22 feet with molded platform; courtesy slips; 4 gas pumps; pump-out station; small ship store with boat accessories, drinks, ice, snacks and fresh deli sandwiches. *Maintenance/Repair:* On-site repair service and parts department with minor fiberglass repair. *Days/Hrs.:* Daily, 8am-5pm (later during summer season). Closed Thanksgiving, Christmas and New Year's. 24-hour security. *Directions:* From I-985 north, take Exit 4 (GA 53/Mundy Mill Road) and turn left. Go about 2 miles to a "T" intersection. Turn right on McEver Road. Go about 4 miles to its end then turn left and go 1.5 miles to the marina. *More Information:* Gainesville Marina, 2145 Dawsonville Highway, Gainesville, GA 30501; 770/536-2171; fax 770/534-2678.

The vessel with the right-of-way is the STAND-ON VESSEL.

Hydrocarbon Pollution

Georgia ranks 14th in the nation in boat ownership. There are 12 million registered motorboats in the United States, and eight million have outboard motors, according to Andre Mele, author of *Polluting for Pleasure* (W. W. Norton and Co., 1993).

What few people realize is that there is a silent villain lurking in our waters that routinely goes unnoticed–hydrocarbon pollution from two-stroke boat engines. The total agglomerate oil and hydrocarbon pollution caused by pleasure boating is 420 million gallons per year–the equivalent of 40 Exxon *Valdez* disasters. According to Mele, two-stroke boat engines and personal watercraft are the largest source of toxic contamination of our nation's waterways, at over one billion pounds annually.

Outboards are designed as either two-stroke engines or four-stroke engines, with the vast majority two-strokes. Every time a piston travels up the cylinder in a two-stroke engine it pushes out some unburned fuel with the exhaust gases. Two-stroke engines spew 25 percent of their carbon intake, fuel and lubricating oil out the tailpipe and into the environment. Generally, two-strokes discharge 200 grams of hydrocarbons per kilowatt hour, whereas four-strokes discharge 6 to 8 grams of hydrocarbons per kilowatt hour.

Ultimately, the consumers of outboard motors must assume responsibility by purchasing their next motor with the environment in mind. While four-strokes are a little more costly than two-strokes (about 10 percent more), they are clearly the right choice for cleaner water, healthy fish and a protected environment.

SUNRISE COVE –This Westrec-owned marina advertises itself as the "most beautiful marina on Lake Lanier." Located in a secluded, deep water cove, it is near to, but out of the way of, congested Lake Lanier traffic. The tree line around the cove protects Sunrise from the northeast winds that blow across the lake, making it a good place for docking sailboats. Indeed, most of the activity here is in sailboats rather than motorboats. Contrasted to Holiday–the other Westrec marina property on Lanier–which caters to the younger crowd, Sunrise Cove's major clientele is age 35 and up. *Facilities:* 589 open slips, 88 covered slips, 23 trailer boat spaces, full electricity and water to each slip; fuel dock; restrooms; ship store with marine hardware, boating apparel, groceries, ice, bait, snack bar; pump-out station. *Maintenance/Repair:* No repairs or service, maintenance is contracted out. Tenants can choose from a list of recommended service people who will come to the marina to do the work. *Days/Hrs.:* Daily, during summer season; Sun.-Thurs.; 9am-5pm; Fri.-Sat., 9am-6pm. Closed on Tues. during the winter season. *Directions:* From I-985 north, take Exit 4 (GA 53/Mundy Mill Road) and turn left. Go to stop light at Oakwood Road and turn left. This road turns into Flat Creek Road and dead ends into the marina. *More Information:* Sunrise Cove Marina, 5725 Flat Creek Road, Gainesville, GA 30504; 770/536-8599; fax 770/532-7667.

AQUALAND –The 144 acres of Aqualand Marina finger out into Lake Lanier between Flowery Branch and Chattahoochee Bays, with docks located in parklike coves spread out and thoughtfully landscaped. A state-of-the-art wave break wall adds to the tranquil setting. Aqualand, which played host to the 1996 Paralympic Yachting Competition, has been owned by one family since the lake filled in in 1958. About 60 percent of the marina's tenants are sailboats. *Facilities:* Sailboats, houseboats, powerboats - 2,000 boats in water, 500 more slips planned; dry storage on trailer, open and covered; 20 courtesy docks; gas; restrooms; large ship store with good variety of stock, including sailboat section, general accessories, deck and top hardware, lighting and electrical instruments, compasses, anchoring, moorings, cordage, wire snaps, horns and paddles, ladders, skis and accessories, flotation, seats and pedestals, trailer equipment, boat covers, fuel delivery, lubricants, fiberglass repair and sealants and clothing; pump-out station. *Restaurant:* One of just three restaurants on Lake Lanier, Dock Side Grill is a well-kept, open-air grill with friendly, hospitable owners and employees. Boaters can dock their boats and walk up to the small wooden building, which is open on three sides, and enjoy a menu that includes grilled tuna steak, fried flounder and grilled chicken breast sandwiches, hamburgers, jalapeno poppers, wings, homemade chili, taco salad, cappuccino and soft drinks. The grill is closed in Dec. and Jan. but opens as early in Feb. as weather permits. Hours vary seasonally but are generally Mon., Wed.-Fri. 11am-6 or 7pm, Sat. and Sun. 8:30am-8pm. Closed on Tues. *Maintenance/Repair:* Self-service boat repair yard with a 25-ton capacity lift. Marina operates the lift, but boat owner brings in own repairman. They have a list of reputable and recommended maintenance people. Repair items must be purchased from Aqualand in order to use maintenance facilities. Lift hours are Mon.-Fri., 8:30am-4pm; Sat. by appointment. *Days/Hrs.:* Daily, 8:30am-5:30pm. *Directions:* From I-985 north, take Exit 3, turning left on Lights Ferry Road, which dead ends into the marina. *More Information:* Aqualand Marina, P.O. Box 1200, Lights Ferry Road, Flowery Branch, GA 30542; 770/967-6811.

STARBOARD MARINA –This nice, quiet marina sits in the middle of Lake Lanier action but out of the way–and out of the wake–at the end of Flowery Branch Bay. Under recent new ownership, the 38.5-acre marina has room for expansion and plans to do so. The marina provides customers with 24-hour boat access and guaranteed ramp parking. Starboard is also the site of the third largest Chaparral dealership in the country. *Facilities:* About 400 slips, 53 dry storage on own trailer, uncovered storage available; gas; ship store with basic marine supplies. *Maintenance/Repair:* All types of maintenance and repairs. *Days/Hrs.:* Tues.-Sat., 8:30am-5:30pm, except for Christmas holidays; Sun., gas dock only. *Directions:* From I-985 north, take Exit 3, turning left on Lights Ferry Road. Turn left on Spout Springs Road following until it dead ends into the marina. *More Information:* Starboard Marina, 6334 Mitchell Street, Flowery Branch, GA 30542; 770/967-2700.

The depth of a vessel below the water line, measured vertically to the lowest part of the hull is known as the boat's DRAFT.

LAZY DAYS MARINA –Lazy Days is less a marina and more a huge dry storage that, with one hour's notice, will launch and retrieve a boat for its customer. In fact, Lazy Day calls itself the largest dry storage on the lake. All boats kept here are placed in the huge light green warehouse-type building and locked at night. *Facilities:* 150 courtesy slips, 575 dry storage accommodating boats up to 30 feet; gas. *Maintenance/Repair:* None on premises; coordinates maintenance with Harry's Marine Service. *Days/Hrs.:* May 15-Labor Day, weekdays, 9am-6pm; weekends and holidays, 8am-6pm. *Directions:* From I-985, take Exit 2 and turn west. Go to GA 13 and turn left. Go to Holiday Road and follow signs. *More Information:* Lazy Days Marina, 6700 Holiday Road, Buford, GA 30518; 770/945-1991.

HOLIDAY –The sign says, "Holiday on Lake Lanier - One of the World's Largest Floating Marinas." Some people say it is also the most popular marina at Lanier. Where it sits on the road to Lake Lanier Islands certainly puts it in one of the most heavily trafficked areas. Westrec, Holiday's owner, is the largest owner of marine properties in the United States and also owns Sunrise Cove Marina on Lanier. However one looks at it, this large marina bustles with people and activity and is one of the lake's hot spots during the summer season. *Facilities:* 1,400 plus wet slips, covered and uncovered, all size boats, no dry storage; 22 gas pumps; large ship store with marine supplies, fishing tackle, action sportswear, swim wear, water toys, groceries, snacks, drinks; 2 pump-out stations. *Restaurant:* Crockers by the Dock is a casual dockside restaurant which serves everything from ribs, steak and hamburgers to catfish fillets, crab cakes and lobster tail. It's open daily, year-round, weekdays, 11:30am-10pm; weekends 11:30am-11pm. The Paddy's Lanier Princess, a dinner boat, also operates out of Holiday (770/736-0000). There are also houseboat and boat rental offices on the backside of the ship store building, facing the docks. Windsong Sailing Academy operates from a dock at Holiday (see page 76). *Maintenance/Repair:* Brown's Bridge Marine handles repairs for Holiday under a sublease arrangement. This is a full-service boat shop that can do fiberglass, wooden boats and overhaul engines on all size boats. They have two wet wells to lift boats out of water. *Days/Hrs.:* Hours

"This is a big lake but it has the smallest watershed in the Chattahoochee basin. Sixty five to seventy five percent of the drinking water for the state of Georgia comes from that watershed. Once it's gone, it's hard to get it back until the good Lord decides it's time to rain on us."

—Philip Burton, manager of Gainesville Marina.

are flexible, especially during the summer months. In general, they are Sun.-Thurs., 8am-5pm (winter); 8am-6pm (summer), Fri.-Sat., 8am-7pm. *Directions:* From I-985, take Exit 2 and turn west. Go to GA 13 and turn left. Go to Holiday Road and follow signs. *More Information:* Westrec Properties, Inc., 6900 Holiday Road, Buford, GA 30518; 770/945-7201.

LANIER HARBOR MARINA AND RESTAURANT –With its white clapboard and blue trimmed buildings complete with an assortment of lounging dogs, this marina looks like a small fishing village. Operators say it is the southernmost marina on the lake, with good access from both I-85/985 and GA 400, making it convenient for people coming from Atlanta. The marina offers a one-hour launch/retrieval service, and it also has one of the few full-service restaurants on the lake. *Facilities:* 400 slips, covered and uncovered; 82 courtesy slips, up to 27 feet; dry storage on trailer; gas dock; ship store with tackle, batteries, film, fire extinguisher, light bulbs, life jackets, soft drinks, snacks. *Restaurant:* The Lanier Harbor Restaurant is a full-service steak and seafood restaurant open during the summer season. The restaurant will also make "On-Board Baskets" featuring barbecue chicken breast, Po Boys and grilled rosemary dijon chicken breast. *Maintenance/Repair:* On-site repair by T&B Marine Service, 1400-sq. ft. wash rack with 4 wash bays including power, 2 tow boats available. *Days/Hrs.:* 24-hour security; daily, 9am-5pm (winter); Mon.-Thurs., 9am-6pm; Fri.-Sat., 9am-8pm; Sun., 9am-7pm (summer). *Directions:* From I-985 north, take Exit 1 and turn left on GA 20, turn right on Peachtree Industrial Boulevard, turn left on Little Mill Road, turn left on Buford Dam Road. Marina is 0.5 mile on right. *More Information:* Lanier Harbor Marina and Restaurant, 2066 Pine Tree Drive, Buford, GA 30518; 770/945-2884.

HABERSHAM MARINA –Habersham Marina advertises itself as the closest marina to Atlanta. And indeed, driving to Habersham is like driving through a typical middle-class Atlanta subdivision. Homes and condos line both sides of the road. But once onto the marina property itself, the atmosphere changes. This is not a typical marina, but rather like a private club or restaurant. Habersham is a valet service marina where owners call ahead for the marina to launch their boat. Then at

On a boat a piece of wood or metal with projecting ends to which lines are made fast is known as a CLEAT.

the end of the day the owner leaves the boat at the dock for the marina to place back into dry storage. At Habersham it is known as "launch and retrieval." The idea is that the boat owner can maximize his time boating, and the marina will take care of the hassles. *Facilities:* 85 to 100 wet slips, 648 dry stack storage for boats 17 to 26 feet; gas dock; small ship store with boat hardware, cleaning supplies, lake maps, life jackets, flotation, skis, ice. *Maintenance/Repair:* Full marine service; mechanic for boat repairs. Repairs and dry storage are handled through Bradley Marine, which is adjacent to Habersham. *Days/Hrs.:* Daily, 9am-5pm. Closed Thanksgiving, Christmas and New Years. *Directions:* From GA 400, go to Exit 14, turn east on GA 20, turn left on Sanders Road, at first stop sign turn right on Buford Dam Road and follow signs. *More Information:* Habersham Marina, P.O. Box 1589, Cumming, GA 30131; 770/887-3107.

BALD RIDGE –Established in 1957, this wooded, nicely landscaped marina lies in a quiet area on Bald Ridge Creek. Known as a family-oriented marina, there is a pleasant picnic ground next to the docks and lots of open space. There is even an open-air utility building with benches used for non-denominational Sunday church services from May to Sept. (It can also be rented out for weddings and other events.) *Facilities:* 660 slips with electricity, water and cable TV hookups; boats up to 75 feet; no dry storage; gas dock; dump station; launch ramp ($4 charge); ship store with chemicals, cleaning supplies, groceries. *Restaurant:* No restaurant, but a deli with fresh sandwiches; the general manager says he has the best turkey around. *Maintenance/Repair:* Full-service maintenance; and carpentry, welding, painting and hull repair on the premises. *Days/Hrs.:* 24-hour security and open docks daily; office open Mon.-Fri., 8:30am-5pm; ship store open daily, Memorial Day to October 1, hours vary. *Directions:* From GA 400 north, take Exit 15 and turn right. Follow until it dead ends into the marina. *More Information:* Bald Ridge Marina, P.O. Box 836, Cumming, GA 30130; 770/887-5309.

LAN-MAR –This locally owned and operated marina has been in business for over 25 years and advertises itself as Lanier's premier marina, with personalized VIP service and the best

The fore or aft movement as the bow and stern rise and fall due to wave action is PITCH.

location on Lake Lanier. Located next to Brown's Bridge, Lan-Mar shares the hilly, mountain type terrain of that area. *Facilities:* 505 wet slips, open and covered with electricity and water; 224 dry stack in fully-enclosed secure building, 150 on trailers; gas dock; pump-out station; small ship store with groceries, life jackets, oil, chemicals; restrooms. *Maintenance/Repair:* Full marina service. *Days/Hrs.:* May 15 to Labor Day - weekdays, 9am-6pm; weekends and holidays, 8am-6pm. Closed for Thanksgiving, Christmas and New Year's holidays. *Directions:* From GA 400 north, take Exit 17, turning right on GA 306. Turn right on GA 369, go about 6 miles and watch for sign to the right. *More Information:* Lan-Mar Marina, 9200 Lan-Mar Road, Gainesville, GA 30506; 770/887-5715.

There are also two private yacht clubs at Lanier:

UNIVERSITY YACHT CLUB –As its name suggests, a person must be a university graduate to be a member of this 45-year old private yacht club. This 200-member club does not solicit membership; instead membership is by recommendation of other members. The club usually adds 10-to-12 new members per year. All facilities here are private. *Facilities:* 190 slips, gas dock, ship store, clubhouse with restaurant. *More Information:* University Yacht Club, 770/967-6450.

ATLANTA ATHLETIC CLUB YACHT CLUB –Founded in 1957, the Yacht Club is operated in conjunction with the Army Corps of Engineers, but it is affiliated with the exclusive Atlanta Athletic Club. All facilities here are for members only. *Facilities:* 201 covered and uncovered boat slips for runabouts, sailboats, cruisers and houseboats; covered and open dry storage for runabouts and jet skis; boat ramp; pump-out station; food service from Apr. until Sept.; clubhouse; private banquet facilities; ships store; electronically controlled entrance gate. *More Information*: Atlanta Athletic Club Yacht Club, 6531 Athletic Club Drive, Flowery Branch, GA 30542; 770-967-BOAT, fax 770/967-6611.

HIKING TRAILS

LAUREL RIDGE TRAIL –Named for the mature stands of mountain laurel which grow along Lake Lanier's hillsides, this well-

The sideward motion of a boat caused by wind and waves is known as ROLL.

marked trail winds around the Buford Dam area, providing great views of the lake, the dam and the Chattahoochee River. The U.S. Army Corps of Engineers at Lake Lanier developed the trail, placing numbered markers along it to indicate points of interest that correspond with a brochure available at the Resource Manager's Office. *Distance:* 3.8 miles, easy to moderate. *Trailhead Location:* Lower Overlook area (see page 53). Can also be accessed from the Powerhouse, Upper Overlook, Buford Dam Park and the Resource Manager's Office. *Features:* The trail, which passes through woodlands, wetlands and around a mountain stream, is a good place to see vegetation of the area such as native azalea, laurel, deerberry, rhododendron, dogwood, river birch, red maple, purple coneflower and black-eyed Susan. Beavers have built a dam on a man-made pond which also attracts heron, raccoon and deer. There are also plenty of interesting views of the structure that created Lake Lanier–Buford Dam.

SIGNIFICANT URBAN EXPERIENCES

ELACHEE NATURE SCIENCE CENTER –Located within the 1,200-acre Chicopee Woods Nature Preserve, Elachee is an environmental education center whose mission is to develop an ecologically responsible community. It is a private, non-profit organization supported by program fees, membership dues, fundraising events, the United Way and private and corporate donations. The center includes a natural history museum, botanical gardens, hiking trails and a scheduled environmental program. Prepared programs are available to school groups from preschool to K-12. Other programs include guided "First Saturday Hikes" into the Chicopee Woods Nature Preserve, wildflower walks, "Celestial Saturday" for learning about the stars, composting workshops and winter survival skills. Three bark and gravel hiking trails wind through about three miles of the Chicopee Woods Nature Preserve. *Days/Hrs.:* Museum, Mon.-Sat., 10am-5pm; trails, daily 8am-dusk. Closed Thanksgiving Day, Christmas Eve Day, Christmas and New Year's Day. *Fees:* Museum, members and children under 2 free, adults $3, children 2-12 $1.50; trails, free. *More Information:*

Elachee Nature Science Center, 2125 Elachee Drive, Gainesville, GA 30504; 770/535-1976.

GAINESVILLE –Long before white settlers arrived to this area, Cherokee nation villages dotted the streams and countryside of what is now Hall County. A trading post, called Mule Camp Springs, sprang up at the confluence of two Indian trails, near a group of springs. This was a stopping place for both Indians and the white traders moving through the area. The federal government acquired this land from the Indians in the treaties of 1817 and 1819, and Hall County was organized under an act of the Georgia Legislature and signed by Governor William Rabun on December 15, 1818. The county was named after Lyman Hall, one of the signers of the Declaration of Independence. In 1821, 50 acres of Lot 148, 9th district, Hall County, was chartered as Gainesville and named for General Edmond P. Gaines. This location was just northwest of Mule Camp Springs.

Two different things stimulated the growth of Gainesville. First was the discovery of gold in the surrounding region in 1828. Miners, merchants and professionals moved in and Gainesville became the trading center for the gold mines. Taverns, stores and offices were erected around the square. Then in 1871 came the first railroad, the Atlanta-Charlotte Airline Railroad, and economic opportunities expanded further. The surrounding springs which had once attracted Indians and traders now attracted tourists, and Gainesville became a resort center. The cool summer climate and healing springs nearby drew the crowds. Springs were marketed for their healing qualities: Iron Springs in City Park for dyspepsia and headaches; Gower Springs for kidney troubles and indigestion; Deal Springs for teething children; and Limestone Springs for its blue flint lime water. There were resort hotels at New Holland Springs and White Sulphur Springs, which catered to the state's wealthy and fashionable. With the tourists came demands for stores, boarding houses, hotels and places of entertainment. Confederate General James Longstreet, who spent the last 30 years of his life in Gainesville, owned the Piedmont Hotel, the most prominent hotel in town. Gainesville was reportedly the first city south of Baltimore to have electric street lights.

LINES ON LAKE LANIER

*Lines are cast, in numerous attempts
To lure all those who daily must feed,
From the dock, few lures have enticed
Them enough to strike, concede.*

*While bread, cast from near water's edge —
No hook — is accepted without fear;
For freedom is the greatest lure
Of the lines on Lake Lanier.*

—Marne H. Finfrock

Fish Consumption Guidelines

Lake Lanier–Bass, no restrictions; catfish, no restrictions; carp over 16", one meal per month. As a general rule, eat smaller fish to be safe.

Source: Georgia Department of Natural Resources, 1997.

By the end of the century there were shoe factories, tanneries, carriage makers, corn mills and cotton gins. Brenau College was established in 1878 as the Georgia Baptist Female Seminary and Conservatory of Music. In 1900, the name became Brenau College Conservatory. Brenau, a word formed from the German word "Brennen"–to burn–and the Latin word "Aurum"–gold–means "refined gold."

Since the founding of Gainesville, Green Street has been one of its most important roads. It had been both stagecoach and freight route to the mining regions and a pleasant way to the Town Spring. Beginning about 1880, many fine homes were built along Green Street; and it became the prime residential district. Today Green Street is a major thoroughfare, although still lined with numerous Victorian and Neoclassical Revival residences from the late 19th and early 20th centuries. The State Department of Natural Resources designated Green Street a Historic District, calling it one of the finest relatively untouched group examples of Neoclassical architecture in North Georgia. Many of the former homes have been remodeled and transformed into office buildings, but their exteriors have been preserved.

A walking tour map of Green Street, available at the Gainesville-Hall County Convention and Visitors' Bureau, locates and describes 32 homes along this historic street. Included are some of Gainesville's oldest houses: a frame, plain style that still has some of the original architectural gingerbread on its exterior; Green Street's best example of a Queen Anne High Victorian style house built in 1886; an example of a plantation plain style built around 1900 and a grand unaltered house with a two-story convex portico built in 1906. *More Information:* Gainesville-Hall County Convention and Visitors' Bureau, 830 Green Street, Gainesville, GA 30501; 770/536-5209.

LANIER MUSEUM OF NATURAL HISTORY –This natural history museum packs a lot of visually interesting information in a small space. Revolving exhibits at the museum highlight the natural, cultural and historical development of Gwinnett County. The museum offers special events and classes where adults and children can learn a long-forgotten art, create nature crafts, study prehistoric earth or see animals in their natural environment. Programs include environmental excursions, day camps and events such as EarthFest, Family Campfire Night and Victorian Holiday. There are teacher training workshops available and a Lanier Museum Outreach program. A newsletter, *The Nature Zone*, features the latest classes and events. *Days/Hrs.:* Tues.-Fri., noon-5pm; Sat., 10am-5pm. *Fees:* Free, with some charges for special events and student and group tours. *More Information:* Lanier Museum of Natural History, 2601 Buford Dam Road, Buford, GA 30518; 770/932-4460.

FISHING

The best fishing on Lake Lanier is for striped bass, black bass, spotted bass, bream, crappie and catfish.

BEST ADVICE –Each lake and every section of river has its own particular bank topography, underwater structure, stream currents and fish population. Professional guides know all the peculiarities of their lake. The most experienced fishermen find that one or two days of guide fees is a good investment before launching out on their own. Inexperienced fishermen or families looking for an enjoyable day's outing will increase their pleasure ten-fold by taking advantage of a professional guide's experience. The best guides not only make sure their customers fish, but provide insights into the fishing habits of different species, lake ecology, weather lore and one hundred-and-one other aspects to enhance the fishing experience.

When booking a fishing guide always check to make sure who is responsible for all tackle (rods, reels, lures), boats and gasoline, all live bait, life jackets, lunch, drinks, snacks, ice and rain gear. Always understand exactly what is included in the guide fees.

GUIDES –The Lake Lanier guides most often recommended by their peers are Jerry Hester (specializing in stripers), 770/479-1584; Randy Steele, 732 Windy Drive, Stone Mountain, GA 30087, 770/921-4530; Mack Farr, 1575 Quail Point Run, Hoschton, GA 30548, 770/271-0851; and Doug Youngblood, P.O. Box 1191, Buford, GA 30518; 770/945-0797.

Ken Sturdivant is a full-time professional guide and fishing educator, offering classroom and on-the-water instruction on

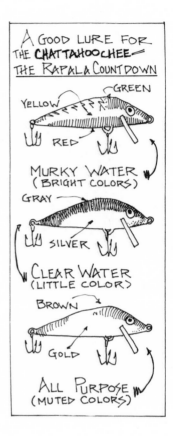

Fish are attracted by underwater conditions. A lake bottom bare of cover usually plays host to few fish. Wise fishermen watch for the ideal combination of a food-producing bottom with protective hiding spots in the same vicinity.

maps, electronics, rods, reels and lures. He conducts fishing schools and seminars and compiles quarterly fishing forecasts. Contact Southern Fishing Schools, 106 Hickory Ridge, Cumming, GA 30130; 770/889-2654.

THE COMMON SNAPPING TURTLE

BEST BOOKS AND MAPS – Fishing Hot Spots publishes a good, waterproof fishing map for Lanier. Available at quality marinas and sporting goods stores. (To order see page 325.) Atlantic Mapping publishes a "Lake Lanier Recreation and Fishing Guide" map that is available at marinas and sporting goods stores. (To order see page 325.)

Fishing guide and instructor Ken Sturdivant has filled a three-ring binder with information on how, when and where to fish Lanier, called *52 Weeks a Year on Lanier.* (To order see page 327.)

U.S. Geological Survey 1:24,000 scale topographical maps covering this section of the river are Lula, Clermont, Murrayville, Coal Mountain, Chestatee, Gainesville, Gillsville, Buford Dam and Flowery Branch. (To order see page 326.)

OTHER SOURCES OF INFORMATION – Tommy Wilkinson, a veteran Lake Lanier fishing guide, writes a "Fishing On Lanier" column in *Lakeside*, a monthly tabloid newspaper. The information is specific and usually tied to seasonal behavior of the lake's fish. *Lakeside* is distributed free at bait and tackle shops and convenience stores around the lake. (To subscribe see page 331.)

BOATING

About 7 million people, many of them repeat customers, visit Lanier each year. On any given hot, sunny summer weekend, there are 30,000 to 50,000 visitors at Lanier, many of them crisscrossing the 38,000-acre lake in powerboats, sailboats, jet skis and fishing boats. Boaters can explore over 100 islands that dot the lake, many of which have secluded coves and beaches. Lanier is the seacoast for the 2.5 million population in the Atlanta metropolitan area.

Ten private marinas and 54 boat ramps with parking areas provide easy access to the lake. Some marinas rent boats, and all have lake maps which show the locations of most lake recreational facilities.

Many lake hazards are marked by standard navigation signs. Boaters should watch for submerged stumps, logs, rocks and shallow water. Boaters are prohibited from dumping raw or treated sewage into the lake. Pump-out stations are available at most marinas (see marina section page 61 - 67). A system of markers maintained by the U.S. Army Corps of Engineers designates the channels of the Chattahoochee and Chestatee rivers and other smaller tributaries.

All federal, state and local laws are enforced. Boating under the influence of alcoholic beverages is a serious offense.

Low water levels can affect the boaters ability to put boats in the water at boat ramps and high water levels can affect bridge and power line clearance for sailboats. Detailed information on sailing is listed below.

The best guide for recreational boaters is a set of topographical maps covering the lake. The 1:24,000 scale topos for Lanier are Murrayville, Clermont, Lula, Coal Mountain, Chestatee, Gainesville, Gillsville, Buford Dam and Flowery Branch. (To order see page 326.) The second best navigation aid is Atlantic Mapping's "Lake Lanier Recreation and Fishing Guide" available at Lanier marinas and area sporting goods stores. Atlantic Mapping also produces a good trout fishing, canoeing and rafting guide to the Chattahoochee River which includes the region from Helen down to Lanier, then jumps Lanier and includes the section of the river from Buford Dam down to Peachtree Creek. This map is a good companion piece for the Lanier map. (To order see page 325.)

North Georgia's Chestatee River lies within the Chattahoochee watershed and was a tributary of the Chattahoochee before Lake Lanier was formed. Lanier power boaters can go up the Chestatee as far as the GA 400 bridge. Use extreme care here. There is a no wake zone about 2 miles below the bridge; strictly observe this zone to preserve the delicate riverbank environment. (See page 40 for Chestatee River canoe trips.)

THE LANGUAGE OF
"WATER"

Chinese–shui
French–l'eau
German–das wasser
Italian–l'acqua
Japanese–mizu
Portugese and Spanish–agua
Russian–vada

SAILING

With a large contingency of racers and sailing clubs, sailing on Lake Lanier is one of the most organized activities on the lake. Sailing is predominantly done in the large, open area of the lake just below Brown's Bridge. Large motorized boats rule the waters on the south of the lake, and sailboats cannot get under Brown's Bridge to go further north. Also, this central portion of the lake is more open to the wind, making better sailing. Sunrise Cove and Aqualand marinas are both located in this area, as well as the Lanier Sailing Club.

These sailing clubs based at Lanier hold numerous events throughout the year. Event and date listings can usually be found in the *Lakeside* newspaper.

LAKE LANIER SAILING CLUB –The Lake Lanier Sailing Club is a private, not-for-profit club that owns 17 acres and leases 50 acres from the Corps of Engineers on Lake Lanier. Most of the one-design fleets at Lake Lanier are based here: Lazer, Sailboard, M C Scow, Snipe, Thistle, Lightning, J-22, J-24, Auxiliary Fleet, C-15 and the Georgia Tech Sailing Club. Membership is through application. The club sponsors the biggest annual regatta on the lake, the Reggae Regatta. It hosts a Junior Week program each summer, teaching juniors to sail and race. Its junior racing fleet travels around the southeast. The club is a member of the U.S. Sailing Association, the Dixie Inland Yacht Racing Association and the South Atlantic Yacht Racing Association. *Facilities:* 88 slips, boat ramps, club house, campground, swimming beach. *More Information:* Lake Lanier Sailing Club, 6206 Commodore Drive, Flowery Branch, GA 30542; 770/967-6441.

BAREFOOT SAILING CLUB –This 135-member club sponsors racing, cruising and social events. It hosts 30 races a year as well as The Barefoot Open Sailing Regatta in the fall. *More Information:* For social events and racing, 404/256-6839.

ATLANTA INLAND SAILING CLUB –This club is strictly racing with few other organized events. The club sponsors the Dogwood Regatta each April as well as a Wednesday-night racing series during the summer months with 20 races. *More Information:* The Weathermark Sailing Center, 770/945-0788.

CATALINA 22, FLEET 58 SAILING CLUB –This nationally chartered fleet falls under the umbrella of the Catalina 22 National Sailing Association. Members of this one-design fleet must own a Catalina 22. The fleet, which is based out of Aqualand Marina, was the national association's 1996 Fleet of the Year. The organization promotes family participation in sailing events, racing, cruising and education. Besides numerous monthly activities, the fleet hosts two annual regattas, the Gone with the Wind regatta the last weekend in September and the Irish Wake on St. Patrick's Day weekend. Boats from all over the southeast attend both regattas. *More Information:* For social events and racing, 770/534-2657.

SOUTHERN SAILING CLUB –Southern Sailing Club has been in operation for about 20 years and its approximately 145 members all live within a 100-mile radius of Atlanta. The club offers monthly racing series as well as several annual regattas. The purpose of the club, however, is "to have more fun with our boats by developing interesting activities in which everyone can participate." In addition to racing, this family-oriented club offers a wide variety of boating and social activities, including a black-tie optional Commodore's Ball, a new member's race and barbecue, a day-sail for local area handicapped young people, beach parties, a club auction, moonlight cruises, a lobster bake and a chili cook-off. *More Information:* For social events and racing, 770/447-8047.

ATLANTA BOARDSAILING CLUB –This club, organized in 1978, is one of the oldest in the country and is a member of US Windsurfing. Membership is around 80 members with most being from the Atlanta area. The club organizes a racing series which includes two major regattas. They also organize trips to Savannah, Cape Hatteras and Florida for recreational sailing weekends. Clinics are offered periodically and new sailors are always welcome. *More Information:* For social events and racing, 404/237-1431.

Some sailing clubs offer instruction for members, but the following sailing schools are open to the public.

LANIER SAILING ACADEMY –Lanier Sailing Academy has been in operation for over 25 years and is a certified American Sailing Association training facility. Courses prepare sailors for ASA

www.chattahoochee.org

ⓖ We welcome your comments, suggestions, recommendations and input regarding this book and the river, via the Internet at the Riverkeeper's website: www.chattahoochee.org.

You can also access the website for additional information regarding the Chattahoochee and the many issues that affect the river.

**ALL IS BORN OF WATER;
ALL IS SUSTAINED BY WATER.**

"Til taught by pain men know not what water is worth."

—Lord Byron

certification in all levels, from Small Boat Dinghy sailing though Bareboat Charter to Celestial Navigation and Ocean Passage-making. *More Information:* Lanier Sailing Academy, 8000 Holiday Road, Lake Lanier Island, GA 30518; 770/945-8810.

WINDSONG SAILING ACADEMY –Windsong offers private and group classes in sailing, bareboat chartering, coastal cruising, coastal navigation, celestial navigation and gourmet cooking. Its programs are sponsored by the parks and recreation service, community adult education programs, marinas and sailing centers in several Georgia counties. Lanier Windsong is based at Holiday Marina. *More Information:* Windsong Sailing Academy, 3966 Secluded Circle S.W., Lilburn, GA 30247; 404/256-6700.

Section 3
Buford Dam to
Peachtree Creek

"It's very frightening for me to see what's taken place. I look at a timeframe of my existence with the Nature Center of eight years. I see what's taken place in that river in an eight-year period and if that continues...

The siltation is so severe today. And it's much more obvious. I think there's exponentially more of it coming down the river corridor. Things are silting in so rapidly today that we're getting land masses where just four years ago we had a good depth of water that we could put our boats in. The river is much more shallow, also, right here in front of the Nature Center. During just regular medium water flows in the river,

Greg Greer

you can walk across the river and not get your hair wet. Eight years ago you couldn't do that. You'd be doing some swimming to get across that river. If they're releasing water at Morgan Falls, which they do almost every evening to generate the supplemental power that's required for the area, we have extensive mud flats that are exposed on all the inside curves of the river. By six o'clock this evening our marsh out here will have no water in it. It will be completely devoid of water. The banks will be just all mud.

There's a lot of rowers on this river. In the evening a lot of people put their sculls in up at the river park, and they row this river. Years ago at the bend in the river where Willeo Creek is, there was plenty of room for five or six or eight canoes and a couple of rowers coming up and down the river and we could pass each other. Today, in the curves of the river, you have to be very careful. Somebody has to often times kind of wait for another boat to get past because the river is so restricted to where there's deep enough water for even boats to pass. All the insides of the curves are silted in.

That river, it's a treasure. There's no other word for it. The importance is that it is the life blood of this region. We get a lot of folks that when they first come to Atlanta they go through a chamber of commerce or call the park service to inquire about what recreational activities are available to people in the area. And often times they're told about the Chattahoochee National Recreational Area units or they're told about the Chattahoochee Nature Center, and we get a lot of those folks on our canoe floats. You get them out there on the river and it opens their eyes up so wide. They just can't believe it. The reaction is one of amazement. They're just stunned with the beauty of that river. And you know, further stunned when you say, 'You realize that we have over two million people now in this area, and you're looking at trees. You're looking at a river that's still flowing.' "

Greg Greer, an environmental consultant and writer, was the Director of the Chattahoochee Nature Center from 1989 to 1997.

THE RIVER

River towns naturally grow up because of a river. Historically, the river served as a means of transportation or the backbone of the economy. But not in Atlanta. Atlanta grew up because of railroads. The Chattahoochee was always at her back door. Atlanta could never be called a river town. But in the last 25 years, metropolitan Atlanta has begun to creep all around the 48-mile stretch of river that runs between Buford Dam and Peachtree Creek.

It is a stretch of river dotted with the history of Indians, white settlers, ferries and Sherman's march to the sea. The Brevard Fault, through which it runs, turns it into a mountain-like river with high rock palisades and numerous shoals. And although the Chattahoochee has never been important to Atlanta in terms of transportation and economy, it is vitally important in terms of water supply, waste water assimilation and, increasingly, in terms of recreation.

On any map of the Atlanta metropolitan area, the red line designating the I-285 perimeter around what we call Atlanta presents a dangerously distorted picture. What we refer to as "Atlanta," when what we really mean is "the Atlanta metropolitan area" has changed dramatically over the past 20 years. The population has shifted and continues to shift north to Cobb, Cherokee, Paulding and Gwinnett counties.

The bull's eye of downtown within the red line of the perimeter highway no longer designates the center of Atlanta. In actuality, it is the blue line marking the course of the Chattahoochee River that serves as the city's heart and center,

Rock climbers at the Lovers Leap cliffs overlooking Vickery Creek

defining and sustaining Atlanta as no strip of concrete can. As planners chart the future course of this region, the priorities at the top of the list are water supply, water supply and water supply.

In the past Atlanta may not have been a river town, but in the future it is going to be a river city.

PARKS AND RECREATION

Although urban sprawl and industrial development heavily affect the Chattahoochee River in certain areas, it is nonetheless one of the most unspoiled, scenic and historic rivers running through any major metropolitan area of the United States. The state Metropolitan River Protection Act, passed in 1973, established a 2,000-foot corridor on either side of the river within which land development is allowed but restricted to protect the river. In August 1978, Congress established the Chattahoochee River National Recreation Area (CRNRA) to preserve and protect the natural beauty, historic aspects and recreational value of the river and authorized the acquisition of up to 6,800 acres, most of it within easy commuting distance of Atlanta.

Today, the CRNRA consists of 48 miles of river and 16 separate land units, or parks, along both sides of its banks. The parks are day use facilities only, made up of hiking trails, picnic grounds, playing fields and, during the summer, two raft/canoe/kayak rental facilities. The river running through it is a stocked trout stream that includes 19 other game fish.

The Chattahoochee corridor has a colorful and interesting history which has been preserved within the National Recreation Area. Numerous rock shelters, once used by nomadic Indian families and later Indian hunting parties, can be explored on the trails at both Island Ford and Palisades East. During the 19th century, the river was the dividing line between the Cherokee and Creek Indian Nations. The Creeks, on the south side of the line, were forced west to Oklahoma in 1828 and the Cherokees, on the north and west side, were forced out in 1838.

The American settlers who followed Removal established cotton plantations and constructed a large number of mills—

grist, lumber, wool, cotton, tanning, whiskey and paper. Within the present boundaries of the National Recreation Area, at least 10 settlers ran ferries across the river. Today, Powers, Pace, Johnson, Heard, Dunwoody, Roswell, Jones, Terrell, Aker, Moore and Abbott are names of landmarks and streets, but once they were names of those early entrepreneurs, their ferries and the roads that led to their mills.

The portion of the river downstream from Jones Bridge receives considerably heavier recreational use than the portion upriver to Buford Dam. The lower section is used primarily for floating, while fishing and picnicking and relaxing in a river environment are more common on the middle and upper sections. The lightest use of the river is seasonal, from September through May.

For rafters, the lower stretch of the river is Class I and II, ideal for beginners and children. A popular trip for rafters is from the Johnson Ferry put-in to the last take-out point in the National Recreational Area at Paces Mill, just past the I-75 bridge. This 3-mile stretch of the river is often referred to as the Atlanta Hooch. Rental facilities, located at Johnson Ferry and Powers Island units, are open on weekends during May and every day from Memorial Day weekend through Labor Day weekend. Shuttle buses run between units. The park's concessionaire is Chattahoochee Outdoor Center. Rafts may be reserved by calling 770/395-6851. In addition to the rental price, a security deposit is required until the boat is returned. Also, visitors are welcome to put in their own watercraft.

Jones Bridge, Island Ford and the Devil's Racecourse, that runs between the Palisades, are good places to put in a kayak or canoe and play, running back and forth in the rapids. All boaters in the park must have a personal flotation device (PFD) with them and children must be wearing one. As the river's waters are a constant 50 degrees fahrenheit, swimming is not recommended. Glass containers are prohibited on the river.

Fishing on this stretch of the river, a designated trout stream, is highly popular and can be quite rewarding. Jones Bridge and Island Ford are two very popular areas among waders fishing mostly for trout. A valid Georgia fishing license with trout stamp is required for anyone 16 years of age or

Kayakers tackling the slalom course at Powers Island

What is a River System?

A river system is a network of connecting channels through which water, precipitated on the surface, is collected and funneled back to the ocean. At any given time, about 1300 km^3 of water flows in the world's rivers. As it moves, it picks up weathered rock debris and carries it to the oceans.

Ken Hamblin, "River Systems," Earth's Dynamic Systems

A FLEDGLING WOOD DUCK PREPARING TO LAUNCH FROM ITS BIRDHOUSE.

older. Fishing is permitted year-round from Buford Dam downstream to the I-285 bridge. On the portion of the river between GA 141 and GA 20, only artificial lures may be used. Refer to current Georgia fishing and trout regulations for further information.

From March through November, guided walks are offered in different park units. Call Park Headquarters or check the bulletin boards in the park units for dates and times. These walks are free to the public.

Although the Chattahoochee River corridor winds through an extremely populated and developed urban area, it is home to an amazing variety of animals, birds and plant life. White-tailed deer, red and gray foxes, mink, river otters and raccoons inhabit the park lands. Great Blue Heron, osprey and golden eagle nest along the river, and great numbers of Canadian geese no longer migrate, but make the Chattahoochee home.

Several city or county parks line the Chattahoochee between Buford Dam and Peachtree Creek. These parks also afford opportunities for launching watercraft, fishing, picnicking and ball playing.

For a map of all parks along the Chattahoochee River corridor, contact the CRNRA Park Headquarters. *Day/Hrs.:* CRNRA units, daily, 7am to dark. *More Information:* CRNRA Park Headquarters, 1917 Island Ford Parkway, Atlanta, GA 30350; 770/399-8070.

The following CRNRA park units, as well as other river parks between Buford Dam and Peachtree Creek, are listed in order from north to south, upstream to downstream.

BOWMAN'S ISLAND UNIT –This is the northernmost unit of the CRNRA. It extends for about two miles along the river between Buford Dam and GA 20, one of the most beautiful sections of river in the metro Atlanta area. The clear, cold waters of the Chattahoochee which run through this unit are more characteristic of a mountain stream environment than any other part of the CRNRA. The river's banks are heavily forested with sycamore, red maple, river birch and ash. The cold lake water released at Buford Dam helps keep the river valley somewhat colder than the surrounding areas. The mountain-like waters provide excellent canoeing and fishing opportunities for rainbow, brook and brown trout. It is heavily wooded with numerous unusual and protected plant species. Topographically it is quite rugged, and there is evidence of prehistoric occupation. There are no developed facilities at Bowman's Island at this time. The Buford Trout Hatchery is located just south of the Bowman's Island Unit on the river's west bank. This hatchery, which is the state's largest, raises over 500,000 stockable brown and rainbow trout for Georgia trout streams each year. Self-guided and group tours are available at the hatchery. *Directions:* This portion of the river can be easily accessed from the Corps of Engineers boat ramp at Lower Pool Park right below Buford Dam (see page 54). There is no parking lot for Bowman's Island. To get to the Buford Trout Hatchery from GA 400 north, turn east on SR 20 (Exit 14). Go about 4 miles and turn left into Chattahoochee River Club subdivision. Take the fourth right onto Trout Place Road. This will dead end into the Hatchery. *More Information:* Buford Trout Hatchery, 3204 Trout Place, Cumming, GA 30131; 770/781-6888. For information on water release schedules and safety information, tune to 1610 AM on the radio or call 770/945-1466. In the event of an emergency on this portion of the river, the following phone numbers are provided: Corps of Engineers, 770/945-9531; National Park Service, 770/952-0370; Georgia Game and Fish, 770/535-5495; Forsyth County Sheriff, 770/887-4330; and Gwinnett County Police, 770/962-1900.

McGinnis Ferry Unit –This is another undeveloped park unit. Its 161 acres stretch about two miles along the river, about eight miles south of Buford Dam. There is no parking lot here, and any access to the river is via undeveloped pathways. *Directions:* From Peachtree Industrial Boulevard north, turn left on McGinnis Ferry Road.

Suwanee Creek Unit –This small unit of the CRNRA is located on the west side of the river, about 10 miles below Buford Dam and north of Rogers Bridge. There is no parking lot in this undeveloped park and access to the river is via undeveloped pathways. *Directions:* From Peachtree Industrial Boulevard north, turn left on Chattahoochee Drive.

Abbotts Bridge Unit –This unit of the CRNRA is about 13 miles downstream from Buford Dam and has the first restroom

Surface Runoff vs. Infiltration

Under natural conditions, from 80 to 100 percent of surface water filters into the subsurface and from 0 to 20 percent flows through the drainage system.

In urban areas, from 0 to 10 percent of surface water filters into the subsurface, and from 90 to 100 percent moves as surface runoff.

WATER RELIGION:
OLD TESTAMENT

The Books of Leviticus and Numbers in the Old Testament requires ritualistic cleansing by water before entry into sacred areas.

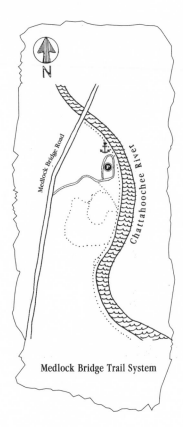

Medlock Bridge Trail System

facilities between here and Lake Lanier. There are no other restrooms until the Jones Bridge Unit, which is another seven miles downstream. This is also the first boat ramp since the ramp below Buford Dam at Lower Pool Park. *Facilities:* Boat/canoe/raft launch, picnic tables, restrooms. *Fees:* Parking, $2. *Directions:* From GA 400 north, exit east on GA 120, State Bridge Road. Follow this until it turns into Abbotts Bridge Road. Follow to the river and watch for the signs.

MEDLOCK BRIDGE UNIT –Four miles downstream from Abbotts Bridge is a tight bend in the river where rock palisades rise above the deep water. This is the 43-acre Medlock Bridge Unit. *Facilities:* Boat/canoe/raft launch, picnic tables, hiking trail (see page 75). *Fees:* Parking, $2. *Directions:* From Peachtree Industrial Boulevard north, take GA 141 (Peachtree Parkway) and watch for the signs. Park is on right.

JONES BRIDGE PARK –This park is on the east side of the Chattahoochee River across from the Jones Bridge Unit of the CRNRA and is part of the Gwinnett County Park System. *Facilities:* Covered group shelter, covered and uncovered picnic tables, grills, viewing deck along river overlooking Jones Bridge Shoals, playground, soccer field, volleyball area, restrooms. *Days/Hrs.:* Sunup to sundown. *Directions:* From Peachtree Industrial Boulevard north, turn left on Peachtree Parkway. Go to East Jones Bridge Road and turn left. Park is at the end of the road.

JONES BRIDGE-BARNWELL UNIT –This 195-acre unit stretches along one of the prettiest sections of the river. From Jones Bridge to Holcomb Bridge is prime canoeing and fishing, especially along the Jones Bridge Shoals. About 100 yards upstream from the unit parking lot are the historic remnants of the old metal Jones Bridge (see page 104), which was built in 1904 to replace the Jones Ferry river crossing. Just below Jones Bridge is a good place to walk across the river on the shoals when the water is not too high. The Geosphere Environmental Education Training Center, managed by the nonprofit organization Friends of Geosphere (FOG), is located on the southern edge of the unit. Here classes and workshops are offered to teachers, scout leaders and other adult educators. The center is not open to the general public except during special events.

Facilities: Concrete ramp for trailers and motorboats, railroad-tie steps launch for canoes and rafts; picnic area with grills; large open grassy recreation area; hiking trail (see page 96); wheelchair accessible viewing deck; restrooms; 2 parking areas. *Fees:* Parking, $2. *Directions:* From GA 400 north, exit east on Holcomb Bridge Road. Go about 4 miles to Barnwell Road and turn left. Go a couple of miles. Entrance to park will be on right side of Barnwell Road.

HOLCOMB BRIDGE UNIT –This unit is an oasis of open fields, forested areas and steeply rising bluffs in the midst of one of Atlanta's fastest growing urban areas. Still undeveloped as a park recreational facility, it contains 30 acres. *Directions:* From GA 400 north, exit east on Holcomb Bridge Road. Follow Holcomb Bridge Road.

ISLAND FORD UNIT –The National Park Service manages the 16 individual units of the CRNRA along 48 miles of river. Park headquarters for the CRNRA is located just off Roberts Road on the river's south side in the Island Ford Unit. At the park information building there is interpretive information about the recreation area as well as maps depicting the hiking trails, facilities, general information and rules for the developed park units. There is also a bookstore and office for the Chattahoochee Outdoor Center in the headquarters complex. The headquarters staff will mail out information about the parks upon request. The Island Ford Unit consists of 297 wooded acres, including the island known as Copeland Island. Some of the best fly and live bait fishing can be done from the shoals along this beautiful section of the river. A fisherman can put in here, fish down a mile or so and walk back to his car with a catch of five or six trout. Island Ford has natural habitats that support muskrat, beaver, fox and raccoon. Huge rock outcroppings along the river were once used by prehistoric man for shelter as well as later Indians who camped here while on hunting parties. The log building located on the property was the summer home for the family of Sam Hewlett, a former Georgia Superior Court Judge. It was constructed in the 1930s, using timber from the Okefenokee Swamp and stone from Stone Mountain. *Facilities:* Headquarters Building for the CRNRA, bookstore, boat ramp (must carry boat to/from ramp),

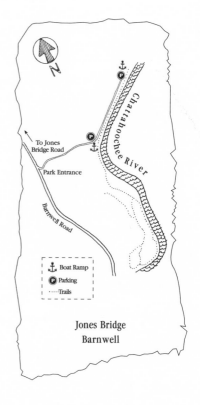

Jones Bridge
Barnwell

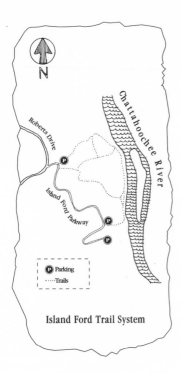

Island Ford Trail System

hiking trail (see page 96), Fallen Branch Shelter, Sam Hewlett Field with picnic tables and grills, wooden deck for river viewing, restrooms, telephone, 3 parking areas. *Fees:* Parking, $2. *Days/Hrs.:* Headquarters, Mon.-Fri., 8am-4:30pm. Closed major holidays. Chattahoochee Outdoor Center hours vary and is not always open if the weather is bad. Call before visiting. *Directions:* From GA 400 north, exit west on Northridge, going toward Roswell Road. Go to Roberts Drive and turn right. Entrance to park is well-marked with signs. *More Information:* CRNRA Headquarters, 1917 Island Ford Parkway, Atlanta, GA 30350; 770/399-8070 or 770/952-4419. Chattahoochee Outdoor Center, 1990 Island Ford Parkway, Atlanta, GA 30350; 770/395-6851; fax 770/396-8911.

VICKERY CREEK UNIT –This unit covers about 254 acres around Vickery Creek, sometimes referred to as Big Creek, a tributary of the Chattahoochee. Steep bluffs of rock create a rugged and varied terrain along the creek. One such bluff, known as Lover's Leap (see page 97), affords a great view and can be reached from a trail on the west side of the creek. The powerful waters of Vickery Creek led Roswell King to build the town of Roswell (see page 107) with cotton mills in the 1830s. Ruins of the Roswell Cotton Mills and mill dam still exist and can be seen from the hiking trail system (see page 96). Near the confluence of Vickery Creek and the Chattahoochee, the Ivy Woolen Mill was built between 1856 and 1857 as well as Allenbrook, which served as home and office for the loom boss. A trail from Allenbrook leads to some ruins of the woolen mill, but it is extremely difficult to find as the trail is nearly impassable around the ruins (see page 97). *Facilities:* Picnic area, viewing areas, hiking trail, fishing on creek. *Fees:* Parking, $2. *Directions:* From I-285, exit north on Roswell Road. Go past the river to the Azalea Drive/Riverside Road intersection and turn right onto Riverside Road. Cross Vickery Creek and take an immediate left into the park. To reach the small, unmarked entrance on the west side of the creek, stay on Roswell Road, crossing the Azalea Drive/Riverside Road intersection. Carefully look for the entrance into Allenbrook on the right-hand side of the street. There is no sign, only a curved brick entrance wall. Turn right and park in the small parking lot.

CHATTAHOOCHEE RIVER PARK –This 770-acre park, managed by Fulton County Parks and Recreation, is very popular and usually crowded. The Atlanta Rowing Club operates from a building here and offers courses in rowing. The Abernathy arts and crafts program also has use of a building here for drawing and painting classes. The park is the site of activities ranging from water ballets to national rowing regattas. Note that this is the last take-out for boaters before Morgan Falls Dam. *Facilities:* Boat/canoe/raft launch, picnic tables, hiking trail, playground. *Days/Hrs.:* Daily, 6am-midnight. *Directions:* From I-285, exit north on Roswell Road. Take Roswell Road until it crosses the river and immediately turn left on Azalea Drive, following it along the river to the park. *More Information:* Fulton County Parks and Recreation, 141 Pryor Street, Suite 8054, Atlanta GA 30303; 404/730-6200; fax 404/730-6206.

GOLD BRANCH UNIT –This 358 acres of woods and marshy environment lies 35 miles downstream from Buford Dam. It is adjacent to Bull Sluice Lake, an impoundment of the Chattahoochee created during the construction of Morgan Falls Dam. There is no boat ramp here. The nearest ramps are at Chattahoochee River Park, two miles upstream from Morgan Falls Dam and Morgan Falls Park, just below the dam. Despite the rapid urbanization around the unit there are many species of wildlife such as beaver, squirrel, rabbit, opossum and raccoon. A large number of nut-and-fruit bearing tees support this substantial wildlife population. *Facilities:* Picnic area, hiking trail. *Fees:* Parking, $2. *Directions:* From I-285, exit north on Roswell Road, turn left on Johnson Ferry Road. Cross the river. Turn right on Lower Roswell Road. Park entrance on right.

MORGAN FALLS PARK –This park is operated by Fulton County Parks and Recreation and sits right below Morgan Falls Dam. This is a large and very nice park, but its emphases are more on ball teams and athletics than on river recreation. *Facilities:* Boat/canoe/raft launch, ball fields, picnic shelter, golf driving range, playground. *Days/Hrs.:* Daily, 6am-midnight. *Directions:* From I-285, exit north on Roswell Road. Turn left on Morgan Falls Road and follow signs. *More Information:* Fulton County Parks and Recreation, 141 Pryor Street, Suite 8054, Atlanta GA

Morgan Falls

Historic is certainly the right word when referring to old stone ruins of gristmills and cotton mills on the river, but somehow it doesn't seem to apply to a huge concrete dam which currently generates hydroelectric power and creates a large capacity reservoir. But Morgan Falls Dam is, in fact, a significant historic structure as it is among the first of the early hydroelectric developments built in Georgia. The use of the river as a source of power took a huge step forward with the construction of Morgan Falls Dam. The Bull Sluice, or Morgan Falls, project began in 1902. When completed in 1904, it produced Atlanta's first hydroelectric power, playing an important role in the city's early industrial growth. *Atlanta Constitution* headlines on March 6, 1904, read "Bull Sluice Dam has Bridled Chattahoochee–Has Cost the Company a Million and Half Dollars to Turn the Powers of the River Into Channels of Commerce." The plant was the South's largest hydroelectric installation. The majority of its 10,500-kilowatt output was initially used to run the Atlanta streetcar system. The generators, designed by Westinghouse, Church, Kerr and Company, are still in operation in the more than 1,000-foot long and 60-foot high structure. The development of hydroelectric power was viewed as the answer to all of the South's and the nation's needs. However, this proved an unwise assumption as early as 1925 when a drought caused a shortage of available water to turn the turbines. The Georgia Power Company owns Morgan Falls. *Directions:* Take Roswell Road north to Morgan Falls Dam Road and turn left. Follow this to its end at Morgan Falls.

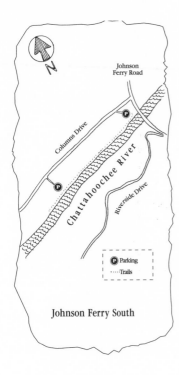

Sopes Creek is named for a Cherokee Indian Old Soap, who lived on the stream in the last days of Cherokee occupation.

—Marion Hemperley, Indian Heritage of Georgia

30303; 404/730-6200; fax 404/730-6206.

JOHNSON FERRY UNIT –For thousands of years humans hunted, gathered, fished and farmed in this unit, relying on the natural environment for all their needs. River cane was woven into baskets. Quartz stones were chipped into arrow points. Nuts and seeds were collected to eat. Fish weirs were built to harvest fish. Just a hundred years ago, Mr. Johnson's ferry traveled silently, carrying travelers back and forth across the river. Named for the 18th-century ferry crossing, the Johnson Ferry Unit is a physiographic continuation of the Cochran Shoals flood plain. It has been divided into two areas separated by Johnson Ferry Road: Johnson Ferry North and Johnson Ferry South.

JOHNSON FERRY NORTH contains over 100 acres of fields, forests, wetlands and four streams. The flat floodplain forest trail, the Mulberry Creek Loop Trail, is excellent for viewing birds, wildlife and wildflowers, and the cold water of the river is great for fishing 22 species of game fish including trout. *Facilities:* Canoe/raft launch, picnic areas, hiking trail (see page 98), restrooms, telephone. The Chattahoochee Outdoor Center has raft rental and shuttle and a concession stand with snack food, water, juices and t-shirts. The Center will also prepare a "river lunch" for boaters which consists of a deli-style sandwich, chips, pickle, pasta or potato salad and a soft drink. Cost per person is $7.25 plus tax. *Fees:* Parking, $2. *Directions:* From I-285, exit north at Riverside Drive, Exit 16. Go 2.3 miles to Johnson Ferry Road and turn left. The entrance to Johnson Ferry North is on the right-hand side of Johnson Ferry Road right after the river. *More Information:* Chattahoochee Outdoor Center, 770/395-6851.

JOHNSON FERRY SOUTH contains about 70 acres of floodplain with large, green open spaces and riverfront hardwoods. In the 1900s this particular tract of land was a farm; however, most recently it served as the home for the Atlanta Polo Club. A dirt farm road that borders about 1.5 miles of the riverbank is the only established footpath in the unit. This unit has two large activity fields that are available for individual and group use. *Facilities:* 3,000-sq. ft. picnic pavilion, 2 large activity fields, hiking trail (see map on this page), good fishing. *Fees:* Parking, $2.

Directions: From I-285, exit north on Riverside Drive, Exit 16. Go 2.3 miles to Johnson Ferry Road and turn left, cross the Chattahoochee River and then take an immediate left onto Columns Drive. The unit will be on the left. The park entrance for Area 1 is 0.1 mile, and the park entrance for Area 2 is 0.7 of a mile.

SOPE CREEK UNIT –This unit connects with the Cochran Shoals Unit and is one of the most historic and interesting areas in the entire CRNRA. Sope Creek is named for a full-blooded Cherokee Indian who lived along its banks. The Indians had been removed by law from the area in 1838, but somehow Old Chief Sope managed to remain. It is said that little boys in the area would run away from home to visit the kindly man who told them stories and taught them Cherokee words.

The stone ruins along the creek are remnants of the Marietta Paper Mill which produced a large portion of the South's paper from 1855 to 1902. Union troops burned the original mills in 1864. Contrary to popular belief, the ruins are from the buildings erected after the Civil War. To reach the mills, visitors must use the car parking lot at Sope Creek on Paper Mill Road and descend on foot to the ruins (see page 99).

The trails on the west side of the creek connect with the Cochran Shoals unit as does the bicycle trail access. Sope Creek and Sibley Pond, in the middle of the unit, are considered year-round fishing spots. *Facilities:* Picnic area, hiking trail, bicycle trail access, fishing. *Fees:* Parking, $2. *Directions:* From I-285, exit north onto Riverside Drive. Turn left onto Johnson Ferry Road. Turn left onto Paper Mill Road. Follow this winding road to Terrell Mill Road and turn left. Entrance to park is on left.

COCHRAN SHOALS UNIT –Joggers, walkers, trail bikers and dog walkers make this one of the busiest park units in the CRNRA. At 9:04am on a Friday morning, 46 cars were counted in the parking lot as health and fitness enthusiasts started their routines. An expansive floodplain and wetlands area, often 2,500-feet wide, parallels the river. Here a 3-mile fitness trail has been installed with 22 exercise stations. This unit also provides access to the only bicycle trail in the CRNRA, a yellow-blazed trail which winds through Cochran Shoals and the neighboring

"It's all interrelated – the air, the surface water, the ground water. We need to look at a watershed as a functioning unit if we are to make ecological and evaluatory sense of it all."

—Howard Marshall, Headwaters of an Endangered River

Sope Creek Unit. Biker speed limit is 10 mph. Dogs are allowed on the trails, but they must be on a leash, and owners must clean up after them. Good trout fishing is also available along the shoals, which can be waded during low water. Higher flows require a float tube or boat. *Facilities:* Picnic area, hiking trail (see page 100), fitness trail, bike trail access (bikes must be registered with the Park), viewing areas, restrooms, telephone. *Fees:* Parking, $2. *Directions:* From I-285, exit west onto Northside Parkway. Turn left onto Interstate North Parkway. Cross the river and turn right into Cochran Shoals parking lot.

POWERS ISLAND UNIT –Powers Island lies directly across the river from the Cochran Shoals Unit and is the put-in for canoeists and rafters of the 3-mile stretch of river, sometimes called the Atlanta Hooch (see page 115). There is also a slalom course about 100 yards long in the inlet between the parking area and Powers Island, which is, unfortunately, rather trashy. The unit is named for James Powers, who began operating a ferry across the river in 1835 and who also developed a large plantation near Vinings. Maps made at the time of the Civil War show over a dozen identified residences in a mile-wide strip on either side of the river from Powers Ferry to Sope Creek. The Powers family retained ownership of their land near Vinings until the 1930s. *Facilities:* Canoe and kayak launch from east bank of Powers Island, raft launch from west bank of island, Slalom course with 20 gates, hiking trail (see page 101), telephone. Chattahoochee Outdoor Center with concessions, raft rental and shuttle. *Fees:* Parking, $2. *Directions*: From Powers Ferry Road, turn right (west) on Interstate Parkway North. Entrance to Powers Island is past the Cochran Shoals entrance, across the river and to the left. *More Information:* Chattahoochee Outdoor Center, 770/395-6851.

PALISADES EAST UNIT –Beginning 0.5 mile below Powers Island and I-285, broken granite bluffs rise abruptly on both sides of the Chattahoochee and the river gradient increases noticeably. These are what's known as the Palisades, a very visual indication of the Brevard Fault (see page 91). Palisades East and Palisades West stretch along both sides of the river.

Palisades East is 393 acres of ruggedly beautiful forested floodplains, ridges and ravines. For thousands of years Native

VIEW FROM THE OVERLOOK AT EAST PALISADES—THIS SECTION OF THE CHATTAHOOCHEE, KNOWN AS THE "DEVIL'S RACECOURSE" IS FORMED AS THE RIVER CUTS THROUGH A HIGH RIDGE LINE OF THE BREVARD FAULT. GREAT FOR KAYAKING!

Brevard Fault

Seen from a globe-circling, picture-snapping satellite high above Earth's surface, the Brevard Fault looks like a monstrous incision across the torso of Georgia made by the Great Physician, operating under battlefield conditions. The massive diagonal scar goes from the patient's left armpit (today's Lake Yonah on the Georgia-South Carolina border) all the way across the chest of Georgia to about the middle of the right rib cage (near Waresville in western Heard County). Even after all these years, the 160-mile cut hasn't healed well. It's full of ridges and valleys, lines where the stitches might have been. The edges of the gash are still rough and ragged.

It just proves that beauty really is in the eye of the beholder. To professional geologists the Brevard Fault scar is a very attractive physical feature. Most have at least heard the name. Not because faults are unusual. Faults are a common feature of the earth's surface. They are the result of one part of the earth's crust moving or slipping in relation to another. There are hundreds of faults, both active and inactive, in the United States. One of the most famous active faults is the San Andreas Fault in California. The Brevard Fault owes its notoriety to location. It is generally accepted that in the southern portion of the United States, the Brevard Fault in part forms the dividing line between two physiographic provinces, the Appalachian Mountains and the Piedmont Plateau.

With that in mind, the fact that the Brevard Fault forms a channel for the Chattahoochee River for some 100 miles of its 540-mile course from the mountains to the sea takes on added significance.

The river and its channel through the fault is a living link between the Appalachian Mountains where the Chattahoochee begins just below Jacks Gap and the Piedmont Plateau. Along the river's course plants and animals have migrated up-and-downstream. Some species of salamanders and birds more common to the mountains than the Piedmont have made their way south along the Chattahoochee corridor thanks to the Brevard Fault.

ATLANTA
CHATTAHOOCHEE RIVER
THE BREVARD FAULT AS IT CUTS ACROSS GEORGIA
COLUMBUS

Sope, Rottenwood and Sweetwater creeks drop off the Brevard Fault Zone's western escarpment (about 1,000 feet in elevation) to the Chattahoochee (about 800 feet in elevation). Steep gradients and fast-flowing currents characterize these creeks which are more like mountain streams than streams of the Piedmont. Sweetwater Creek, for example, drops 120 feet from Austell to the Chattahoochee; it drops 80 feet within the boundaries of Sweetwater Creek State Park alone.

North-facing coves on these creeks, as well as other locations along the river within the Fault Zone, harbor trees, shrubs, herbs and wildflowers usually associated with the Appalachian Mountains to the north. Dr. Charles Wharton, in

his classic work, *The Natural Environments of Georgia* published in 1978, refers to this area as "Bluff and Ravine Forests of Northern Affinities." The "Northern Affinities" meaning that many of the plants and trees found here are usually associated with the north Georgia mountains. Beech trees, white oak, northern red oak, black oak, umbrella magnolia, big leaf magnolia, tulip popular, chestnut oak, sourwood, black locust, serviceberry, Carolina rhododendron, rosebay rhododendron, mountain laurel, wild hydrangea, sweetshrub, northern madenhair fern, lady fern, marginal wood fern, solomons seal, false solomon seal, alum root, northern ginger, dolls eyes, grass of parnassus, spring beauty, lousewort, gentians, tooth wort, goats beard and lobed strawberry survive in the rich productive environment created by the combination of the Brevard Fault and the Chattahoochee River.

This section of the river has nurtured human as well as botanical diversity. Early settlers located grain, paper and textile mills on fast flowing mountain streams like Vickery, Sope, Rottenwood and Sweetwater creeks. The remains of those mills, which date from the mid-1800s, can still be seen today.

In terms of geological importance, the Brevard Fault is far more significant and more interesting than its cousin, Stone Mountain. Almost everybody has heard of Stone Mountain. Visited by six million people a year, it is the most popular state park in Georgia. Almost no one outside of professional geologists, however, has ever heard of the Brevard Fault. Its problem is exposure, public relations; it's an image thing. There's plenty of the Brevard Fault, but it's difficult to see. Many of those who have seen the Brevard Fault don't even know it. Perhaps the best place in all the South from which to observe the fault is the overlook

mud and silt near the edge of an ocean basin. They were buried under even more sediments. In a process that occurred two or three miles below the surface, they metamorphosed into the rocks seen today. They were forced to the sur-

up and over another. This 36-degree dip is an easily identifiable characteristic of rocks throughout the palisades area and helps the visitor see the direction of the fault's thrust.

Looking upstream the river here is flowing faster on the eastern bank, or the right side. That process is cutting into the right river bank. Sediments are deposited by the slower moving currents on the west, or left bank and form the sandy beach or "point bar" on that side of the river visible from the overlook.

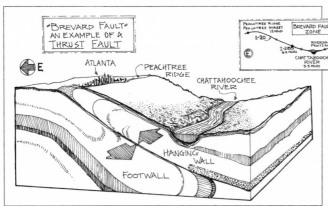

In the late 1800s traders steered small barges downriver through this section. On the return trip they poled their boats upstream. Getting through these rocks was "the devil," and this section acquired the name "Devils Racecourse." The channel visible in the middle of the river was blasted with dynamite during this time to make an easier course through the rocks. A second channel just below the tree line is visible during leafless winter months.

platform in the Palisades section of the Chattahoochee River National Recreation Area. The overlook is reached after a one-mile hike, which includes uphill walking.

The overlook itself is located on one of the highest and hardest ridges of the Brevard Fault. The ridge line forms a "strike" which runs at a bearing of north 36 degrees east that is 36 degrees east of north. Geologists call this line the "strike line." The ridge line continues on the other side of the river. The river has cut through the ridge line and left rocks and shoals that are known today as Devil's Racecourse.

From the overlook platform a person's line of vision is upstream, or north. Here the river has changed its southwesterly direction and is flowing more directly south, cutting through the quartzite ridges in the Brevard Fault which trends in a northeast to southwest direction.

These rocks that we call the Palisades are some 400 million years old. They originated as sand,

face during the kinds of cataclysmic upfolding that caused the Brevard Fault. When they were first formed, these mountains were several thousand feet, perhaps as much as a mile, higher than they are today. Over millions and millions of years these mountains have eroded down to the remnants seen today. The minerals, feldspar, mica and quartz, eroded from these and other rocks of the Appalachian Mountains, form the beaches of the Gulf Coast, barrier islands and river deltas. While river currents, rain, wind and ice have eaten away at all of the rocks and minerals of the mountains—mica, schist, feldspar and quartz—the harder, more resistant minerals—feldspar and quartz—have resisted the longest. It is those minerals that make up the shoals in today's river.

The layering of the rocks of the river's shoals below dip 36 degrees to the southeast, a direction that corresponds to the southeast to northwest movement of the thrust fault as one line of rocks pushed

Known locally as the "Atlanta Hooch," the three-mile section of river from Powers Island to Cobb Parkway is the most popular section of the river for canoeists, kayakers and rafters. This is where the river cuts through the Brevard Fault creating interesting shoals and rapids. Competitive canoeists and kayakers, some of whom compete internationally, practice here several days a week during the winter months. The many variations of Class I and II rapids allow them to perfect paddling techniques that they will use on streams with Class IV and V rapids. From October to May a 0.25 mile slalom course used by these paddlers hangs on the section of river visible from the overlook. Beginning

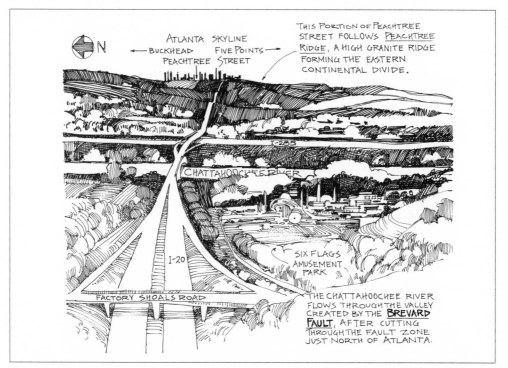

Within the illustration:

⊕ N

ATLANTA SKYLINE
←BUCKHEAD   FIVE POINTS→
PEACHTREE STREET

THIS PORTION OF PEACHTREE STREET FOLLOWS PEACHTREE RIDGE, A HIGH GRANITE RIDGE FORMING THE EASTERN CONTINENTAL DIVIDE.

I-285

CHATTAHOOCHEE RIVER

I-20

SIX FLAGS AMUSEMENT PARK

FACTORY SHOALS ROAD

THE CHATTAHOOCHEE RIVER FLOWS THROUGH THE VALLEY CREATED BY THE **BREVARD FAULT**, AFTER CUTTING THROUGH THE FAULT ZONE JUST NORTH OF ATLANTA.

paddlers find that this section of river is also ideal for learning to paddle in fast-moving water.

While the overlook platform may be the best place from which to see the Brevard Fault, there are other places in the Atlanta area where the dramatic scale and scope of the Fault can be observed.

I-75 NORTH AT THE CONNECTOR –From downtown Atlanta, take the Connector (combined I-75 and I-85) north to where the two freeways divide. Take I-75 north. Immediately on the right under the Fairfield Inn sign and extending to an area below the Equifax building are the cliffs of the Brevard Fault. This section of the Fault is known as the Clairmont formation.

I-285 NEAR I-20 –From downtown Atlanta, take I-20 west. At the I-285 interchange, go south on I-285. The exit cuts right through the Fault Zone. The cliffs on both sides

of the exit ramp are part of the Brevard Fault Zone.

I-20 WEST OF THE CHATTAHOOCHEE — The best place to observe the dramatic scale of the Fault is from I-20 about 2.2 miles west of the Chattahoochee River. From the Thornton Road exit on I-20, Exit 12, go east on I-20 toward Atlanta. About 1.4 miles from Thornton Road, I-20 crests and the Atlanta skyline is straight ahead. The Chattahoochee River flows through the foreground but is not visible. This hilltop where Factory Shoals Road crosses I-20 is the western side of the fault. It extends east about 5 miles to I-285 where rock cliffs mark the eastern side of the fault. The Chattahoochee River runs through the lowest section of the fault.

Beyond the fault the skyline of Atlanta is visible. Most of the skyscrapers on the horizon are built

along or just off Peachtree Street which follows the crest of Peachtree Ridge running north and south through the city. This portion of Peachtree Ridge is the eastern continental divide, meaning that the rain which falls on the western side of the ridge flows into the Chattahoochee and eventually into the Gulf of Mexico. Rain that falls on the eastern side of the ridge flows east and ends up in the Atlantic Ocean.

There is no more interesting and geologically significant view in this region. As one proceeds down the slope of I-20 toward the river, the panorama widens and becomes more dramatic. The distance from Factory Shoals Road on I-20 to the river is about 2.2 miles, and it is about 2.4 miles from the river to I-285, making the width of the Brevard Fault in this section a little less than five miles.

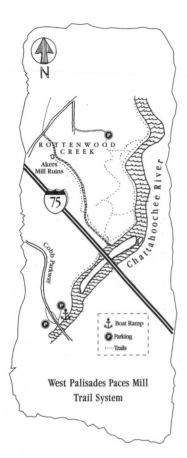

West Palisades Paces Mill
Trail System

Americans lived along this river, their villages flourishing then vanishing. They camped in the shelter of granite overhangs. One of the largest rock shelters in the park is located approximately 0.5 mile upstream from Long Island Creek (see page 102). An Overlook Trail, which begins west of Indian Ridge trailhead, leads to a wooden platform where hikers can witness a spectacular view—the Devil's Racecourse Shoals, which were named by early river boatmen because the shoals were the "devil" to navigate. During this same period, the rugged granite palisades were dubbed "Devil's Stairstep." Bird and mammal tracks can be spotted all along the river's edge, and Great Blue Herons and kingfishers dive among the shoals to capture their dinner as mallards turn tail up to feed in the river. There are plenty of places along the river for an informal picnic or just experiencing the astounding beauty of this scene right in the middle of the largest metropolitan area of the south. *Facilities:* Picnic area, hiking trails, fishing, viewing platform, 2 parking areas. *Fees:* Parking, $2. *Directions:* From I-75, exit north onto Mt. Paran Road. Turn left onto Harris Trail. Turn left onto Whitewater Creek Road. This leads to the main park entrance. A second parking lot can be reached by continuing on Harris Trail, taking a left on Northside Drive and a left on Indian Trail. A third, but unofficial, way to access the park is to take I-75 to the Northside Drive Exit and exit (east). Turn right onto Powers Ferry Road. Take this to a driveway on the left leading into Ray's on the River Restaurant and an office complex. Turn here and go straight ahead until it dead ends into a building. Turn right and go to the back of the parking lot to the river. Park along the back row and access the unit from a trailhead on the left.

PALISADES WEST UNIT –This unit consists of 302 acres and covers the west side of the river along the Palisades. The canoe and raft launch at the Paces Mill area just past the I-75 bridge marks the end of what is known as the Atlanta Hooch (see page 115). Big signs on the river point out what is the last boat ramp in the CRNRA. Equipment rented from the Chattahoochee Outdoor Center must be turned in here. Hiking trails here wind through the floodplain and across the ridges of the Palisades. *Facilities:* Canoe/raft launch, picnic tables and grills along the river, concession stand, hiking trail (see map on page 94), restrooms, telephone. This is the take-out for raft rentals and shuttle service provided by the Chattahoochee Outdoor Center. The Center also operates a concession stand with snack foods, water and juices. *Fees:* Parking, $2. *Directions:* From I-285, exit south onto Cobb Parkway/US 41. Turn right into the park just before the Chattahoochee River bridge. To reach the gravel parking area on the northeast border of the park, go north on Cobb Parkway from the river. Turn right (east) on Akers Drive, also the entrance to Wood Mill and The Highland at Akers Mill apartments. Turn right and follow the signs to the parking area for the trail known as the Trout Lily Trail.

HIKING TRAILS

It is one thing to enjoy the Chattahoochee River corridor from the seat of a canoe or raft. It is truly another experience to see it from the hiking trails which weave along its banks. Climb the cliffs and ledges of the Palisades to get a sense of the awe-inspiring architecture of the Brevard Fault. Sit in the shelter of an Indian cave along the river's banks. Hike the hills and ravines of Vickery or Sope creeks, discovering the mill ruins at both, to understand how this terrain was used by white settlers. Follow Rottenwood Creek to the old Akers Mill ruins and witness what modern development is doing to the wonderful mountain canyon atmosphere that nature has given to this area. The following hiking trails are all within the Chattahoochee River National Recreation Area and are listed from north to south along the river corridor. *Days/Hrs.:* Daily, 7am to dark. *Fees:* Parking, $2. *More Information:* CRNRA Park Headquarters, 1917 Island Ford Parkway, Atlanta GA 30350; 770/399-8070.

MEDLOCK BRIDGE –This hike explores a particularly scenic area of the river—the big bend of the Chattahoochee right above Medlock Bridge Road. *Distance:* Nearly 3 miles, easy to moderate. *Trailhead Location:* CRNRA Medlock Bridge Unit (see page 84). *Features:* This trail follows the big bend in the river, looking up at the rock palisades that rise up over the water, which is particularly deep and still in this part of the

www.chattahoochee.org

 We welcome your comments, suggestions, recommendations and input regarding this book and the river, via the Internet at the Riverkeeper's website: www.chattahoochee.org.

You can also access the website for additional information regarding the Chattahoochee and the many issues that affect the river.

**ALL IS BORN OF WATER;
ALL IS SUSTAINED BY WATER.**

Rottenwood Creek is named for a Cherokee Indian, Rottenwood, who lived on a stream in that area.

—Marion Hemperley, Indian Heritage of Georgia

Vickery Creek Trail System

river. It also loops into the dense forest areas.

JONES BRIDGE –The trails in this system either follow along the riverbank or meander through fields and woods. *Distance:* Over 2 miles, easy to moderate. *Trailhead Location:* CRNRA Jones Bridge Unit (see page 84). The northernmost portion of the river trail can be accessed from either parking lot. The southernmost portion of the river trail as well as the forest trail can be accessed from the first parking lot. *Features:* The blue-blazed river trail follows the Chattahoochee riverbank except for where it diverts around some private property. This part of the river has beautiful shoals and is quite picturesque with trout fishermen and Canada geese wading in the rapids. The rusted, half structure of Jones Bridge can be seen from a viewing deck. Red-blazed trails loop off of the main trail and through the woods. *Hiked by Riverkeeper staffer Dana Poole.*

ISLAND FORD –The Island Ford Shoals can also be reached from this trail. The river here is shallow enough to cross by wading and walking on the numerous rock outcrops and small islands that punctuate it. It's a pretty picture—fishermen in the fall and winter, sunbathers as soon as the weather warms. Other parts of the trail system lead into the woods along the ridges. *Distance:* 3 miles, easy to difficult. *Trailhead Location:* CRNRA Island Ford Unit (see page 85). Blue-blazed trail can be accessed from the parking lot near the entrance. All trails can be accessed from the main parking lot at the Park Headquarters. *Features:* Like several other sites along the river, man's prehistoric habitation is evident here. Several huge rock outcroppings, where Indians are believed to have camped while on hunting parties, can be seen from the river trail.

VICKERY CREEK –This system of trails winds along the cliffs of Vickery Creek Gorge. Not only does the gorge provide some spectacular landscape, but the creek itself is a history lesson in the early settlement and industry of the area. Vickery Creek is another Atlanta tributary which, due to the terrain created by the Brevard Fault, was the perfect site for dams and mills. From the northernmost edge of the park unit, the trail runs along the creek where Roswell King built his textile mills in the 1830s, mills which led to the founding of the town of Roswell, provided industry for the area and played a significant role in the production of grey woolen material for Confederate uniforms during the Civil War (see page 107). The ruins of the Roswell Cotton Mills and the mill dam can be seen across the creek from the trail. A bridge crossing the creek leads out of the park unit but provides a view of the dam and mill ruins from the Roswell side of the river. *Distance:* About 6 miles, easy to difficult. *Trailhead Location:* CRNRA Vickery Creek Unit (see page 86) entrance parking lot off Riverside Road. *Features:* This system of trails runs through wooded gorges and over the steep bluffs and rock outcroppings along the east side of Vickery Creek from where it winds through the town of Roswell to its confluence with the Chattahoochee. A short, blue-blazed trail starting at the parking lot leads to the creek's edge and the cliffs area. This is directly opposite from Lover's Leap (see below) behind the historical home of Allenbrook. A red-blazed trail climbs up the ridges and winds around the park. Trails are well-maintained with fallen trees cleared away, but the trail markings are at times confusing. Historic Roswell signs suddenly appear, leading to the part of the creek that looks out at the mill ruins on the other side. *Hiked by Riverkeeper member Steve White.*

ROCK CLIMBING ON LOVERS LEAP AT VICKERY CREEK PARK

LOVER'S LEAP –Known as Lover's Leap, Lover's Rock, Allenbrook or Vickery Creek Overlook, this is one of the area's most rugged and scenic vistas. It is found at the end of a very short but steep path that begins behind historic Allenbrook, a pre-Civil War home and office for the loom boss of the Ivy Woolen Mills, which were located downstream. The mill ruins, which are surrounded by privet hedge, are difficult to reach or see. They were built at the confluence of Vickery Creek and the Chattahoochee River in 1857 by James Roswell King and Thomas Edward King, sons of Barrington King and grandsons of Roswell King. *Distance:* Less than a 0.25 mile to Lover's Leap, about 1 mile easy to moderate river trail. *Trailhead Location:* CRNRA Vickery Creek Unit (see page 86). Allenbrook parking lot, which is on the west side of the creek about 300 yards past the Chattahoochee River bridge, leads to the trailhead which is behind the house. *Features:* Steep, railroad-tie stairs lead down to a path which follows the creek. This is not a well-marked trail. At the bottom of the steps, look for the

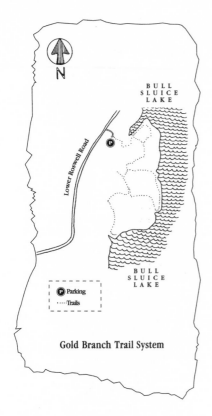

Gold Branch Trail System

short path which leads straight to the edge of the cliffs. This 100-foot cliff overlooks Vickery Creek Gorge. This is a particularly inspiring view in the winter when the trees are bare. The rest of this trail follows the creek downstream to where it meets the river, following the ridge for a while and then descending to the creek bed. The ruins of the Ivy Mills are located near the confluence, but once the trail gets to the bridge over Vickery Creek, it becomes overgrown with kudzu and briars. It is impassable, making the ruins impossible to reach.

CHATTAHOOCHEE NATURE CENTER WETLANDS TRAIL –This trail is a well-interpreted boardwalk through wetlands created when the Chattahoochee was dammed at Morgan Falls. Hundreds of years ago this area was a lush forest lining a rocky, rolling river. During the mid 1800s settlers converted it to farmland. After Morgan Falls Dam was constructed a few miles upstream in 1904, the Chattahoochee's banks overflowed, flooding this area and producing this productive wetland habitat. *Distance:* 0.5-mile loop, easy. *Trailhead Location:* East side of Willeo Road, across from the entrance to the Chattahoochee Nature Center (see page 106). *Features:* Both swamp and marsh environments present; red-bellied woodpeckers spotted; overlook areas with seating, wheelchair accessible, braille signage, self-guided brochure. *Hiked by Riverkeeper Member Brenda Paine.*

GOLD BRANCH –This system of trails winds through secluded wooded areas, marshy environments, open fields which once were rich farmlands and along Bull Sluice Lake, the impoundment created by Morgan Falls Dam. *Distance:* 7 miles, easy to difficult. *Trailhead Location:* CRNRA Gold Branch Unit parking lot (see page 87). *Features:* The red-blazed trail winds to an endpoint at Bull Sluice Lake. There are two loops off this trail: a shorter yellow-blazed loop and a longer blue-blazed loop that follows the lake shoreline, providing great views of the river and the riverside homes. Especially picturesque in the fall are the rowing teams practicing for the regatta. The blazes are not always obvious, and paths through the system can be difficult to follow when fall leaves cover the ground. *Hiked by Riverkeeper member Kathryn Hutton.*

JOHNSON FERRY NORTH –Because this is a floodplain area, the Johnson Ferry trail system is an easy, "intown" walk, mostly on level ground. Known as the Mulberry Creek Loop Trail, this unmarked but easy-to-follow trail, crosses several streams and follows along the river. *Distance:* 2.5-mile loop, easy walking. *Trailhead Location:* CRNRA Johnson Ferry North Unit (see page 88) trailhead in parking area. *Features:* Several footbridges cross the four creeks which flow through the wetlands and into the river. There's a diversity of wildlife, including herons, beavers and otters. At the mouth of Mulberry Creek, which is the easternmost creek in the trail system, look for the dark "V" pointing downstream. This is the remains of a fish weir or fish trap that early settlers built for harvesting fish. Also watch for the signs warning about a petroleum pipeline which is mostly underground and zig-zags through the area. *Trail hiked by Riverkeeper member Michelle Hamel.*

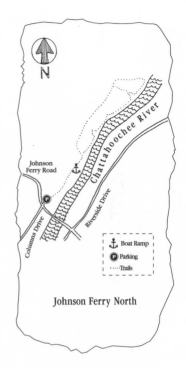

Johnson Ferry Road

Columns Drive

Riverside Drive

Chattahoochee River

⚓ Boat Ramp
Ⓟ Parking
····Trails

Johnson Ferry North

SOPE CREEK –During the last half of the 19th century, this part of Sope Creek was the location of the Marietta Paper Mill, one of the area's principal industries during that period. A number of stone buildings which lie in ruins along both sides of the creek south of the Paper Mill Road bridge were once part of this mill operation. These ruins, crumbling and covered with vines, add a haunting quality to a creek that is already endowed with great natural beauty. *Distance:* Numerous short and long loops give many options to the hiker concerning distance and degrees of difficulty. This system also links to the Cochran Shoals trail system. *Trailhead Location:* CRNRA Sope Creek Unit (see page 89) entrance parking lot. *Features:* These trails loop through moderately steep to rolling hills which lead to lush ravines and wooded areas, a small fishing lake called Sibley Pond and the Marietta Paper Mill ruins. The ruins, which stretch along both sides of Sope Creek, are the largest mill ruins on CRNRA property. Built in the mid-1850s, the original mills were incorporated in 1859. The rugged terrain of Sope Creek Gorge created by the Brevard Fault made this an ideal location on which to harness water power. The mills processed cotton stalks, wood and rags into tissue paper, newsprint, stationery and wrapping paper.

After the outbreak of the Civil War, the mills produced cartridge paper as well as paper stock for printing Confederate money. On July 6, 1864, the Union Army burned the mills. The

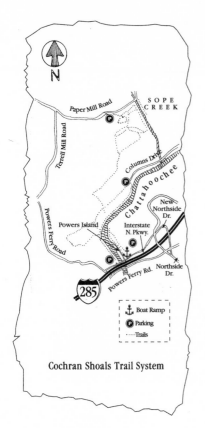

Cochran Shoals Trail System

factories were rebuilt after the war and manufactured twine, newsprint and blotting paper. A fire in 1902 ended operations, and the mills never ran again. By that time, two conditions made the mills uneconomical to operate: their 7-mile distance from the railroad in Marietta and the development of electric engines, which reduced the need for water power in manufacturing. There are nine ruins in the area, five of which are easily seen from the path along the creek. *Directions:* CRNRA Sope Creek Unit (see page 89). To reach the ruins, use the car parking lot at Sope Creek just off Paper Mill Road and descend on foot to Sope Creek. *Hiked by Riverkeeper members Michelle Hamel and Steve White.*

COCHRAN SHOALS –The popular Cochran Shoals Unit of the CRNRA gets about 3 million visitors a year, making it the most heavily used unit in the park system. Most of these visitors are here to use the 3 miles of 12-foot-wide path that run along the river and meander through the park's 968 acres, but they aren't just out to take a hike through the woods and enjoy nature. Many are here for jogging, speed walking and biking, making trails at Cochran Shoals a hazard to your health on a spring day in Atlanta. Although bikers are not allowed on the fitness trail, only on the bike trail, they sometimes get confused. Sometimes they even go over the 10mph speed limit posted on the biking trail. And although pets are only allowed on leashes, they sometimes get away from their owners. There is a movement to ban bikers and dogs from the park, but so far, they are still welcome. The park is home base for the 400-member Chattahoochee Road Runners Club, a group of athletes who train with their dogs and cross-train by cycling. *Distance:* 3-mile flat, fitness trail and several miles of easy to difficult hiking trails. *Trailhead Location:* CRNRA Cochran Shoals Unit (see page 89) parking lot. *Features:* This is a good place for views of the river, wetlands ecology and people watching. Hikers or walkers can hike the mountain bike trails, which wind through hardwood forested ravines and ridges, with lots of ups and downs. The fitness trail is totally flat, follows the river for 1.5 miles and contains a 22-station fitness course with pull ups, sit ups and other activities near its south end. There is also a new nature boardwalk that goes back into the swamp area. There are lots of wetlands between the river and the ridges. Hawks, owls, raccoons, beaver, opossum, fox and ducks all make this area home. Trails are well-marked with detailed maps posted. There are several observation decks and a restroom along the way. Possibly the best time to hike here is in the winter when there are less people. The low point of this hike is always the sewage smell. *Hiked by Riverkeeper member Steve Walburn.*

POWERS ISLAND –Although Powers Island is busy in the summer with rafters and kayakers, this hiking trail is much, much less used than the trails directly across the river at Cochran Shoals, which are full of joggers, walkers and bikers. *Distance:* About a 1-mile loop, easy to moderate. *Trailhead Location:* CRNRA Powers Island Unit (see page 90) parking lot. At back, or north end, of parking lot. *Features:* Just a nice, easy walk along the river and through hardwood forest.

PALISADES EAST –The trails in the Palisades East trail system lead to one of the most beautiful places found along the Chattahoochee River. This is a 90-degree bend in the river surrounded by the canyon walls of the Palisades. Rapids cascade over the eddies and shoals of the river here. An overlook high on the east cliffs provides hikers with a beautiful view, but perhaps the most serene spot to witness this scene is from the banks of the river itself right at this bend. The ruins of a homesite sit here surrounded by the forested cliffs of the Palisades. *Distance:* Approximately 5 miles, easy to strenuous. *Trailhead Location:* CRNRA Palisades East Unit (see page 90). Blue-blazed trail begins in main parking lot at park entrance off Whitewater Creek Road. To locate the lesser used red-blazed trailhead, take Powers Ferry Road to Ray's on the River driveway and turn left. Go straight to last office building complex and turn right. Go to the back of the parking lot which is along the river. Trailhead is on the left. *Features:* This area is as diverse in terrain as it is beautiful. Easy walking can be found along the blue-blazed trail which begins in the parking lot off Whitewater Creek Road and follows the river banks. The red-blazed trail which begins at the end of the parking lot on Powers Ferry Road is mostly steep and strenuous climbing over cliffs and along narrow ledges. The history seen from these trails is also diverse: Palisades formed by the Brevard Fault,

East Palisades Trail System

The Urban Chattahoochee

Reece Turrentine has canoed the Chattahoochee and other rivers of the south for more than 50 years.

"Not long ago, I was walking upstream along the East Palisades river's edge trail, looking for a better location to beach canoes. When I'm guiding a group down this 'city section,' I always like to stop them here for a hike into the woods and up the cliffs of the old 'Indian Shelter.' It's a 30-foot deep rock overhang archaeologists determine nomadic Indians, following the river's course, used for shelter for 6-7,000 years. The river trails were Atlanta's original interstate highway.

I had just seen the I-75 bridge in the distance. Where I stopped now, I could no longer see it, but I could still hear the roaring engines and speeding tires slapping the bridge joints of the pavement. So close and yet so far. They couldn't see me. When you're bumper to bumper at that speed, nobody has time to look out at a river.

For a moment, my imagination ran away with me and I thought I could hear the traffic

Indian caves (see below), the ruins of an early homesite, the darkened channel of the river (supposedly dynamited by early traders) and the slalom course fences dotting the river throughout the colder months. Trails can be hard to follow here, signage is scarce. Also, beware of poison ivy. *Hiked by Riverkeeper member Julie O'Kelly.*

INDIAN CAVE HIKE –Caves have provided shelter for people along the Chattahoochee River corridor for thousands of years. This hike follows the banks of the river and leads to what is perhaps the biggest such cave in the area. It is located on the Palisades East hiking trail system, (listed above), but is listed separately here because it is difficult to spot. *Distance:* About 1.5 miles round trip, easy to moderate. *Trailhead Location:* CRNRA Palisades East Unit (see page 90) entrance off Whitewater Creek Road. At end of parking lot near river. *Features:* This blue-blazed trail follows the east bank of the river. After about 0.5 miles start looking for the cave, which is about 200 yards up from the trail. This very large cave is visible through the trees from the river trail. Spot the cave and then look for a path up. There is no marked cave path, but there are several ways to get there. This climb is steep but quite manageable.

AKERS MILL HIKE –This hike up Rottenwood Creek is not very picturesque for the first 0.25 to 0.5 mile. The hike is no longer on the CRNRA's Palisades West trail system map, and the trail itself does not appear to be maintained—briars and kudzu cover the path in some areas. In the summer, it might be better to get off the trail where the undergrowth is thick and walk up the stream on boulders. The last half of the hike is well worth any trouble, however, because of the beautiful mountain-like terrain and the stone ruins of the old Akers gristmill. *Distance:* About 2 miles round trip, easy to moderate. *Trailhead Location:* CRNRA Palisades West (see page 94). "Rottenwood Creek Access" sign at left of Chattahoochee Outdoor Center. Follow path under I-75 bridge and over bridge at Rottenwood Creek; sign points left to Akers Mill Trail. *Features:* Rottenwood Creek is reminiscent of a North Georgia mountain creek with its large boulders and canyon-like walls covered with bright-colored leaves in the fall. At one point the trail follows an Atlanta sewer pipe which crosses the creek. Located at the end of the trail are the ruins of Akers Mill, a 19th-century gristmill operated by the Akers brothers. In 1880, The Marietta Journal reported that the mill had recently installed a new process of milling that increased from 39 to 43 pounds the amount of flour produced from a bushel of wheat as well as providing a finer grade of flour. The flour mill could produce 200 barrels of flour every 24 hours, and the corn mill could produce 1,500 bushels of cornmeal. The power for the flour mill was a 36-inch turbine, supplemented by an 80-horsepower engine used when water was scarce. The Akers family cut out and graded new roads to the mill and farmed the nearby land. The mill employed about 60 people, who lived in a small village–now long vanished–constructed by the proprietors.

HISTORIC SITES

HIGHTOWER TRAIL –This trail was an old Indian path which crossed the Chattahoochee River at the Shallowford, just a short distance downstream from the present Roswell bridge. This path is the present boundary line between Gwinnett and DeKalb counties. It intersected the present Peachtree Road at the county line of Gwinnett and DeKalb, crossed the river and continued northwest to the Etowah (or Hightower) River. *Directions to Historical Marker:* Go north on Roswell Road and cross the river. Turn left on Azalea Drive. The marker is on the left.

JOHNSTON'S RIVER LINE –When Gen. Joe Johnston and his Confederate troops were forced to retreat from the Kennesaw Mountain Line they had held against Sherman's army, they fell back to well-prepared works on the north bank of the Chattahoochee that have come to be known as Johnston's River Line. Instead of a vulnerable army anxiously attempting to cross the river, Sherman found the Confederates awaiting him from behind a formidable line of fortifications 5.5 miles long and one mile deep. The line occupied high ground from a ridge overlooking Nickajack Creek to the left and the Chattahoochee to the right. Engineered by Gen. F. A. Shoup, Chief of Artillery of Johnston's army, the entrenchments were built by slave labor and the troops of the Georgia Militia. Log

of I-285 upstream and around the bend to my right. It was some kind of distant roar. I looked under limbs upstream and saw the source of the muffled roar. I was relieved. It was not the traffic. It was Thornton Shoals, bubbling over its rocks. It was sounds of wilderness, not interstates. Although the two worlds are competing for dominance out here, this spot at least looked and sounded like wilderness. What a strange place I was standing on. To my left, downstream and around the bend, was a mixture of Long Island Shoals and I-75. To my right, upstream and around the bend was Thornton Shoals and I-285. Similar sounds from different worlds. But that wasn't the end of it. In front of me was the river, teeming with fish and wildlife. Beyond the river and over the hill was Rottenwood Creek and the old flagstone foundations of the Akers gristmill, which operated until the late 1800s. But almost scraping the mill's foundation stones was the gouging of giant earthmovers, carving out yet another larger multi-lane interstate interchange. The creek and mill foundations were saved by a matter of feet. Behind me was yet another contrast. Some of Atlanta's finest homes are just past the river on streets like Mt. Paran, Harris and Northside. But before you can get to them are the cliffs of East Palisades containing Atlanta's oldest home: the old Indian shelter. Worlds collide, but as of now, the river rolls on. I stood on an almost holy place. Just beyond ear and eye a great city was grinding away. But where I stood was a pocket of pure wilderness."

Fog

Wonder why mists often shroud rivers, creeks and valleys during cloudless nights in the summer and fall? During these times of year the sun warms up the water, causing it to evaporate a lot of moisture into the air next to it.

Throughout the night, however, the water surface and adjacent humid air lose heat rapidly to the colder atmosphere above. During calm and clear nights, the temperature of the humid surface air often falls below the dew point. When this change happens, the air cannot hold as much moisture as before and condenses to form innumerable water droplets that form a fog.

If the air is windy, the fog tends to blow over the water and dissipate. If the sky is overcast, there usually is enough heat radiating from the clouds back to the earth to prevent cooling of the surface air to the dew point and the consequent formation of fog.

and earthworks forts, with walls 12-feet thick, were located at 60 to 175 yard intervals and linked by vertical log stockades. These massive earthen structures could absorb the impact of artillery fire and were designed to be manned by a company of 80 riflemen. Huge siege cannons, requisitioned from the defenses of Mobile, Alabama, and positioned at strategic angles, augmented Johnston's field guns. The fortifications covered the railroad bridge over the Chattahoochee, a major wagon bridge and three pontoon avenues that Johnston installed to ensure safe passage if he were forced to withdraw quickly. Even going against an old military rule, "never fight a battle with a river at your back," Old Joe Johnston's army seemed impenetrable. Sherman called it the best line of field entrenchments he had ever seen—and began to look for a way to go around it. *Directions:* Take I-285 to Veterans Memorial Highway Exit (formerly Bankhead Highway). Go east about 3 miles to Oakdale Road. To get an idea of Johnston's position, drive along Oakdale, which follows the ridge of the river line.

JONES BRIDGE –About 100 yards upstream from the CRNRA Jones Bridge Unit parking lot is the historic remnants of the old metal Jones Bridge which was built in 1904 to replace the Jones Ferry river crossing. It is an eerie site, a frail-looking rusted structure which extends halfway across the river. According to the Jones's family diaries, their ancestor, John Martin, purchased the land on both sides of the river back in 1818. Martin built a home on the Gwinnett side of the river and operated a ferry to get back and forth from his land on the Gwinnett side to his land on the Fulton County side. This was called Martin's Ferry. Through marriage, the operation of the ferry was turned over to the Jones family and renamed Jones Ferry. Jones Bridge was built in 1904 to replace the ferry. By the 1930s the oak boards of the bridge had deteriorated and given way, making the bridge unsafe. The two counties could not agree on repairing the bridge, so it was closed. Local legend has it that a group of workers dismantled half of the bridge for scrap metal in the 1940s. Neighbors who saw the workers cutting down the bridge didn't realize that they were actually stealing the metal until it was too late. *Directions:* CRNRA Jones Bridge

Unit (see page 84). About 0.5 mile upstream from the main parking lot.

SHERMAN'S RIVER CROSSINGs –When Sherman decided against a frontal assault on Johnston's fortified "River Line," he deployed troops to begin looking for a place upstream to cross the Chattahoochee. He ordered Maj. Gen. John M. Schofield to select a river crossing on Johnston's right flank, between Pace's Ferry and Roswell. The spot chosen was Isom's Ferry where Sope Creek entered the Chattahoochee River, six miles above Pace's Ferry. Here, an observant Union calvary soldier spotted the remains of an old stone fish dam a half mile upstream. On July 8, 1864, Daniel Cameron's 2nd Brigade of Jacob Cox's 3rd Division waded across at the fish dam and Col. Lawrence H. Rousseau's 12th Kentucky Regiment shot out from the mouth of Sope Creek in pontoon boats. A small Confederate cavalry outpost armed with a single piece of artillery was their only opposition, and the crossing was made without losing a man. The next day, Wilder's Lightning Brigade of Kenner Garrard's cavalry division crossed the river at Shallow Ford, about a mile below the Roswell bridge. Later that day a third crossing was made by a detachment of the 1st Tennessee Regiment of Edward McCook's cavalry, under Col. James Brownlow. The cavalry dismounted, and carrying their guns over their heads waded nude except for their hats at Cochran's Ford, half a mile below Sope Creek. Finding himself outflanked, Johnston was forced to abandon the impregnable River Line. During the night of July 9, he withdrew across the Chattahoochee, burned the railroad bridge behind him and deployed his men to the outer defenses of Atlanta located on a ridge overlooking Peachtree Creek just several miles north of the main fortifications of the city. *Directions:* To reach ruins of old paper mill on Sope Creek, take I-75 to Exit 111. Go east on Delk Road. Turn right on Powers Ferry Road. Turn left on Terrell Mill Road. Go to Paper Mill Road and the CRNRA.

STANDING PEACHTREE –In the days when the Chattahoochee River was the basic dividing line between the Creek and Cherokee Indian Nations, Indian towns and villages dotted its banks. One of the most important Indian villages in the vicinity of what is now Atlanta was Standing Peachtree. This village

The ruins of the Roswell Manufacturing Company cotton mills stand along Vickery Creek.

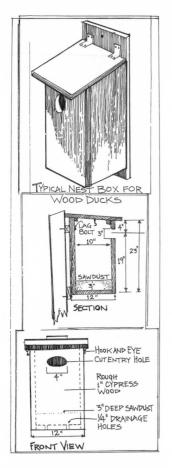

TYPICAL NEST BOX FOR
WOOD DUCKS

SECTION

LAG
BOLT 3" 4"
10"
23"
19"
SAWDUST
3"
12"

FRONT VIEW

HOOK AND EYE
CUT ENTRY HOLE
4"
ROUGH
1" CYPRESS
WOOD
3" DEEP SAWDUST
1/4" DRAINAGE
HOLES
12"

Wood Duck Boxes

The wood duck is a bird that lives in the woods of southern Canada and throughout the United States. The male is the most colorful of North American ducks. Its upper feathers glitter with green, blue and purple. Underneath, it is red, yellow and white. Females are brown above and yellowish below. Both males and females have large crests. The birds measure about 20 inches long and have short necks and long tails.

Wood ducks spend much time in ponds and streams near woods, going into the woods for nuts and insects. They nest in hollow trees, sometimes 40 feet

probably extended along the southeast bank of the river at its confluence with Peachtree Creek, back eastwardly along Peachtree and Nancy creeks and possibly even on the north bank of the river. Standing Peachtree, strategically located for both river traffic and trading, was a point of entry for licensed white traders who were permitted to enter Indian country or trade with them. River traffic here was heavy with canoes and crude boats going up and downstream to the other villages. During the War of 1812, Fort Peachtree was built at Standing Peachtree to protect the white settlers from the Creek Indians who were allied with the British. A road connecting Standing Peachtree with another fort, Fort Daniel at Hog Mountain, was opened in 1814. That 30-mile stretch of road became Atlanta's original Peachtree Road. *Directions:* Take Moores Mill Road to Ridgewood and turn into the Fort Peachtree parking lot.

SIGNIFICANT URBAN EXPERIENCES

CHATTAHOOCHEE NATURE CENTER –The banks of the Chattahoochee River provide a natural setting for one of the largest and busiest nonprofit, nongovernmental educational facilities in the Southeast. Built in a marshland that was created when Morgan Falls dam silted in, the Chattahoochee Nature Center teaches the importance of wetland, riverine and river bank environments. Through hands-on interaction with nature, the Center enlightens an average of 100,000 visitors annually, 60,000 of them children. Guided canoe floats; raptor, reptile and bald eagle exhibits; guided nature walks; pond studies; native plants and animals; fern, bog and butterfly gardens; woodland and wetland trails; and after-school programs are just some of the activities the Center sponsors. About 1,200 injured and ill wild animals are brought each year to the center's clinic for treatment and subsequent return to the wild, if possible. *Days/Hrs.:* Mon-Sat, 9am-5pm; Sun, 12noon-5pm. *Admission:* Adults, $2; children/senior citizens, $1; children under 3 and members free. *Directions:* From Roswell Road heading north, turn left on Azalea Drive, the first left after crossing the Chattahoochee River. Go to the 2nd traffic light and turn left on Willeo Road. The Nature Center is 0.5 mile on the right. *More Information*: Chattahoochee Nature Center, 9135 Willeo Road, Roswell, GA 30075; 770/992-2055.

ANTEBELLUM ROSWELL –Roswell King was a man with vision and shrewd business sense. In the mid 1830s, he traveled from his home in Darien on the Georgia coast to Dahlonega in North Georgia, the site of a gold mining operation. In route he explored the area where the town of Roswell now stands. The Indians had recently been forcibly removed from the region; boom towns had sprung up in north Georgia as a result of the Dahlonega gold rush in 1828. Twenty miles to the south, Atlanta had been designated the terminus for the Western and Atlantic Railroad and migration to this part of Georgia from the coastal region was increasing. A canny businessman and entrepreneur, King envisioned what was to come. He saw the rolling terrain, steep bluffs and tumbling, powerful waters of Vickery Creek as a natural site for cotton and woolen mills. With the help of his son, Barrington King, he oversaw the development of a mill on the banks of Vickery Creek. Other family members and friends joined the Kings in their venture, accepting their offer of homesites and the opportunity to buy stock in the mill.

The Roswell Manufacturing Company, a successful venture from the start, became one of the biggest and most productive mills in the Southeast. By 1852 there were two cotton mills, a woolen mill, a flour mill and a tannery employing some 250 people. Ivy Mill, built at the mouth of Vickery Creek in 1857, was part of this complex. By 1861 the mills employed 350 people, mostly women. The mill's company store was a profit-making venture charging 40 cents a yard for calico and 25 cents a pound for coffee. Since hard currency was limited, a barter system was in place with the company store making a profit on the resale of items bartered. The combination of low pay and the company store economics kept workers indebted to the mill.

On July 6, 1864, Union cavalry arrived in Roswell and inspected the Ivy Woolen Mill, finding "CSA" woven into the gray wool fabric. Union soldiers burned the woolen mill and two cotton mills, then bivouacked in and around Roswell in preparation for the assault on Atlanta. The mill workers, who

from the ground and usually in the woods away from the water. Female wood ducks lay 8 to 15 creamy-white eggs.

Wood ducks have been in decline along the Chattahoochee in recent years mainly because they have lost much of their nesting sites due to development along the river. Eagle Scouts, in cooperation with the Chattahoochee Nature Center, have instituted a program of building and placing wood duck boxes throughout the nature center for nesting. Many private individuals have done the same on their river property.

SMITH ACTION OPTICS POLARIZED SUNGLASSES $129.95

WATERSKIP TRADING COMPANY FLY FISHING HAT $49.95

SAGE FLY ROD $580.

SCIENTIFIC ANGLER MASTERY XPS WEIGHT FORWARD FLOATING LINE $49.95

BRODIN ANGLING NET $66.

GOLDENEYE FISHING VEST $160.

SIMMS WINDSTOPPER FLEECE JACKET $189.95

STAINLESS STEEL FILLET FISHING KNIFE $54.95

100% "DEET" INSECT REPELLENT SPRAY $24.95

ABEL FLY REEL $410.

SIMMS GORE-TEX WADERS $349.

WATER WISP DRY FLY $2.45

J.W. OUTFITTERS FLOAT TUBE $225.

Trout fisherman at Island Ford in full battle gear.

were mostly women, were rounded up and deported to the north along with women from the mills on Sweetwater Creek (see page 123). When mill owners returned to Roswell in 1865, they found mills destroyed and homes ransacked but still standing. They began rebuilding the mills. A new mill built in 1882 operated until 1975.

Today, 90 percent of the structures built by these founding fathers before the Civil War remain. What sets Roswell apart from other Georgia towns that have preserved their antebellum architecture is that the buildings are representative of the entire spectrum of social classes. Wealthy mill owners, upper middle-class gentleman farmers, mill managers and poor illiterate mill hands are all represented in Roswell architecture. Besides that, the ruins of the Roswell Manufacturing Company venture, dams and vine-covered brick building, still stand along the banks of Vickery Creek—silent now, but a reminder of man's ability to take the natural resources around him and harness them for his own gain.

The Roswell Visitors Center conducts guided walking tours of Roswell which leave from the Center on Wednesdays at 10am and Saturdays at 1pm. The Center also has maps available for a self-guided tour of Roswell and guide books available for a walking tour of the mill site. Visitors can explore the mill ruins along Vickery Creek where there are interpretive displays for a better understanding of the mill operation. *Directions to mill ruins at Vickery Creek Park in Roswell:* From I-285, take Roswell Road north to Roswell. Cross the river and go to the square. At the north end of the square, turn right on Sloan Street. Follow it, bearing to the left. Park in the parking lot across from Founder's Cemetery and follow the trail down to the creek and the ruins. *More Information:* Roswell Visitors Center, 617 Atlanta Street, Roswell, GA 30075; 770-640-3253 or the Roswell Historical Society, Inc., 227 S. Atlanta Street, Roswell, GA 30075; 770/992-1665.

FISHING

The Chattahoochee from Buford Dam to Georgia 400 Bridge is the most productive and popular trout stream in

Georgia. For 46 miles the Chattahoochee River tailwater is stocked with brown, rainbow and brook trout. "Tailwater" is the term applied to water released off the bottom of lakes through dams. The depth of the water keeps it permanently cold, and the turbulence produced by the water releases creates oxygen. The combination, unintended when the dams were built for flood control and the production of hydroelectric power, results in a favorable downstream habitat for rainbow, brook and brown trout. The hatchery below Buford Dam is the southernmost trout hatchery in the United States. The Chattahoochee tailrace has no closed season, making year-round fishing possible.

BEST ADVICE –Every section of river has its own particular bank topography, underwater structure, stream currents and fish population. Professional guides know all the peculiarities of their area. The most experienced fishermen find that one or two days of guide fees is a good investment before launching out on their own. Inexperienced fishermen or families looking for an enjoyable day's outing will increase their pleasure tenfold by taking advantage of the experience of a professional guide. The best guides not only make sure their customers fish, but provide insights into the fishing habits of different species, lake and river ecology, weather lore and other aspects that will enhance your fishing experience.When booking a fishing guide always check to make sure who is responsible for all tackle (rods, reels, lures), boats and gasoline, live bait, life jackets, lunch, drinks, snacks, ice and rain gear. Be sure to understand exactly what is included in the guide fees.

GUIDES –Chris Scalley (770/650-8630) and Harlan Trammell (404/352-9828) provide guide service for this section of river. Both drive flat bottom "jet" boats which allow them to navigate upstream as well as down to places that may not be accessible to conventional outboard motor-powered boats in normal water conditions. Phil Sharpe (770/319-7012) is a fly-fishing guide and instructor of basic and advanced fly fishing techniques. His instruction employs wading, float tubes or a combination of the two.(See Fishing Guides on page 334).

BEST BOOKS AND MAPS –Jimmy Jacob's *Tailwater Trout in the South, An Angler's Guide*, provides a comprehensive guide to

Buford Dam Water Release

The waters released at Buford Dam during the production of electricity rise suddenly and swiftly. Warning horns located along the river between the dam and the GA 20 bridge will sound prior to the release of water.

When the horns sound, anyone standing in the river should move immediately to the riverbank. If you do not hear the warning horns and you notice the water rising, you should move immediately to the riverbank. Since riverbanks are steep in many places, you should always plan an escape route. Inexperienced boaters should not attempt to "ride the flow" during power generation. Rising waters are capable of swamping open boats. The swift water may render your craft difficult to control or cause you to become trapped against fallen trees in the river. Conditions stabilize only after the rock shoals have been covered with water. It is recommended that all fishermen, boaters, canoeists and kayakers wear a Coast Guard approved personal flotation device while on the river.

I may not catch a lot of fish but I show those worms who's boss.

—Tee-shirt seen in elevator of Atlanta skyscraper

Buford Tailwater

"The story behind the conversion of the Chattahoochee tailwater to a trout fishery is a bit unusual in that the state fishery managers played no role in the original endeavor. When Buford Dam was closed in 1957, there were no plans to introduce trout into the river. At the time, a program of stocking and stream renovations was in progress in the mountainous northern portion of the state, and the old Georgia Game and Fish Commission was trying to draw anglers to those northern counties. At that time, it had no interest in creating a competing trout fishery closer to the center of population in metro Atlanta.

In 1959 the local chapter of the Izaak Walton League obtained about 5,000 rainbow trout fingerlings and surreptitiously released them into the tailwater below the dam. Once the fish had grown to catchable size, club members invited the state biologists to join them for a day of fishing the new trout water. Needless to say, such actions today with regard to amateur stocking projects would be illegal, but the state fisheries managers quickly climbed aboard this bandwagon when the river's trout potential was demonstrated."

Jimmy Jacobs from Tailwater Trout in the South.

fishing the Chattahoochee River from below Buford Dam to Peachtree Creek, including the tailwater at both Buford Dam and Morgan Falls Dam. Jacob's book, used in conjunction with the Atlantic Mapping map of the Chattahoochee River, would be the best combination of guides to fishing this section of the river. (To order see page 328).

Atlantic Mapping's "Map of the Chattahoochee River" shows the section of the river from Buford Dam to Peachtree Creek in good detail. This map combines much of the historical information on the National Park Service map with topographical and highway information and presents it to the reader on a scale large enough to include details and information. For example, the map shows the locations of most of the river islands and shoals in this section of the river. The map also shows boat ramps and access roads. (To order see page 325).

U.S. Geological Survey 1:24,000 scale topographical maps covering this section of the river are Buford Dam, Suwanee, Duluth, Roswell, Mountain Park, Norcross, Chamblee, Sandy Springs and Northwest Atlanta. (To order see page 326).

OTHER SOURCES OF INFORMATION –Gary Merriman and his laid-back staff at the Fish Hawk (see page 335) in Atlanta's Buckhead neighborhood are good sources of information on Chattahoochee tailwater fishing. They can supply beginning and experienced fishermen with books and maps, sell them all the quality gear they could possibly need and recommend good fishing locations or professional guides.

TACKLE AND BAIT –Rods normally range from 4 to 6 feet and feature very light action while retaining sensitivity. Match one of these to a spinning or spincast reel. Use a good quality 4-to-6-pound test line. Recommended baits are 1/24 to 1/8 ounce Rooster Tails. Smaller spoons work. Night crawler worms are very effective. Use a small split shot and drift these with the current. Other very productive baits include brightly colored salmon eggs and Berkley Power Worms.

INSIDER TIPS AND HOT SPOTS –The Chattahoochee is a low-water fishery. When Buford Dam is generating, the river is high and muddy and trout fishing is poor. The best section of the river for catching trout is the 2.5 miles between Buford Dam and the GA 20 bridge. The Buford Trout Hatchery is located just north of the bridge. The hatchery releases about 250,000 9-to-10-inch rainbow, brown and brook trout each year into the Chattahoochee. The water released from the dam comes from the bottom of the lake, 200 feet deep at that point and remains at a constant year-round temperature of about 48 degrees. The extremely cold water from the lake provides good year-round temperature for the trout. Power releases from the dam scours the rock, gravel and sand keeping away aquatic insect life. Competition for meals is fierce. Trout are hungry and bite easily. Fishermen normally catch recent stockers, but occasional browns of 20 inches or better are caught. Generally speaking, the closer to the GA 20 bridge, the bigger the fish.

Bowman's Island (see page 82), which is within sight of the dam, is the one easily wadable shoal on this part of the river. But water releases from the dam can turn it into a raging torrent in a matter of minutes. For water release information, call 770/945-1466.

The 15 miles of river between GA 20 and Medlock Bridge (GA 141) is stocked with rainbows, brown and brook trout. Like the section above, the river flow tends to scour the stream bed and banks, resulting in little aquatic insect life and hungry fish. The best fishing is from a boat or float tube. The river is wadable at Fish Weir Shoals.

Fish for large trout and stripers at the base of Morgan Falls Dam. Use a Carolina rig and big minnows to catch stripers. There is a boat ramp at the base of the dam on the east side of the river at Morgan Falls Park (see page 87).

Striped bass, originally a saltwater fish which routinely swims 20 miles a day, migrating 60 miles upstream from West Point Lake eat most of the 125,000 fingerling brown and rainbow stocked trout in this portion of the river. Experienced fishing guides report catching few trout from Peachtree Creek or Paces Mill Park on Cobb Parkway to Morgan Falls Dam. The Georgia Department of Natural Resources has discontinued stocking stripers in West Point Lake, much to the vociferous objections of West Point Lake guides and fishermen, and that may positively effect the trout population below Morgan Falls Dam in years to come.

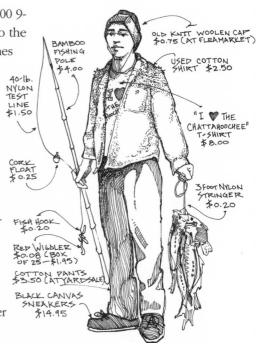

Fisherman below Morgan Falls Dam, economy model.

Fish Consumption Guidelines

Buford Dam to Peachtree Creek–Brown trout, no restrictions to Morgan Falls Dam; rainbow trout, one meal per week to Morgan Falls Dam; carp, one meal per month to Morgan Falls Dam; spotted sucker, no restrictions to Morgan Falls Dam; yellow perch, rainbow trout, largemouth bass, one meal per week to Morgan Falls Dam; carp, one meal per month Morgan Falls Dam to Peachtree Creek; bass, no restrictions below Morgan Falls Dam. As a general rule, eat smaller fish to be safe.

Source: Georgia Department of Natural Resources, 1997.

Fishing with Harlan

Harlan Trammell is a professional fishing guide and Upper Chattahoochee Riverkeeper boat captain.

Harlan went after his fish with the intimidating concentration of a major league closer going after the last out. Eyeing the water near the bank where he believed the trout waited, he used a six-pound rod to whip a rapala lure to the desired spot.

"You wanna catch a big trout?" he asked, directing his question more to the water than to his fishing companion. "Pick one mile of river and fish every log there."

Harlan was following his own advice. We were fishing below Buford Dam on the Chattahoochee River. He cast ten times and pulled in six fish. Brown trout. Harlan wanted rainbows.

"They know what happens when they get a boat like this... frying pan... I'll take 'em home and eat 'em."

He changed rapalas, looking for some magic to match the day's light and water color.

"Don't ask me why a fish would eat that thing, but they do," he said. "As I have proven... neon green and red neon and neon orange. Wood and painted metal. Let me have that other pole right there if you don't mind."

We passed Chris, another Chattahoochee River guide, steering upstream in his 21-foot boat powered by a 40 horse-power mercury jet engine. Two customers sat toward the bow. Caught in the November sunset, the threesome looked like an Orvis ad. Harlan fished in a baggy, tan, cotton sweater, tight faded Levis and high-topped black canvas basketball shoes.

"Chris's a good guy, but you don't need all that stuff to catch

BOATING

Canoeists can navigate the entire 48-mile stretch of the Chattahoochee between Buford Dam and Peachtree Creek. Most paddlers prefer the 9-to-10-mile section below Morgan Falls Dam. The 3 miles from Powers Island to the Paces Mill Unit of the Chattahoochee River National Recreation Area, which includes the beautiful Palisades and the rapids of Devil's Racecourse, are the most popular paddling sections of the river whether for canoes, kayaks or rafts.

Fishermen and pleasure boaters with a small outboard powered boat (a 12-foot jon boat with a 9.9 horsepower motor is the ideal boat) can navigate much of this section of the river. In fact the adventurous boater who is willing to get into the water periodically and walk or rope his craft over shallow shoals can navigate much of this section from Buford Dam to Morgan Falls. Quite a Chattahoochee adventure. Not something for the inexperienced or timid boater, but doable and a fun, rewarding way to experience this section of river.

Note that all of the put-in and take-out points below can be used for canoes for tubers or for fishermen floating the river. *Fishermen and tubers in particular should be cautious about checking times and distances between put-ins and take-outs.*

BUFORD DAM TO ABBOTTS BRIDGE –The river explorer to whom an "in the boat out of the boat" approach is appealing will enjoy this 13-mile motorized float from the boat ramp at Lower Pool Park below Buford Dam to the boat ramp at the Abbotts Bridge Unit of the CRNRA. Boaters should be experienced and competent with oars. *Put-In:* Lower Pool Park (see page 54), just below Buford Dam. *Take-Out:* Abbotts Bridge (see page 83). *Distance:* About 13 miles. *High Points:* Buford Dam and the U.S. Army Corps of Engineers' power generating plant is an awesome, intimidating sight. Taking into account power generation; flood control; riverside development, which could not have taken place without this dam; the recreational popularity of Lake Lanier, which the dam backs up; and Lanier's importance to the water supply of Atlanta, few man-made structures in all of the Southeast have as much impact on as many people as this dam does. The view from the top of the dirt mound downstream is dramatic, taking in Bowman Island and the shoals surrounding it. An old fish weir is located below GA 20. Scenic cliffs rise up from the east side of the river near Level Creek. *Hazards:* The release of water from Buford Dam can imperil the most experienced boaters. It's a good idea to call 770/945-1466 for water release information before launching a boat anywhere on this section. It's critical to call if launching in the 2-mile zone directly below the dam. Life jackets must be worn at all times in the 2-mile zone. The release of water from Buford Dam also determines the water level and, therefore, what kind of boat, if any, can negotiate the shoals. The shoals on both sides of Bowman's Island present an immediate problem for the boater launching from below Buford Dam. Boaters must be prepared to walk and rope their craft through them. A shoal area just north of McGinnis Ferry is an obstacle for motorized boats. Be prepared to use oars or rope boats over shoals at some water levels. *USGS Topos:* Buford Dam, Duluth and Suwanee.

ABBOTTS BRIDGE TO JONES BRIDGE –Abbotts Bridge is a perfect put-in location for boaters who want to explore 4 or 5 miles upstream and 6 miles downstream from the put-in without encountering shoals. Small motorized boats can go upstream to McGinnis Ferry Road and downstream to just above the boat ramp at the Jones Bridge Unit of the CRNRA without encountering difficult shoals. *Put-In:* Abbotts Bridge (see page 83). *Take-Out:* Abbotts Bridge for boaters exploring upstream and down. Jones Bridge for boaters willing and able to rope or oar over the shoals above the Jones Bridge boat ramp (see page 84). *Distance:* 7 miles from Abbotts Bridge boat ramp to Jones Bridge boat ramp. *High Points:* An unusual opportunity to explore this 12-mile section of river in a small motor-powered boat. *Hazards:* Shoals 1.5 miles south of Jones Bridge (the old metal bridge ruins upstream of the Jones Bridge boat ramp). *USGS Topos:* Duluth, Roswell, Mountain Park, Chamblee and Norcross.

JONES BRIDGE TO CHATTAHOOCHEE RIVER PARK –The segment between Jones Bridge boat ramp and the downstream end of the Island Ford Shoals is for experienced boaters who do not object to roping or walking their boats over shoals. Two sets

any fish. Buy a trout stamp and a cheap rod and reel and a worm and catch a fish in this river. Make your kid happy. You don't even need a boat."

We passed through the Jones Bridge rapids. With his left hand, Harlan used one long oar to steer the 19-foot outboard around the shoals while he continued to cast with his right.

"These are some bitchin' shoals. As you can see...You wash through one of those rapids, get sideways against one of those rocks and you're toast." We brushed by a submerged boulder. *"That's* a widow maker..."

While he steered and talked, he whizzed the rapala. "Trout find little spots. They usually stay right where they're dumped. But they do move around. Particularly in high water. Water quality deteriorates, they go somewhere else."

It was getting late. Gray clouds darkened the river valley. It was beginning to rain. "This ain't nothing but drizzle. We'll run down there and head back. This ain't no heavy rain or nothin'." Harlan spoke off the side of the boat, toward the fish.

"These fish down here must've stepped on a rusty nail and got lock jaw."

Another cast.

"It's gonna' be Taco Bell on the way home. I believe I could've put on a piece of turkey sandwich and threw it back up there where those big ones were and they would've ate it," he said, intensely staring toward the bank as he whistled a new rapala that way.

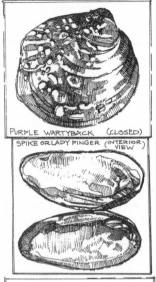

PURPLE WARTYBACK (CLOSED)
SPIKE OR LADY FINGER (INTERIOR VIEW)

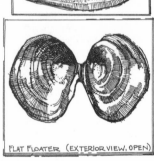

FLAT FLOATER (EXTERIOR VIEW, OPEN)

of shoals, 1 to 1.5 miles above Island Ford and then the Island Ford Shoals make this a challenging section for motorized boaters. Here is a suggestion for exploring this section in a jon boat with a small outboard: Put-in at the Fulton County Chattahoochee River Park boat ramp and motor upstream as far as Island Ford Shoals, which is just north of GA 400. Then go downstream to Bull Sluice Lake and Morgan Falls Dam. This is an interesting and beautiful section of the river that gives boaters an opportunity to see shoals at Island Ford, wetlands around Bull Sluice Lake and the historic Morgan Falls Dam built in 1904 and still churning out electricity with the original generators. *Put-In:* Jones Bridge (see page 84), or alternatively, Chattahoochee River Park (see page 87). *Take-Out:* Chattahoochee River Park. *Distance:* 11 miles from Jones Bridge boat ramp to Chattahoochee River Park boat ramp. Four miles from Chattahoochee River Park to Morgan Falls Dam. *High Points:* Shoals and scenic bank environment around Island Ford. Granite cliffs that jut up from the river north of Morgan Falls Dam. Riverside banks of rhododendron and mountain laurel north of Morgan Falls Dam are dramatic echoes of the north Georgia mountains. *Hazards:* Extensive shoals at Island Ford. Bull Sluice Lake formed by Morgan Falls Dam is extensively silted. Motor boats must follow river channel or creek channels or risk getting stuck. Morgan Falls Dam is 67 feet high on the lake side, but the lake at the dam is waist deep today as a result of 93 years of siltation. *USGS topos:* Duluth, Norcross, Roswell, Chamblee, Mountain and Sandy Springs.

MORGAN FALLS DAM TO JOHNSON FERRY NORTH –This is the beginning of the most popular canoeing, kayaking and rafting section of the entire 540-mile-long river. Small motorized boats can operate in this section but should do so with extreme caution and with concern that their wake might interfere with non-motorized craft. *Put-In:* Morgan Falls Park boat ramp (see page 87), on the east side of the river just below Morgan Falls Dam. *Take-Out:* Johnson Ferry North Unit of the CRNRA (see page 88). *Distance:* About 1 mile. *High Points:* The put-in and the pool below Morgan Falls Dam offer an unusual opportunity to view this historic hydroelectric dam built in 1904 and still operating with the original generators. The red brick-and-concrete dam and powerhouse are quite beautiful in their own industrial way. The location was chosen because a great waterfall, Morgan Falls, at this point on the river provided a natural site for the power plant. Fisherman pull big bass from this pool and from the river just downstream. *USGS Topos:* Chamblee and Sandy Springs.

JOHNSON FERRY NORTH TO POWERS ISLAND – This 4-mile stretch is the beginning of the most popular rafting section of the river. In season, Chattahoochee Outfitters runs a shuttle service from here downstream to the CRNRA's Powers Island Unit and Paces Mill take-outs. *Put-In:* Johnson Ferry North (see page 88). *Take-Out:* Powers Island (see page 90). *Distance:* About 4 miles. *USGS Topos:* Sandy Springs.

POWERS ISLAND TO PACES MILL –This 3-mile section known as the Atlanta Hooch is the most scenic and popular section of the river for canoeists, kayakers and rafters. It is well used in summer, but in fall and winter true paddling aficionados find solitude on this beautiful stretch of waterway. The take-out at Paces Mill is well-marked for those who need to turn in rental equipment to the Chattahoochee Outdoor Center. *Put-In:* Powers Island (see page 90). *Take-Out:* Paces Mill (see page 94). *Distance:* About 3 miles. *High Points:* High cliffs of the Palisades formed by the river cutting through the Brevard Fault (see page 91) are arguably the most dramatic features of the river along its entire length from Chattahoochee Gap to Apalachicola Bay. The rapids, known as Devil's Racecourse, are never more than Class I or II water but provide a variety of white-water experience. National and international canoe and kayak competitors come here to practice skills they use on Class IV and V water. Rhododendron and mountain laurel along the steep rocky banks create a mountain environment reminiscent of the river's origins in the north Georgia mountains. The rhododendron banks between I-285 and Cobb Parkway are the southernmost stand of that species along the river, although mountain laurel can be found much farther down river. *USGS Topos:* Sandy Springs and Northwest Atlanta.

PACES MILL TO STANDING PEACHTREE –Due to a difficult take-out and a potentially dangerous waterfall at the City of Atlanta's

Freshwater Mussels

A mussel is an animal that lives in water. A protective shell, made up of two similar pieces called valves, covers the mussel's body. The valves are joined at one point by a hinge and can be opened and closed somewhat like a powder compact. The mussel's body lies within the shell and consists of various organs including the foot, gills, stomach and heart. Freshwater mussels live in streams and lakes while sea mussels live in the ocean. Their presence or lack of presence in a lake or stream is indicative of water quality; they don't like pollution or filtration. Few are seen on the Chattahoochee between Lake Lanier and West Point Lake. According to a 1992 American Fisheries study, of the 297 native American freshwater mussels, many are considered "endangered, threatened or of special concern. Only 70 percent are listed as currently stable."

Cubic feet per second, an accurate method of expressing river flow in terms of function of flow and volume is commonly abbreviated as cfs.

water intake, few canoeists continue past Paces Mill although Goat Island Shoals below Paces Mill Road provides 0.25 mile or more of interesting varied shoals across a river that widens considerably at this point. *Put-In:* Paces Mill (see page 94). *Take-Out:* There is no boat ramp here. Boaters must carry up a steep rip rap bank on Peachtree Creek, just upstream of the creek's confluence with the Chattahoochee. To reach the parking lot, take Moores Mill Road to Ridgewood and turn into the Fort Peachtree Park. A dirt road to the left leads to the parking area. *Distance:* 3 miles. *High Points:* Interesting shoals below Paces Mill Road. A 3-to-4-foot high waterfall constructed to back up water for the City of Atlanta water intake provides a challenging white-water practice area for some kayakers and canoeists. However, the setting by the water intake, always littered with plastic bottles, styrofoam cups and waterlogged day-glow tennis balls, seems environmentally out of sync with the canoe and kayak experience. *Hazards:* Conoeists must negotiate the 3-to-4 foot high manmade waterfall, which at low water can be very dangerous, prior to reaching the confluence of Peachtree Creek and the only take-out. *USGS Topos:* Northwest Atlanta.

MORGAN FALLS DAM

Section 4
Peachtree Creek to
West Point Lake

"'d been Riverkeeper only a couple of months when we went canoeing from South Fulton County down to Sixteen Bridge. There were two or three canoes of us. I'd never been canoeing on that part of the river before. It was after a couple of days of pretty heavy storm so the volume of water was high, and it was moving fast. I can remember just being amazed that 40 miles south of Atlanta you could still smell sewage in the air and coming out of the water. You could look around, and there was farmland and you didn't see people. You didn't see anything. But you could still smell Atlanta in the river.

From Peachtree Creek down to that South Fulton Camp Creek discharge the river is disgusting. It's been written off for decades. There's no way to get on it. Because nobody wanted to get on it. It smells like chlorine. Or sewage. Or other strange chemicals. The trash is unbelievable. And many people just decided to say, 'That's gonna' be the industrial section of the river. So be it.' I think that's unconscionable. That the state, the city and everybody involved has allowed 20 or 30 miles of river to be just totally written off and abused in the way it has. And the abuse is not just the waste water discharge. You've got junk yards, industries, industrial parks, people building too close to the river.

Somewhere in South Fulton County the river opens up. It becomes a more relaxing experience. That 40-mile stretch of river down to Franklin is a little-known gem. There are floodplains filled with arrowheads and pottery; white water at Bush Head and Daniel Shoals; unexplored islands and excellent fishing. I've seen a deer swimming across the river there. It's a part of the river I'd like to be able to take my children to, but there's no way to get on it. And unfortunately, there are times when it smells bad and there's bacteria in the water so it's not safe.

Rivers can be restored, and the river south of Atlanta can and will be restored. Sewage treatment technology is not rocket science. The technology is available. It's just a matter of making sewage a priority. Of building sufficient capacity and having a metropolitan area that's willing to put the bucks into it. The question is how long is it going to take. I would like to see all dischargers meeting their clean water permits. I'd like to see

Sally Bethea

them move from chlorine to ultraviolet disinfection so you don't have that horrendous chlorinated smell in the air and that bad taste in your mouth as you travel past those white foamy discharges into the river. I'd like to see a place where there would be a public access point for educational trips so people could understand what rivers can absorb and what they can assimilate. How we use rivers to take away our waste. How we've got to be careful not to abuse that privilege. Where we get our drinking water. You get out on the river and see that there is wildlife and that the river doesn't have to smell and look bad.

Given the infrastructure needs that have to be in place for the city of Atlanta, if we get going now, we'll see improvements in five years and major differences within 10 years. That's not that long a period of time when you think about it, given that the city has known about the sewage in our urban streams for 25 years and has done very little about it.

I want to end forever the Atlanta-based notion that the Chattahoochee ends at Peachtree Creek. And I want to open people's eyes to the surprising beauty and wonderful remoteness of the Chattahoochee as it winds out of South Fulton and Douglas counties and flows downstream through Coweta, Carroll, Heard and Troup counties to West Point Lake. This is not Atlanta's river. It's not Georgia's river. It's a Southern river. It's a regional river. People in Alabama love this river just as much

KINGFISHER

as Georgians do. The folks in Florida have a resource they treat very well—the bottom 107 miles of the Chattahoochee called the Apalachicola. Apalachicola Bay is the richest and most diverse estuary in this part of the world.

We have an unbelievable resource. It's part of an ecological system. And the more we realize we're a piece of that whole system and not get caught up in our own small part of the landscape the better off we'll be. And the better off the river will be."

Sally Bethea is the Upper Chattahoochee Riverkeeper.

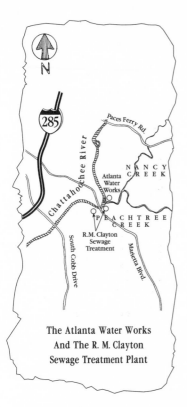

**The Atlanta Water Works
And The R. M. Clayton
Sewage Treatment Plant**

THE RIVER

This 65-mile section of the river from Peachtree Creek to West Point Lake is the most polluted section of the entire 540-mile long Chattahoochee. This is especially true of the 15-mile segment from Peachtree Creek to the GA 166 Bridge. It is in this segment that Atlanta's infamous R. M. Clayton waste water plant, the largest such facility in the southeast, is located.

It is also in this section that Riverkeeper Sally Bethea and her boat captain Harlan Trammell have personally discovered three spills of untreated sewage flowing into the Chatta-hoochee, after claims by the city of Atlanta that such spills could not occur. A front-page picture in the March 17, 1997, edition of the *Atlanta-Journal Constitution* showed Riverkeeper attorney David Moore standing on the riverbank near the Clayton plant, holding a glass jar of untreated human waste that he had scooped up off of an urban stream which flows into the river. All of the runoff from the massive Six Flags over Georgia amusement park flows into the river in this section, as well as runoff from junkyards and industrial facilities.

The beautifully named Peachtree, Nickajack, Utoy, Proctor and Sweetwater creeks were important parts of this region's cultural and economic history. Early settlers lived by them and built gristmills on their rapids. Now they ooze a grey-brown liquid into the river or send in a torrent of foamy, chlorine-smelling chemical water. On any given day a boat ride along this part of the river can result in burning eyes. The smell of chlorine produces a queasiness bordering on nausea.

And yet...As it leaves Fulton County and heads toward more rural Carroll, Coweta and Heard counties, the river demonstrates its incredible capacity for self-healing. As the boater continuing downstream reaches the GA 166 Bridge, the river banks begin once more to look like river banks rather than the banks of a sewage ditch. At the 487-acre McIntosh Reserve the river splashes over picturesque shoals. Further down Hilly's Mill Creek and Red Bone Creek enter the river like mountain streams, the way Sweetwater, Nickajack and Peachtree creeks used to. Fishermen congregate at the foot of Daniel Shoals during spring spawning runs of crappie and bass.

PARKS AND RECREATION

SWEETWATER CREEK STATE CONSERVATION PARK —Sweetwater Creek State Conservation Park is a 1,986-acre area that was created to protect the natural character of the Factory Shoals section of Sweetwater Creek and the historic integrity of the New Manchester Manufacturing Company mill and town site ruins. The Brevard Fault zone which runs directly through the Sweetwater Creek basin created a higher elevation which gives the area a more mountainous environment than surrounding communities. The 1849 mill was located along the creek for these very reasons. The elevations drop rapidly—60 feet in a 2,000 foot stretch. There are no overnight facilities here, but there is good fishing in the 215-acre lake and along Sweetwater Creek. There are also more than nine miles of hiking through rugged, wooded terrain and past the historic mill site which has remained virtually untouched since it was burned in the Civil War (see page 129 for a self-guided tour). The park offers a variety of interpretive and programming services ranging from scheduled special events and walking tours to ranger-guided natural/historical interpretive programs for organized groups. There are also annual special events, including New Manchester Commemoration, History Lecture Series, Spring Wildflower Walks and Fall Foliage Walks. *Facilities:* 75 picnic tables with grills; 11 picnic shelters with grills, water and electricity; a 150-person group shelter; bait shop; rental boats; fishing; hiking; playgrounds; restrooms. *Days/Hrs.:* Park, daily, 7am-10pm.; trails, daily, 7am-sunset. Bait Shop (varies seasonally), Tues.-Sun., 7am-7pm. Closed Mon. Park office, daily, 8am-5pm. *Fees:* Parking fee. *Directions:* 15 miles west of Atlanta. Take I-20 west to Thornton Road (Exit 12). Turn left, cross bridge and go 0.25 mile to Blairs Bridge Road. Turn right and go until Blairs Bridge Road dead ends into Mt. Vernon Road. Turn left and go 0.5 mile to the entrance of the park. *More Information:* Sweetwater Creek State Conservation Park, P.O. Box 816, Lithia Springs, GA 30057; 770/732-5871.

THE MCINTOSH RESERVE —This 487 acres of land adjacent to the Chattahoochee River is a historic site and a recreational area. In the park is the site of Chief William McIntosh's planta-

Point and Nonpoint Source Pollution

Pollution sources can be categorized as either "point source" or "nonpoint source" in their origin. A point source means a discharge of chemicals, sewage, garbage and other wastes into a stream through some sort of pipe, culvert or ditch, while a nonpoint source describes a discharge from a non-discrete source, such as storm runoff from construction activities, agriculture and forestry.

Although point sources of pollution have been the focus of much successful regulatory attention over the past 25 years since the passage of the federal Clean Water Act in 1972, problems remain. In the upper Chattahoochee River basin (headwaters to West Point Dam), there are 159 facilities, such as municipalities and industries, which are permitted to discharge their treated wastewater into the river or a tributary.

Upper Chattahoochee Riverkeeper routinely monitors compliance reports from these facilities to determine whether or not they are meeting permit requirements. Those which are chronic violators receive attention through Riverkeeper's legal action program, if the state and/or federal regulatory agencies have not already pursued an enforcement action. Interestingly, municipal (local government) sewage treatment plants were the most egregious violators in the upper Chattahoochee basin with more than 70 percent of the permit infractions during the two-year period 1995-1996.

Sally Bethea, Upper Chattahoochee Riverkeeper

Georgia Adopt-A-Stream

The Georgia Adopt-A-Stream program is a hands-on way to learn more about and to protect local streams. Administered by the Department of Natural Resources Environmental Protection Division, the program provides the tools volunteers need to assess the habitat, water quality and biological life found in streams. More than 4,000 volunteers throughout Georgia participate in some type of Adopt-A-Stream activity–everything from conducting regular cleanups to monthly monitoring and stabilizing streambanks with vegetation. Usually, a group will adopt a stream for one year and then choose to participate in Level I, II or III. The levels of involvement provide something for everyone.

Level I involves setting up a project, finding a stream and partners, registering with the program, walking a watershed and participating in quarterly visual assessments and clean-ups. Level II adds to the project monthly chemical testing, quarterly biological monitoring or a habitat improvement project. Level III recognizes those volunteers who do all of the services listed in Level II. All levels send their results to the Georgia Adopt-A-Stream program. Groups receive an official certificate of stream adoption when they register their program.

Georgia Adopt-A-Stream provides manuals and videos on how to get started and instructions for chemical and biological monitoring. Volunteers should attend a training workshop before starting monitoring activities. Workshops are offered every month in the metro Atlanta area and frequently throughout Georgia. The annual conference in October is also a great way

tion, known as Lochau Talofau, or Acorn Bluff, as well as the grave of McIntosh himself. Chief McIntosh was the son of William McIntosh, a Scottish Captain in the British Army, and Senoi, a full-blooded Creek Indian woman belonging to the influential Wind Clan.

McIntosh's place in history comes from his participation in Indian Wars and his willingness to cede Indian lands to the federal government. In 1805, the 27-year-old McIntosh helped President Thomas Jefferson extend the area of white settlement into Georgia to the Ocmulgee River. During a civil war between the Upper Creeks and Lower Creeks in 1813, McIntosh fought with General Andrew Jackson when federal troops intervened in the war. In 1818-19 during the Seminole Wars in Florida, McIntosh, now a general, fought with the Lower Creeks and the U.S. troops against the Seminoles—and many of the Upper Creeks, who had fled to Florida territory.

But finally in February 1825 after McIntosh had negotiated the questionable Treaty of Indian Springs where vast Creek lands were ceded to Georgia for white settlers, the Upper Creeks plotted their revenge. They had sworn death to anyone ceding land to whites without a vote by all Creek tribes. Under the command of Menawa, a Redstick who had fought against McIntosh and Jackson at the Battle of Horseshoe Bend, the Creeks came to the plantation to carry out the Creek National Council's order of "Fire and Blood." On May 1, 1835, they killed McIntosh and one of his followers, burned the plantation and destroyed what livestock they could not carry off; but they spared the lives of all women, children and one white man. McIntosh's eldest son, Chilly, escaped by swimming across the river. He rode bareback all night long to Milledgeville, then the state capital, to get help from Georgia Governor George M. Troup, his father's first cousin. Chilly wanted protection for his mother, Eliza, and other family members. Help was never sent, and the government never assisted the McIntosh family.

In 1978, Carroll County acquired this acreage where McIntosh operated his backwood plantation, tavern and ferry and where he met his fate. This park along the river preserves a bit of history and provides visitors with some nice recreational opportunities in a serene setting. *Facilities:* Primitive camping (weekends only), picnic tables, pavilion, river overlook, ball field, walking trails, horse trails, restrooms. *Fees:* $8 per unit per night camping fee. *Days/Hrs.:* Daily, winter, 9am-6pm; spring and summer, 9am-8pm. *Directions:* From Newnan, take US Alt 27 to Whitesburg. Turn left on GA 5. Go about 2 miles to entrance. Access to the park is provided by a county-maintained road that connects with GA 5. *More Information:* McIntosh Reserve Park, P.O. Box 249, Whitesburg, GA 30185; 770/830-5879.

HISTORICAL SITES

COCHRAN MILLS –The ruins of old gristmills dot the landscape of much of the Chattahoochee River Valley. This particular one, built by Cheadle Cochran in the early 1800s, sits on Little Bear Creek in what is now a Fulton County Park. When Cochran died in 1854, his estate included 700 acres of land, 40 slaves and a rustic gristmill which his son Owen continued to operate. Later in 1870, Owen's older brother Berry built a small, wood-frame gristmill on the main branch of Bear Creek. Both of these mills have been destroyed by vandals. The first mill's wooden structures were burned in 1967. The fieldstone dam, which was originally 80 feet long, was dynamited several years ago. The second Cochran mill was destroyed in 1972, but the 48-foot long fieldstone dam was left intact. Parts of the cleaning sluice and penstock remain. *Directions:* The first Cochran Mill is located a few hundred feet off of Cochran Mill Road. The second mill can be reached by following a dirt path (part of the old Cochran Mill Road) for about 0.5 mile. *More Information:* Fulton County Department of Parks and Recreation, 141 Pryor Street., Suite 8054, Atlanta, GA 30303; 404/730-6200, fax 404/730-6206.

NEW MANCHESTER –People who lived and worked in the mill towns which sprang up along the Chattahoochee River in the 1800s seldom knew each other. But they were connected by the work they did and the lives they led. The people of New Manchester would become greatly connected to the people of Roswell, some 16 miles to the north. But whereas Roswell thrives and flourishes today, New Manchester is a ghost town.

for volunteers to expand their knowledge of water issues, meet other volunteers and learn more about the program.

There are several organizations that sponsor local Adopt-A-Stream programs. About a dozen cities and counties have staff that help local volunteers and coordinate activities on area streams and rivers. There are networks of teachers and students along the Chattahoochee, Altamaha and Savannah rivers that conduct regular monitoring and share their results with each other. Nonprofit groups, like the Upper Chattahoochee Riverkeeper and Trout Unlimited, also sponsor individual volunteers.

All together, these volunteers are making a real difference in protecting and improving water quality and the health of streams all over Georgia. Adopt-A-Stream is expanding to provide guidance on volunteer monitoring of lakes and wetlands. *More Information:* Georgia Adopt-A-Stream, see page 322; The Upper Chattahoochee Riverkeeper Adopt-A-Stream Network, see page 324.

Laurie Hawks, Former Adopt-A-Stream Coordinator

A cartoon in the New Yorker shows a scowling mafia-like figure being examined on the witness stand. "All I can figure," he says to his questioner, "is that he must have been inspecting the water quality of our lakes and rivers when he became entangled in cement."

Whittier Mills Village

Tucked away in a corner of northwest Atlanta is Whittier Mills Village, another reminder of how the Chattahoochee River was a source of income and a way of life for hundreds of people who lived along its banks.

Whittier Cotton Mills of Lowell, Massachusetts, was first documented in Atlanta in 1895, the year of the Cotton States and International Exposition. The company purchased 1,080,000 square feet of land on the south bank of the Chattahoochee River, due west of Bolton. Originally part of the Creek Nation, the parcel was about two miles downstream from the site of Standing Peachtree.

The mill itself closed in 1971 and most of its buildings were destroyed in 1988. Only two buildings remain: the four-sided, three-story red brick tower of the original cotton mill and a single-story carpentry shop, constructed in 1900, where mill workers cut pieces for Ideal American Jigsaw puzzles in the evening to make extra money during the Depression. These structures stand uncared for and deteriorating on the derelict 17 acres of the original mill site.

However, unlike so many other southern mill villages, Whittier Mills Village never declined into disrepair or abandonment. Its white frame houses, with steeply pitched roofs, are and have generally been very well tended. Antique red roses still bloom in the neighborhood's many flower gardens. Equally important, because it is physically isolated in a small river valley between two brick plants and divided from the rest of the area by Southern Railway tracks and the river itself, the community has remained largely intact, both architecturally and socially, and

There are no photographs of the mill which was once a state-of-the art factory, five stories tall. There are no photographs of the houses that were here. Except through local folklore, there is little known of the people who once walked these roads along Sweetwater Creek. There are many lost and forgotten mill towns near the river, but few are the result of one pivotal day in history. New Manchester, Georgia, has that distinction.

In the 1800s Sweetwater Creek was seen as one of the best water power sources in the state. The topography along Sweetwater Creek created by the Brevard Fault provided an ideal location for a water-powered factory. In 1849 two entrepreneurs, Colonel James Rogers of Milledgeville and former Georgia Governor Charles J. McDonald of Cobb County, incorporated the Sweetwater Manufacturing Company to "manufacture, bleach, dye, print and finish all goods of which cotton or other fibrous materials form a part, and to manufacture flour from wheat or grain of any kind, and all machinery used for such purposes or any other, and to erect such mills and other works as may be necessary to carry on their business." In 1857 Charles McDonald reorganized the company into the New Manchester Manufacturing Company, outfitted the factory with new machinery and tripled the output. Assets of the company were listed at $50,000.

The New Manchester Manufacturing Company owned the property on both sides of the creek, and a typical mill town grew around it. The company built houses on the ridges along the creek which the mill workers and their families rented. Rent was taken out of the their wages. The company store was the only one in town, but it carried the necessities. The worker was also indebted to it. There were probably 70 or so men, women and children working at the mill and about 200 living within a mile of the factory.

There is little known about the life of the New Manchester employees. It is known that the mill itself was the only large building in town so it was a favorite place to hold weddings. Production would stop as a minister married a couple standing beside a loom or spinning frame. It's also known that these couples' children made up part of the labor force. A bell in the mill tower regulated the pace of life, and working hours were from daylight to sunset. Low water, as well as flooding, affected the mill's capabilities, and repairs to the mill could cause a shutdown, meaning impromptu holidays for the mill workers. Sundays were for religious meetings and for Sunday School, which functioned as a "real" school teaching the three R's to the children of the town. Swimming and fishing along the creek behind the mill was probably a favorite activity.

In 1860, New Manchester was taking in about 700 pounds of cotton per day and turning out 120 bundles of yarn and 500 yards of osnaburg, a coarse cotton cloth. With the addition of more machinery in 1861, production jumped to 6,700 bundles of yarn per month at 5 pounds per bundle and 12,000 yards of osnaburg.

In 1861 with the outbreak of the Civil War, the Confederate government contracted the factory to weave uniform cloth, make shoes and repair wagons and equipment. Mules and wagons hauled cotton to the factory from Marietta and Atlanta. Each wagon carried four bales of cotton, and the trip took two days. The company paid from 75 cents to $1 per pound in Confederate money for cotton in 1864.

Unfortunately, by aligning with the South's war effort, the New Manchester operation became a legitimate military target. When General Joseph E. Johnston withdrew the Confederate Army across the Chattahoochee River in his efforts to protect Atlanta, he left factories along the river unprotected. Union General William T. Sherman ordered the destruction of the mills at New Manchester as well as those at Roswell, Georgia (See page 107.)

Union General Kenner Garrard, commanding the Second Division of the Cavalry Crops, moved quickly to seize the mill and destroy it. Two regiments of Yankee cavalry commanded by Colonel Silas Adams (1st Kentucky) and a strong force of infantry under Major Haviland Thompkins (14th Illinois) of General Stoneman's staff appeared on the high ground across Sweetwater Creek where they set up artillery within sight of the factory. Not a shot was fired as they approached the mill under the watchful eyes of the anxious employees. At first, the mill workers were merely arrested and sent to their homes under guard to await arrival of wagons to deport them to west

undeveloped—only three houses have been built since the mill owners' expansion of the village in 1927.

While unique in character, the history of Whittier Mills Village is also representative of the establishment, development and decline of the southern cotton mill industry.

Laura Lieberman and Don Rooney, Whittier Mills Village residents

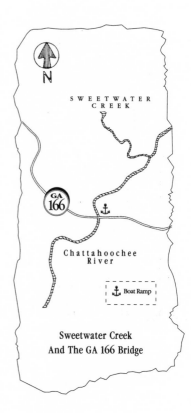

Sweetwater Creek
And The GA 166 Bridge

Rivers: Movers and Shapers

The most vigorous mover and shaper on terrestrial earth is running water. Seen from space, the most noticeable landforms on the planet are stream valleys, which resemble in their patterns the shape of an outspread tree without leaves: intricate, delicate filaments at the top, like twigs at the end of a branch; strong, thick near the bottom, like the base of a trunk.

Rivers are alive, growing, maturing and responding to the elements around them. The main force by which a river changes shape is the channel's gradient, or slope, which is generally steep near the headwaters and flat near the mouth.

As a stream flows, it constantly tries to balance the flow of water while moving the sediment in it. A river is in equilibrium if the channel shape and gradient are equalized so that neither erosion nor sediment deposition takes place. Rivers constantly adjust to reach this ideal condition.

Downcutting, when sand and gravel moving downstream scrape the sides of a channel, is a primary means of erosion in a river. Streams have a tendency to erode headward, or upslope, and to increase the lengths of their valleys until they reach the watershed divide. Sometimes tributaries of one stream creep upslope and reach the channel of another stream, redirecting the headwater of one stream to another. The Chattooga, for example, once fed the Chattahoochee River until the Savannah, eroding northward, captured it. Look closely at a Georgia map; it seems apparent. Connect the dots between them and the rivers run along the same line.

Rivers naturally flow into Georgia. They were told that they would not be hurt if they did not try anything foolish.

Meanwhile, Major Thompkins led part of the cavalry force in his command up the Chattahoochee to the mills at Roswell, Georgia, where they met up with Frenchman Theopholie Roche who attempted to save those mills by running up a French flag and claiming protection under it. This so infuriated General Sherman that he raged to General Garrard, "I repeat my orders that you arrest all people, male and female, connected with those factories, no matter what the clamor, and let them foot it, under guard, to Marietta, where I will send them by cars to the North." "If you hang Roche," he screamed, "I approve the act beforehand!"

Fearing the rage of Sherman, Major Thompkins burned the Roswell Mills and hurried back to New Manchester to do the same. A detachment of eight men set fire to the factory, the company store, the machines shops and the homes around the mill. A battery of guns ripped great holes into the 300-foot-long wooden dam, sending massive timbers sailing into the air and releasing the power of Sweetwater Creek.

During the 16-mile trek to Marietta, the Union soldiers constantly raped and abused the women of New Manchester. These women were then placed with women from the Roswell Mills—400 in all—and were thereafter known as the "Roswell Women," or the "Factory Hands," their identity forever lost.

The battered women, who were housed in the Georgia Military Institute building in Marietta, were an embarrassment to the Union Army, and Sherman ordered that they "be disposed" and "sent to Indiana."

With nine days rations, the women were placed on trains on July 15 and sent to a distribution point in Nashville, and then moved to Louisville on July 20. After that, they were to be sent north; but there are no records of their wherabouts beyond July 20.

When the war ended in April 1865, people all over the South returned to their homes. But not one New Manchester woman ever did. Only a handful of men came back, and these were the only ones within the state who had first-hand knowledge of the New Manchester events. Only one husband is known to have found his wife in Louisville. The rest died never knowing the whereabouts of their wives and children.

Directions: Sweetwater Creek Park. 15 miles west of Atlanta. Take I-20 west to Thornton Road (Exit 12). Turn left, cross bridge and go 0.25 mile to Blairs Bridge Road. Turn right and go until Blairs Bridge Road dead ends into Mt. Vernon Road. Turn left and go 0.5 mile to the entrance of the park. *More Information:* Sweetwater Creek State Conservation Park, P.O. Box 816, Lithia Springs, GA 30057; 770/732-5871.

SWEETWATER CREEK AND ITS GEOLOGY

Sweetwater Creek, near Austell, Georgia, has served many purposes. To the beaver that inhabit its banks, Sweetwater Creek is home–signs of their work are visible along the park trails. To the botanist the creek is an ideal place to study various plants unique to this area; and to the geologist it is a spot where the past is revealed in the rocks and changes in the land's surface can be seen taking place day by day.

The mill ruins within Sweetwater Creek State Park are the visible remains of a once-prosperous factory and town. The New Manchester Manufacturing Company was one of several factories located on tributaries of the Chattahoochee River in the 19th century. Water from the local creeks provided power for the factories' machinery. During the Civil War, the workers at the Sweetwater Creek factory produced cloth for Confederate uniforms until the Union Army destroyed the factory and surrounding towns, leaving only the ruins that remain today (see page 123).

During this century Sweetwater Creek provided water for both Austell and East Point, Georgia. In recent years the land within the creek's drainage basin has undergone considerable development. Towns near the creek have grown, and residential areas have increased in size and number. Some industries have also located along the creek or on its tributaries. Pavement and buildings now stand where trees and vegetation once were, leading to an increase in runoff water. As a result, recent flood levels along Sweetwater Creek are higher than in the past. Floodwater generally recedes within a day; but while

increasingly winding and crooked paths. When they run into obstacles, the water deflects to the opposite side, which creates a bend. On such a curve, water strikes the outer bank and causes rapid erosion. In time as the current chips away at it, the bend grows progressively larger, more pronounced and becomes a meander.

In contrast to the outside of a meander where the water quickens its pace, the flow slows on the inside, where it deposits sediment to form sand or gravel bars. Because erosion takes place on the outside and deposition on the inside, meanders move over time in a lateral direction. They also advance downslope because more erosion takes place on the downstream side of a meander.

As a meander becomes more pronounced, it resembles a loop. Eventually the current cuts across the neck of the loop, which can create an island in midstream, an oxbow lake or a combination of the two.

Sweetwater Creek is named for a Cherokee chief, Sweet Water, also known as AmaKanasta, his Cherokee name.

—Marion Hemperley, Indian Heritage of Georgia

Buzzard's Roost Island and Sandtown

Perhaps the best documented and most important archaeological site in northwest Georgia is the Buzzard's Roost and Sandtown area near the Fulton, Cobb and Douglas county borders. These sites stretch for about one mile north and south from Buzzard's Roost Island on both banks of the Chattahoochee. In addition, the Sandtown Trail, perhaps the oldest road in the southeast, which led from the Alabama and Tennessee frontiers east, is believed to have crossed the Chattahoochee at Buzzard's Roost Island. Evidence of both Woodland (1000BC to 900AD) and Mississippian (900 to 1600AD) villages, as well as Paleo-Indian (10,000 to 8,000BC) mounds have been found throughout the area. A number of burial mounds run along the river. There is also evidence of an "earth lodge" existing in Douglas County. Buzzard's Roost has been a settlement site for a number of Native Americans throughout history. More recently the area has been home to Nickajack (late 1700s), Creeks (beginning 1813 to Red Stixx Wars), the Pony Boys, Cherokees and finally Europeans (around 1830). Many of the maneuvers along Sherman's far right flank during the Atlanta Campaign of the Civil War were staged from the Buzzard's Roost area.

flooding is at its peak, water covers portions of the park trails and the creek becomes a raging torrent. This is when the largest amount of erosion takes place.

Sweetwater Creek's drainage basin encompasses an area of 246 square miles within the Georgia Piedmont. The northern and southern sections of the creek are distinctly different in character. The northern section flows quietly through a wide, often swampy, stream valley. In the northern section, from where it originates near New Georgia in Paulding County, until it reaches Austell, Sweetwater Creek flows in an eastward direction.

Sweetwater Creek State Park lies along the southern portion of the creek. At Austell the creek bends to flow in a southeasterly direction until it enters the Chattahoochee River. The characteristics of the creek change as well as its direction as it encounters the resistant rocks of this area. Relief increases, the creek valley sides steepen and fall and turbulence disrupts the previously tranquil creek. This section of Sweetwater closely resembles a mountain stream.

The Chattahoochee River floodplain lies within the Brevard Fault zone at a lower elevation than the surrounding portion of the Piedmont. Sweetwater, as well as the other creeks that enter the river, is constantly downcutting in its effort to reach the lower elevation of the Chattahoochee. From Austell to its junction with the river, Sweetwater Creeks drops 120 feet in elevation, 80 feet of which are inside the park. This change in gradient was an important factor in the choice of the Sweetwater factory site.

Before Sweetwater Creek enters the Brevard Fault zone and the Chattahoochee River, it crosses a series of northeast-trending rock units. Some of these rocks, such as quartzite, are more resistant to erosion than the surrounding rocks. These quartz-rich rocks divert the creek at right angles to its southeastward direction of flow. Other rocks in the creek contain open joints and allow the creek to flow through these openings and across the rock units. This control of the creek's direction by the rocks and the structures within them gives Sweetwater Creek a rectangular drainage pattern characterized by right angle bends.

WALKING TOURS

SWEETWATER CREEK TOUR –Leave the Sweetwater Creek Park parking area and follow the trail that leads to the mill ruins. This roadbed, while not a primary route in use by the New Manchester community, may well have been a lane leading to nearby private property or homesites.

Upon reaching Sweetwater Creek, turn right on Factory Ruins Trail.

This roadway paralleling the creek was the New Manchester community's main street. Approximately 0.5 mile upstream, or north, was the location of Ferguson's Crossing. For several generations, into the early 20th century, the Ferguson family operated small sawmills and gristmills at Ferguson's Crossing. Ferguson's Crossing was also the last bridge across Sweetwater Creek before the stream emptied into the Chattahoochee River several miles downstream. Important during the operation of the New Manchester factory, this bridge lay along the route to the railhead in Atlanta and played a critical tactical role in the advance of Union troops toward New Manchester in July 1864. From Ferguson's Crossing south to the New Manchester factory, this route was called Sweetwater Factory Road. Immediately upstream from here, a century of water fluctuations have washed out an entire section of the roadbed.

Take the first trail on the left. This is a short trail that leads over some rock outcrops and down to the creek.

The rock outcrop on your left before reaching the creek is a garnet-mica schist. The most interesting feature of this rock is the garnets. Garnet is a common rock-forming mineral in the Georgia Piedmont. Most of the garnets here are small, reddish-brown and "wart-like." On closer examination of the rock, a second, flattened type of garnet can also be seen. In some parts of the United States, garnets are mined for use as gemstones or abrasives. However, garnets found here have little or no commercial value because they lack the size, form and quality necessary for such uses.

Walk a few feet toward the creek on this same trail. At this stop the creek turns almost 90 degrees. Return to the main

Hiking along the Factory Ruins Trail at Sweetwater Creek

WATER RELIGION:
EASTERN CHRISTIANS

During the Feast of Theophany on January 6, Eastern Christians drink holy water, blessed because the liquid represents the primal element of creation and the baptism of Jesus.

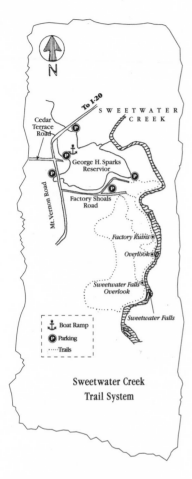

Sweetwater Creek
Trail System

"The name of this river derived from Chatto, a stone, and hoche, marked or flowered; there being rocks of that description in the river above Hoitbletigau at an old town Chattahoochee."

—Indian Agent William Hawkins Letters, 1799.

trail and continue downstream.

The land on either side of the creek throughout this area was owned by the New Manchester Manufacturing Company (originally the Sweetwater Manufacturing Company). New Manchester, Georgia, (see page 123) was a typical mill town of the 19th century with the company providing housing for many of the workers and their families. Houses were built on the ridges along the creek.

The excavated depression to the right of the trail was the site of the store owned by the New Manchester Manufacturing Company. Operated in the classic "mill town" fashion, this store was the source of the basic needs of the community: food, clothing, even hardware items. Liberal use of credit ensured that valuable labor would not leave town while in debt to the company. Three stories tall, retail space and storage shared the two first floors. As was customary in mill towns such as New Manchester, space at the company store was allocated to the town post office. The storekeeper was allowed to live on the third floor with his family. When Union troops burned the mill on July 9, 1864, the people of the New Manchester community were invited to take from the store what they would need for their journey before it was set afire.

To the left of the trail is the beginning of the millrace, a channel into which water is sent to the factory, supplying power for the operation. This one is a man-made ditch built with manual labor and lined with stones from the area. A dam was constructed across Sweetwater Creek at the entrance to the millrace, backing water upstream as far as Ferguson's Mill. A series of gates were located along the millrace to control the flow of water.

The rock spanning the creek at this point was a major factor in the site selection of the millrace entrance. The rock provides a natural basis for a dam to divert water into the millrace. It also marks the beginning of a major increase in the slope of the stream. This change in stream level, or gradient, allowed the mill, located downstream, to be at a lower level than the entrance to the millrace. This difference in the level of the millrace entrance and the mill provided the slope necessary to generate the water energy to turn the mill wheel.

Return to the main trail.

A short distance along the trail on the right is a spring which is fed by underground water passing through joints in the rock beneath the ground surface. Even in years of drought this spring was a reliable source of cool, clean drinking water. Locations such as this also served as handy gathering places where personal news and gossip were exchanged, serving much the same function as the village courthouse squares in larger communities.

Stand on the bridge and look immediately downstream in the millrace. Only a few short years ago the large flat rock on the right side of it was almost under the bridge. The force of the creek water keeps moving it downstream a bit at the time. The rock exposed at this stop shows weathering along foliation planes. The almost horizontal ridges in the rock are formed by erosion along the foliation.

The stone wall to the left of the trail marks the outer edge of this section of the millrace. The natural slope of Sweetwater Creek began to get steeper than desired by the designers of the millrace system. To keep the millrace water at a lesser rate of fall on its approach to the factory, this hand-laid stone wall was built on the side of the hill. This section of millrace has been dry since the loss of the control gates (located where the millrace changes from wet to dry). The cylindrical holes made by quarrying equipment can be seen on some of the rocks in the wall. Foliation played an important part in the quarrying operation. By splitting along the foliation, quarrying was made easier, enabling the builders to provide rocks that had at least two regular smooth, flat surfaces. Joints, although not as common as foliation, were also used as an aid in quarrying. In the construction of the wall, the builders used a combination of joints and foliation to form rectangular blocks. Joints also played another role in the millrace wall. Continuing through the millrace, observe how the builders used the joint surfaces of the large rock outcrops to the right as part of the millrace wall. This portion of the wall is formed by natural joint surfaces.

In the stream directly in front, there are examples of a well-developed pothole and well-developed joints. Potholes are erosional features usually found in the rock in fast-moving

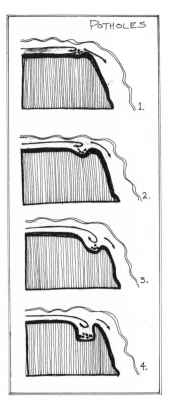

POTHOLES

1.

2.

3.

4.

Potholes

Potholes are deep holes in a streambed caused by the abrasive action of sand, pebbles and cobbles trapped in a depression and swirled around by currents. This rotational movement acts like a drill, cutting the deep holes. As the pebbles and cobbles are worn away, new ones enter the depression and continue drilling into the streambed.

A hiker rests on the rocks along Sweetwater Creek

Centralhatchee Creek in Heard County means "Perch Creek" from the Creek Indian "sundal" meaning "perch" plus "hachi" meaning "stream" or creek."

—Marion Hemperley, Indian Heritage of Georgia

streams. These circular depressions in rocks are formed by the grinding action of trapped sand and gravel being swirled around by the strong currents within the creek. Starting points for potholes are usually niches or breaks in the rock, such as poorly developed joints or along foliation planes, where the water flow becomes disturbed and begins to swirl and erode (see page 131). The pothole seen at this stop was initiated along a poorly developed joint. Look toward the opposite bank of the stream. The influence of many joints on the creek is apparent. The water finds the open joints much easier to flow along and to erode down through than the less open foliation.

Continue to the factory ruins.

At five stories, this factory building was taller than any building in Atlanta in 1860. The lumber was cut and sawmilled locally. The bricks were made on the property, and the foundation stones were quarried downstream from this site. Looking at the building, notice how the windows flare outward towards the inside of the wall. Since open flame light sources were not allowed in the mill for fear of fire, this window design allowed natural light from outside to disperse into the interior, maximizing the light inside the factory. Bales of cotton, brought from the railhead in Atlanta, were converted at the New Manchester mill to cotton yarns and a material known as osnaburg, a loose weave material lighter than canvas but heavier than linen. The machinery required for cleaning raw cotton, spinning and coloring yarns and weaving the fabric was powered by the water of Sweetwater Creek. The millrace funneled creek water into the arch on the west side of the building. Flowing through the factory and out the arch on the creek side, a huge water wheel turned. Unlike the slim, upright water wheels of common gristmills, this water wheel resembled a large barrel placed on its side. Weighing 50,000 pounds (25 tons), this wheel provided a tremendous amount of energy. A series of shafts, gears and leather belts distributed this energy to the machines throughout the building.

Rocks used for the mill base are found locally, but no abandoned quarry, necessary for the large amount of rock used, has been found as a source for these rocks. An interesting feature in the rocks used for the base is the presence of large elliptically shaped feldspars (white). The distinctive appearance given by these elliptical feldspars within the rock is termed "augen" (German for "eyes"). A good example of the augen is found in the bottom cornerstone of the mill. There, a series of augen is visible within a band of feldspar in the rock.

Continue along the main trail behind the mill. Behind the mill note the well-developed joints in the rock on the right.

Nearing the creek, observe the two large blocks of rock on the opposite bank that have fallen down the hillside. These blocks are an indication that the stream is widening its channel and, therefore, is undercutting the rocks along the banks. The lighter colored rock near the bank of the creek is called "pegmatite." Look diagonally across the creek in an upstream direction to see that the pegmatite extends across the width of the creek. The darker rock on either side of the pegmatite is "metagreywacke." Joints are poorly developed or are not present in the pegmatite. The pegmatite was injected as a hot liquid into the metagreywacke after metamorphism, and therefore, lacks the foliation present in the metagreywackes. It also has much larger crystals than the metagreywacke because it cooled slowly. The lack of uniformity with the surrounding rocks caused the pegmatites to react differently than the metagreywackes to the joint forming stresses, resulting in a lack of joints in the pegmatites.

Sweetwater Creek begins to bend at this point due to the influence of the pegmatites within the stream. As the creek bends, it once more flows near right angles to the joints and parallel to the foliation. Further south, the creek bends again to flow through the joint openings. Continue along the trail to the overlook platform for dramatic views up and down the creek.

Directions: Sweetwater Creek Park (see page 121), 15 miles west of Atlanta. Take I-20 west to Thornton Road (Exit 12). Turn left, cross bridge and go 0.25 mile to Blairs Bridge Road. Turn right and go until Blairs Bridge Road dead ends into Mt. Vernon Road. Turn left and go 0.5 mile to the entrance of the park. Trail begins in parking area. *More Information:* Sweetwater Creek State Conservation Park, P. O. Box 816, Lithia Springs, GA 30057; 770/732-5871.

Fish Consumption Guidelines

Peachtree Creek to West Point Lake–Bass, one meal per month; carp, one meal per month; channel catfish, one meal per week; striped bass, one meal per month. As a general rule, eat smaller fish to be safe.

Source: Georgia Department of Natural Resources, 1997.

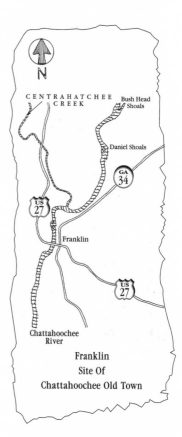

Franklin
Site Of
Chattahoochee Old Town

Monica and Joe Cook

In 1995 Monica and Joe Cook canoed the entire length of the Chattahoochee to photograph it and compile an audio visual presentation which they show to schools and clubs. This is an excerpt of an interview with them about their trip.

Question: Would you repeat your trip?

Monica: Absolutely...Why are you looking at me like that?

Joe: Well, you've said we wouldn't do all of it at one time. That we would do parts of it again.

Monica: We said we would do it again if we had the time. We just don't have...

Joe: It's a fun trip; but what we always tell people is that people go to Yosemite, they go to Yellowstone, they go to Alaska, they want to see wilderness, they want to see breathtaking

SIGNIFICANT URBAN EXPERIENCES

COCHRAN MILL NATURE CENTER –An air of friendliness and cooperation prevails at this private, non-profit organization and is exemplified in their mission statement, "To teach the importance of our roles in respecting the earth and each other through environmental education, conservation and outdoor recreation activities." Volunteer labor built the log cabin structure which serves as the Cochran Mill Nature Center. The center sits on 50 privately owned, heavily wooded acres in South Fulton County. The Center cooperates with the adjacent Cochran Mill Fulton County Park by joining up with their trail system to make six miles of hiking trails that explore the diverse forest, rock and water landscapes which surround the area.

The Center is a licensed rehabilitation facility and is home to a variety of both native and non-native wildlife species. The Center cares for animals which may have been orphaned or permanently injured and are unable to survive in the wild. Wildlife that recover from injuries are released back into their natural habitat.

Environmental education programs on topics such as ecology, forests, solutions for solid waste, pond and stream ecology, natural history of Georgia and endangered species are available to schools and organized groups for a small per person fee. Ropes courses are offered to schools, small businesses, families, support groups and corporations. Special activities include week-long adventure and nature camps, a 3.5-mile race, a 1-mile Fun Run and a Father's Day Fishing Derby. *Fees:* $1 adults and children over 12, $.50 children 12 and under. Yearly memberships available. *Days/Hrs.:* Year-round, Mon.-Sat., 9am-5pm; Mar.-Oct., Sun., 1pm-5pm. *Directions:* From Atlanta, take I-85 south to Exit 16. Stay left and follow sign to Spur 14. Follow Spur 14 (South Fulton Parkway) approximately 15 miles until it ends. Turn right onto Rivertown Road. Follow Rivertown Road about 2 miles to the first stop sign. Turn left onto Cochran Mill Road. The Nature Center is 200 yards on the left. *More Information:* Cochran Mill Nature Center, P.O. Box 911, Fairburn, GA 30213; 770/306-0914.

FISHING

BEST ADVICE –Catch and release techniques are recommended due to a variety of contaminants in this section of river and the issuance of fish consumption guidelines by the state for certain species. Below GA 166 and particularly below the GA 16 Bridge, the river begins to recover, at least in appearance if not in water quality; and the prospects for fishing brighten.

INSIDER TIPS AND HOT SPOTS –The section of river between the GA 16 Bridge and West Point Lake is almost all the private preserve of a few lucky land owners who live along the river. It is fairly inaccessible except to boaters in canoes or hardy boaters in jon boats with small outboard motors who are willing to walk or rope their craft over shoals at various water levels. Daniel Shoals blocks the route upstream from West Point Lake for most boats. There is good fishing around Bushhead and Daniel shoals for fishermen adventuresome enough to get to these beautiful and productive spots.

BEST BOOKS AND MAPS –U.S. Geological Survey 1:24,000 scale topographical maps covering this section of the river are Northwest Atlanta, Mableton, Ben Hill, Campbellton, Winston, Palmetto, Rico, Newnan North, Whitesburg, Lowell and Franklin. (To order see page 326.)

BOATING

PEACHTREE CREEK TO GA 166 BRIDGE (CAMPBELLTON HIGHWAY) –This 15 miles is the most intensely polluted and abused section on the entire Chattahoochee River from its origin at Chattahoochee Gap to where it flows into the Gulf of Mexico as the Apalachicola River. *Put-In:* There is no boat ramp here. Boaters must carry down a steep rip rap bank. To reach the parking lot, takes Moores Mill Road to Ridgewood and turn into the Fort Peachtree Park. A dirt road leads to the parking area. *Take-Out:* Boat ramp at GA 166 Bridge. *Put-In/Take-Out:* Boat ramp is on the northeast side of the river where GA 166 crosses. *Distance:* About 15 miles one way. *Low Points:* Anyone remotely interested in the environment, water and the future of the Chattahoochee River should make it a point to take this

beauty, spectacular vistas. You'll find that on the Chattahoochee, but you'll also find all the other junk. Trash floating in the river and the outfall from the sewer treatment plants and the homes right on top of the river. And so, you see some spectacular beauty, but you also see how we use the river and how we abuse it. So, it's more of an educational trip. It's more of a...What's the word I'm searching for?
Question: What are the physical features of the river that you remember most?
Joe: The headwaters. Particularly, the part from the Chattahoochee River Campground down to Robertstown. It's so wild. There's some spectacular waterfalls.
Monica: Once we left Anne Gale's (the Wildwood Shop). South of there. I liked that.
Joe: Alum Bluff is a big surprise.
Monica: Owl Creek was a really good find.
Joe: From Columbus south there's these huge sandbars. The sandbars are really beautiful.
Joe: We saw Jeff Blauser and Greg Maddox fishing on the river. They were in a boat right above Jones Bridge.
Question: Any special memories?
Joe: We were paddling south of Atlanta. It was late in the afternoon. The wind was blowing the cottonseed. The sun was backlighting it and it looked like snow. It was very peaceful and beautiful land. We were right there south of Atlanta and that to me just kinda said something about, you know, it's a beautiful river. But while we were seeing this, we were smelling this stench coming from the waste water treatment plants. Smelly, but it was so beautiful and peaceful. The experience we got from the river was, oh gosh, what a beautiful place, but *gosh*.

How the Chattahoochee Got Its Name

As early as the 17th century, English traders venturing out from the South Carolina coast had referred to the river as some phonetic variation of the word Chattahoochee, although there was no consensus as to the exact pronunciation. A year before the American Revolution began, wandering botanist William Bartram, crossing the river at Coweta, put the name down in print as Chatta Uche, which he thought was named after the nearby village of Uche. No ethnologist, Bartram had unfortunately misunderstood the river's name. The wild popularity of his *Travels* across the Atlantic, however, ensured that his misconception lingered in some form for a century or more.

The first authentic documentation of the most likely origin of the name of the Chattahoochee River came in 1799 from the travel log of Indian agent Benjamin Hawkins, an excellent linguist. He wrote: "The name of the river derived from Chatto, a stone, and hoche, marked or flowered; there being rocks of that description in the river above Hoithletigua at an old town Chattahoochee." The exact location of the old town Chattahoochee remains a mystery, although most authorities place it near the present town of Franklin in Heard County, just north of the vicinity of Hoithletigua, also known as Burnt Village.

Matt Gedney, who has written a history about Helen's pioneer families called *Living on the Unicoi Road*, says the headwaters of the Chattahoochee were in Cherokee territory. There, the river was known by its Cherokee name, Chota River or Chota Creek. This name came from the

trip. Boaters pass these historic and now abused tributaries: Peachtree Creek, Proctor Creek, Nickajack Creek, Utoy Creek and Sweetwater Creek. The city of Atlanta's waste water treatment plants and the Cobb and Fulton County sewage treatment plants discharge into the river in this segment. *Hazards:* A visual disaster. Bank side vegetation appears to be sprouting plastic soft drink bottles, muddied yellow tennis balls, styrofoam cups, plastic streamers and, at times, toilet paper and other bathroom items. On any given day chlorine fumes inflame eyes. Drinking this water can cause serious illness. *USGS Topos:* Northwest Atlanta, Mableton, Ben Hill and Campbellton. *Guides and Outfitters:* Riverkeeper staff who have personally identified raw sewage flowing into the river will escort down this river section small groups of elected officials from Atlanta and other municipalities as well as others interested in the future of the Chattahoochee. *More Information:* Riverkeeper office, 404/352-9828.

GA 166 Boat Ramp to GA 16 Boat Ramp –The river demonstrates its remarkable regenerative powers. Below GA 166 the chlorine smell dissipates. The river banks appear to be river banks rather than sides of a drainage ditch. *Put-In:* Boat ramp is on the northeast side of the river where GA 166 crosses. *Take-Out:* Boat ramp is on the northeast side of the river where GA 16 crosses. *Distance:* About 25 miles. *High Points:* The old metal bridge north of the present GA 16 was the route of the Old Carrollton Road between Newnan and Carrollton. A wooden bridge built by Horace King once spanned the river at this location. *Gauges:* The locked gauge at the GA 16 Bridge is U.S. Government operated, and the data is not available to boaters on the river. *USGS Topos:* Campbellton, Palmetto, Winston, Rico, Newnan North and Whitesburg.

GA 16 Boat Ramp to Franklin –Canoeists will enjoy this section of river. River explorers with small jon boats with small outboard motors may be able to navigate downstream at moderate water levels, but they should be prepared to rope or walk boats over McIntosh Reserve, Bushhead and Daniel shoals as well as other shoal areas on river. *Put-In:* Boat ramp is on the northeast side of the river where GA 16 crosses. *Take-Out:* Riverside Park boat ramp in Franklin just below the US 27

Bridge. Other Heard County boat ramps are at Snake Creek Park (see page 145) and Brush Creek Campground (see page 153) in the headwaters of West Point Lake. *Distance:* About 25 miles. *High Points:* McIntosh Reserve (see page 121) about 4 miles below the GA 16 bridge includes a beautiful shoal area. Banks studded with huge boulders rise 80 feet above the river. The rugged landscape is evidence of the Brevard Fault (see page 91) zone so prominent along the section of the river which flows through the Palisades below Morgan Falls Dam. A hiking trail follows the river bank. Overnight camping is allowed on weekends. An Indian fish weir is visible at low water levels on the left side of the river opposite the Reserve.

In the early days of Heard County, which this portion of the river flows through, poled barges transported cotton downstream to Columbus where it was transferred to steamboats and transported to market in Apalachicola and New Orleans. Several ferries crossed the river along this section. Bowens Ferry and Webbs Ferry were two of them. Union cavalry troops making their way back to Sherman's headquarters in Marietta crossed the river at Bowens Ferry after their defeat at the Battle of Brown's Mill in July 1864.

Hilly's Mill Creek joins the Chattahoochee via a waterfall visible from the river. This was the site of a gristmill that operated in the last century. Red Bone Creek, a mile farther downstream, is a miniature version of Hilly Mill's. Like McIntosh Reserve upstream, these waterfalls and rocky creeks are the last reverberation of the Brevard Fault zone along the Chattahoochee. At this point the fault zone continues in a southwesterly direction into Alabama. The river leaves the fault zone and flows in a more southerly direction forming the border between Georgia and Alabama.

The river widens at Bushhead Shoals. The shoals extend all the way across the river with a small island splitting the current. The banks are wooded, and the scene here is one of the most beautiful on the entire river, yet few people see this spot. Drifting here below the shoals, the disgusting 15 miles of river just a few miles north seem remote and of little consequence. Unfortunately, they are not. *Hazards:* None, except that boaters attempting this segment in a jon boat with a small out-

Cherokee town of Chota which was located in the Nacoochee Valley. So, where the river flowed through Creek Territory it was called the Chattahoochee; but once it reached the boundary between the Creek and Cherokee Indian nations, it became the Chota.

Gedney points out that early maps had the Chattahoochee beginning about 25 river miles below its source high on the Blue Ridge, at the point where the Chota River merged with the Soquee River. "Later, an 1820 Georgia surveyor's map moved the start about eight miles further upstream to where the river was joined by Sautee Creek at the lower end of Nacoochee Valley. Above that point and on up through the Helen valley, the main channel was still identified as the Chota River."

Gedney has found that one of the last references to Chota River appears in Adiel Sherwood's 1837 *Gazetteer of Georgia.* "Under the entry for Chattahoochee River, the *Gazetteer* said the river was formed by two principal branches, the Chota and the Sokee...which unite 8 miles below Clarkesville. The western branch now, however, is called the Chattahoochee, instead of Chota as it was by the Indians."

With the removal of the Cherokee Indians from the Nacoochee Valley, the memory of their name for their river, the Chota, quickly faded. Says Gedney, "The map makers eventually traced the river to its source, following the larger stream at every junction to bestow the title upon a small spring which lies a short distance below the crest of the Blue Ridge."

Billy Winn

Billy Winn is editorial page editor of the *Columbus Ledger Enquirer* and author of *The Old Beloved Path: Daily Life Among the Indians of the Chattahoochee River Valley*.

"The first mention that I know of in literature about the river occurs in Indian agent Benjamin Hawkins's travel log of the Chattahoochee River and the Creek country in the year 1798, 1799. And basically, what Hawkins says in there is that Chattahoochee was a town north of us here at that time, which he says is the founding town on this part of the river. And he says that it got it's name from the Creek 'Chatto,' a stone, and 'hoche,' marked or flowered. There's no way to spell it exactly because the Creeks didn't have a written language at the time, but basically it would be Chato oochee.

Unfortunately, the elements in the words that supposedly mean all that also appear in other words which are translated variously as stony creek or red river and so Chattahoochee meaning river of painted rocks or river where there are marks on the rocks is merely the most generally accepted translation, but I

board motor should bring oars, be competent in using them and be prepared to rope and walk their boats over several sets of shoals. *USGS Topos:* Whitesburg, Lowell and Franklin.

SWEETWATER CREEK –Sweetwater Creek runs south over the Brevard Fault zone through Sweetwater Creek State Park and into the Chattahoochee River southwest of Atlanta. Before entering the state park, the creek loops around populated Austell, then runs for her life under the heavily traveled bridges of I-20. Such environs could not be expected to help Sweetwater live up to her name. These waters offer to viewers a collection of cast-off tires, Big Wheel tricycles and clusters of styrofoam containers.

Sweetwater Creek has three distinct faces. The first four miles are lazy and smooth. This is a good section to fish in or listen to the towhee or watch the red-tailed hawk sail overhead. Boaters can stretch their legs by hiking up the cascading spillway behind the state park or exploring some of the hiking trails in the park. But inside the boundary of the state park and around the curve lies the second face of Sweetwater–the rapids. For the next three miles boaters twist and bump, pry and brace their way down some of the best chutes and slides in Georgia. The ruins passed on the right are of the old New Manchester Manufacturing Company, where confederate clothing was made under the management of William J. Russell, grandfather of the late Senator Richard Russell (see page 123).

Old Factory Shoals is a long river-wide ledge with an island in the center. In lower water, there is a nice smooth ride to the left of the island, but this becomes difficult in higher water, when the right side again becomes runable. At any level, this stretch is a three-mile bucking bronco that will put to test every stroke in the canoeing textbook. Don't run blindly up on these shoals. Heavy rains that cause a gauge reading of two feet or more will require some falls and slides to be portaged. Below two feet, the shoals are runable, but it's pick-and-pay all the way.

The last two miles present yet another face of Sweetwater Creek. Sandy banks, narrow channels and fallen trees become the order of the afternoon. The challenge now is to maneuver among the fallen trees, staying in the narrow channel and off the sandbars. The current remains brisk so watch those overhanging limbs; being swept into limbs will upset a canoe quicker than rapids. *Put-In:* Beneath the bridge on Blairs Bridge Road. Take I-20 to Thornton Road (Exit 12). Turn left, cross bridge and go 0.25 mile to Blairs Bridge Road. Follow to bridge. *Take-Out:* Bridge on Riverside Parkway, formerly Lower River Road. Continue south on Thornton Road to Riverside Parkway and turn left. Follow to bridge. *Gauges:* Height of Sweetwater is a crucial factor in determining how difficult her rapids will be and which course to take through them. Check the water gauge at the put-in before starting. At 1.6 feet, the creek is at its lowest navigable level, and shoals at this level will be scrappy. Regular readings should be two feet. Above two feet, shoals will be heavy and in some spots dangerous. Scout all shoals and be prepared to portage around some. *Hazards:* Sweetwater is a wide and fast creek, and her shoals can be dangerous for the inexperienced. Lower sections have a few fallen trees and overhanging limbs which should be treated with caution, since the current continues to run fairly fast through to the Chattahoochee. *USGS Topos:* Mableton, Austell, Ben Hill and Campbellton.

Rapids at Sweetwater Creek, which flows through the Brevard Fault and into the Chattahoochee

have a lot of trouble with that, too. Mainly because of vowel shifts and the way that the English, French and Spanish transposed prefixes and suffixes and garbled Indian words. For example, Chattahoochee is very close to Chatahachee which means red creek or red river. 'Chata' being the Creek word, the Muscogee word, for red and 'hachee' for stream or creek. So it could very easily, in my mind, mean red river or red stream. Which would make some sense. However, in the absence of any other concrete evidence most people rely on Hawkins. After all, he was here, and he was a very good linguist, and he had a chance to interview Indians that lived on the river; and according to him, they say that the word meant river of painted or marked rocks.

Well, I can live with the river of marked or painted rocks; but the only problem is I've spent my lifetime on the Chattahoochee and I've never seen a marked or painted rock. And of course, that doesn't mean that at one time they weren't here. It could refer to something as simple as a place where the moss grew on the rocks in a peculiar way or lichens had marked the rocks or the rocks were stained red with a particular kind of algae or something. It could mean all of those things. But the Indians also were good linguists, and they were very careful about words. So I think it's up in the air, and I don't think we'll ever know."

Section 5
West Point Lake

Pete Cavender

"I'm 56 years old and born and raised in Palmetto. Daddy had a fish camp out on the river. Dad fished it all his life. He fished trot line, set switch, all that. We got a lot of our food from the Chattahoochee River, to be honest with you.

My Daddy started in the cotton mills when he was 12 years old. When his daddy died, he went to work in the cotton mill. When I turned 16, I had a job offer startin' me off at a dollar; and I think it was fifty cents an hour. But Daddy wouldn't let me take it. He said, 'Nope, I started in the cotton mill at twelve and never got out, and you're not going in it.'

If you go out Hutchinson Ferry to Jones Ferry and take it to where it dead ends, it dead ends into the place I'm talkin' about—the fish camp. The river at that point was approximately 80 yards wide. It was a huge place. If I had a river map, I could show you how far it went on the river. It must have been 10 miles of frontage or more on the river. And this gentleman let daddy build a cabin there. He had three old buildings. One he had an old wood stove set up in it. He called that our kitchen. One had a table in it. That's where we ate. One was a big cabin. Looked more like an army barracks. We slept in it. Had an old pot-bellied stove in it to stay warm. We stayed out there winter and summer, huntin' in the winter, fishin' in the summer.

The river was clean when I first remember it. We could swim in it. Do whatever we wanted to. By the time—I'm gonna' say in the mid-fifties—especially when we had that big drought and the river got so low you could walk across it in a lot of places, I saw catfish and carp dyin' in the pollution. That's how bad it had gotten somewhere from the mid-to-late fifties. And after that, we caught 'em strictly for the sport cause they weren't fit to eat. That's when Dad and them started fishin' 40 miles south of here, roughly, and a few years later it was just as bad down there.

I'm not a scientist or anything else, but it goes into the chemical factor. I personally wouldn't eat a fish out of the upper part of this lake right now."

Pete Cavender managed West Point Landing Marina from December, 1993, until July, 1997.

THE LAKE

West Point Lake straddles the Georgia-Alabama border right where the Chattahoochee River makes its big left-hand turn to head due south to Florida's Apalachicola Bay. This Corps of Engineers lake, which extends 35 miles along the river between Franklin and West Point, Georgia, has more than 500 miles of shoreline and 26,000 acres of water surface. Construction of the lake was authorized by the Flood Control Act of 1962 with actual construction beginning in 1965 and impoundment beginning in October 1974. The lake is part of the Apalachicola-Chattahoochee-Flint Waterway System which runs 260 miles from Apalachicola, Florida, to Columbus, Georgia. Water released from West Point Lake helps keep lakes and channels downstream deep enough for navigation. Water stored here during rainy seasons protects downstream towns and farms from flooding.

THE BALD EAGLE

The 57,000 acres of land used to build West Point Lake shares the same history as many other areas along the Chattahoochee. Here, in this fertile bottomland, the Lower Creek Indians cultivated fields and built large villages of clay-covered, wooden houses. They used the river for fishing and transportation. European traders entered the picture next, using the navigable parts of the river to transport goods. By the early 1800s white settlers drove out the Creeks and began establishing farms, trade routes, cotton plantations and water-powered mills for sawing timber or grinding wheat and corn.

In 1886, the river town of West Point flooded for the first time. The Chattahoochee River waters crested at 26 feet, washing out the bridge which spanned it and severely damaging most houses and businesses. In December 1919, the river rose to over 29 feet, producing the town's most devastating flood; and in February 1961, it crested at 24 feet, killing one person, covering the entire downtown area and causing one million dollars in damage. But still the people of West Point rebuilt in the river's floodplain, and in 1962 Congress authorized West Point Lake and Dam.

West Point Lake, 60 miles south of Atlanta's I-285 perimeter, provides a stark and fascinating contrast to its U.S. Army Corps

"Whiskey is for drinking, water is for fighting."

—Mark Twain

of Engineers sister lake, Lake Lanier, 30 miles north of the Atlanta perimeter. West Point Lake extends 35 miles along the Chattahoochee and has a shoreline of more than 500 miles. Lanier extends 44 miles up the Chattahoochee and 19 miles up the Chestatee, and has a shoreline of approximately 540 miles, depending on the pool level. Lanier has 10 large, lively marinas; West Point has two lazy ones. While on a busy summer weekend thousands of pleasure boats navigate Lanier, only a fraction of that crisscross West Point Lake. Many of West Point Lake's day use parks, particularly those on the northern end of the lake, have a forlorn, abandoned appearance while their counterparts on Lanier are beehives of activity. West Point Lake fishing is good–exceptional really–although serious sport fishermen who love to fish the lake will tell you quickly, and emphatically, that they do not eat the fish they catch. The geography is scenic. A strictly enforced 100-yard setback for residential development keeps the landscape uncluttered. It is located near Callaway Gardens, a beautiful and popular resort. In addition to the Chattahoochee, scenic rocky streams like Wehadkee Creek feed the lake.

Ironically, West Point Lake is the first project in the Corps of Engineers South Atlantic Division to have recreation considered as a prime benefit along with the generation of electricity and flood control. Because of this and because of West Point's proximity to three major metropolitan areas–Atlanta, LaGrange and Columbus–the project was identified by the Corps of Engineers as a recreation demonstration project.

It's hard not to blame the lake's high pollution levels–and thus the city of Atlanta–as the reason that West Point Lake has not achieved the level of popularity envisioned for it by the Corps of Engineers. Who really wants to sail or ski on a settling pond for metro Atlanta's development and often untreated sewage? Phosphorus levels in the lake have improved, diminishing the problem of excessive algae growth, and sewage plant upgrades for Atlanta facilities appear to be underway.

PARKS AND RECREATION

West Point Lake was the first Corps of Engineers lake in the

South Atlantic Division to have had recreation in mind when it was planned. Lake campgrounds and day use areas, therefore, offer many recreation facilities not normally found at Corps lakes. This includes ball fields, basketball and tennis courts, amphitheaters and fish attractors placed under the fishing piers, which are accessible to the handicapped. The Corps operates and maintains seven campgrounds and 26 day use facilities. At least one campground stays open year-round. The other facilities usually open in March or April and close sometime in September or October. Campgrounds are unlocked from 7am-10pm. Several recreational areas have established user fees which are used to maintain and operate the parks. Present fees include $2 per day for use of a boat launching ramp and $1 per person per day for use of swimming beaches, with no more than $3 per car. Children under 12 are free. Contact the Resource Manager's Office concerning current fees, campground openings and to obtain a map on campground locations and facilities. The Resource Manager's Office is worth a visit to see several interesting exhibits. One called "Life Along the Chattahoochee" illustrates the lifestyle of the Creek Native Americans who inhabited the riverbanks in the 17th and 18th centuries. Another depicts 19th century attempts at navigation and has photos of flood damage from the turn-of-the-century. A multi-paneled interactive display demonstrates power generation from the dam. Visitors can respond in the role of the Water Resource Manager to crisis situations. *More Information:* West Point Lake, Resource Management Office, 500 Resource Management Drive, West Point, GA 31833-9517; 706/645-2937.

Other parks on the shores of West Point Lake are operated either privately or by county or municipal park authorities. Most are located on the Corps of Engineers lake map.

The following campgrounds and parks are listed clockwise around the lake, beginning with Snake Creek Park, the northern most facility on the east side of the lake.

Snake Creek Park –This Corps park is located just below Franklin on the east side of the Chattahoochee where it converges with Snake Creek. *Facilities:* Boat ramp, picnic grounds, picnic shelters, restrooms, drinking water. *Directions:* From Franklin, take South River Road south and follow the signs.

Rivers Shape the Earth

Running water is part of the Earth's hydrologic system and is the most important agent of erosion. Stream valleys are the most abundant and widespread landforms on the continents.

Ken Hamblin, "River Systems," Earth's Dynamic Systems

RINGER CAMPGROUND AND DAY USE PARK –This campground is located right above Fish Creek. It is the only Corps campground at West Point Lake that is free. The area is open year-round, but it is primitive camping with no facilities. *Facilities:* Primitive campsites, boat ramp, picnic grounds, restrooms, drinking water, playground. A 0.5-mile nature trail allows good views of the lake and rock outcroppings. *Directions:* From LaGrange, take US 27 north about 5 miles and follow the signs.

CROSSROADS PARK –The Troup County Engineering Department maintains this boat ramp located on the upper northern portion of the lake across from the West Point Lake Management Area. *Facilities:* Boat ramp. *Directions:* From LaGrange, take GA 219 north to Wares Cross Road. Turn right and go about 1 mile. Park entrance is on left.

GEORGIA PARK –This boat ramp is located on the northern portion of the lake on the main river channel. *Facilities:* Boat ramp, portable restrooms, hand-pumped water. *Directions:* From LaGrange, take GA 219 north and follow the signs.

YELLOWJACKET CREEK RECREATION AREA –This is the busiest Corps recreation area on West Point Lake. It is located on the lower west side of Yellowjacket Creek where it merges into the Chattahoochee River. *Facilities:* Boat ramp, beach, picnic grounds, reservation shelter, restrooms, drinking water, playground, tennis courts. *Fees:* Boat ramp, $2; swimming beach, $1 per person but no more than $3 per car. Under 12, free. *Directions:* About 2 miles north of downtown LaGrange. From LaGrange, take Cameron Mill Road north and follow the signs.

SUNNY POINT PARK –This day use area is located within the city limits of LaGrange on the west side of Yellowjacket Creek. *Facilities:* Boat ramp, picnic grounds, picnic shelters, restrooms, drinking water. *Directions:* From LaGrange, take GA 219 north and follow the signs.

CLARK DAY USE PARK –This park is on the upper west shore of Yellowjacket Creek. *Facilities:* Boat ramp, picnic grounds, restrooms, drinking water. *Directions:* From LaGrange, take US 27 north and follow the signs.

HALFMOON CREEK PARK –This park is located on the east side of the lake on Halfmoon and lower Yellowjacket creeks. *Facilities:* Picnic grounds, restrooms. *Directions:* From

LaGrange, take Cameron Mill Road north and follow the signs.

3 CREEKS CAMPGROUND –This privately-owned campground, located on the east side of the lake, has access to the lake and is also just a 0.25 mile from McGee Bridge Park. *Facilities:* Campsites with electricity, water, sewer and TV hookups; primitive campsites; stocked catfish pond; boat storage; bathhouses; laundry. *Days/Hrs.:* Daily, year-round, 24 hrs. *Directions:* From LaGrange, take GA 109 west to Old Roanoke Road. Turn right and follow signs. *More Information:* 3 Creeks Campground, 305 Old Roanoke Road, LaGrange, GA 30240; 706/884-0899 or 706/884-5041.

McGEE BRIDGE PARK –Named after the Old McGee Bridge which once spanned the river here, this day use area is located on the east side of the river next to Perch Creek. This is one of three parks which has a barrier-free fishing pier. *Facilities:* Fishing pier, boat ramp, picnic grounds, picnic shelters, handicap facilities, restrooms, drinking water. A 0.2-mile walking trail here is especially designed for disabled persons. *Directions:* From LaGrange, take GA 109 west for 2 miles. Go right on Vernon Ferry Road and follow the signs.

PYNE ROAD PARK –This park and campground is operated by Troup County Parks and Recreation. It is located on the east side of the lake above Wilson Creek. *Facilities:* 24 hookups with electricity and water, 10 primitive sites, boat ramp, picnic grounds, restrooms, showerhouse, drinking water, ball field, dump station. *Fees:* Hookups, $10 per night; primitive, $8 per night. *Days/Hrs.:* Mar.-Nov. *Directions:* From LaGrange, take GA 109 west for 3 miles. The park is before the bridge. *More Information:* Troup County Parks and Recreation, 706/884-1414.

GLASS BRIDGE PARK –Glass Bridge is located on the east side of the lake where Rainbow Creek feeds into the Chattahoochee. *Facilities:* Boat ramp, picnic grounds, picnic shelters, restrooms, drinking water. *Fees:* Boat ramp, $2. *Directions:* From LaGrange, take US 29 south to Upper Glass Bridge Road. Turn right and follow the signs.

EARL COOK RECREATION AREA –This recreation area is located on the east side of the lake near Rainbow Creek. *Facilities:* Boat ramp, beach, bath change house, picnic grounds, picnic

WATER RELIGION:
CHRISTIANITY

Soon after Christianity began, the Jews took up the practice of baptizing converts a week after their circumcision. To erase sin, John the Baptist immersed followers far out in the desert in the Jordan River, a radical change from the ritual water of purified pools used by most Jews at the time. After his baptism by John in the Jordan River, Jesus began his life of preaching.

shelters, reservation shelters, handicap facilities, restrooms, drinking water, playground, tennis, basketball, softball. A 0.4-mile nature trail winds around the lake. *Fees:* Boat ramp, $2; swimming beach, $1 per person but no more than $3 per car. Under 12, free. *Directions:* From West Point, take US 29 north to Lower Glass Bridge Road. Turn left and follow the signs.

LONG CANE PARK –This is a nice, large well-shaded park which lies on the east side of the lake on Maple Creek. Picnic tables line the wooded banks of the creek. This park's 2-mile hiking trail is one of the longest on the lake. *Facilities:* Boat ramp, picnic grounds, picnic shelters, reservation shelter, restrooms, drinking water, a 2.1-mile hiking trail. *Directions:* From West Point, take US 29 north and follow the signs.

R. SHAEFER HEARD CAMPGROUND –This campground on the southeast side of the lake near the dam is the only campground with electricity and water that stays open year-round. On a nice February weekend there were quite a few RVs, inhabited by professional campers, who camp year-round, moving from one campground to the next and putting out mailboxes and yard decorations—Smokey the Bear or George and Martha Washington holding American flags. During the summer, rangers host nature programs on Saturday evenings in the amphitheater. *Facilities:* 117 campsites with water and electricity hookups, boat ramp, bathhouses, drinking water, playground, tennis, basketball, softball, dump station, amphitheater. *Directions:* From West Point, take US 29 north about 3 miles. Turn left on West Point Dam Road. Entrance is on the right. More Information: R. Shaefer Heard Campground, 706/645-2404.

R. SHAEFER HEARD DAY USE AREA –This day use facility is located on the extreme southeast side of the lake near the dam. *Facilities:* Boat ramp, picnic grounds, picnic shelters, restrooms, drinking water, playground, tennis, basketball, softball. There is a 0.7-mile nature trail with playground and benches along the way. *Fees:* Boat ramp, $2. *Directions:* From West Point, take US 29 north about 3 miles. Turn left on West Point Dam Road. Entrance is on the right.

EAGLE VIEW PARK –This park lies between the West Point Dam and the Resource Management Office. Due to its proximity to the dam, there is no boat ramp; but there are picnic shelters which can be reserved. *Facilities:* Picnic shelters, grills, playground, restrooms, drinking water. *Directions:* From West Point, take US 29 north about 3 miles. Turn left on West Point Dam Road. Go about 1.5 miles. Entrance is on the right.

HARDLEY CREEK PARK –This recreation area is located on the west side of the Chattahoochee River right below West Point Dam. The Creek Indians settled in this area partially because the riverbed was shallow here and filled with rocks, making it easy to cross. Nicely wooded picnic areas line the river. There is no boat ramp, but there is a barrier-free fishing pier as well as a fishing pond for children and handicapped fishermen. The Powerhouse Visitor Center is also located here. *Facilities:* Fishing pier, preteen fishing pond, picnic grounds, picnic shelters, reservation shelter, handicap facilities, restrooms, drinking water, playground, tennis, basketball, softball. A 0.9-mile walking trail winds through the area with nice views of the river. *Directions:* From West Point, take State Line Road (CR 212) north about 2 miles. Entrance is on the right.

WEST OVERLOOK –This area located on the lower southwest section of the lake is for scenic viewing only of the dam and lake. *Facilities:* Overlook shelter. *Directions:* From West Point, take State Line Road (CR 212) north and follow the signs.

ANDERSON PARK –This park is directly across from West Overlook on the southwest side of the lake. There is a good, unofficial swimming cove here. *Facilities:* Boat ramp, courtesy dock for loading and unloading, picnic grounds, picnic shelters, restrooms, drinking water, playground. *Fees:* Boat ramp, $2. *Directions:* From West Point, take State Line Road (CR 212) north about 3 miles. Entrance is on the right.

PINE COVE SHOALS –This privately-owned campground is located on the west side of the lake next to West Point Landing Marina. *Facilities:* 87 campsites with combinations of electricity, water and sewer hookups; primitive campsites; bathhouses; laundry; clubhouse with store and cafe; pool; drinking water; telephones; playground; basketball; softball; shuffleboard; volleyball. *Days/Hrs.:* Daily, year-round; 24-hr security; office open 9am-10pm. *Directions:* From West Point, take State Line Road (CR 212) north about 4 miles. Entrance is on right. *More*

West Point Dam

West Point Dam rises about 97 feet above the existing riverbed. The concrete dam, with its two connecting earth embankments, is 7,250 feet long. The concrete structure includes the non-overflow section, the intake-powerhouse and the spillway. The spillway section has six tainter gates, each 50 feet wide and 41 feet high between 10-foot thick concrete piers supported on the overflow section. The project was designed to permit construction of a navigation lock through the portion of the main earth dam, lying west of the powerhouse switchyard on the Alabama side, should such an improvement ever be warranted.

Congress authorized the project in 1962 for flood control, hydroelectric power, navigation, fish and wildlife development and general recreation. It was the first U.S. Army Corps of Engineers project in the Southeast to be constructed with recreation as one of the prime benefits. As with all dams, turbulent water is present in areas immediately above and below the dam. Be aware of posted signs and safety rules; and when recreating downstream of the dam, be prepared to leave the area immediately when the warning horn sounds and water is released. *Directions:* From West Point, take US 29 north about 3 miles. Turn left on West Point Dam Road. Go about 1.5 miles. Dam is on the right.

Information: Pine Cove Shoals, 5006 County Road 212, Lanett, AL 36863; 334/499-2131.

AMITY CAMPGROUND –This large Corps campground is located in the area between Alligator and Indian creeks on the west side of the lake. It is easy to bring a boat around to a campsite here and anchor it. This campground has the best campsite fishing at West Point. Get a site at the far point of the peninsula, under the shady trees. Kids can bring their bikes and pedal to the playground. *Facilities:* Campsites with electricity and water hookups, primitive campsites, boat ramp, bathhouses, drinking water, playground, tennis, basketball, softball, dump station, amphitheater. Two hiking and nature trails and one interpretive trail wind through the campground. The interpretive trail connects with the Alligator Creek trail for another 0.8-mile hike. *Directions:* From West Point, take State Line Road. (CR 212) north about 4 miles. Entrance is on right. *More Information:* Amity Campground, 334/499-2404.

ALLIGATOR CREEK PARK –This day use area is located on the west side of the lake on Alligator Creek. This is a favorite place for the blue herons that frequent the lake. *Facilities:* Boat ramp, picnic grounds, restrooms. A 0.8-mile hiking trail connects with the interpretive trail in Amity Campground for a hike through some nice environments. *Directions:* From West Point, take State Line Road (CR 212) north to CR 222. Turn right and go 1 mile. Entrance is on the right.

ROCKY POINT RECREATION AREA –Rocky Point is located on the west side of the lake where Alligator, Veasey, Stroud and Wehadkee creeks merge into the river. This is one of just three Corps day use facilities on West Point Lake with a barrier-free fishing pier. There is a nice, sandy beach here and a big wading pool. This is a popular place for church picnics and family reunions. *Facilities:* Fishing pier, boat ramp, beach, bath change house, picnic grounds, picnic shelters, reservation shelter, handicap facilities, restrooms, drinking water, playground, tennis, basketball, softball. The Rocky Point trail system consists of two trails: a 0.5-mile hiking trail and a 0.5-mile nature trail designed for disabled persons. *Fees:* Boat ramp, $2; swimming beach, $1 per person but no more than $3 per car. Under 12, free. *Directions:* From West Point, take State Line Road (CR

212) north to CR 222. Turn right and follow the signs.

VEASEY CREEK PARK –This park is located on the west side of the lake on the south banks of Veasey Creek. *Facilities:* Boat ramp, picnic grounds, picnic shelters, reservation shelter, restrooms, drinking water. *Directions:* From West Point, take State Line Road (CR 212) north to CR 222. Turn left and follow the signs.

STATELINE CAMPGROUND –Straddling the Georgia-Alabama border, this campground sits on the west side of the lake on a finger of land between Stroud and Wehadkee creeks. *Facilities:* Campsites with electricity and water hookups, primitive campsites, boat ramp, beach, bathhouses, drinking water, playground, tennis, dump station. There are two separate hiking and nature trails here totaling 1 mile. *Directions:* From LaGrange, take GA 109 west about 7 miles. Turn left on Old State Line Road which dead ends into the park. *More Information:* Stateline Campground, 706/882-5439.

DEWBERRY PARK –Located on the west side of Wehadkee Creek, this boat ramp was crowded with boat trailers on a February weekend. One fisherman indicated it was because of the good crappie fishing on Wehadkee and Cainey creeks. *Facilities:* Boat ramp, restrooms. *Directions:* From LaGrange, take GA 109 west about 7 miles. Turn left on Old State Line Road. Entrance is on the left.

EVANSVILLE PARK –This park is located on the upper west side of Wehadkee Creek. *Facilities:* Boat ramp, picnic grounds, restrooms, drinking water. *Directions:* From LaGrange, take GA 109 west about 7 miles. Turn right on Old State Line Road. Go about 1 mile. Entrance is on the right.

WEHADKEE PARK –This day use facility on Wehadkee Creek is just a boat ramp and a parking lot, but it is crowded on a winter day with crappie fishermen. *Facilities:* Boat ramp, restrooms. *Directions:* From LaGrange, take GA 109 west about 6 miles. Entrance is on the left.

HOLIDAY CAMPGROUND –This campground sits at the confluence of the river's main channel and Wehadkee Creek. *Facilities:* Campsites with electricity and water hookups, primitive campsites, group camping, boat ramp, bathhouses, drinking water, playground, tennis, basketball, softball, dump sta-

STRIPER

"The Chattahoochee is a microcosm of all other river systems. They have the same stories as far as watershed is concerned, only no one has accumulated them yet."

—Howard Marshall, EPA, Water Quality Branch, Atlanta

Boating Safety Guidelines

These guidelines are from The American Whitewater Affiliation's safety code.

A. Be a competent swimmer with ability to handle yourself underwater.

B. Wear a life jacket.

C. Keep you craft under control. Control must be good enough at all times to stop or reach shore before you reach any danger. Do not enter a rapid unless you are reasonably sure you can safely navigate it or swim the entire rapid in the event of capsize.

D. Be aware of river hazards and avoid them. Following are the most frequent killers.

1. High water. The river's power and danger, and the difficulty of rescue, increase tremendously as the flow rate increases. It is often misleading to judge river level at the put-in. Look at a narrow, critical passage. Could a rise in the water level from sun on a snow pack, rain, or a dam release occur on you trip?

2. Cold. Cold quickly robs your strength, along with your will and ability to save yourself. Dress to protect yourself from cold water and weather extremes. When the water temperature is less than 50 degrees, a diver's wet suit is essential for safety in event of an upset. Next best is wool clothing under a windproof outer garment such as a splashproof nylon shell; also carry matches and a complete change of clothes in a waterproof package. If, after prolonged exposure, a person experiences uncontrollable shaking or difficulty talking and moving, warm them immediately by any means available.

3. Strainers. Brush, fallen trees, bridge pilings or anything else that allows river current to sweep through but pins boat

tion, amphitheater. There are a total of 3 hiking and nature trails totaling 1.9 miles that wind through the campground. *Directions:* From LaGrange, take GA 109 west about 4.5 miles. Turn left on Thompson Road which dead ends into the campground and follow the signs. *More Information:* Holiday Campground, 706/884-6818.

WHITETAIL RIDGE CAMPGROUND –This campground is located on the west side of the main channel of the river. *Facilities:* Campsites with electric and water hookups, boat ramp, bathhouses, drinking water, playground, dump station. A 0.9-mile nature trail winds around a duck pond. *Directions:* From LaGrange, take GA 109 west about 4.5 miles. Turn left on Thompson Road. Entrance is on the left. *More Information:* Whitetail Ridge Campground, 706/884-8972.

HORACE KING PARK –This park is named after the ex-slave who was a master bridge builder in the Chattahoochee Valley. The park lies directly below the GA 109 bridge on the west side of the Chattahoochee River. *Facilities:* Boat ramp, picnic grounds, picnic shelters, restrooms, drinking water. *Fees:* Boat ramp, $2. *Directions:* From LaGrange, take GA 109 west about 4 miles. Cross the bridge. Entrance is on the left.

INDIAN SPRINGS GROUP CAMPING AREA –This campground, on the west side of the lake adjacent to the GA 109 Bridge, has the basics only. The nearest boat ramp is across the road at Horace King Park. *Facilities:* Primitive camping, group camping, drinking water. *Directions:* From LaGrange, take GA 109 west about 4 miles. Entrance on right. *More Information:* Indian Springs Group Camping Area, 706/884-8972.

WHITEWATER PARK –This facility is located where Whitewater and Turkey creeks converge on the west side of the lake. *Facilities:* Boat ramp, restrooms, drinking water. *Directions:* From Glenn, take Antioch Road south to Neely Road. Turn right and follow the signs.

LIBERTY HILL –This boat ramp is located on the west side of the Chattahoochee north of where the river converges with Yellowjacket Creek. *Facilities:* Boat ramp, restrooms, drinking water. *Directions:* From Glenn, take Antioch Road south to Liberty Hill Road. Turn left and follow the signs.

WEST POINT LAKE MANAGEMENT AREA –This wildlife management area consists of nearly 10,000 acres and is located at the upper end of the lake. It provides a habitat for many kinds of game and non-game wildlife, including deer, turkey, dove, quail, wood ducks and other waterfowl, and is a bald eagle nesting area. It is operated by the Game and Fish Division of the Georgia Department of Natural Resources. Hunters with a Georgia Wildlife Management Area stamp can hunt seasonally and participate in special quota hunts. *More Information:* Heard County Commissioner Office, 706/675-3821.

BRUSH CREEK CAMPGROUND –This Heard County park is near the town of Franklin on the upper west end of the lake. *Facilities:* Campsites, boat ramp, picnic grounds, restrooms, bathhouses, drinking water, playground, ball field, hiking trail, dump station. *Fees:* User fees. *Directions:* From Franklin, take Bevis Road south and follow signs. *More Information:* Heard County Parks and Recreation, 706/675-3778. Camp reservations, 706/675-CAMP.

RIVERSIDE PARK –This park in the middle of Franklin is operated by Heard County Parks and Recreation. *Facilities:* Boat ramp, picnic grounds, restrooms, ball field, hiking trails. *Days/Hrs.:* Daily. *Directions:* On US 27/GA 100 in Franklin on south side of bridge over river. *More Information:* Heard County Parks and Recreation, 706/675-3778.

MARINAS

HIGHLAND MARINA AND RESORT –This 200-acre marina is located where Yellowjacket Creek merges with the Chattahoochee. Highland offers repair services as well as boat sales and rentals. *Facilities:* Over 300 wet slips; dry storage, covered and uncovered; fuel docks; ship store with fishing tackle and bait, snacks, recreational supplies; boat rentals; campsites with electricity and water; 33 fully-equipped 1-and-3 bedroom cottages with central heat and air, color TV, phone, decks with grill and private boat docks available; bass boats, pontoons for rent. *Restaurant:* The Waterfront Restaurant concentrates on serving breakfast and lunch to hungry boaters and fishermen. Breakfast buffets are popular on the weekends. Depending on the weather and the activity on the lake, the restaurant opens daily

and boater against the obstacle. Water pressure on things trapped this way is overwhelming, and there may be little or no white water to warn of danger.

4. Weirs, reversals and souse holes. Water drops over an obstacle, then curls back on itself in a stationary wave, as is often seen at weirs and dams. The surface water is actually going upstream, and this action will trap any floating object between the drop and the wave. Once trapped, a swimmer's only hope is to dive below the surface where current is flowing downstream or to try to swim out the end of the wave.

E. Boating alone is not recommended–the preferred minimum is three craft.

F. Have a frank knowledge of your boating ability and don't attempt waters beyond it.

G. Be in good physical condition consistent with the difficulties that may be expected.

H. Be practiced in escape from an overturned craft, in self-rescue, and in artificial respiration. Know first aid.

I. The Eskimo roll should be mastered by kayakers and canoeists planning to run large rivers or rivers with continuous rapids where a swimmer would have trouble reaching shore.

J. Wear a crash helmet where an upset is likely. This is essential in a kayak or covered canoe.

K. Be suitably equipped. Wear shoes that will protect your feet during a bad swim or a walk for help, yet will not interfere with swimming (tennis shoes recommended). Carry a knife and waterproof matches. If you need eyeglasses, tie them on and carry a spare pair. Do not wear bulky clothing that will interfere with your swimming when waterlogged.

Skipper's Terms

Distinguishing between port (left) and starboard (right) can be confusing for new boaters. Remember that "port" and "left" match up as four-letter words, while "right" and "starboard" have more letters. Port and starboard colors follow the same rule: port is red (short); starboard is green (longer). Port, left and red are all short words. Starboard, right and green are longer words.

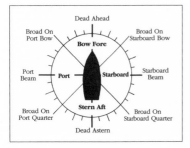

in March until October. Hours vary seasonally, but generally are from 6am-5pm. *Maintenance/Repair:* On-site repair facility with a Master Technician on duty 6 days a week. Several fishing guides are based out of Highland Marina. *Days/Hrs.:* Spring-summer, 6:30am-8pm; winter hours vary. *Directions:* From LaGrange, take GA 109 west and follow the signs. *More Information:* Highland Marina, 1000 Seminole Road, LaGrange, GA 30240; 706/882-3437. Waterfront Restaurant, 706/885-0031.

WEST POINT LANDING MARINA –This family-oriented marina is located on the lower west side of the lake. Home to many of the sailboats docked at West Point Lake, it is the only marina located on the large mass of water between West Point Dam and the GA 109 Bridge. The West Point Sailing Club is based out of West Point Landing. *Facilities:* 140 slips, covered with electricity and water, uncovered with water; storage for trailers only; fuel docks; ship store with tackle, live bait, boating accessories, oil, groceries, ice, cold beverages, fishing licenses; restrooms; campground; 2-bedroom waterfront cabins with fully-equipped kitchens, large decks; 5-bedroom house, fully furnished and equipped. *Restaurant:* This small dockside grill is connected to the ship store. Menu items include pancakes, eggs, egg muffins, burgers, hot dogs, onion rings, cheese sticks and smoked turkey sandwiches. The grill cooks on demand daily from 6am-11pm. *Maintenance/Repair:* No repair done on premises but will recommend services. *Days/Hrs.:* Daily, 9am-5pm. *Directions:* From West Point, take State Line Road (CR 212) north and follow the signs. *More Information:* West Point Landing Marina, 1133 County Road 294, Lanett, AL 36863; 334/644-3881. West Point Lake Sailing Club, Commodore Mike Dooley; 770/251-6463.

SIGNIFICANT URBAN EXPERIENCES

LAGRANGE –After the Creek Indians sold their land in this area to the U.S. government in 1825, Troup was one of five counties created from property located between the Chattahoochee and Flint rivers. LaGrange was designated the site of the county seat and incorporated on December 16, 1828. The town was named after the country estate of French nobleman General Marquis de LaFayette. The general was a member of General George Washington's staff and fought for American freedom in the Revolutionary War. His estate was known as the Chateau de LaGrange.

Roads and bridges were planned and laid out to make it easy for persons traveling to the new county seat; and by 1830, LaGrange had a population of nearly 1,500 persons, or one-fourth of the county's total. The first industries in the area were the grist, flour and saw mills, and later, the cotton and textile mills which flourished along the tributaries of the Chattahoochee.

La Grange, like other southern towns, suffered the effects of the Civil War. Much of the town was burned and trans-portation facilities were destroyed. In the 1880s, LaGrange businessmen saw the advantage of industrializing. The result of this was textile mills that would make LaGrange a leading industrial center in the state.

Some interesting places to see in LaGrange include:

LaFayette Square–A bronze statue, made in LePuy, France, from a mold of the original sculpted by Ernst Eugene Hyolle, of General LaFayette stands in the center of the square.

Gallery on the Square–Former slave and master covered bridge builder, Horace King, built this structure around 1870. The interior has a pressed tin ceiling.

Chattahoochee Valley Art Museum–This 1892 Victorian building was originally constructed as the Troup County Jail. Today it houses a contemporary art gallery, offices and class-rooms where changing exhibits showcase paintings, sculpture, crafts, photography and prints by the Southeast's best artists. *Days/Hrs:* Mon.-Fri., 9am-5pm; Sat., 11am-5pm. *Fees:* Free admission to all exhibits and many other programs and lec-tures. *More Information:* 706/882-3267.

LaGrange College–Opened in 1831 as the LaGrange Female Academy, the college is the oldest non-tax supported institu-tion of higher education in Georgia.

Bellevue–Built in 1854-55, this Greek Revival mansion was the home of United States Senator Benjamin Harvey Hill. *Days/Hrs:* Tues.-Sat., 10am-12pm and 2pm-5pm. *More Information:* 706/884-1832.

www.chattahoochee.org

 We welcome your comments, suggestions, recommendations and input regarding this book and the river, via the Internet at the Riverkeeper's website: www.chattahoochee.org.

You can also access the website for additional information regarding the Chattahoochee and the many issues that affect the river.

ALL IS BORN OF WATER; ALL IS SUSTAINED BY WATER.

Bellevue, home of United States Senator Benjamin Harvey Hill (1823-1882), was built in 1854-55 and typifies the Greek Revival architecture popular in the Old South. Jefferson Davis and other Confederate celebrities were frequent guests here. At the urging of Senator Hill, lawyer, one of Georgia's foremost orators and champion of the South during Reconstruction days, President Hayes withdrew Union occupa-tion troops. In 1942 Bellevue was presented to the LaGrange Women's Club by the Fuller E. Callaway Foundation. It is now main-tained by the Club.

—Historical marker located on Broad Street at Ben Hill Street, LaGrange, Georgia.

Spring Spawning Run on West Point Lake

"There's a flat I can show you five minutes from here that you and I could be sittin' in the boat when the sun hits the trees and from then 'til dark we may put a hundred fish in the boat. Hybrids, white bass, stripers, largemouths, all mixed together. You catch a different one on every cast. They herd the shad onto these flats. When they go to doin' it, there may be fifteen boats sittin' there and every boat is catchin' 'em just as fast as you do. As soon as it gets dark, they shut off. I've seen a place three acres wide that looks like piranhas working in the water. And you sittin' in the middle of it catchin' fish on every cast. If you miss one, BOOM!, just keep crankin', another one will hit it. I got a four-year-old grandson and me and him and my son was in the boat up here on this flat last year; and I hung a hybrid, my son hung one off the back of the boat and all at once my little four-year-old grandson standin' in the middle hollerin', 'I got one too.' "

Pete Cavender

Confederate Cemetery–LaGrange was the site of many hospitals during the Civil War and over 300 soldiers from every state in the Confederacy are buried here. Outside the fence are the graves of former slave and master bridge builder Horace King and his son.

Callaway Memorial Tower–This tower was built in 1929 as a tribute to textile magnate Fuller E. Callaway, Sr., founder of the Callaway Mills. Callaway Mills employees erected the tower. It was patterned after the Campanile of St. Mark's Square in Venice, Italy.

FISHING

The most sought after fish on West Point Lake are largemouth bass, hybrid striped bass, striped bass, white bass and crappie. Special rules: West Point Lake has a 16-inch limit, approximately three pounds, on large mouth bass. They have to be 16 inches to legally keep.

BEST ADVICE – Each lake and every section of the river has its own particular bank topography, underwater structure, stream currents and fish population. Professional guides know all the peculiarities of their lake. The most experienced fishermen find that one or two days of guide fees is a good investment before launching out on their own. Inexperienced fishermen or families looking for an enjoyable day's outing will increase their pleasure ten-fold by taking advantage of the experience of a professional guide. The best guides not only make sure their customers catch fish, but provide insights into the fishing habits of different species, lake ecology, weather lore and other aspects that enhance the fishing experience. When booking a fishing guide, always find out who is responsible for all tackle (rods, reels, lures), boats, gasoline, live bait, life jackets, lunch, drinks, snacks, ice and rain gear. Understand exactly what is included in the guide fees.

GUIDES –For the occasional fisherman or the individual introducing his family to fishing, West Point Lake provides the most rewarding fishing experience on the Chattahoochee. Guide Tommy Mike takes out parties of up to 10 fishermen and comes back with fish, regardless of weather or time of year.

Mike is a native of LaGrange and hunted and fished the area's hills and valleys before they were flooded by impoundment in 1975. He has a master's degree in fisheries biology from Auburn University and is one of the most respected fishing pros in Georgia. He seems to know the address and eating habits of every fish in West Point Lake—large mouth bass, crappie, stripers, spotted bass and white bass. He says, "I like to think that a fishing trip is more than just fishing. I hope that it is a learning experience, too. During the course of a day, I try to teach clients something about the lake's geography, map reading, seasonal fishing patterns, fishing equipment and tackle. Plus, we have a good time."

There is no better way to introduce a child to the joy of fishing than with Tommy Mike on West Point Lake. One caution: be sure when you contract with Mike that he will personally guide the trip. He sometimes subcontracts his trips to other guides on the lake who are not nearly as qualified as he. He is the man you want to fish with. Tommy Mike Guide Service, 4006 White Oak Lane, LaGrange, Georgia 30240; 706/882-8187 or 800/829-MIKE.

Another fishing guide respected and recommended by his peers is Ron Savage. Savage is an expert on wide mouth bass fishing and is known to be the artificial lure guru of West Point Lake. He is the lake's only full-time artificial lure fishing guide. Ron Savage, P.O. Box 2602, LaGrange, GA 30241; 706/884-6232.

BEST BOOKS AND MAPS –Fishing Hot Spots' "West Point Lake" fishing map is the best fishing resource for the lake. It locates 46 good fishing spots with helpful tips on how to fish each one. For example: "Area 38. The Highway 27 Bridge over Yellowjacket Creek is a good place to fish for crappie on summer nights. Use lights or lanterns to attract baitfish and crappie. Small Minnows or jig/minnows combos are deadly presentations." "Area 9. During winter, largemouth bass anglers should work the old mouth of Wehadkee Creek with a Texas-rigged worm or jig n' pig combo. Summer hybrids roam the area and respond to live bait." The map also has a section on special features and characteristics of the lake, basic fishing tips and locations of all boat ramps, buoys, fish attractors, marinas, access

The Bass, the Heron and the Hawk

"One day I was up on the Chattahoochee River fishing on an underwater hump, and we were catching one largemouth bass after another. Of course, we like to catch and release everything, especially largemouths. But one fish got hooked a little too deep and when we turned him loose he floated off and died. There was a blue heron sitting about 200 yards away on a red clay point. A little breeze was blowing, and the ripple on the water was slowly drifting this largemouth bass toward that blue heron. The fish was so large the heron wasn't strong enough to go out in the water, pick him up and carry him back, so he just sat on the point and watched and waited. The fish got closer and closer. When he got within a few yards, all of a sudden out of nowhere, a giant American bald eagle, so big he blocked the sun, came right down in front of the blue heron and grabbed that fish in one talon and flew off like he didn't have anything in his claw. You should have heard that old blue heron squawk."

Tommy Mike, West Point Lake Fishing Guide

What is a Thermocline?

Just ask a fisherman about a thermocline. Its location determines the location and health of his quarry. In the winter, lack of heat and sunlight results in a constant temperature in a lake. In the summer, however, the water often divides or stratifies into different horizontal layers. On top is the warm, flowing epilimnion. On the bottom is the cool, stagnant hypolimnion. In the middle is a thin layer in which the greatest temperature changes occur, the thermocline.

In late spring, the hypolimnion loses oxygen due to limited mixing with the epilimnion, which receives air from the surface. If the thermocline is relatively deep in the lake, the hypolimnion receives no oxygen from photosynthesis.

Nutrients like nitrogen and phosphorus concentrate in the hypolimnion and occasionally go up to the epilimnion, where they contribute to feeding frenzies by algae known as blooms. The little green organisms proliferate and gorge until they run out of food and die en masse.

Seasonally, blooms happen in the fall when the epilimnion cools and falls below the temperature of the hypolimnion, which then rises, bringing up nutrients to trigger algae blooms. Excess nutrients like phosphorus and nitrogen from human sources, however, can significantly amplify blooms, throwing the seasonal pattern out of whack and in extreme cases leading to massive fish kills.

roads, structures and vegetation. Hot Spot maps are available at outdoor stores and marinas. (To order see page 325.) Tommy Mike served as a consultant for the Hot Spots map and personally selected many of its top fishing locations. A Hot Spots map may be ordered directly from Tommy Mike for $9.50.

Atlantic Mapping's "West Point Lake Map" (1994 Revision) is a large fold-out, waterproof map that shows the lake with 160 fish shelters and structure sites which can be located with a Global Positioning System (GPS) instrument. It also includes topographical features of the lake and surrounding area, access roads, campgrounds, parks, marinas, bait stores, boat ramps and other recreational facilities. Atlantic Mapping maps are available at outdoor stores, marinas, bait and tackle stores. (To order see page 325.)

U.S. Geological Survey 1:24,000 scale topographical maps covering the lake are Franklin, Hillcrest, Hogansville, LaGrange, Abbottsford, Five Points and Lanett. (To order see page 326.)

OTHER SOURCES OF INFORMATION –Pete Cavender, the manager of West Point Landing Marina, is an experienced fisherman who can point out hot spots and mark your map. Also, ask at the numerous bait shop/convenience stores near the boat ramps. Employees usually know where they are "hittin'."

INSIDER TIPS AND HOT SPOTS –West Point Lake's fishing event of the year is the crappie spawning in late winter and early spring. The water temperature warms, and crappie migrate up into the creeks and up on the banks to spawn. The fish are easy to catch. Fishermen in boats as well as on the banks haul in plenty of fish. Use jigs trolled slowly early in the spawning period, then as the fish go further into the spawn use live minnows on a cork floated in the area where the fish are.

Hybrid stripped bass make a strong run up the Chattahoochee River to the shoals above Franklin from mid-march to mid-April. This happens when the water gets around 58 degrees for the white bass and a little warmer for the hybrids and stripers. This can happen in February, but it usually occurs in March. The fish congregate above New River, above Glovers Creek, above the bridge at Franklin and all the way to the shoals where there are plenty of sand bars. Fishermen follow. Pickups and boat trailers fill the single ramp at Franklin, and a hundred boats crowd the river until there's hardly a place for another one. Catches can be a hundred fish a day. This lasts between four and six weeks, depending on the water temperature. To fish, go up river and take any kind of lure that looks like a shad, tie it on a spinning rod, throw it on the bank and reel it back. Use live bait when the fish get farther up the river. Real simple fishing. After a hard rain the river gets muddy and the fishing drops off accordingly, but the water clears quickly. When the river is muddy, some fishermen continue to catch bass using chicken livers on a Carolina rig and letting it lay on the bottom. Note: Do not throw leftover livers in the water. This is a type of nonpoint source pollution.

In summer, fish looking for cooler, oxygenated water and food go very deep in West Point Lake. Find them on humps, underwater roads, bars, ridges, flats and ledges. Also in summer, the white bass, hybrids and stripers are mostly caught on live bait. A deep diving crank bait with a buck tailed jig tied about three feet in front of it works good. Umbrella rigs have proven to be successful on West Point. Guide Tommy Mike's favorite technique is to find the fish, lower shad to the bottom right in front of them, raise it up a little bit and, "catch 'em and catch 'em and catch 'em and have a ball."

West Point Lake fishing is better from Monday through Friday when the Corps of Engineers is generating power through the gates at West Point Dam. The current's movement over humps, bars, ridges and points breaks up schools of shad allowing bass to see individual bait fish rather than a school, like a wolf picking a stray out of a flock. The entire food chain in the lake is operative when the current is flowing. The flowing water brings oxygen down to a deeper level, stimulating fish activity. Call 706/645-2929 for generating times.

The reduction of phosphorous levels in West Point Lake, thanks primarily to a ban on phosphate detergents in metro Atlanta, has increased the width of the thermocline. As a result, fish have gone deeper and deeper in the lake. Many bass fishermen have not yet figured out how to catch the fish in 28 to 32 feet of water. Those who have reap the rewards.

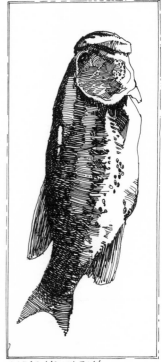

LARGE-MOUTH BASS

Fish Consumption Guidelines

West Point Lake–Carp greater than 12", one meal per week; hybrids greater than 12", one meal per week; catfish greater than 12" but less than 16", one meal per week; catfish greater than 16", one per month, crappie, no restrictions. As a general rule, eat smaller fish to be safe.

Source: Georgia Department of Natural Resources, 1997.

"I'd rather throw the wrong lure in the right place than the right lure in the wrong place. Find the fish. That's the most important thing."

—Tommy Mike, West Point Lake fishing guide

BOATING

CLINCH
KNOT

For a boating tour of the lake, contact fishing guide Tommy Mike. He is not only an expert fisherman, but he is a person with immense knowledge about the ecology, biology and environment of the lake.

Boaters who wish to get an overview of the lake should obtain Fishing Hot Spots' "West Point Lake" fishing map available at the area's marinas and at most large sporting goods stores. (To order see page 325.) This map lists good fishing areas, shows boat access to recreational areas and locates all boat ramps. Another helpful map for the recreational boater is the U.S. Army Corps of Engineers West Point Lake map available from the Resource Management Office, 500 Resource Management Drive, West Point, GA 31833-9517; 706/645-2937.

U.S. Geological Survey 1:24,000 scale topographical maps covering the lake are Franklin, Hillcrest, Hogansville, LaGrange, Abbottsford, Five Points and Lanett. (To order see page 326.)

Section 6
West Point Lake to
Walter F. George

Frank Schnell

"'m convinced that the Chattahoochee was one of the most important trade routes in prehistoric times. One of the most important prestige items in prehistoric times was shell. The large whelk shell found in southern Florida was the most prestigious and most widely traded of all the sea shells. It was the best one for making certain artifacts. The shell gorgets made from whelk shells are found all over the eastern United States.

The best route to get from southern Florida to the interior of the United States was up the Chattahoochee River. Otherwise you gotta' come up the coast of Florida and then make a long detour over to the mouth of the Mississippi and then up again. But if you can just come up the Peninsula of Florida, hit the Apalachicola, come up the Chattahoochee and make a little jump, and you're over on the Tennessee and into the central core of the Mississippian and Woodland centers for the United States.

The Corps of Engineers once asked me how many archeological sites were under their responsibility, and I said there are two sites; there's the Georgia site and the Alabama site. The lower Chattahoochee probably has the largest concentration of archaeological sites in the state of Georgia. There are literally hundreds of archaeological sites all up and down here, with every culture from Paleo Indian times to historic Creek.

The richest land is right below the Fall Line. Water came down the Chattahoochee and hit the Fall Line, immediately expanded into the big bottom lands and dropped its load of soil. So you get natural refertilization of the bottom land. And of course the Creeks, above all, were farmers. So this, in terms of agricultural property, is the most valuable property in the Chattahoochee Valley, right here, below the Fall Line. It extends for about 15 to 20 miles. It's easy to see when you start looking at the important historic Creek towns because there's a huge concentration of them starting here at the Falls and going down. Now you get further downstream and you get pockets of outstanding land and you get very important archaeological and historic sites. At the mouth of almost every one of the major streams there was a mound. Immediately south of the Alabama State Docks was Coweta Town. In the fifteen and sixteen hundreds, places like Coweta Town and Cusseta Town and Apalachicola Town had thousands of inhabitants. How many thousands I'd be afraid to guess. I'm pretty sure that at around 1800 the largest Indian town in the Southeast was Cusseta Town. It may have rivaled Charleston in population.

James Oglethorpe came here to Coweta Town in 1739 to negotiate the peace treaty with the Creek nation. Essentially, that was the treaty that allowed the Colony of Georgia to continue to exist. Indian towns and settlements ranged all the way down to Little Sowokli which probably didn't have a hundred people in it. There was a whole bunch of little farmsteads all scattered down the river with corn fields in between them.

One of the things that badly disrupted the Indians on the Chattahoochee when the English trade got firmly entrenched was that the English were not interested in corn and beans and squash and things like that. They were interested in deer skins and beaver pelts, and that's what they wanted in return for guns and knives and axes. And the Indians very quickly had to readapt back to their old hunting customs. So basically, the English trade was destroying the agricultural economy because the Indians were having to go back into the woods and spend endless hours hunting to trade for the axes, knives and guns that almost instantly became necessities. The English seemed to be primarily interested first in the trade and then actually taking the land for farming... Which is what eventually happened."

Frank Schnell is a historian and archaeologist for the Columbus Museum in Columbus.

THE RIVER

From West Point Dam to Lake Walter F. George, the river no longer meanders westward across the state, but takes a sharp turn to the south, forming the border between Georgia and Alabama on its path to the Gulf of Mexico. Along the first stretch of this section, the river historically thundered over the Fall Line. Dropping more than 300 feet over 38 miles, the river raced over a long series of waterfalls and shoals where the rolling hills of the Piedmont meet the flats of the Coastal Plain. Millions of years ago, the Fall Line marked the edge of the gulf

Steamboats

For over a century, 200 riverboats chugged up and down the 262-mile waterway between the Columbus steamboat wharf and the Gulf of Mexico port of Apalachicola. The first was the *Fanny* in 1828. The last to dock in Columbus was the *George W. Miller* in 1939. Stacked high with cotton bales on the trip down and loaded with groceries, manufactured goods and Apalachicola Bay oysters–kept alive with cornmeal sprinkled in wooden barrels–on the way up, the riverboats stopped at any number of 240 landings or towns along the way. Boiler explosions, fires, changing river currents and sand bars made steamboating on the river dangerous. The sunken remains of some lie hidden in the muddy depths.

Coweta is the name of a Lower Creek town in today's Russell County, Alabama. The name may mean "falls" or "where there were falls" from the falls on the Chattahoochee at present-day Columbus.

—Marion Hemperley, Indian Heritage of Georgia

Coast. In modern times, it marks the end of navigable waters from the gulf.

Mound builders of the Mississippian culture lived in the valley from 1,000 to 1,500 AD, relying in large part on fish from the river to supplement their maize, squash and bean harvest, grown in Chattahoochee River Valley soil made fertile by seasonal floods.

Some of the older peoples include Hitchitees. But the Muskogees, or Creeks, occupied this section of Georgia and Alabama when the Europeans arrived. Creek trails from all over the southeast intersected just below the Fall Line rapids, where sand bars naturally accumulated, offering relatively easy passage across the river. The two largest towns of the Lower Creek nation were on this part of the Chattahoochee: Coweta, the capital of politics and war, on the western bank of the river, just below present-day Phenix City, Alabama, and Cusseta, the peace and religious capital, on the eastern bank where today stands Lawson Air Field at Fort Benning, Georgia.

The Spanish saw the falls along the Chattahoochee as early as 1639 and tried to establish exclusive trade with the Creeks. In 1689 they built a fort at Apalachicola, named for a Creek town, to keep an eye on English traders. Two years later Spanish troops abandoned and destroyed their northernmost outpost in the New World, 17 miles south of present-day Phenix City, to return to Florida because of a threatened French attack.

Naturalist William Bartram, traveling the Eastern continent for an English patron interested in American plant species for his garden, crossed the Chattahoochee at the mouth of Oswichee Creek, a few miles south of Columbus on what is now Fort Benning property. On the eastern bank, he visited the villages of Chehaw and Usseta, now Columbus. On the western bank, some miles downstream, he saw the town of Apalachicola, whose exact location remains a mystery.

The Georgia Legislature established Columbus in 1828 as a trading town. At the head of navigable waters on the Chattahoochee, Columbus was a strategic place from which to send much of the cotton and other goods produced in Georgia and Alabama on their journey down the Apalachicola River to the Gulf of Mexico and beyond. In a Machiavellian sense, the city served another practical purpose for the American settlers, as a buffer against the Creeks, forced by treaty and threats west of the river.

In the 1850s, railroads began to overtake steamboats as the primary means of commercial transportation. But the Chatta-hoochee offered one more benefit which ensured the Columbus area's success as an industrial hub for years: energy. Harnessing the power of the river along the Fall Line, giant saw, grain processing and textile mills sprang up on both banks between Columbus and West Point from the late 1820s until the early 1900s. In the 1830s, Columbus erected the first dam to divert water to its business district. In the 1850s, the city ranked second only to Richmond, Virginia, as an industrial center in the south.

Dams continue to tame the river. Today four span the Chattahoochee in Columbus, with five more north of the city up to West Point. Six of these generate hydroelectric power. Several of the larger ones help control the floods which histor-ically inundated the valley.

The majority of dams are spillways, meaning most of the water flows over their tops; the river channel's flow is not affected greatly. But two of the river plugs, Oliver Dam and Bartletts Ferry Dam, back up the river to create large lakes, bringing fishermen to their waters and home builders to their shores.

Recreational boating and fishing on Lake Harding and Lake Oliver have boosted the economy in recent years. But some local outdoorsmen dream of turning downtown Columbus into a kayaker's paradise. Just downstream of the three most southerly dams in the city are impressive rocks and shoals, reminders of the mighty Coweta Falls which once roared underneath the pent-up waters. Breaching the lowest two, City Mills and Eagle-Phenix Dams, neither of which is in use, would create perhaps the finest urban white-water run in the world. Whether the citizens of Columbus, very proud of their rich history on the river, would approve is another matter.

Langdale To Lake Harding

"We arrived at the banks of the Chata Uche river opposite the Uche town; where, after unloading our horses, the Indians came over to us in large canoes, by means of which, with the cheerful and liberal assistance of the Indians, ferried over the merchandize, and afterwards driving our horses altogether into the river swam them over: the river here is about three or four hundred yards wide, carries fifteen or twenty feet of water and flows down with an active current; the water is clear, cool and salubrious."

—*William Bartram*, Travels

LAKES

Of the nine dams which span the Chattahoochee River from West Point to south Columbus, only three have sizable reservoirs: Lake Harding, the largest, backs up 5,850 acres of surface water behind Bartletts Ferry Dam, 17 miles north of Columbus; Lake Oliver, created by the Oliver Dam in north Columbus, is a distant second at 2,150 surface acres; and Goat Rock Lake, between the two on the river, is third at 1,050 acres. In the warmer months, water and jet skiing and fishing are popular pastimes on the lakes, which can rise or drop a foot or more each day as hydroelectric plants release water downstream. Georgia Power signs above the dams warn boaters of intake currents and open spillways, like the one at Goat Rock. Signs below the dams caution everyone to keep their distance because water releases can cause unpredictable turbulence.

LAKE HARDING –Bartletts Ferry Dam creates the largest and most popular recreation lake, Lake Harding, near Columbus. Its southernmost section being 17 miles north of the city, Lake Harding has a shoreline that spans 156 miles and is 120 feet deep at the concrete dam, built in 1926. Ranch houses intermingled with small public and private marinas or boat ramps line the banks on much of the southern section of the lake, particularly on the Alabama side. There is no bridge crossing the lake. Motorists from the Alabama to the Georgia side must either go south to Columbus or north to US 85. CR 379 does cross the main lake tributary, the backed-up waters of Halawakee Creek in Alabama. Much of the northern shore, particularly on the Georgia side, remains undeveloped, most of it land owned by Georgia Power. During the summer, hordes of jet skiers and anglers bump into each other. Later in the day everyone rubs elbows and mixes drinks on Ski "Island," in the middle of the channel close to the dam. Numerous recreation areas and marinas are scattered around the rim of the lake, including Chattahoochee Valley Park (see page 170) on the Alabama side and Blanton Creek Park (see page 170) on the Georgia side. In the northern outreaches of the lake as the Chattahoochee narrows, several undeveloped islands, part of the Blanton Creek Wildlife Management Area (see page 169),

WATER RELIGION:
BRAZIL

Immersion under streams or waterfalls is a common ritual to symbolize initiation. For example, the Akwe and Chavante of Brazil expose initiates to water for long periods of time to recall when legendary heroes created the world during a flood.

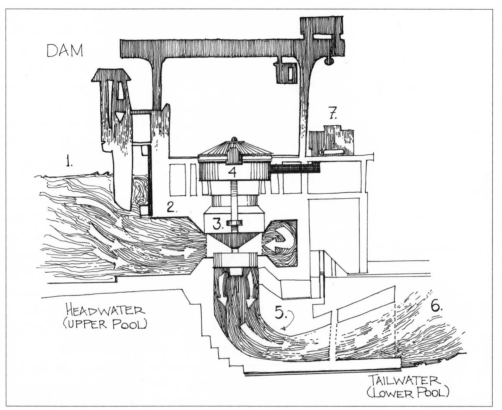

DAM

7.

1.

4.

2.

3.

HEADWATER
(UPPER POOL)

5.

6.

TAILWATER
(LOWER POOL)

How Hydroelectricity Works

The principles used in a modern hydro plant are the same as those used centuries ago. Then, the natural energy of falling or flowing water was harnessed and changed into mechanical energy by paddle wheels, like those seen at old grist mills and textile plants. The water turned the wheels and the wheels turned the machinery.

In the late 1800s, hydro energy was first changed into electrical energy by allowing water to spin turbines connected to electric generators instead of paddle wheels. To meet the evergrowing demand for energy, dams were built to hold and store the enormous amounts of water (called reservoirs) needed to produce thousands of kilowatts of electricity.

In this illustration, you can see how the Chattahoochee Hydro Group uses the natural power of water to generate electricity:

Falling water from the reservoir (1) passes through the penstock (2) to enter the powerhouse. The flowing water turns the propeller-like water wheel or turbine (3), which is connected by a shaft to the generator (4), which spins and produces electricity.

The same water that flowed through the turbine (3) is then discharged through the draft tube (5), where it enters the tailrace (6) and returns unaltered to the river below the dam.

The electricity produced by the spinning generator (4) is conducted to the power transformer (7), where the voltage is increased. The high-voltage electricity is then fed into Georgia Power's transmission lines for distribution throughout the state to electricity customers.

While each plant has on-site controls (typically located in the powerhouse) by which it can be manually operated, all but Langdale and Riverview are managed by remote control from the Bartletts Ferry plant, operating headquarters for the Chattahoochee Hydro Group. Those controls are manned around-the-clock.

The Fall Line

Sixty million years ago a trip to the Georgia coast meant Augusta, Macon or Columbus, the last place where the Chattahoochee exited into a sea. Over time the ocean receded, but the geological feature of the old coastline remained, running along the Southeast through Richmond, Baltimore, Raleigh, Columbia and Montgomery. Known as the Fall Line, it divides the hard crystalline rock of the Piedmont Plateau–the lower reaches of the Appalachian Mountains–from the softer sediments of the Coastal Plain, deposited in the prehistoric ocean. Early towns sprang up along the Fall Line, so called because of the preponderance of waterfalls along the zone, created as rivers and streams cut into the Coastal Plain's softer sediments. The whitewater shoals offered an incredible source of power as settlers dammed up the rivers and creeks to run grain and textile mills. They also mark the end of upstream navigation, making cities along the Fall Line ideal inland ports.

Above the Fall Line, the Piedmont is characterized by the familiar red clay soil. Below, ocean deposits left soft sandy sediments and limestone, the remains of ancient tiny sea organisms. And south of it are prehistoric sand dunes and sand hills, where collectors find shark teeth from dinosaur days and other oddities. Above the Fall Line, rivers run in narrow, well-defined channels through hard rock. But below it, they meander and spread out into wide, swampy floodplains.

offer remote hunting in the winter and quality bird watching in the summer. They can be reached only by boat and the nearest launch is Blanton Creek Park. *Directions*: To access Lake Harding from Blanton Creek Park from Columbus, take GA 219 north to its intersection with Bartletts Ferry Road and Lick Skillet Road. Head north on Lick Skillet Road for about 5 miles. Turn left (west) at sign on entrance road to the park.

GOAT ROCK LAKE –One of the smallest and least developed reservoirs on the Chattahoochee River in the Columbus area, Goat Rock Lake, between Lake Harding to the north and Lake Oliver to the south, has a shoreline of only 25 miles and is 68 feet deep from the top of the stone masonry dam, built in 1912. It's not so much a lake as part of the Chattahoochee whose water seems slightly elevated. A few people put in their motor and ski boats from Goat Rock's one public boat access point, Sandy Point Recreation Area, just southwest of Bartletts Ferry dam. But the relatively undisturbed atmosphere of the lake and shore attracts a diversity of wildlife. All three of the resident bald eagles in the area make their home near Goat Rock. Tradition has it Goat Rock acquired its name from a herd of goats that hung out on a giant boulder buried by backwater just north of the dam on the Alabama bank. Today skiers stumbling on the rocks just below the surface give new meaning to the name. *Directions:* To access Goat Rock Lake from Sandy Point Recreation Area from Phenix City, AL, go north for 7 miles on US 280/431. Turn right (northeast) on CR 379 for about 4 miles, then go right (east) on CR 334 for almost 4 miles. Turn right (south) at sign to recreation area.

LAKE OLIVER –Many of the well-to-do in Columbus weekend at expensive homes along the banks of Lake Oliver in developments with names like Rock Island and Green Island Hills, neither of which is actually separated from the mainland. Created by Georgia Power in 1959 with a 70-foot-high concrete dam, Lake Oliver has 40 miles of shoreline. Public boat access is limited to the Municipal Marina (see page 175) just northeast of the Lake Oliver Dam in Columbus, and Goat Rock Recreation Area (see page 171), just southwest of the Goat Rock Dam in Alabama. *Directions:* To access Lake Oliver from City Marina in Columbus, take River Road (GA 219) north. After passing under the North By-Pass (US 80), take first left into marina on Lake Oliver Road.

PARKS AND RECREATION

Most of the parks along this stretch of river are developed on Georgia Power property and open to the public. The exception to this is Uchee Creek Recreation Area on Fort Benning. The following recreational areas are listed north to south. *More Information:* Georgia Power Company, Land Department Field Office, 1516 Bartletts Ferry Road, Fortson, GA 31808; 706/322-0228.

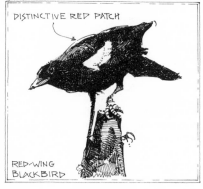

DISTINCTIVE RED PATCH

RED-WING BLACKBIRD

BLANTON CREEK WILDLIFE MANAGEMENT AREA –This 4,758-acre property, prior to Georgia Power's acquisition of it in 1983, was primarily used for pasturing, farming and timbering. It sits on gently rolling terrain that changes into steep ravines and rocky ridges along the Chattahoochee in the upper reaches of Lake Harding, about 26 miles north of Columbus. The power utility company continues to cut timber, but in irregular patterns to create tree stands of different ages. About two-thirds of the WMA is covered by pine or hardwood trees. Wetlands, either marshes periodically flooded along the river or ponds created by beavers, cover about 212 acres, with ten miles of shoreline. The area is leased to the Georgia Department of Natural Resources, which manages it for public use, primarily hunting. *Facilities:* Two primitive camping areas, a 1.2-mile nature trail with a few interpretive signs for children, a 28-acre marsh project created as a refuge for migratory waterfowl. *Days/Hrs.:* Open during deer, turkey, small game, dove and waterfowl hunting seasons from Sept. to May. During breaks in the hunting seasons or the remainder of the year, the WMA is generally gated and closed. Georgia Power land resource officers or the WMA on-site caretaker sometimes open it by appointment for recreational users like bird watchers. Johnson Island, near the northern boundary, was incorporated in the wildlife management area in 1990. Camping is not allowed there, but hunting and nature watching are. Access is by boat only. The nearest boat ramp is Blanton Creek Park. *Fees:* None to enter or camp, but hunters must have wildlife conservation stamps.

In most cases, states mark their respective boundaries in the center of a river. But wherever the Chattahoochee divides Georgia and Alabama, the first state boasts ownership all the way to the river's western bank. This boundary was established by the U.S. Supreme Court in a case (The State of Alabama v. The State of Georgia) which was decided in 1859.

Fossil Generation on the Chattahoochee

About 90 percent of the electricity generated by Georgia Power comes from coal-fired plants. The remainder is supplied by nuclear and hydroelectric units. Georgia Power operates three fossil-fueled electric generating plants on the Chattahoochee River. They all operate on the same principle. Coal, which has been ground into a fine powder by a pulverizer, is blown into a furnace-like device, called a boiler, and burned. The heat produced is used to convert water, which runs through a series of pipes, into steam. The high pressure steam turns the blades of giant turbine generators to produce electricity.

Constructed in the early 1960s, Georgia Power's McDonough Electric Generating Plant is located about six miles northwest of Atlanta on the river. During its early years, the plant was the largest and most powerful generating station in the Georgia Power system. The plant is capable of producing about four billion kilowatt-hours of electricity annually–or enough electricity to supply approximately 400,000 average homes a year.

Located on the river near Newnan, Plant Yates is one of Georgia Power's oldest and largest fossil power plants. Having units built during the 50s and the 70s and ranging from 100 to 350 megawatts capacity per unit, Yates is a good example of how power generation and consumption has changed over the years. The plant operates seven generating units with a total capacity of 1,250 megawatts.

Plant Wansley, located along the river in Heard and Carroll counties, covers more than 5,000

Directions: From West Point, take GA 103 south for ten miles. At sign turn right to check station.

BLANTON CREEK PARK –The most developed Georgia Power recreation site on this stretch of the Chattahoochee, Georgia's Blanton Creek Park offers many recreational amenities and camping sites right on the edge of Lake Harding. *Facilities:* 40 RV camp sites with water and electricity hookups, picnic tables and grills; 8 tent sites with picnic tables and grills; group wilderness camping; restrooms with hot showers, dump station, laundry room, soda machine, pay phone, ice for sale; day use area with picnic tables, 2 large pavilions with grills, restrooms, volleyball court and playground. Day use and camping facilities are handicapped accessible; 2-lane paved boat ramp. *Days/Hrs.:* Apr. 1 to day after Labor Day, Sun.-Thu., 7am-9pm, Fri.-Sat., 7am-10pm. A park attendant closes the gates at night. *Fees:* Camping, $10 a night for RVs, maximum of 8 people; $8 a night for tent sites. Seniors with Golden Age Passports get $2 off either one. Day use costs $2 daily for automobiles, buses or motorcycles. *Directions:* Two miles northeast of Bartletts Ferry Dam, at the intersection of GA 219, Bartletts Ferry Road and Lick Skillet Road, head north on Lick Skillet for approximately 5 miles. Turn left (west) at sign on entrance road to the park. *More Information:* Blanton Creek Park, 706/643-7737.

CHATTAHOOCHEE VALLEY PARK –Georgia Power had planned to further develop this park in Alabama on Lake Harding. A sign indicates camping is permitted for up to 72 hours, and the first of two loop roads through the hilly pine woods of the park looks like people have parked their RVs beside it, but Georgia Power says staying overnight is not allowed. There's no water either. The park borders secluded residential properties on either side. *Facilities:* Paved boat ramp, small dock. *Days/Hrs.:* Officially for day use only from Apr. 1 until day after Labor Day. However, when it's open, the gates are not closed at night. *Directions:* On CR 379, 0.5 mile north of Halawakee Creek (the main Alabama tributary of Lake Harding) go right (northeast) on CR 380, then 0.25 mile later turn right (east) again on CR 369. A big sign indicating a left turn into the park soon appears.

PO BOYS LANDING –This is nothing more than a highway stop on Lake Harding. *Facilities:* Boat ramp, small picnic area. *Days/Hrs.:* Daily, year-round. *Directions:* From Phenix City, AL, go north for 7 miles on US 280/431. Turn right (northeast) on CR 379 for about 4 miles, then go right (east) on CR 334 for almost 2 miles. Park is on left.

IDLE HOUR PARK –This is a fairly remote boat launch on Lake Harding. *Facilities:* Boat ramp. *Days/Hrs.:* Daily, year-round. *Directions:* From Columbus, take GA 219 north. At the intersection of GA 219, Bartletts Ferry Road and Lick Skillet Road, head north on Lick Skillet for about 4 miles. Turn left (west) on Mountain Drive. Take to the park.

SANDY POINT RECREATION AREA –Similar to Goat Rock Recreation Area (below), this one is little more than a clearing in the woods with an unimproved boat ramp. Just below the Bartletts Ferry Dam on the Alabama bank, it offers the only public boat access to the Goat Rock reservoir, which is not so much a lake as a run of the river impoundment. It has significantly less boat traffic than elsewhere in the Columbus area, partly because of all the hidden rocks underneath the water, partly because it is small and partly because of the lack of public access. *Facilities:* Unimproved boat ramp, picnic tables, parking area. *Days/Hrs.:* Daily, year-round. Camping is not encouraged, but some people do anyway. *Directions:* From Phenix City, go north for 7 miles on US 280/US 431. Turn right (northeast) on CR 379 for about 4 miles, then go right (east) on CR 334 for almost 4 miles. Turn right (south) at sign to recreation area.

GOAT ROCK MARINA –Don't pull into Goat Rock Marina expecting a marina. There's no gas, no bait and tackle, no snacks or ice. This is not really a marina but a small mom-and-pop operated campground and boat ramp, located on the Georgia side of Goat Rock Lake. *Facilities:* Boat ramp, campsites with hookups. *Directions:* From Columbus, take GA 219 north to Goat Rock Road/GA 315. Turn left. Go to Adcock Road and turn right. *More Information:* Goat Rock Marina, 465 Peggy Lane, Fortson, GA 31808; 706/322-6076.

GOAT ROCK RECREATION AREA –This clearing in the woods with a gravel boat ramp on the Chattahoochee just downstream of

acres. The plant's two coal-fired units are capable of producing about 1,730,000 kilowatts. Its first unit began producing electricity in 1976 and Unit 2 was completed in 1978.

"About 70% of the body is made up of water. It is a vital resource and a precious fluid absolutely essential for life. Water has hundreds of important functions: it regulates body temperature, carries nutrients and oxygen to cells, lubricates the joints, helps maintain proper muscle tone, removes wastes and protects organs and tissues."

—Sign in Bill Stanton's Health Food Store, Atlanta

William Bartram

While collecting plants in the Southeast for an English patron, naturalist William Bartram wrote and illustrated a diary of Indian life that captured the imagination of Europe, inspiring the poetry of Wordsworth and the politics of Voltaire. Bartram reached the Chattahoochee near modern-day Columbus in 1775.

"We arrived at the banks of the Chata Uche river opposite the Uche town....The river here is about 300 or 400 hundred yards wide, carries 15 or 20 feet of water and flows down with an active current; the water is clear, cool and salubrious."

"The Uche town is...the largest, most compact and best situated Indian town I ever saw; the habitations are large and neatly built; the walls of the houses are constructed of a wooden frame, then lathed and plastered inside and out with a reddish well-tempered clay or mortar, which gives them the appearance of red brick walls; and these houses are neatly covered or roofed with Cypress bark or shingles of that tree. The town appeared to be populous and thriving, full of youth and young children. I suppose the number of inhabitants...might amount to 1,000 or 1,500, as it is said they are able to muster 500 gun-men or warriors. Their own national language is altogether...different from the Creek or Muscogulge tongue...They are in confederacy with the Creek, but do not mix with them."

the Goat Rock spillway waterfall attracts anglers and locals. Compared to other parts of the river near Columbus, this wooded section of the Chattahoochee near Georgia Power property is not heavily visited. It boasts the only bald eagles in this vicinity south of West Point Lake. *Facilities:* Boat ramp. *Days/Hrs.:* Daily, year-round. Camping is not encouraged, but some people do anyway. *Directions:* From Phenix City, go north about 8 miles on US 280 (also US 431). Turn right (west) on CR 249 for 4 miles. At the intersection of CR 318, stay on 249, which becomes an unpaved, winding road, for a little over a mile. Follow the sign on the right (west) to the recreation area.

FORT BENNING/UCHEE CREEK RECREATION AREA –The good news is this popular campground and marina at the confluence of the Chattahoochee River and Uchee Creek in Alabama has more conveniences, recreational facilities and things to rent than any other park in the Columbus area. The bad news is only military and related government personnel or their families can rent anything. But if a person works for the Defense Department, the Red Cross, or visits with someone who does, they can often qualify and take advantage of the low prices and great facilities. Uchee Creek has the only canoe rentals on the Chattahoochee in the Columbus area. One exception, anyone can use the boat launch here, the only one on the river between Rotary Park (see page 185) and River Bend Park (see page 199) at the head of Lake Walter F. George. *Facilities:* 32 cabins; 85 campsites, 50 with water, electricity and sewer, 35 with water and electricity only; boat ramp, dump stations, laundromat, shuffleboard, playground, pool, volleyball and basketball courts, baseball field. The park rents self-contained campers, canoes, jon boats, bass boats, pontoon boats and camping equipment. The marina has boat docks, boat slips and a convenience store with bait and tackle shop. Next door there's a short order grill with burgers, pizza and beer. *Days/Hrs.:* Daily, everyday but Christmas, 9am-6pm during winter and 7am-7pm in the summer. *Fees:* Boat launch costs $1 for military and $2 for civilian users. Prices for cabins, camp sites and other rentals vary according to rank of sponsoring party. Call or write for specifics. *Directions:* From Fort Mitchell, head south on AL 165 for 1.5 miles. Turn left at the Uchee Creek Recreation Area/Fort

Benning Sign. The road bends south and passes a Schools of the Americas training area. A total of 3.5 miles after getting off AL 165, take a left (east) at sign for the park. The road soon dead ends into it. *More Information:* General Manager, P.O. Box 53323, Fort Benning, GA 31905; 706/545-7238.

CHATTAHOOCHEE INDIAN HERITAGE CENTER –From a historic marker in this park, 0.5 mile east toward the river following the old Federal Road, once stood Fort Mitchell, an early 19th century federal garrison. Fort Mitchell was one of the principal gathering points for the forced removal of Creek Indians. Some refused to go, hiding in the Alabama interior or joining Seminole Indians on the Apalachicola River in Florida. But most of the others–starving, stripped of their land and possessions–began the walk, known as the Trail of Tears, to a resettlement reservation in Oklahoma. Many died along the way.

The purpose of the Chattahoochee Indian Heritage Center is to celebrate the culture and accomplishments of the Indians who inhabited the Chattahoochee River Valley for at least 12,000 years before their removal by the U.S. Government. The names of all the Indian heads of household who passed through Fort Mitchell on the journey are inscribed on metal tablets surrounding a symbolic recreation of a square ground in a Creek village.

Interpretive signs describe the heart of a typical Creek village, a centralized public plaza with an open hearth: sacred ground with sacred fire. The square ground was where all matters of importance were discussed. The symbolic square is on top of a hill overlooking the Chattahoochee River Valley to the east. Under the hilltop is a large field cleared to play stick ball, a wildly popular Indian game. Participants would catch and throw a deerskin ball, often filled with rabbit fur to make them lively, with handcrafted sticks that had small loops on the end. A nearby pavilion is a frequent picnic spot and several miles of narrow dirt roads in wooded areas are often used as jogging trails. The heritage center has no other facilities, but there are plans to rebuild a portion of Fort Mitchell and develop an interpretive trail in the near future.

Directions: From Phenix City, take AL 165 south 10 miles. Just past Fort Mitchell National Cemetery is the entrance to the

Uchee is the same as "Oochee," "Yuchee" and "Yuchi" and was one of the sub-tribes of the Creek Confederacy.

—Marion Hemperley, Indian Heritage of Georgia

Fort Mitchell County Park/Chattahoochee Indian Heritage Center on the left (east). *More Information:* Chattahoochee Indian Heritage Association, 334/687-9755.

MARINAS

CHAMBLEY'S MARINA –This marina is in Alabama, on the northern bank of Halawakee Creek, the main tributary of Lake Harding. *Facilities:* Dock space for about 25 boats, dry dock storage, boat ramp, groceries, gas, fishing, ship store with marine supplies, snack bar. *Days/Hrs.:* Daily, winter, 8am-11pm; summer, 7am-midnight. Schedule varies but generally summer season hours last 4 months. *Directions:* In Alabama, just north of Halawakee Creek on CR 379, turn west on CR 364 and follow signs. *More Information:* George Chambley, owner, Chambley's Marina, 120 Lee Road, #802, Valley, AL 36854; 334/749-5417.

HALAWAKA CAMPGROUND AND MARINA –A small, cozy outfit on a peaceful Alabama bank of Lake Harding, Halawaka has catered to recreational boaters and anglers since 1991. *Facilities:* 6 RV hookups; 6 tent sites; 4 cabins each with one bedroom with two full-size beds, kitchen, bath, air conditioning, carpet and deck with picnic table; boat dock; gas; ship store with bait and tackle. *Days/Hrs:* Daily, Nov.-Feb., 7am-7pm; 7am-9pm the rest of the year. *Fees:* $15.90 per night, RV hookups; $12.72 per night, tent sites; $42.40 per night or $212 a week, cabins. *Directions:* From I-85 Exit 79, take US 29 south about 4 miles. Turn left onto CR 279 and go about 7 miles. Marina on left. *More Information:* Randy Hudman, owner., Halawaka Campground and Marina, 8180 Lee Road 279, Valley, AL 36854; 334/749-4912.

JAY'S MARINA –A Lake Harding marina near the Bartletts Ferry Dam on the Georgia side. *Facilities:* 10 wet slips; dry storage 0.5 mile away; gas; ship store with snacks, beer, cigarettes, groceries, some boating accessories, bait and tackle. Everything is water access only, no road traffic. *Days/Hrs.:* Daily, Mar. 1-Oct. 31, 9am-9pm; closed Nov.-Feb. *Directions:* From the intersection of GA 219, head west on Bartletts Ferry Road toward the Bartletts Ferry Dam and take the second right (northwest)

Hitchetee Creek's name comes from the Hitchitees who were one of the main divisions of the Creek Confederacy. Their main town was just downstream from today's Columbus.

—Marion Hemperley, Indian Heritage of Georgia

about 0.33 mile later on the marina entrance road. *More Information:* 45 Bartletts Ferry Road, Fortson, GA 31808; 706/596-0026.

MUNICIPAL MARINA –Also called City Marina, this marina is located on Lake Oliver on the Georgia side just east of the dam. *Facilities:* Dock space for about 35 boats, boat ramp, picnic area with pavilion, gas, bait and tackle shop, restroom. *Days/Hrs.:* Bait and tackle shop, 6am-dark. Park, 5am-11pm. *Directions:* From Columbus, take River Road (GA 219) north. After passing under the North Bypass (US 80), take first left into marina on Lake Oliver Road. *More Information:* Bob Barron, B. & R. Enterprises, 5501 River Road, Columbus, GA 31904; 706/323-0316.

SIGNIFICANT URBAN EXPERIENCES

COLUMBUS –As much as any other Georgia city, Columbus has relied on a river for its livelihood. In Atlanta, the Chattahoochee seems like an afterthought, tucked away in remote parts of the city. In Columbus, the river is the focal point of its past and present. In downtown, the river is threaded with old bridges, blocked by stone mill dams and flanked by turn-of-the-century factories. Sunken steamboats lurk beneath its muddy red waters. Old military forts decay on its banks.

The banks are lined with tasteful brick river walks, modern amphitheaters and brand new corporate headquarters. The local newspaper, chamber of commerce and convention center all view the river. Should a minor leaguer with the Columbus Red Stixx knock one out of the park, it might plunk in the Chattahoochee.

In 1827 the Georgia Legislature selected a site near Coweta Falls to become a trading city because it was at the foot of a long series of falls which afforded great potential for water power and at the head of river navigation on the Chattahoochee River. A reservation of 1,200 acres was allotted for the town and commons in 1827. By the end of 1829, the city had 1,000 inhabitants.

The first mills didn't spin thread but ground corn and flour.

"Whence we may conclude that the water goes from the rivers to the sea and from the sea to the rivers, thus constantly circulating and returning, and that all the sea and the rivers have passed through the mouth of the Nile an infinite number of times."

—Leonardo da Vinci, 1452-1519

CITY MILLS = SITE OF THE FIRST DAM ACROSS THE CHATTAHOOCHEE AND THE
OLDEST MANUFACTURING OPERATION ON THE RIVER, BUILT 1828 IN COLUMBUS.

A NATIONAL HISTORIC LANDMARK- THE INDUSTRIAL RIVERFRONT DISTRICT-

THE CHATTAHOOCHEE RIVERWALK, DILLINGHAM STREET BRIDGE, AND PHENIX CITY AMPHITHEATER.

LDRED FEEDING HER PIGEONS NEAR THE RIVERFRONT.

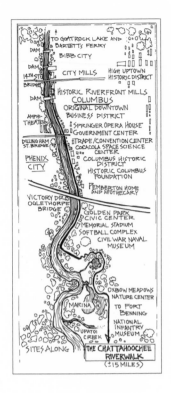

Seaborn Jones, having won the first lot in the state lottery, a 5.5 acre plot next to Coweta Falls, built a gristmill in 1828. The original dam was of wooden construction, but in 1907 the City Mills Company completed a stone dam at the site.

The second oldest dam on the Chattahoochee River in the Columbus area was built to power the circa 1851 Eagle Mill. One of the city's pioneer textile plants, the mills, organized by William H. Young, a merchant from Apalachicola, manufactured cotton and woolen goods. By 1860, the city ranked second only to Richmond, Virginia, as an industrial center in the south, boasting a paper mill, cotton gin maker, furniture factory and several iron works in addition to the textile mills. Whether in raw or finished form, crops or goods from all over the region floated down the river from Columbus on steamboats to Apalachicola, the Gulf of Mexico port city in Florida that, like Columbus, rose to economic prominence soon after its founding in the early 19th century.

During the Civil War, Columbus supplied many goods to the Confederacy. The Eagle Mill churned out gray uniform tweed, cotton duck for tents, cotton stripes for army shirts, cotton jeans, osnaburgs, sheetings, rod and India rubber cloth. The Columbus Iron Works forged cannons, mortars, steam engines and boilers. The Haimon Brothers became the largest maker of swords for the South. A naval yard produced a Confederate boat.

On April 16, 1865, in one of the last major land battles of the Civil War, 13,000 Federal cavalry troops invaded the city from Alabama and burned all of the war-related mills, warehouses and foundries. The war had officially ended a week earlier, but news of General Robert E. Lee's surrender had not reached either side.

Despite its losses, the city rebounded quickly. The Eagle Mill was rebuilt and renamed the Eagle & Phenix Mills to signify its rebirth. From 1868 to 1878, it quadrupled its output, becoming the largest textile mill in the south.

The Columbus Iron Works rebuilt and re-tooled to turn swords into plowshares, organizing the Southern Plow Company in 1877. Another iron works affiliation, the Columbus Muscogee Ice Company, became a world leader in the manu-

Upatoi is the name of a Creek Indian settlement in today's eastern Muscogee County. The exact meaning is unknown, but it could have meant some type of sheet-like covering from "apata-i" meaning "I cover." It has also been suggested that the word meant "bullfrog" from "apatana." A third possibility is "last" or "farthest off" referring to the location of a village away from its main affiliate town. Utoy Creek in Fulton County is the same word as Upatoi.

—*Marion Hemperley*, Indian Heritage of Georgia

TODAY, COTTON WAREHOUSES AND TEXTILE MILLS ARE STILL AN IMPORTANT PART OF THE COLUMBUS RIVERFRONT.

FROM AN OLD POSTCARD – UNLOADING COTTON AT COLUMBUS WHARF ON THE CHATTAHOOCHEE. C.1900 – STEAMBOATS COULD TRAVEL THE RIVER FROM THE GULF OF MEXICO TO COLUMBUS, ENABLING THIS CITY TO THRIVE AS A TRADING AND MANUFACTURING CENTER

facture of ammonia absorption machines for large scale refrigeration and ice-making. Interestingly, John Gorrie, a physician at the other end of navigation on the river, Apalachicola, had created the first ice-making device several decades earlier. His attempts to market the invention failed.

The mills and factories kept coming: Muscogee Manufacturing Company in 1867, Swift Manufacturing Company in 1887, Paragon Mills in 1888, Columbus Manufacturing Company in 1899 and Bibb Manufacturing in 1900, which soon became a textile plant larger and with more spindles than any other in the nation. The Bibb mill used hydroelectric power from the river, not mechanical. The North Highlands Dam, then the largest in the south, turbines connected to electrical generators, instead of paddle wheels, connected to mechanical gears. The technological triumph would eventually change the relation between the river and the city. As hydroelectricity moved farther from its original source, the mills no longer had to be close to the Chattahoochee to receive their energy supply.

Over the years, many manufacturing giants moved their operations away from the river because of the risk of flooding. Others closed because of foreign competition. The process continues today. Many of the historic red brick warehouses are being torn down. And in 1997 two historic mills are only running skeleton crews—Bibb and Fieldcrest Cannon, formerly Muscogee Manufacturing.

Yet Columbus, a city of 180,000 residents, has undergone a river renaissance in recent years. The risk of floods, which in the old days reached as far as Front Street, subsided after several large dams were built north of the city in the mid 1900s. People gawk inside the cavernous old Columbus Iron Works, transformed into an unusual, award-winning convention center that retains much of its original character. Pedestrians, joggers and bikers zip up and down the Columbus Riverwalk, a multimillion dollar brick path that follows the banks of the river from downtown Columbus to Fort Benning.

The Columbus Convention and Visitors Bureau offers maps of three historical walking or driving tours around downtown Columbus: Uptown (business district), the Historic District and High Uptown (residential districts). The Historic Columbus Foundation conducts Heritage Corner Tours, a walk-through of five historic properties beginning with its own at the corner of Broadway and Seventh Street. Tours are Monday through Friday, 11am and 3pm; Saturday and Sunday, 2pm except holidays. Cost is $3 per person with a minimum of two on tour. *More information:* Columbus Convention and Visitors Bureau, 1000 Bay Avenue, Columbus, GA 31902; 706/322-1613 or 800/999-1613. Historic Columbus Foundation, 700 Broadway, Columbus, GA 31906; 706/323-7979.

THE COLUMBUS MUSEUM –This 86,000-square foot museum devoted to American art and history with special emphasis on the Chattahoochee Valley region is perhaps one of the finest museum experiences to be found in the southeast. Of particular note, the exhibit Chattahoochee Legacy, which presents the history of the region in a chronological format ranging from prehistoric times to the present. The museum's art collection contains works by American masters of the 19th and 20th centuries. Educational programs are designed for all ages and include lectures, films and demonstrations. *Facilities:* 30,000-square feet of exhibition galleries, 2 classrooms, a teaching darkroom, an orientation theater, a 298-seat auditorium, meeting room, gift shop. *Days/Hrs.:* Tues-Sat., 10am-5pm; Sun., 1pm-5pm; closed Mon. and legal holidays. *Admission:* Free, donations accepted. *Directions:* From I-185 south, take Exit 4, Wynnton/Macon Road and turn right. Museum is on the right, just past 13th Avenue intersection. *More Information:* 1251 Wynnton Road, Columbus, GA, 31906; 706/649-0713.

PHENIX CITY –The origins of Phenix City began sometime before 1820 as a trading post, known as Girard, in Creek Indian territory on the west bank of the Chattahoochee River. The town consisted of a few log houses and a little cleared land. But soon after John Godwin and his slave, Horace King (see sidebar page 182), built the first bridge across the river in 1832, the city attracted a railroad line, textile plant, paper mill and hundreds of small homes for commuters to Columbus mills.

One of the final land battles of the Civil War destroyed much of the city. Seven days after General Robert E. Lee surrendered, Union General James Harrison Wilson and his army, marching through Alabama on what later became US 80, broke through a desperate line of defense in Girard, manned by inexperienced, ill-equipped troops, to take over Columbus under the cover of darkness. The Confederates had stopped a Union advance earlier in the day by destroying the lower or city bridge, which King had built. Bright flames soon lit up both towns, whose industrial or military sections were set afire by the victors. A message from Confederate forces in Macon would not inform Columbus of the truce to end the war for four more days.

In 1889 a suburb of Girard called Brownville became Phenix City. In 1923 the two cities were merged under the second name.

Today there is still evidence of Phenix City's early days as Girard. On Broad Street are some of the town's oldest surviving homes. The circa 1851 Collins Scott House one block north

"The rain falls, runs down the creek, fills the river that flows by our house on its way to the Ohio on its way to the Mississippi on its way to the Gulf and from there almost anywhere... And what do I do? I keep my canoe under lock and key."

—Jonathan Greene

Horace King

Famous for his skill as a bridge builder in the early years of Chattahoochee Valley history, Horace King was a slave owned by John Godwin of Cheraw, South Carolina. Godwin came to Columbus after his bid of $14,000 had been accepted to build the first bridge to connect Columbus with Girard, the present day Phenix City, Alabama. But his slave Horace King was the real bridge builder.

King was part Catawba Indian and part Negro. A skilled carpenter, he designed and supervised the construction of at least six bridges across the Chattahoochee, including the first toll bridge built in West Point.

It is said that Godwin promised King his freedom if he could complete building a bridge across the river in a given time. King succeeded and Godwin kept his promise. Not only did King go on to build more bridges with his sons John, Marshall and Washington King; but he was also twice a member of the Alabama legislature–with the good wishes of southern whites– during the Reconstruction period.

Upon Godwin's death, King erected a marble monument with the inscription: "Erected to the Memory of John Godwin, by his friend and former slave, Horace King."

of the Dillingham Street Bridge is considered the oldest. The pale green wooden house survived Union pillaging reportedly because a Yankee sympathizer owned it. Across the street at 1040 Broad Street is the Russell County Historical Commission's headquarters in a renovated white cottage. Other historic houses along Broad have been restored and converted into law offices.

Evidence of a Confederate fort, Fort Gilmer or Fort # 5, a pentagon-shaped breastworks, remains in the northwestern part of Phenix City, right off US 431, one block north of Crawford Road. A historical marker is at the north end of the K-Mart shopping center there. The well-preserved breastwork has three cannon emplacements, designed to protect the Confederate naval yard and iron works. Lack of manpower left the fort unmanned during the attack by Wilson's Raiders. The 30-foot high earthworks can be detected from the parking lot, behind some pine trees at the top of the more northern of two hills behind the shopping center. The fort is on private land and closed to the public.

Horace King, who was freed by Godwin in 1846, became a member of the Alabama Legislature in 1869 and the foremost covered bridge builder in the region. His bridges were the first to cross the Chattahoochee at West Point, Eufaula and Fort Gaines. In the Godwin private family cemetery King placed a stone obelisk over the tomb of Godwin, who died in 1859. It reads: "Erected to the memory of John Godwin, by his friend and former slave, Horace King." *Directions:* To reach the cemetery, turn south on 17th Avenue off 14th Street and take an immediate right (west) on 13th Place. One block later at 18th Avenue, turn right (north) into the graveyard on a short dirt road. Marker is next to two large cedars. *More Information*: Russell County Historical Commission, 334/297-8225.

WALKING AND DRIVING TOURS

RIVERWALK –As a steamboat highway and hydroelectric power source, the Chattahoochee was once the lifeblood of Columbus. But as railroads and electricity came of age, the city no longer relied on the river; and the waterfront became neglected, unkempt and a place for the city to dump trash and sewage. To boost tourism and attract businesses, the city has again looked to the riverfront, transforming it in recent years into a center of recreation and civic life that draws heavily on its past. The hallmark of the river renaissance is the Chattahoochee Riverwalk, a landscaped, paved path that extends 10 miles south from the end of 12th Street in Uptown Columbus to the entrance of Fort Benning.

The project has an interesting history. Federal law required many cities to divide old rain water collection and sewer lines by 1996. Since Columbus had mulled over building a Riverwalk for years, it decided to combine both projects, running the new sewer line next to the river and building the Riverwalk above. The trail has become extremely popular with cyclists, joggers and pedestrians; and Columbus plans to expand it seven miles north to Lake Oliver Dam.

Begin a tour of the Riverwalk from its north end:

Corner of 12th Street and Bay Avenue. From the large parking lot here is one of the best views of Columbus' history on the river. Nearby on the grass is a life-size bronze statue of a young woman sketching the scene: old mills, dams and whitewater rapids on the river. Just upstream is the historic Eagle & Phenix Mill Dam. Below that is an impressive stretch of whitewater rapids where Indians once fished for shad. Today, sea gulls and blue herons flock to the large rocks.

Dillingham Street Bridge, mile 0.3. This was originally a covered bridge built in 1832 by Horace King, a slave who would later receive his freedom, become the most successful bridge builder in the region and win a seat in the Alabama legislature. Low water sometimes exposes sections of King's work. At night hundreds of light bulbs light up the underlying brick arches of the current Dillingham Street Bridge built in 1912.

Steamboat Landing, mile 0.4. South end of Bay Avenue. For more than a century, 210 steamers used the Columbus Steamboat Wharf, the last upstream stop on the river before the Fall Line rapids and rocks made passage impossible. The first was the *Fanny* in 1828, and the last was the *George W. Miller* in 1939. Chugging 360 miles from Columbus to Apalachicola, a port city on the Gulf of Mexico, the riverboats were loaded

The Bridge Between

Before this bridge with its arches fair
Another all wooden and covered stood there.
Built by a man, Horace King was his name,
Master builder of bridges led to his fame.

His life was a symbol, a bridge between men,
Can we let it happen through us yet again?
By letting this span with its lights all aglow,
Bring cities together and unity show.

O tell of the river, the rapids and bends,
And sing of its beauty as onward it sends,
A message of hope and strength to begin,
New pages in history where dreams find an end.

The bridge as a beacon, its lights cross the way,
Shining in darkness toward a much better day,
For bridges are for people to closer draw and be,
Bound with the promise of unfailing harmony.

Peggy Usher Theus

Fish Consumption Guidelines

Goat Rock Lake–Black crappie, no restrictions; channel catfish 12 to 16", no restrictions; spotted sucker over 16", one meal per week; largemouth bass 12" to 16", one meal per week; hybrid bass, one meal per month; channel catfish over 16", one meal per month; largemouth bass over 16", one meal per month.

Lake Harding–Crappie, no restrictions; hybrid bass under 12", one meal per week; largemouth bass 12 to 16", one meal per week; channel catfish under 12", one meal per week; hybrid bass over 16", one meal per month; channel catfish over 12", one meal per month; largemouth bass over 16", one meal per month.

Lake Oliver–Bluegill under 12", no restrictions; redear sunfish under 12", no restrictions; largemouth bass 12 to 16", one meal per week; catfish over 12", one meal per month, largemouth bass over 16", one meal per month. As a general rule, eat smaller fish to be safe.

Source: Georgia Department of Natural Resources, 1997.

with cotton bales and other agricultural goods. On the return trip, stopping at any number of 240 steamboat landings or cities along the way, they carried manufactured products, dry goods, groceries and Apalachicola Bay oysters, kept alive by sprinkling corn meal in barrels. Boiler explosions, fires, changing river currents and sand bars made steamboating on the Chattahoochee dangerous. One modern-day riverboat, the *Chattahoochee Princess*, still uses the wharf. An 18-plank paddle wheel powers her from the stern while a striking, Indian princess wooden figure guides her from the bow. The sternwheeler has daily afternoon river rides without reservations and nightly dinner and late night cruises with reservations from May to September. There are afternoon river rides and dinner cruises on weekends only during the rest of the year. For specific schedules, reservations or prices, call Captain Jim Kittrell at 706/324-4499 or 800/934-2628.

Coca Cola Space Science Center, mile 0.8. Part of a national network of science education centers for children established in memory of the crew of the Space Shuttle Challenger, the center has a space shuttle mission simulator, an 150-seat planetarium and an observatory connected by remote link to observatories around the world. *Days/Hrs.:* Tues.-Fri., 10am-4pm; Sat., 7-9pm. *More information:* 701 Front Ave., Columbus, GA 31901; 706/649-1479.

South Commons, mile 2. South end of Veteran's Parkway. The Woodruff Museum of Civil War Naval History in the Commons has an outdoor display of two Confederate vessels, the C.S.S. *Chattahoochee* and the C.S.S. *Jackson.* The *Chattahoochee,* a 130-foot long sail-and-steam powered gunboat, was scuttled at the war's end to prevent Union capture. Her first captain was C. R. Jones, better known as the commander of the *Merrimack,* which challenged the *Monitor* in the only battle of ironclad vessels in the Civil War. The *Jackson,* a 225-foot long ironclad built in Columbus with six heavy cannons, was set afire at the steamboat landing by invading Federal forces on April 17, 1865. It floated some miles downstream and sank, burned to the waterline. The interior museum exhibits a wide range of salvaged artifacts, like torpedoes made from wooden kegs and glass jugs. *Days/Hrs.:* Tues.-Fri.,

10am-5pm; Sat.-Sun., 1-5pm. *More Information:* 202 4th St. Columbus, GA 31906; 706/327-9798.

The Commons also contains Golden Park, site of 1996 Olympic women's fast pitch softball and home of minor league baseball's Red Stixx; and the Civic Center, home to the city's new professional hockey franchise, the Cottonmouths.

Rotary Park, mile 2.3. This area has parking, a riverboat ramp and the Bulldog Bait and Tackle Shop, open 7 days a week, 7am-6pm.. *More Information:* Bulldog Bait and Tackle Shop, Richard Thomasson, 706/322-5331.

Rigdon Park, mile 4. Closed and scheduled to be rebuilt by 1998.

Oxbow Meadows Environmental Learning Center, mile 6. Around mile 5.2, the walk meanders away from the river toward Oxbow Meadows, once the site of a landfill in the vicinity of the old Bickerstaff clay mines, dug for brick material. The city capped the landfill with three feet of compacted dirt and sank monitoring wells. In 1995 it opened the environmental learning center on 1,600 acres of reclaimed land. The pits are now wetland ponds, and a 300-year old natural oxbow lake gives the area its name. There is a lot of river wildlife, including turtles, snakes and fish, for visitors to see; and a short trail around a nearby wetland pond. *Days/Hrs.:* Mon.-Fri., 11am-5pm; Sat., noon-3pm; and Sun., 11am-3pm. *More Information:* Oxbow Meadows Environmental Learning Center, 3491 S. Lumpkin Road, Columbus, GA 31901; 706/687-4090.

The river bends close to the Riverwalk at mile 7, but only momentarily. At mile 9 it crosses Upatoi Creek, enters Fort Benning and ends at the National Infantry Museum.

National Infantry Museum, mile 10. This relatively unknown museum of national significance features an extensive collection of military art, artifacts and weapons. The museum is a fascinating chronicle of two centuries of the American foot soldier. *Days/Hrs.:* Mon.-Fri., 8am-4:30pm; Sat.-Sun., 12:30-4:30pm. Tours may be arranged by calling the museum. *More Information:* National Infantry Museum. Ft. Benning, GA 31905; 706/545-2958.

Langdale Dam

When West Point Manufacturing Company completed this dam in 1908, it cranked out 4,000 kilowatts of power for its Langdale textile plant, four miles south of West Point. Together with the nearby Riverview plant, it supplied enough power to operate 7,000 spindles. Langdale's original units have retired, but two completed in the 1920s continue to generate electricity for Georgia Power, which bought Langdale and Riverview in the 1930s. The stone masonry dam is 15 feet high and spans 1,362 feet across the river. The reservoir covers 152 acres of surface water; the crest elevation is 548 feet. The open spillway bends in the middle, making a "V" with the point facing downstream. The powerhouse is located on the Alabama bank. *Directions:* On US 29 about 2 miles south of US 85 intersection, go left (east) on 59th Street just before the Langdale Mill, then first left (north) on 16th Avenue. Go right (east) into a parking area and continue on a road behind the mill. The powerhouse is unmanned and closed to the public.

Crow Hop Dam

Many people either consider this dam to be a part of Riverview Dam or don't know that it exists at all. Like Riverview, Crow Hop is a stone masonry dam with a free-flow spillway. The dam was built after Riverview and is 15 feet high and 944 feet long, extending from Hills Island to the eastern bank of the river. The function of this dam is to push the river to the western channel around Hills Island to provide more water to the generators.

A dam usually marks the upstream limit for fish intent on moving upstream. They will congregate near the base if for no other reason than they can go no farther. In addition there are other attractions: a deep pool, aeration and currents to stir up food. Fish will lie downstream from the drop-in, but others will lie close against the dam. The aerated water will mean good fishing in the stretch immediately downstream, so try this as well as the pool at the base of the dam.

FISHING

Largemouth bass, an angler's favorite, thrive in these lakes. Other fishes found in this stretch of the river include spotted bass, hybrids, black crappie and bream. There's catfish too, but those from Lake Oliver are inedible due to Chlordane, a DDT-like pesticide. Other chemicals detected in the river and lakes, such as mercury and PCBs, also pose risks to water species and those who eat them. Pollutants have all but wiped out fresh-water mussels in this region. Once plentiful, they live only in one or two isolated pockets. But pollutants aren't the only things that have harmed some fish species; dams have cut them off from their natural migrations.

BEST ADVICE –Lake Harding, Goat Rock, Lake Oliver, the lakes clustered along this section of the river are seemingly the private fishing grounds of area residents; no professional guides work the area. The best advice for newcomers is to inquire in person at the marinas listed below for recommended baits and best locations.

BEST BOOKS AND MAPS –Atlantic Mapping's Lake Harding and Lakes Oliver & Goat Rock fishing map includes geographic coordinates of 34 selected fish shelters and structure sites. (To order see page 325.)

U.S. Geological Survey 1:24,000 scale topographical maps covering this entire stretch of river are Lanett North, Lanett South, Whitesville, Beulah, Bartletts Ferry Dam, Smiths Station, Fortson, Phenix City, Columbus, Fort Benning, Fort Mitchell, Union, Omaha and Twin Spring. (To order see page 326.)

Lake Harding is a 5,850-acre Georgia Power reservoir between LaGrange and Columbus with two private and four public boat ramps. Specific fishing information for Lake Harding is as follows:

BEST BOOKS AND MAPS –U.S. Geological Survey 1:24,000 scale topographical maps covering this lake are Lanett South, Whitesville, Beulah and Bartletts Ferry Dam. (To order see page 326.)

OTHER SOURCES OF INFORMATION –George Chambley owns and operates Chambley's Marina (see page 174), the largest marina and bait-and-tackle store on the lake. It is on the Alabama side on Halawakee Creek, 205/749-5417

Goat Rock is a 1,050-acre Georgia Power reservoir located 15 miles north of Columbus. It is an old reservoir, initially impounded in 1912, with one private and one public boat ramp at opposite ends of the lake. The public ramp, Sandy Point Recreation Area (see page 171) is located on the Alabama side at the upper end of the reservoir and is operated by the Georgia Power Company. Specific fishing information for Goat Rock is as follows:

BEST BOOKS AND MAPS –U.S. Geological Survey 1:24,000 scale topographical maps covering this lake are Bartletts Ferry Dam and Smiths Station. (To order see page 326.)

OTHER SOURCES OF INFORMATION –Goat Rock Marina, 707/322-6076 (see page 171).

INSIDER TIPS AND HOT SPOTS –Hybrid and white bass fishing is usually excellent at the upper end of the lake, below Bartletts Ferry Dam. Best times are during the two power generations periods which occur early in the morning and late in the afternoon. The hybrids and whites congregate in this highly turbulent water, and fishermen can sometimes catch their limit in a short period of time.

Lake Oliver is a 2,150-acre Georgia Power reservoir located within the city limits of Columbus. A city marina (see page 175) has two double-wide boat ramps, a handicapped accessible fishing pier, a small bait and tackle store and a picnic area. The DNR maintains three fish attractors in this lake which are marked by buoys. Due to its location and the heavy use by recreational boaters, summer fishermen usually resort to early morning or late afternoon fishing. Specific fishing information for Lake Oliver is as follows:

BEST BOOKS AND MAPS –U.S. Geological Survey 1:24,000 scale topographical maps covering this lake are Smiths Station and Fortson. (To order see page 326.)

INSIDER TIPS AND HOT SPOTS –Two O'clock Hole in Standing Boy Creek is locally known as a favorite spot for bass. Lake Oliver is probably best known for its bream. April through May, many bluegill up to 0.75 pound are caught with crickets fished in the backs of coves. Red-ear sunfish up to 1.5 pounds are commonly caught with worms near the mouth of Standing

Riverview Dam

Built in 1918 one river mile downstream from Langdale, the Riverview Dam and hydroelectric plant originally powered several West Point textile mills. In the 1930s Georgia Power took over the plant. Riverview consists of two stone masonry dams, both with free-flow spillways that create scenic, long waterfall drops. The older one is 10 feet high and extends 200 feet from the Alabama bank to Hill Island. The circa 1918 powerhouse located at the west end has two units that still produce 500 kilowatts. The later upper dam is Crow Hop Dam (see page 186). The dam and plant are directly behind the Riverview Mill, as is a small day-use Georgia Power park with a footbridge to a small island next to Hills Island. There are short trails to the lower spillway dam and the river. *Directions:* From CR 379 in Riverview, turn east at Milner's Grocery & Deli and take the first left (north) almost immediately. At 0.5 mile the road forks into three sections. Take the one on the far right.

A bobber should always be used in still fishing over weed beds. Without a bobber, the bait quickly sinks into the weeds where it cannot be seen to lure the bass. Adjust the bobber so the bait floats just clear of the weedy largemouth bass haunts. Lift bait occasionally to be sure it is free.

Bartletts Ferry Dam

Named for Rev. Simpson Wilson Bartlett, a 19th century minister and doctor who operated a ferry on the Chattahoochee here, this hydroelectric plant dwarfs the others in the vicinity. Its red brick warehouselike plant began delivering 30,000 kilowatts to Columbus in 1926. Within 25 years the capacity had more than doubled. And in 1985 Georgia Power spent $100 million to fix up the plant, boosting output to 173,000 kilowatts. The 120-foot high and 1,900-feet long concrete dam impounds Lake Harding. Underneath the gated spillways, Bartletts Ferry Dam has "lift buckets," resembling giant, widened water slides. Their curved shape lifts water into the air to dissipate its full force before crashing into the concrete at the bottom. Otherwise the dam's foundation would quickly erode. On the dam's top are two cranes capable of lifting 150 tons, poised to lift 20 flood gates to unleash excess water. The headquarters of the Georgia Power division that manages the region's hydroplants, Bartletts Ferry controls by remote control the gates and generators of Riverview, Langdale, Goat Rock, Oliver Dam and North Highlands. *Directions:* From GA 219 about 13 miles north of Columbus, turn left (west) on Bartletts Ferry Road. Continue 2 miles until the road dead ends in front of a gate. A short walking path to the left (south) leads to the dam. A side road that goes to the left shortly before the road dead ends does cross the dam, but it is closed to public traffic and often gated.

Boy Creek. The tailwater fishery below Lake Oliver also produces some excellent bream fishing, but receives very light fishing pressure due to limited access.

BOATING

WEST POINT DAM TO LANGDALE, OR 'CROOKED" DAM –The best boating in this portion of the river occurs when water is being released from West Point Dam and is moving down the river. When water is not being released, the river is less than a foot deep in most areas. A 12-foot jon boat with a motor no bigger than 15 horsepower or a canoe would be the boats of choice in this segment. Even with small outboards, boaters can expect to hit some rocks. Dam releases cause currents that move sandbars altering navigation patterns. *Put-In/Take-Out:* The only boat ramp between West Point Dam and Langdale Dam is in front of the West Point fire station at 1st Avenue and West 7th Street in West Point. Boaters can go as far upstream as 200 feet below West Point Dam and downstream as far as Langdale Dam. *Distance:* About 10 miles. *High Points:* This is an excellent fishery for bass, bream, crappie and stripers. An overlook at the base of West Point Dam provides an introductory view downstream. Hardley Creek Park has recreational facilities and restrooms and is a good place to view the river. (See page 149.) *Hazards:* 200 yards below West Point Dam is a boat safety zone, with a positive barrier blocking boats from approaching too close to the dam. This section of the river is designated a "hazardous area" due to the fluctuations in water level caused by releases from West Point Dam. All passengers in a boat must wear a U.S. Coast Guard approved personal flotation device which is properly fitted and fastened. Langdale Dam is a low head dam, meaning that water flows over the top of the dam. It is hard to see and boaters should use maximum caution when approaching near the dam. *USGS Topos:* Lanett North and Lanett South.

BELOW LANGDALE OR "CROOKED" DAM TO CROW HOP DAM –This is not a recommended boating section. If the water is not generating from West Point Dam, it is low and scrappy. If the water is generating, it is very fast. It is not particularly scenic, and there are lots of islands and rocks. *Put-In/Take-Out:* Boat ramp below Langdale Dam. Going south on US 29 in Langdale turn left on 20th Avenue in front of the Langdale United Methodist Church, the big curve known locally as Johnson's Curve. Bear left and continue down a dirt road to the boat ramp. *Distance:* About 1 mile. *Hazards:* Proximity to West Point Dam and its water releases make this a designated "hazardous area" of the river. Boaters must wear a personal flotation device which is properly fitted and fastened. Crow Hop Dam is another low head dam. Dams like this are hard to detect from boat level and should be regarded with maximum caution. *USGS Topos:* Lanett South.

RIVERVIEW BOAT RAMP UPSTREAM TO CROW HOP DAM AND DOWNSTREAM TO LAKE HARDING –This segment of the river can be considered on its own or as part of the Lake Harding impoundment. River explorers with a taste for adventure can put in at Riverview boat ramp and go as far upstream as Crow Hop Dam, if the water level and their own boating skills will allow them. The extensive shoal just north of Flat Shoals Creek will limit access to the upper portion of this segment for most boats at most water levels. Immediately downstream of the boat ramp is canoe and jon boat territory. (Georgia Department of Natural Resources enforcement officers operate large outboards as far upstream as the Riverview boat ramp, but they are intimately familiar with the river channels.) About a mile downstream from the boat ramp, the river deepens to four or five feet as the Lake Harding impoundment starts backing up. *Put-In/Take-Out:* Riverview boat ramp. In Langdale, take US 29 south to 20th Avenue. At Riverview Church, turn left onto Lower Street and follow to the end. Boaters can also use any of the other boat ramps on Lake Harding listed below. Vandalism has been a problem at this boat ramp. Do not leave a car overnight. *Distance:* About 5 miles. *High Points:* The river is 300 or 400 yards wide through this section. Although there are a number of islands in the river, navigation is fairly simple. Nevertheless, for first time-explorers, a topographical map would be a useful navigation tool. This is a pretty rural area with a few houses on the Alabama side where locals sit out on their porch and strum banjos. On the Georgia side of the river

Goat Rock Dam

The most historic plant in the Columbus area, Goat Rock's concrete dam and red brick powerhouse on the Alabama bank remain essentially unchanged since their construction at the beginning of the 20th century. A goat served as mascot during construction, but the name reportedly came from a herd of his cousins that hung out on a giant boulder jutting from the Alabama bank. Boys from Georgia playing in the river yelled at the goats to watch them scale the cliff. Today Goat Rock is covered by the backwater of the Goat Rock Dam. The original two units put out 6,000 kilowatts, but by 1956 a total of six pumped out 26,000 kilowatts for the Georgia Power plant. This open spillway dam is high, long and straight over the entire river, making an unbroken waterfall 68 feet high and 1,320 feet across. Of all the dams in the area, this one has the most attractive historic structure and spillway and should be visited first. *Directions:* The plant is closed to the public, but the Goat Rock Recreation Area (see page 171) just downstream on the Alabama side offers a panoramic view of the dam. About 9 miles north of Phenix City on US 431, turn right (east) on CR 249. About 3.5 miles later the pavement ends, but continue another mile or two, then turn right (east) at the sign for the Goat Rock Recreation Area.

Oliver Dam

On the site of the 19th century Clapp's Factory textile mill in Columbus, Oliver Dam boasts the first completely automatic, remote-controlled hydroelectric plant in Georgia. Completed in 1959, its four generators on the Georgia bank produce 60,000 kilowatts. The concrete dam, 70-feet high and 2,021-feet long, has about 30 blue iron spillway gates with sloping lift buckets underneath. It impounds Lake Oliver, a reservoir eight miles long with 2,150 surface acres and 40 miles of shoreline. Below the dam the river slows to a trickle. Most of the underlying rock bottom is exposed. During normal conditions, the dam releases a strip of water only several dozen feet across. *Directions:* From Columbus, go north on River Road. Just after the bypass, turn left (west) on Lake Oliver Road. Less than 0.5 mile later the road dead ends near the eastern end of the dam.

is the Blanton Creek Wildlife Management Area (see page 169) and Blanton Creek Park (see page 170), owned and operated by Georgia Power Company, where there is a boat ramp. *Hazards:* No serious hazards. First time boaters on this section would be wise to take a topographical map as a navigation aid due to the river's width and the number of islands. *USGS Topos:* Lanett South, Whitesville, Beulah and Bartletts Ferry Dam.

LAKE HARDING –Lake Harding is the weekend retreat for area residents who can afford the luxury of a lake home. *Put-Ins/Take-Outs:* 9 boat ramps dot the shore of Lake Harding. Clockwise around the lake starting with Riverview Boat Ramp (above) they are: Blanton Creek Park (see page 170), Idle Hour Park (see page 171), Po Boys Landing (see page 171), Halawaka Campground (see page 171), Chambley's Marina (see page 174), 2 boat ramps on the Alabama side just north of the 379 Bridge over Halawakee Creek and Chattahoochee Valley Park (see page 170). *Distance:* About 10 river miles. *High Points:* Between West Point Dam and Bull Creek which enters the river in south Columbus, the natural river corridor of the Chattahoochee drops over 300 feet over a dramatic geological feature knows as the Fall Line. (See page 168.) Before electric power, mills were built at these strategic places on the river. Later hydroelectric power plants like the one at Bartletts Ferry Dam were built on the Fall Line where elevations dropped precipitously through narrow channels creating made-to-order sources of electric power. Perhaps no place along the Chattahoochee better or more scenically illustrates this than the location of Bartletts Ferry Dam. Taking in the hydroelectric power plant, the canyon walls where the river flows over the Fall Line and the beautiful bend in the river as it continues downstream from Lake Harding is one of the great views of the Chattahoochee Valley. There is no public access road across the top of Bartletts Ferry Dam, but those wishing to enjoy the view from the top of the dam can get there from both sides of the river. *Hazards:* Lake Harding is a very "fast" weekend lake, the busiest Georgia Power lake in Georgia. Lake residents and weekend visitors favor big power boats and jet skis creating wakes which can annoy and endanger operators of small jon boats or canoes. Fishermen and operators of small boats should plan to use the lake early in the mornings or on weekdays. *USGS Topos:* Beulah and Bartletts Ferry Dam.

GOAT ROCK LAKE –Goat Rock is known as the fishing lake in Harris County, Georgia. Everything bites here from catfish to crappie, bream, stripers and bass. In 1995 Goat Rock held the state record for hybrid bass. A lot of fishermen go up to the base of the falls at Mulberry Creek and fish for catfish. Goat Rock is a deep lake, over 100 feet at the base of the dam. It's not until boaters are within eyesight of Bartletts Ferry Dam on the north end of the lake that the water gets significantly shallower. At the same time there are several oxbow lakes (see page 253) where fishermen can test shallower water. *Put-Ins/Take-Outs:* There are 2 boat ramps on the lake. To reach the Sandy Point Recreation Area ramp (see page 171) on the Alabama side of the river from Phenix City, AL, take US 280/431 north for 7 miles. Turn right (northeast) on CR 379 for about 4 miles, then go right (east) on CR 334 for almost 4 miles. Turn right (south) at sign to recreation area. On the Georgia side is Goat Rock Marina (see page 171), a ramp owned by a private individual who charges a small fee for launching. To reach the marina from Columbus, take GA 219 north to Goat Rock Road/GA 315. Turn left. Go to Adcock Road and turn right. Follow the signs. *High Points:* Mulberry Creek Falls is one of the most spectacular spots on the entire 540 miles of the Chattahoochee. Like the scene at Bartletts Ferry Dam, it illustrates the dramatic impact of the Fall Line on this section of the river. It is similar to the mountain-like scenery produced by the Brevard Fault along Sweetwater Creek. The fall is surrounded by private property and should only be accessed from Mulberry Creek. The creek enters the lake about two-thirds of the way down on the Georgia side. *Hazards:* No significant hazards. *USGS Topos:* Bartletts Ferry Dam and Smiths Station.

LAKE OLIVER –Lake Oliver is the Columbus, "let's get in a couple of hours fishing after work," lake, as contrasted to Lake Harding, which is more of a weekend retreat. Lake Oliver, too, is high traffic, with power boats and jet skis; but it's about half the size and not as busy as Harding. Small jon boats and even canoes have a place here, though wakes from larger power

North Highlands Dam

Built in 1899, the first large dam in the South powered the Bibb Cotton Mill in Columbus, about a mile south of Oliver Dam, which at the turn of the century had more spindles than any other mill in America. A 1901 flood almost destroyed North Highlands, the oldest dam in the Columbus area. When rebuilt two years later, two dams directed water to two power-houses, one generating 5,000 kilowatts of electricity and the other using rope drive to power the Bibb Mill. In 1963 a $7.6 million, four-unit station generating 29,600 kilowatts replaced the old electrical powerhouse. But the original stone masonry dam, 33 feet high and 728 feet across, remains in use. The reservoir has only 131 acres of surface water and three miles of shoreline. The crest elevation is 269 feet above sea level. Completely automatic, North Highlands is remote controlled from Bartletts Ferry. *Directions:* From downtown Columbus, head north on 1st Avenue which dead ends in Bibb City. Dam is to the left.

The geographical drop of the river expressed in feet per mile is called the GRADIENT.

City Mills and Dam

Seaborn Jones, having won the state lottery for the first property in Columbus, a 5.5-acre spread next to Coweta Falls, built a mill to grind cornmeal in 1828. The mill's original dam was wooden, but in 1907 the City Mills Company replaced it with stone. Today the once prosperous mill lies abandoned, its neat rows of huge windows in red brick are cracked or boarded, its giant white painted letters faded and peeled. The open spillway makes a 10-foot waterfall spanning the river, bent slightly in the middle like the letter "V," the point facing downstream. *Directions:* Located at the intersection of 1st Avenue and 18th Street in downtown Columbus.

boats may make it rocky at times. *Put-Ins/Take-Outs:* The Municipal Marina (see page 174) is the main put-in and take-out point. From Columbus, take GA 219 north to Lake Oliver Road. Turn left into marina. *Distance:* Oliver is about 2,150 acres. *Hazards:* No serious hazards. *USGS Topos:* Smiths Station and Fortson.

BIBB POND –Below Lake Oliver, the body of water known locally as Bibb Pond extends south to North Highlands Dam. This section of river is used primarily as a gathering pond for the next hydroelectric generating plant at North Highlands Dam. *Put-In/Take-Out:* There is one boat ramp in Phenix City, AL, just north of the North Highlands Dam which is sometimes closed. Scout first. *Distance:* About 1 mile long. *Hazards:* Rocky and shallow. The water fluctuates when the North Highlands hydroelectric plant is generating. North Highlands Dam is low-head, meaning water flows directly over the top of the dam creating a hazard for upstream boaters. *USGS Topos:* Smiths Station, Fortson, Phenix City and Columbus.

NORTH HIGHLANDS DAM TO CITY MILLS DAM –This stretch of river is called City Mills Pond. *Put-In/Take-Out:* There is no public access to this body of water. *Distance:* About 1 mile. *USGS Topos:* Phenix City and Columbus.

CITY MILLS DAM TO EAGLE PHENIX DAM –This is the river area between the two oldest mills in Columbus. *Put-In/Take-Out:* There is no public access between these 2 dams. *Distance:* Less than a mile. *USGS Topos:* Columbus and Phenix City.

EAGLE PHENIX DAM SOUTH TO FLORENCE MARINA STATE PARK AND THE WALTER F. GEORGE IMPOUNDMENT –Here at the Fall Line, the prehistoric coastline where Piedmont meets Coastal Plain, boaters with almost any size boat can put in and navigate all the way to the Gulf of Mexico without exiting the river. *Put-In:* At Rotary Park (see page 185). *Take-Out:* Boaters can adjust the length of this trip to suit their own time, interest and craving for adventure. A good take-out is Florence Marina State Park (see page 200). *Distance:* About 42 miles. *High Points:* Motoring upstream as far as the shoals at the base of the Eagle Phenix Dam puts the boater at the heart of the most interesting urban scene in the Chattahoochee Valley. The three bridges here, the 14th Street Bridge, the Dillingham Bridge and the

Oglethorpe Bridge are the most frequent series of bridges along such a short stretch of river anywhere in the valley. Columbus' historic mills extend along the east bank. The picturesque 10-mile Riverwalk follows the line of the river. Phenix City's Amphitheater adorns the west bank. The Georgia state line extends to the normal high water mark on the west bank of the river, so technically none of the Chattahoochee belongs to Alabama. For this reason, all the mills and industry are Georgia's, explaining the states' rich cousin-poor cousin relationship. This is also an urban scene that is rapidly changing. A large new bridge spans the river, and the 14th Street Bridge and the Dillingham Street Bridge will probably be converted to pedestrian only. Total Systems, the huge financial services and credit card processing company, is building a 5,000-employee complex on the riverbank, and the city is carving out a new large green space. Columbus makers and shakers say these developments will transform not only Columbus but this entire section of the Chattahoochee Valley. The view here dramatically illustrates how the river–not railroads, not roads and highways, not air transportation, but the river–molded the destiny and character of Columbus.

Downstream the boater passes a historically rich landscape. From prehistoric times until Indian removal in the 1830s, Indian villages lined the banks along the entire length of the Chattahoochee, particularly along this section of river because of the rich soil that washed down and settled in the flood plains immediately below the Fall Line. In the few miles below Columbus the boater passes the sites of Coweta Town, Cusseta Town, Yuchi Town, Chiaha Town, Oswichee Town and a dozen others, as well as Rood Mounds, one of the largest concentrations of Indian mounds in the Chattahoochee Valley. On the west bank of the river below Columbus are the visible remains of a Spanish-built wooden fort and moat. Georgia founder James Oglethorpe signed an Indian treaty at Cusseta Town. The Old Federal Road connecting Washington and New Orleans crossed the river a few miles below Columbus near Fort Mitchell which was visited by Lafayette in 1825. Explorer and naturalist William Bartram crossed this section of the river and visited Indian villages along it. Florence Marina State Park,

Eagle & Phenix Mills and Dam

The second oldest dam on this part of the Chattahoochee, a small, straight spillway across the river, powered the Eagle Mills, a pioneering textile mill founded by William H. Young, a merchant from Apalachicola. During the Civil War it churned out grey uniform tweed, cotton duck for tents, cotton stripes for army shirts, cotton jeans, and osnaburg. Union raiders torched the mill in April of 1865, a week after the war officially ended. Rebuilt a year later, it became the Eagle & Phenix Mills to signify its rise from the ashes. Within 15 years it quadrupled its output, becoming the largest textile mill in the South. The impressive 100-yard stretch of rocks and rapids below the dam gives the best glimpse of the mighty white water that once roared over the fall line. Adventurous kayakers sometimes work the boiling waters, although water releases from upstream dams make the current fluctuate unpredictably. *Directions:* 1229 Front Avenue in downtown Columbus.

www.chattahoochee.org

We welcome your comments, suggestions, recommendations and input regarding this book and the river, via the Internet at the Riverkeeper's website: www.chattahoochee.org.

You can also access the website for additional information regarding the Chattahoochee and the many issues that affect the river.

ALL IS BORN OF WATER;
ALL IS SUSTAINED BY WATER.

the take-out point for this section, is near the site of Roanoke, a settlement of 200 people which was burned by the Indians in 1836. *Hazards:* No significant hazards. First time boaters will find a topographical map useful in navigating the curve. *USGS Topos:* Phenix City, Columbus, Fort Benning, Fort Mitchell, Union, Omaha and Twin Springs.

Old mill foundations typical of those that sit along many tributaries of the Chattahoochee

Section 7
Walter F. George
to Seminole

Tom Mann

"We's Cherokees on both sides. We came from North Carolina. It was in the 1800s. My grandmother and her five sisters all married white men and part white men. I was born in Chambers County on a farm. We plowed mules and raised cotton and corn and food to survive on. Our pastime was huntin' and fishin', so we learned. Back where I was raised you didn't just hunt the land you owned. You hunted thousands of acres. There wasn't many folks there anyways. They didn't care if you went on their land. Your land was their land, theirs was yours. It wasn't like it is today. I studied fish since I was six years old. I'd go down on the creeks and watch fish. There's just something that fascinated me about even the slightest minnow. I's always fascinated in 'em, and I learned their movements. I studied weather all the time. I could tell you what kind of thunderstorm that was and what this one was gonna do and that one. I was almost like a weatherman. I learned about all wildlife like that. It's just been a great love of me all my life. My daddy was that way. And he taught me. So it come down through the old Indian heritage.

When I come off the farm, I got me a job in a cotton mill. I made lures and sold 'em to my friends on the river banks and creek banks. I'd make all my fishing money selling 'em. And then my wife started working with me. I used calf tails; I used fox tails, squirrel tails. I design all my own lures. I don't use any lure except what I design and hadn't for forty years.

Those fish are harder to fool than you think they are. You can sometimes throw your arm off with an artificial bait and you can't get a bite. You throw a live bait and they'll, "bang," just like that. You can't see that much difference in yourself, but them fish see it. They know colors, and they can tell one color from another. You can throw one color at 'em for a long time and they'll get wise to it and they won't hit it. And then you can switch another color and they'll hit it 'cause it's something different. I come out with these forage fish colors that looks exactly like a fish. And if you'll notice all of 'ems got some red. And all game fish got some type of red on 'em somewhere. Where it's his belly you got some chartreuse on it. And you got some white pearl. He's got those in 'em. They're built in 'em no matter what fish it is you'll find a touch of chartreuse, white and red in 'em, all of 'em.

Well, in my mind I see those fish. I know exactly what they're doing and when they bunch up like that. Now they don't do it all the time. It's a certain time of year they do it. It's got to be, normally, when they leave migration routes and come from spawning and go up in creeks. They go just like ducks and quails and anything else. They go in a covey and they move back and they go to a certain place and they stop and they'll stay there a few days. The moon's gotta be right and everything's gotta be just right and they'll bunch up and they'll stay congregated there for maybe as much as three weeks. And they'll do it every year, same places. But you gotta know when to be there. What kind of a moon. Now you may go here eleven o'clock today and they're not there, and at one o'clock they're there. Once you get the moon phase it may be one thirty tomorrow, two the next day, three the next day, and on down until they disappear."

Tom Mann is a professional fisherman and lure designer.

THE RIVER

This section of the Chattahoochee includes the river from where it begins to back up for Lake Walter F. George to where it begins to back up for the Lake Seminole impoundment, a total of 114 river miles. Walter F. George, often referred to as Lake Eufaula, extends 85 miles along the Chattahoochee with 640 miles of shoreline. Lake George W. Andrews is a 1,540-acre impoundment operated by the Corps of Engineers for navigation. The Lake Andrews reservoir is actually a 29-mile long widened stretch of the river running from the Walter F. George Dam, south to the George W. Andrews Dam. The impoundment is more like a large river than a lake.

Before there were locks and dams and water releases to control its flow, this was a working section of river. Indian dugout canoes, trade barges, 300-ton steamboats—all moved up and down this stretch of river. Indian mounds prove the earliest existence, old fort sites bear witness to the importance of the river as a means of transportation and antebellum homes

Lock and Dam Names

Walter F. George–Walter Franklin George was born on a farm near Cordele, Georgia, in 1878 and was a United States Senator from 1922 until his death in 1957. Having chaired the Foreign Relations Committee, George exercised great influence on both foreign and economic policy. In recognition of Senator George's distinguished public service, the dam was named for him in 1958.

George W. Andrews–George William Andrews was born in Clayton, Alabama, in 1906 and served as a United States Representative from 1944 until his death in 1971. Andrews chaired the Legislative Subcommittee and sat on the Department of Defense Subcommittee. His active role in the Public Works Subcommittee directly benefitted the Chattahoochee Valley. The project was originally named the Columbia Lock and Dam and was renamed for Congressman Andrews in 1972.

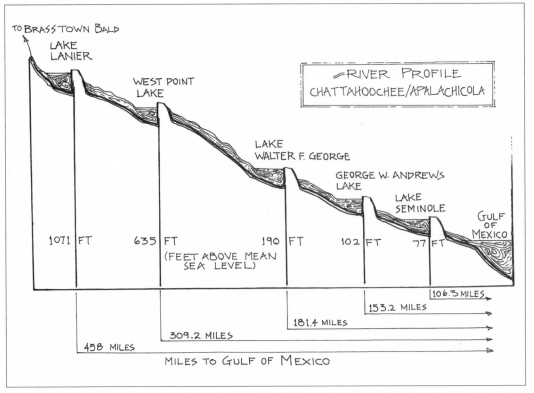

TO BRASSTOWN BALD

LAKE LANIER

WEST POINT LAKE

RIVER PROFILE
CHATTAHOOCHEE/APALACHICOLA

LAKE WALTER F. GEORGE

GEORGE W. ANDREWS LAKE

LAKE SEMINOLE

GULF OF MEXICO

1071 FT   635 FT   190 FT   102 FT   77 FT

(FEET ABOVE MEAN SEA LEVEL)

106.3 MILES

153.2 MILES

181.4 MILES

309.2 MILES

458 MILES

MILES TO GULF OF MEXICO

show the wealth of the early towns that dot the river's banks.

PARKS AND RECREATION

There are a number of campgrounds and day use parks along lakes Walter F. George and George W. Andrews. The Corps of Engineers manages most of them. The Corps offers both fee and non-fee campgrounds. The fee campgrounds have hookups for water and electricity, grills, picnic tables and shower facilities with laundries. There are control gatehouses with attendants, and park ranchers patrol for security. Campers may stay as long as 14 consecutive days. Camping fees are $14 per night with boat launching included. Most of the boat ramps in the day use parks have a $2 charge for launching. Areas of White Oak and Cotton Hill campgrounds are open year-round. All other campgrounds and day use areas are usually closed from December through February. The season varies, however, and it is best to check with the Resource Manager's Office.

Hours for all Corps facilities are 7am-10pm. *More Information:* U.S. Army Corps of Engineers. Visitor Information Center/Resource Manager's Office, Route 1, Box 176, Fort Gaines, GA 31571; 912/768-2516.

This area also has six state parks on or near the river. The parks listed below are in order from north to south along both sides of the river.

RIVER BEND PARK –This Corps of Engineers park is the northernmost recreational facility on Walter F. George. The day use section is closed for an undetermined length of time for renovations, but the adjacent boat ramp is open. The park and ramp are next to a great big river bend with a series of oxbow lakes filled by the backwaters of Walter F. George. Shallow and containing many small islands, the river bend discourages fishermen, but attracts canoeists, who consider this section of the Chattahoochee–spread out into a series of old channels–one of the finest to paddle in the Columbus area. It's near Fort Benning so visitors might hear rumbling artillery fire in the distance. *Facilities:* Boat ramp, picnic pavilion, pit toilets, no drinking water. Although closed and not maintained, people can park outside the gate and use the picnic area, according to the Corps. *Days/Hrs.:* Day use area closed indefinitely. Boat landing is always open. *Fees:* None. *Directions:* From Cusseta, take US 27 south about 2 miles. Turn right at the sign on River Bend Road, which dead ends 10 miles later into the park.

BLUFF CREEK PARK –This campground is located on the Alabama side of the Chattahoochee River where Bluff Creek converges with it. This is north of Walter F. George, and the river is more like a river than a lake. Mostly used by people in RVs fishing the river, this Corps of Engineers camping area is heavily paved. Yet much of it is wooded with Spanish moss-covered trees, and some sites directly overlook the backed-up waters of the Chattahoochee or Bluff Creek. *Facilities:* 88 camp sites with all hookups except sewer, boat ramp, picnic tables, grills, pullouts for campers, fire rings, restrooms, showers, drinking water, dump station, fish cleaning station. *Fees:* User fee. *Directions:* On AL 165 about 20 miles south of Phenix City in Loflin, turn left (east) at the sign on mile-long road which dead ends into the access area.

Considering going through the Walter F. George Lock, a boater asked veteran lock master James Gilley, "How big a boat can you handle?"

"If it fits, we'll take it," Gilley said.

"How small?" the boater ask.

"If you come through on a pretty sturdy log, we'll lock it through," Gilley answered.

A Lake with Three Names

For over 30 years, the reservoir impounded by Walter F. George Lock and Dam has not had one common name with which people on both sides of the lake could be happy. Signs welcoming visitors to Eufaula, Alabama, read "Welcome to Historic Eufaula: Home of Lake Eufaula" while similar signs in Fort Gaines, Georgia, read "Welcome to Historic Fort Gaines" Home of Lake Walter F. George. A lone Lake Chattahoochee sign further complicates the issue.

Why all the confusion? It seems that about the time the U.S. Army Corps of Engineers completed the Walter F. George lock and dam to form the huge reservoir, the states of Alabama and Georgia adopted resolutions to name the lake. According to a boundary established by the U.S. Supreme Court in 1859, Georgia owns the lake up to the western bank. But on June 25, 1963, both Houses of the Alabama Legislature as well as the entire Congressional delegation endorsed the name Lake Eufaula in honor of the Creek Indians who once lived throughout the Chattahoochee Valley. Georgia took the name from the river which created the lake and endorsed the name Lake Chattahoochee in a House resolution dated March 12, 1965. The Corps initially referred to the lake as the Walter F. George Reservoir and later changed the name to Lake Walter F. George after the U.S. Senator from Georgia who was an active supporter of the project. It might be noted that the Corps usually designates a body of water impounded by a lock and dam by the name of the lock and dam; and besides, the Corps already had one Lake Eufaula in Oklahoma.

BRIAR CREEK PARK –Operated by Russell County, AL, this park is way up the Hatchechubbee Creek before it enters the Chattahoochee on the Alabama side of Walter F. George. *Facilities:* Boat ramp, pit toilets. *Days/Hrs.:* Daily. *Directions:* Between Cottonton and Pittsview, AL on CR 4.

HATCHECHUBBEE CREEK PARK –This day use facility sits on the west side of the river, just south of the bridge over Hatchechubbee Creek. *Facilities:* Boat ramp, picnic area, picnic shelter, drinking water, restrooms. *Fees:* Boat launching, $2. *Directions:* From Cottonton, take AL 165 south. Entrance is on the left just south of the bridge over Hatchechubbee Creek.

FLORENCE MARINA STATE PARK –Located at the northern end of Walter F. George on the Chattahoochee River, this 150-acre state park was once a private recreation area owned by the W. C. Bradley Company. There is a natural deep-water marina with six large, covered docks. The Kirbo Interpretive Center is an educational museum located on the park grounds. Displays here depict the removal of the Creek Indians from the Florence area from 1715-1836 as well as artifacts from the prehistoric Paleo-Indian period through the early 1900s. There are also displays about the influence of cotton on the development of towns along the Chattahoochee and the story of the steamboats which traveled the river from 1828 to the 1930s. Special tours leave the Kirbo Center for the Rood Creek Indian Mounds, an Indian village which existed more than 600 years ago, and to Fort McCreary, a reproduction of an authentic 1820s - 1830s wooden blockhouse built to protect the frontier settlers from Native American attacks. Special annual events at the park include a March Crappie Tournament, an Easter Egg hunt, Native American Day in September and Astronomy Evening in November. *Facilities:* Marina with 66 slips, gas, 10 rental cottages, 44 tent and trailer sites with electricity, water and sewage hookups, picnic tables, picnic shelter, clubhouse, jon boat and canoe rentals, swimming pool, tennis courts, public fishing pier, miniature golf and trading post with snack and fishing supplies, nature trails, museum, restrooms. *Days/Hrs.:* Daily. Park, 7am-10pm; park office, 8am-5pm; Kirbo Interpretive Center, 8am-5pm. *Fees:* User fees. *Directions:* From Lumpkin, take GA 39C west for 16 miles. Park entrance located at end of

39C. *More Information:* Florence Marina State Park, Route 1, Box 36, Omaha, GA 31821; 912/838-6870. For reservations, 800/864-7275. Kirbo Interpretive Center, 912/838-4706.

PROVIDENCE CANYON STATE CONSERVATION PARK –This 1,108-acre state park is called Georgia's "Little Grand Canyon" because of the pink, orange, red and purple hues of its soft canyon soil. An interpretive center explains how the massive ditches, the deepest being 150 feet, were caused by erosion due to poor farming practices in the 1800s. The canyons are named for the Providence Church, organized in 1832-33. The church, moved because of canyon erosion, originally stood on land that is now between two of the ravines. Hikers can enjoy views of the canyon from the rim trail, and backpackers can stay overnight along the backcountry trail. Pioneer camping is allowed, which Georgia State Parks define as camping for organized groups under the active supervision of adult leaders. Sites are semi-remote and without shower facilities. Special events include spring and fall Wildflower Days and a Kudzu Takeover Day in August. *Facilities:* Pioneer camping, 65 picnic sites, 2 picnic shelters, group picnic shelters, interpretive center, 3 miles of hiking trails, 7-mile backcountry trail. *Days/Hrs.:* Daily. Park, Sept. 15-Apr. 14, 7am-6pm; Apr. 15-Sept. 14, 7am-9pm. Park office, 8am-5pm. *Fees:* User fees. *Directions:* From Lumpkin, take GA 39C west for 7 miles. Park entrance on left. *More Information:* Providence Canyon State Conservation Park, Route 1, Box 158, Lumpkin, GA 31815; 912/838-6202.

EUFAULA NATIONAL WILDLIFE REFUGE –In 1964, the U.S. Fish and Wildlife Service established the Eufaula National Wildlife Refuge in cooperation with the Corps of Engineers to provide habitat for wintering waterfowl and other migratory and resident species. The 11,160-acre refuge lies on the upper reaches of the Walter F. George Reservoir on either side of the Chattahoochee River in Alabama and Georgia. At one time, this area was heavily forested, but past land practices that involved agriculture and clear cutting resulted in landscape and wildlife changes. The refuge is managed to protect diverse species in greater numbers than the area could under natural conditions. This is accomplished by managed farmlands, grasslands,

At an early date, efforts were undertaken to get Alabama and Georgia to agree on one name. Lake Alaga was proposed (combining the abbreviations of the two states) but the name was never taken seriously.

All three governmental bodies have erected highway signs with their designated name. Consequently, there are visitors to the lake who are trying to find Lake Walter F. George but are bewildered by the Lake Eufaula signs. There are other visitors looking for Lake Eufaula but can't find it on a highway atlas.

Right or wrong, the name most commonly associated with the lake by sportsmen is Lake Eufaula. This is in spite of the fact that Lake Walter F. George is the name used in virtually all atlases and on the Georgia highway map. Many believe that the popularity of the name "Lake Eufaula" can be attributed to the intense promotion of the lake by the Eufaula Chamber of Commerce, City of Eufaula and Eufaula Tribune.

Even so the debate–and the confusion–continue.

Eufaula's name came from the Creek settlement located on the present site of Eufaula. The Creek word Eufaula is a proper name and does not translate into English.

—Marion Hemperley, Indian Heritage of Georgia

woodlands and wetlands. There's a self-guided wildlife drive, interpretive trail and observation tower. Fishing is allowed throughout the refuge. Doves, ducks and deer may be hunted during special refuge-conducted hunts. Boat ramps are available at the Florence Marina State Park and Rood Creek Landing Recreation Areas adjacent to the refuge and the Gammage Road access point on the refuge. Camping is not permitted. Bicycles and horseback riding are permitted on the gravel roads only. *Facilities:* Boat ramps, observation tower, wildlife driving trail, interpretive nature trail, refuge headquarters. *Days/Hrs.:* Daily, Mon.-Fri., 7:30am-4pm CST. *Directions:* From Eufaula, AL, take US 431 north for 5 miles to Lakepoint State Park. Turn right on Old Hwy 165. Go 2 miles and follow the signs. *More Information:* Refuge Manager, Eufaula National Wildlife Refuge, Route 2, Box 97-B, Eufaula, AL 36027-9294; 334/687-4065.

ROOD CREEK PARK –This non-fee camping area sits on the east side of Walter F. George right above the mouth of Rood Creek and adjacent to the Rood Creek Indian Mounds (see page 210). *Facilities:* Primitive camping, boat ramp, picnic area, pit toilets, drinking water. *Fees:* Boat launching, $2. *Directions:* From Georgetown, take GA 39 north. Turn left into the well-marked entrance and follow the dirt access road 1 mile south into the park.

LAKEPOINT RESORT STATE PARK –This 1,200-acre Alabama state park sits beside Cowikee Creek on the northern end of Walter F. George and adjoins the Eufaula National Wildlife Refuge. The resort hotel has a restaurant and banquet and convention facilities. The park's naturalist staff hosts a year-round schedule of recreational and educational programs from the parks' Community Building, which includes environmental slide shows, guest speakers, bird-watching and nature walks. Tours and activities can be tailored to guest's age and interests. A special summer environmental camp teaches about conservation. The Alabama State Parks Division and the U.S. Fish and Wildlife Service offer a cooperative Watchable Wildlife Program each year at Lakepoint for 2 nights and 3 days. *Facilities:* Marina with fuel dock; boat launch; overnight docking; permanent wet storage; fishing and pontoon boat rental; 101-room

WATER RELIGION:
ESKIMOS

The mother of all sea creatures, the water goddess Sedna dispatches famine and chaos when Inuit Eskimos violate their taboos.

resort motel with restaurant and convention center; 29 fully-equipped cabins; 244 campsites with water and electricity hookups; nature center with trained park naturalist; beach area with white sand and bath house; picnic area with pavilions, tables, grills and playground; 18-hole golf course; 6 lighted, all-weather tennis courts; swimming pool; 5 miles of hiking trails. *Days/Hrs.:* Daily. Lodge, 24 hrs. a day. Campground, 8am-5pm. *Fees:* User fees. *Directions:* 7 miles north of Eufaula, AL, off US 431. *More Information:* Lakepoint Resort State Park, P.O. Box 267, Eufaula, AL 36072-0267. Park, 334/687-6676. Resort, 334/687-8011 or 800/544-LAKE. Alabama State Parks Central Reservation Service, 800/ALA-PARK.

OLD CREEK TOWN PARK –This Eufaula public park named for an old Indian village is on the Alabama side of Walter F. George. *Facilities:* Boat ramp, fishing pier, picnic area, picnic shelter, swimming beach, playground, ball fields, drinking water, restrooms. *Days/Hrs.:* Daily, daylight-10pm. *Fees:* $2 per vehicle. *Directions:* From Eufaula, take US 431 north. Turn right at marked access road. *More Information:* 334/687-1213

RIVER BLUFF PARK –This Corps day use area is on the east side of Walter F. George near the city of Georgetown. *Facilities:* Boat ramp, picnic area, fishing pier, restrooms, drinking water. *Fees:* Boat launching, $2. *Directions:* From Georgetown, take GA 39 north. Look for marked access road, leading to the park.

BARBOUR CREEK LANDING –Eufaula operates this park on Barbour Creek. *Facilities:* Boat ramp, picnic area. *Days/Hrs.:* Daily, daylight-10pm. *Fees:* $2 per vehicle. *Directions:* From Eufaula, AL, take US 431 south. Park is on the north side of the 431 Bridge at Barbour Creek. *More Information:* 334/687-1213.

CHENEYHATCHEE CREEK PARK –This day use area is located on the Alabama side of Walter F. George at the mouth of Cheneyhatchee Creek. *Facilities:* Boat ramp, pit toilets. *Fees:* Boat launching, $2. *Directions:* From Eufaula, AL, take US 431 south, turn east onto the access road to the park.

COOL BRANCH –This former Corps campground, located on the east side of Walter F. George, is now a day use facility. *Facilities:* Boat ramp, picnic shelter, restrooms, showers, drinking water. *Fees:* Boat launching, $2. *Directions:* From GA 39, take Hwy 22 west to the park.

God said, "Let the water team with living creatures, and let birds fly above the Earth across the vault of the heavens...Let the Earth bring forth living creatures, according to their various kinds"... And He saw it was good.

—Genesis 1:20, 24, 25

WHITE OAK CREEK PARK CAMPGROUND –This is one of two Corps campgrounds that has some areas open year-round. It lies on the west side of Walter F. George at the mouth of White Oak Creek. *Facilities:* Campsite with water and electricity hookups, boat launch, picnic shelter, swimming beach, playground, restrooms, showers, pit toilets, drinking water, information center. *Fees:* User fee. *Directions:* From Eufaula, AL, take US 431 south to AL 97. Campground is just before the bridge over White Oak Creek.

WHITE OAK CREEK DAY USE PARK –This day use area is adjacent to White Oak Creek Campground and lies on the west side of Walter F. George where White Oak Creek converges with the lake. There is no boat launch. *Facilities:* Picnic area, picnic shelter, swimming beach, playground, restrooms, drinking water. *Fees:* None. *Directions:* From Eufaula, AL, take US 431 south to AL 97. Day use area is just before the bridge over White Oak Creek.

PATAULA CREEK PARK –This park is on the east side of Walter F. George at the mouth of Pataula Creek. *Facilities:* Boat ramp, picnic area, picnic shelter, restrooms. *Fees:* Boat launching, $2. *Directions:* From Fort Gaines, take GA 39 north. Cross Pataula Creek and look for park signs.

THOMAS MILL CREEK PARK –The Corps has closed this camping area on the west side of Walter F. George at the mouth of Thomas Mill Creek. The boat ramp is still open and leased to Alabama. *Facilities:* Boat ramp. *Days/Hrs.:* Daily, year-round. Directions: From Eufaula, take US 431 south to AL 97. Follow well-marked access road which turns west into park.

SANDY BRANCH PARK –This day use area, located on the east side of Walter F. George near Sandy Creek, is managed by the city of Fort Gaines. *Facilities:* Boat ramp, picnic area, pit toilets, drinking water. *Days/Hrs.:* Daily, year-round. *Directions:* From Fort Gaines, take GA 39 north. Turn left into park on CR 2411.

COTTON HILL PARK –Cotton Hill Park is located on the east side of Walter F. George at the mouth of Sandy Creek. It is one of two Corps campgrounds that has areas open to campers year-round. The boat ramp is for campers only. *Facilities:* Campsite with water and electricity hookups, boat ramp, picnic shelter, swimming beach, playground, information center, restrooms, showers, dump station, drinking water. *Fees:* User fee. *Directions:* From GA 39, take Hwy 82 west a short distance to the first road on the left and follow the signs.

GEORGE T. BAGBY STATE PARK –This 300-acre Georgia state park is located near the southern end of Lake Walter F. George. The park's 30-room lodge has meeting room space for up to 125 people. The Pilothouse Restaurant overlooks the lake and serves a la carte and buffet style meals. There is a marina with slips available for monthly or daily rental and a public boat ramp open for all park visitors. Pontoon boat excursions go to the lock and dam located at the southern end of the lake. There is no camping available, but the nearest campground is less than a mile away. Special events hosted here include a Fathers Day Sunday in the Park, a July 4th Celebration and a Christmas Craft Workshop. *Facilities:* 34 boat slips; gas dock; 30-room guest lodge with meeting rooms; Pilothouse Restaurant; 5 fully-equipped, 2-bedroom cottages; 1 covered picnic shelter; 50 picnic sites; swimming beach; pedal boat, canoe and fishing boat rental; public boat ramp; bait and tackle shop. *Days/Hrs.:* Daily, park, 7am-10pm; park office, 8am-5pm. Swimming beach, Memorial Day-Labor Day. *Fees:* User fees. *Directions:* From Fort Gaines, take GA 39 north for 4 miles. Entrance on left side of road. *More Information:* George T. Bagby State Park, Route 1, Box 199, Fort Gaines, GA 31751; 912/768-2660. Walter F. George Lodge, George T. Bagby State Park, Route 1, Box 201, Fort Gaines, GA 31751; 912/768-2571.

HARDRIDGE CREEK PARK –Hardridge Creek Park lies on the north shore of Hardridge Creek where it enters Walter F. George on its south end. *Facilities:* Campsite with water and electricity hookups, boat ramp, picnic area, picnic shelter, swimming beach, restrooms, pit toilets, drinking water. *Fees:* Camping fee; boat launching and/or swimming, $2. *Directions:* From Eufaula, AL, take US 431 south to AL 97. Entrance is on the left before crossing the Hardridge Creek bridge.

EAST BANK PARK –This day use area sits in the southeast corner of Walter F. George just north of the dam. *Facilities:* Boat ramp, picnic area, picnic shelter, swimming beach, fishing pier, drinking water, restrooms. *Fees:* Boat launching, $2. *Directions:* From Fort Gaines, take GA 39 north to lake. Entrance on left.

"Everybody needs more water when there's less of it."

—*Woody Miley, Apalachicola*

RESOURCE MANAGER'S OFFICE –On the east side of Walter F. George near the dam, the Resource Manager's Office and Visitor Information Center is a good place to stop for information on the lakes. The Visitor Information Center has interpretive displays on the lake history, regional history and the area's flora and fauna. *Facilities:* Picnic area, restrooms, drinking water. *Days/Hrs.:* Office, daily, 8am-4:30pm; Visitor Information Center, Mon.-Fri., 8am-4:30pm. *Directions:* From Fort Gaines, take GA 39 north. Turn left into well-marked entrance. *More Information:* Lakes Walter F. George and George W. Andrews, Resource Manager's Office, Route 1, Box 176, Fort Gaines, GA 31751-9722; 912/768-2516. Alabama, 334/585-6537.

HIGHLAND PARK –This day use facility lies near the southwest corner of Walter F. George. *Facilities:* Boat ramp, picnic area, swimming beach, pit toilets. *Fees:* Boat launching and/or swimming, $2. *Directions:* From Eufaula, AL, take US 431 south to AL 97. Follow to the park area which is on the left.

WALTER F. GEORGE DAM AREA –This day use area is located on the west side of the Chattahoochee River directly next to the Walter F. George Dam. *Facilities:* Fishing pier, restrooms, drinking water. *Directions:* From Fort Gaines, take AL 46 and turn north onto the access road to the dam area. *More Information:* For group tours of dam and powerhouse call 912/768-2635.

FRANKLIN LANDING –This area lies on the west side of the river below the Walter F. George Dam. This site was previously the Indian town of Cheeska Talofa and is near the site of the frontier village of Franklin. Established in 1814 by Colonel Robert Irwin, who operated a log ferry across the river, Franklin was the first colonial village in east Alabama. Fort Gaines was constructed to protect Franklin, a promising port, from the Creek Indian Nation. However, the town never recovered from the destructive flood of 1888. *Facilities:* Boat ramp, pit toilets. *Fees:* Boat launching, $2. *Directions:* From Fort Gaines, take AL 46 to the well-marked access road on the right.

KOLOMOKI MOUNDS STATE HISTORIC PARK –This 1,293-acre state historic park is an important archaeological site as well as a recreational area. There are seven mounds within the park which were built during the 12th and 13th centuries by the Swift Creek and Weeden Island Indians. These include

Kolomoki is probably a Creek word meaning "where there are white oaks" with a terminal element for "water."

—Marion Hemperley, Indian Heritage of Georgia

Georgia's oldest great temple mound, two burial mounds and four ceremonial mounds. The Kolomoki museum interprets the mounds and this Indian culture. *Facilities:* Campsites with electricity and water hookups, pioneer camping, group camping, 71 picnic sites, 7 picnic shelters, 2 group shelters, 2 lakes with boat ramp and dock, fishing and canoe boat rental, fishing, swimming pool, nature trails, museum, restrooms. *Days/Hrs.:* Daily, park, 7am-10pm; park office, 8am-5pm. *Fees:* User fees. *Directions:* From Blakely, take GA 27 for 6 miles. *More Information:* Kolomoki Mounds Historic Park, Route 1, Box 114, Blakely, GA 31723; 912/723-5296.

ABBIE CREEK PARK –This campground lies at the mouth of Abbie Creek where it enters the west side of Lake George W. Andrews. "Abbie" is said to be a Creek Indian name meaning "a grove of dogwood trees." *Facilities:* Camping, boat ramp, picnic area, pit toilets. *Directions:* From Shorterville, take AL 97 south. Entrance is on the left.

ODOM CREEK PARK –This day use area is located on the east side of Lake George W. Andrews at the mouth of Odom Creek. *Facilities:* Boat ramp, picnic area, pit toilets. *Directions:* From Fort Gaines, take GA 39 south to CR 1691, turning right onto Odom Creek Road.

COHEELEE CREEK PARK –This campground lies just downstream from the Coheelee Creek Covered Bridge (see page 209) which crosses Coheelee Creek on the east side of Lake George W. Andrews. It is managed by Early County. *Facilities:* Primitive camping, boat ramp, picnic shelter, pit toilets, drinking water. *Days/Hrs.:* Daily, dawn to dark. *Directions:* From Fort Gaines, take GA 39 south to CR 1691. Park is where the bridge crosses Coheelee Creek.

COLUMBIA BOAT RAMP –A boat ramp is the only facility here at this spot on Lake George W. Andrews operated by Columbia, AL. *Facilities:* Boat ramp. *Days/Hrs.:* Daily, dawn to dark. *Directions:* From Columbia, AL, take AL 52 southeast to the river and follow the signs.

OMUSSEE CREEK PARK –This park is located on the west side of Lake George W. Andrews at the mouth of Omussee Creek and is leased by the Corps to the state of Alabama. *Facilities:* Boat ramp, picnic area, restrooms, drinking water. *Days/Hrs.:*

"While the human body can survive for weeks without food, it can survive only a few days without water. Water should be consumed regularly throughout the day, at least eight ounces about eight times a day."

—Sign in Bill Stanton's Health Food Store, Atlanta

Daily, dawn to dark. *Directions:* From Columbia, AL, take AL 52 west. Turn left on AL 95 and follow the signs.

GEORGE W. ANDREWS LOCK AND DAM –This day use area is on the east side of the Chattahoochee River just below the George W. Andrews Lock and Dam. *Facilities:* Boat ramp, restrooms, drinking water. *Fees:* None. *Directions:* From Hilton, GA, take GA 62 west to Andrews Dam Road and follow the signs.

WEST BANK DAMSITE AREA –This area is on the west side of the Chattahoochee River just below the George W. Andrews Lock and Dam. *Facilities:* Picnic area, fishing pier, restrooms, drinking water. *Fees:* None. *Directions:* From Columbia, AL, take AL 52 west. Turn left on AL 95 and follow the signs.

CHATTAHOOCHEE STATE PARK –This 600-acre Alabama State Park sits about 4 miles from the Chattahoochee River. Fishing for bass, bream and shellcracker on the stocked, spring-fed lake is the principal attraction of the park. Several hiking trails wind through the flat land. There is plenty of wildlife, including raccoons, opossum, fox, coyote and wild turkey. *Facilities:* Primitive camping, picnic tables with grills, group shelter, 15-acre lake with boat ramp, boat rentals, hiking trails, restrooms. *Days/Hrs.:* Daily, 7am-sunset. *Fees:* User fees. *Directions:* From Gordon, AL, take AL 95 south about 9 miles. *More Information:* Chattahoochee State Park, 250 Chattahoochee State Park Road, Gordon, AL 36343; 334/522-3607.

MARINAS

CHEWALLA MARINA –This 43-acre full-service marina is the only privately owned and operated marina on Lake Walter F. George. It is located right off the main channel on Chewalla Creek in Eufaula. *Facilities:* 87 wet slips, covered and uncovered with electricity and water hookups; dry storage on trailer only; all types of boats; boat ramp with $2 fee; gas dock with diesel on request; ship store with basic marine supplies, picnic items, snacks, sandwiches, soft drinks, beer and ice. *Maintenance/Repair:* This is a full-service facility with a 15-ton lift. It has a certified MerCruiser, Mariner and Mercury service department. *Days/Hrs.:* Tues.-Sun., 9am-5pm. *Directions:* From Eufaula, AL, take US 431 north to Chewalla Creek and follow

RED FOX

signs. *More Information:* Chewalla Marina, 580 Chewalla Road, Eufaula, AL 36027; 334/687-5751.

HIKING TRAILS

CHATTAHOOCHEE STATE PARK HIKING TRAIL SYSTEM –Nine individual trails, some linked together, form this trail system which winds around the lake and through the flat terrain of this 600-acre Alabama state park. Trails are well-marked and named for some of the plant and wildlife features that can be found along their paths. *Distance:* Over 7 miles. *Trailhead Location:* Chattahoochee State Park (see page 208). *Features:* A Civilian Conservation Corps (CCC) camp was once located on the park grounds and several of the trails pass the foundations and cabin chimneys of these historic camps. Raccoon, opossum, squirrel, fox, coyote, wild turkey, snake, lizard and turtle are plentiful. A trail map can be obtained from the park office.

HISTORIC SITES

COHEELEE CREEK COVERED BRIDGE –The Coheelee Creek Covered Bridge is the southernmost covered bridge still standing in the United States. In 1891 about three dozen workers built the bridge from foundation to shingles in just four months at a total cost of $490.41. Today its weathered timbers still span the 96 feet across Coheelee Creek about 0.5 mile from where the creek flows into the Chattahoochee River. *Directions:* From Fort Gaines, take GA 39 south to CR 1691, or Old Covered Bridge Road. Follow to bridge.

KOLOMOKI MOUNDS –Long before European explorers walked this continent, Kolomoki was a major population and ceremonial center. Located along Kolomoki Creek a few miles from the Chattahoochee River, this site held a Woodland Indian village where as many as 3,000 Indians may have lived and worshiped during the 13th century. The Kolomoki inhabitants created huge mounds of earth upon which they practiced their religion and buried their dead. It is estimated that two million basket loads of dirt carried by perhaps 1,000 workers were necessary to build the largest mound, the Great Temple which

"What people have to remember is the river is the river is the river... that's all there is. There isn't any more."

—Trout fisherman Ken Worsham quoted by Clint Williams in The Columbus Ledger Enquirer.

rises 56 feet above the surrounding plain and covers nearly 1.5 acres. From its summit, the chief priest led the riverine agriculturalists in the elaborate religious rituals which governed their lives and deaths. Directly in front of the Great Temple Mound, a large plaza served as a village commons and playing field. Scattered around the perimeter of the plaza are two burial mounds and four ceremonial mounds. The Woodland Indians placed their dead in carefully prepared log-lined graves which they covered with a layer of rock and a thick mantle of earth. Typical of the Woodland culture, a variety of goods such as beads, pottery bowls and clay effigies were buried with the dead. The 300-acre historic site lies within the Kolomoki Mounds State Historic Park (see page 206). *Directions:* From Blakely, take GA 27 for 6 miles. *More Information:* Kolomoki Mounds State Historic Park, Route 1, Box 114, Blakely, GA 31723; 912/723-5296.

ROOD CREEK INDIAN MOUNDS –The Rood Creek Indian Mounds are from an Indian village more than 600 years old which probably was abandoned before the Spanish came to the area. The mound site, consisting of a large multiple mound Mississippian ceremonial center with nine temple mounds fortified by two moats, has remained virtually untouched except for the brush and forest that have grown around them. The earthworks are known as the Rood Mounds because the Rood family owned a plantation on this land. The U.S. Army Corps of Engineers now owns the property, and it is closed to the public with the exception of a tour leaving from the Kirbo Educational Museum in Florence Marina State Park (see page 200). The 1-mile walk through the site lasts about 1.5 hours. *More Information*: Kirbo Interpretive Center, 912/838-4706.

SIGNIFICANT URBAN EXPERIENCES

EUFAULA PILGRIMAGE –Eufaula is an Alabama river town which shares the same history as many of the towns along the Chattahoochee, a history inherently dependent upon the river. It is believed that "Eufaula" is a Creek Indian word which means "high bluff." Prehistoric Indians probably roamed Eufaula's bluffs; Indian mounds in Barbour County show evidence of an early Lower Creek population. In the early 1800s, the Winslett brothers from Georgia found the Creek Indians cultivating the fertile river bottom lands on each side of the Chattahoochee. They liked what they saw and settled, adopting the Creek village's name. Eufaula grew as other whites came. For a while the settlers worked and lived peaceably with the Eufaula clan of the Creek tribe. But as they infringed more and more on the Indian lands, conflict broke out. The Indians were, of course, the losers and eventually were removed to Oklahoma—which they named Eufaula.

In late 1834, Seth Lore, an entrepreneur working for the Summerville Land Company, laid out streets with wide parkways in the downtown district. The most important thoroughfares, Livingston, Orange, Randolph and Eufaula, spelled out "LORE." Seth apparently wanted to make sure he was not forgotten. Settlers from Georgia, the Carolinas and Virginia flocked to Eufaula to buy the cheap land.

General William Irwin, an Indian War hero and one of the most prosperous men in the area, used his influence to promote the area's development and established the first steamboat wharf along Eufaula's high bluffs. This set the stage for the commercial rise of the town which was grateful enough to change its name to Irwinton in 1837. Due to post office confusion with the town of Irwinton in Georgia, the name reverted back to Eufaula in 1843.

From 1840 to 1860, Eufaula enjoyed great prosperity owing to its location as a Chattahoochee riverboat landing. Cotton, grown on the large surrounding plantations, was shipped down river to Apalachicola, Florida. From there, it traveled to the world markets at New York City and Liverpool, England. Mercantile trade flourished as caravans of wagons came from all over Alabama to buy merchandise from Eufaula stores. Impressive homes and businesses began to line Seth Lore's planned parkways.

The Civil War interrupted the boom in Eufaula, but it was spared any destruction and by the 1870s boom times returned. It was said that "all roads lead to Eufaula." Goods sold from store counters all over the area came from the wholesale and general stores of Eufaula. More beautiful homes were built.

"I'm sure that by the next presidential election, the environment will become a major issue. My father was a sociologist, and he used to claim that it's in human nature to wait until things get really bad before there's a great rush to try and correct it. We're beginning to see that great rush now."

—Dr. Eugene Odum quoted in Chattooga Quarterly, Spring, 1997

Cotton was still the main source of revenue, and Eufaula was the shipping point or market for a large cotton producing section. Many thousands of bales were shipped from Eufaula every year. But Eufaula's commercial preeminence slipped away as the railroads became the major means of inland transportation. Textiles, lumber and other industries gained in importance, but the town changed very little through the World Wars and the Depression.

The river, once again, was the source of Eufaula's second boom. Construction of the Walter F. George Lock and Dam and the river's 9-foot deep navigable channel have spurred industrial development in the city. Recreational activities on the lake bring many tourists who then discover the wide parkways that Seth Lore laid out and the beautiful homes that river trade money built.

Today the Seth Lore and Irwinton Historic District is the largest in East Alabama. The town boasts over 700 structures listed on the National Register of Historic Places. A brochure for a self-guided walking and driving tour can be picked up at the Eufaula Chamber and Tourism offices. Any time is good to visit the district, but a special time is during the annual Eufaula Pilgrimage in April when many of the historic homes are open for tours and there are antique, needlework and art shows as well. Some of the structures included on the tour are:

Shorter Mansion–Built by Eli and Wylena Shorter in 1884, this home is recognized by the National Trust for Historic Preservation as an excellent example of Neo-Classical Revival architecture. It is furnished with antiques and serves as the headquarters for the Eufaula Heritage Association.

The Tavern–Eufaula's oldest frame structure was originally an 1830s inn for Chattahoochee River travelers. It once housed a Confederate hospital as well as an Episcopal church.

Couric-Smith Home–This 1850 Greek Revival home was one of the first homes built along North Eufaula Avenue. It was the homestead of Charles M. Couric, a French expatriate and ancestor of television news anchor Katie Couric.

Kendall Manor–Materials for this home were purchased before the Civil War, but the house was not finished until 1872. It is one of the finest examples of Italianate architecture in

Alabama. It is now a bed and breakfast inn and open for tours.

Fendall Hall–Ann Fendall Beall and E. B. Young, a banker and merchant who built the first tall bridge across the Chattahoochee, constructed this house in 1860. It has Waterford chandeliers, hand-stenciled walls and murals and is now owned by the Alabama Historical Commission. Days/Hrs.: Mon., Thur., Sat., 10am-4pm (CT).

Pitts-Gilbert Home–Built in 1895, this two-story, Queen Anne home is typical of Victorian architecture with its large porches and banisters, gingerbread trim and large front gables trimmed with elaborate woodwork.

More Information: Eufaula/Barbour County Tourism Council, 102 N. Orange Street, Eufaula, AL 36027; 334/687-5283 or 800/524-7529. Eufaula Heritage Association, 340 N. Eufaula Avenue, Eufaula, AL 36027; 334/687-3793.

Tom Mann's Fish World –Tom Mann's Fish World, owned by fishing guide Tom Mann, is a large freshwater aquarium. Visitors can view huge largemouth bass along with many other native species of fish swimming in a completely natural under-water setting. The largest aquarium is 40 feet long, 20 feet wide, 8 feet deep, and contains 38,000 gallons of fresh water. There are also aquariums containing individual species of fish which are native to Alabama water. In the main building is a natural flowing stream with waterfalls and a number of differ-ent fish species swimming through it. On the grounds of Fish World, there is a man-made lake stocked with huge catfish; the largest one weighs around 35 pounds. The fish can be viewed in their natural habitat through an underwater tunnel.

Mann, who is an Indian, has also put together an Indian museum featuring paintings of many famous Indian chiefs and a large collection of Indian relics. Next door to Tom Mann's Fish World Aquarium is Tom Mann's Fish World Factory Outlet which sells Fish World and brand name tackle. *Days/Hrs.:* Daily, summer, 9am-5pm; winter, 9am-4pm. *Directions:* From Eufaula, AL, take US 431 north for 4 miles. *More Information:* Tom Mann's Fish World, Route 2, Box 84C, Eufaula, AL 36027; 334/687-3655 or 334/687-7045.

Westville –Mule-drawn wagons rounding the bend of a dirt road, frame buildings, newly plowed fields, the clink of a

"For the first time it occurred to me this afternoon what a piece of work a river is — a huge volume of matter ceaselessly rolling through the fields and meadows of this sub-stantial earth, making haste from the high places, by stable dwellings of men and Egyptian pyramids, to its restless reservoir, one would think that by a very natural impulse, the dwellers upon the headwaters of the Mississippi and the Amazon would follow in the trail of their waters to see the end of the matter."

—Henry David Thoreau, September 5, 1838

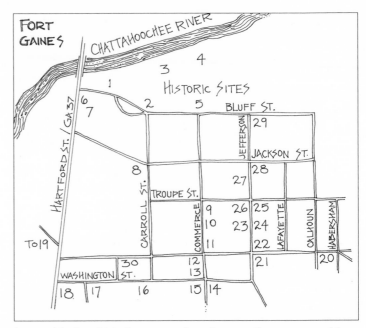

heavy blacksmith's hammer, the chatter of women quilting. This is Westville, "Where it's always 1850." Westville, in Lumpkin, Georgia, is a living history village which realistically depicts 1850 Georgia's pre-industrial life and culture. Westville sprang from a collection owned by Dr. John Word West who spent a lifetime collecting antique farm tools, buildings and artifacts. After his death in 1956, Dr. Joseph Mahan and a group of far-sighted individuals purchased the collection.

This private, not-for-profit educational museum has relocated original structures from around the state and authentically restored and placed them in the landscape of an early Georgia town. Two structures, the Bryan-Worthington House and the Pottery Shop, were moved from locations along the Chattahoochee River in Stewart County. Another structure, the Adams Store, was originally located on GA 27. Supplies brought up the river went to this store for distribution to Lumpkin and the surrounding area.

Westville hosts events all year, including a Spring Festival in conjunction with the Eufaula Pilgrimage (see page 210) and an 1836 Creek Indian War re-enactment weekend with soldier re-enactors and Indian camp demonstrations. *Days/Hrs.:* Tues.-Sat., 10am-5pm; Sun., 1-5pm. Closed New Year's Day,

Thanksgiving, Christmas and the first full week of Jan. Open on Mon. only on major Federal holidays. *Directions:* In Lumpkin at the intersection of US 27 and GA 27. *More Information:* Westville, P.O. Box 1850, Lumpkin, GA 31815; 912/838-6310, 888-SEE-1850.

WALKING TOURS

FORT GAINES WALKING TOUR –Fort Gaines, Georgia, sits on the southern end of Walter F. George, high on a bluff overlooking the Chattahoochee River. This prominent position on the river has contributed to the interesting history of the town. Artifacts place a large prehistoric Indian village on the site between 900 and 1400 AD, and more than two centuries ago the Creek Indians had a town of some size here. After the first Creek War in 1814, General Edmund Pendleton Gaines established a frontier fort on the site. Gaines was later noted for arguing against Indian removal. Built in 1816, the 100-square foot fort was enclosed by a stockade eight feet high and garrisoned by Federal troops under General John Dill, who would later build a large home in the town. In 1836 a second fort was constructed to provide settlers with protection from Indian attacks. (The third, built in 1863, was intended to keep Union troops from going upriver to Columbus, an important city to the Confederacy for its shipbuilding, iron works and textile plants.) In the 1830s, Fort Gaines was chartered as a town and its real heyday began. One historical marker calls the town "Queen City of the Chattahoochee." And so it was. A shipping point for cotton planters for many miles on both sides of the river, it was one of the most important points between Apalachicola and Columbus until the railroads arrived in 1858. Huge warehouses along the river held thousands of bales of cotton for shipping on large steamboats. Traces of the old cotton slide, leading down to the river warehouses can be seen down the bluff. Boom times came again after the Civil War, as merchants came from Alabama and all around to sell their cotton. The town boasted several hotels, two newspapers and saloons everywhere. The decline set in with the ominous boll weevil depression of the 1910s.

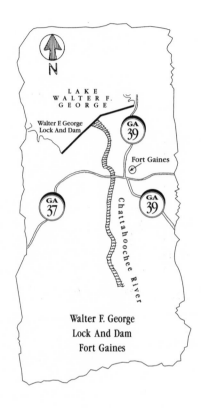

Walter F. George
Lock And Dam
Fort Gaines

Today Fort Gaines is a little worn at the heels. It is the county seat of Clay County, which, according to the 1990 census, is the poorest in Georgia. Much of the downtown and houses built in the 1870s and 1880s are still here. Because of the economy, it is the least changed of the river towns—which can be good for visitors who want to experience a Chattahoochee river town as it once looked.

The best place to start any tour of Fort Gaines is on Bluff Street where the town's history began.

THE BLUFF (1) overlooking the river is at this point about 130 feet above the Chattahoochee. Standing on this bluff and looking at the magnificent view brings a startling revelation as to why Indian sites and forts were built on bluffs in the first place. The river view extends in both directions. This site is the perfect place from which to guard the river, the standard means of transportation for friend and foe alike. Walking along this bluff brings history to life.

CORNELIA CLUB HOUSE (2), erected in 1927, is at the site where the three forts prominent in the town's early history were located.

This CONFEDERATE CANNON (3) is in its original position. From this position above the river Confederate artillerymen had a commanding view. A second cannon was a few yards to the south, and a third was below the bluff in a bend of the river.

TOLL HOUSE (4), the white two-story building with the single chimney rising from the center of its roof, is where in the 1820s people paid tolls for the ferry across the Chattahoochee to Indian Territory (now Alabama). Later, a covered bridge was built. It was the first home of fort commander John Dill.

THE LOG HOUSE (5) was built by the Boy Scouts in the early 1930s and was Fort Gaines' first community library. Today, it is used for civic events.

Go south on Bluff Street to the road down the hill.

THE STATUE (6) facing the river commemorates Otis Micco, a Creek leader. In 1816, by order of General Andrew Jackson, Otis Micco and his people abandoned their village here, fleeing to Spanish Florida. The statue was carved by local artist Philip Andrews from a tree section measuring three feet around and 10 to 12 feet long. Much of the work was done with a chain saw. It is illuminated at night and makes an imposing sight from GA 37 far below.

FRONTIER VILLAGE (7), a collection of authentic frontier structures, is part of an ambitious project to re-create Fort Gaines as it might have looked during the town's earliest days, using only original buildings. There are log houses, a syrup cooker and a cane press.

Go back up the hill and then turn right onto the traffic circle, then right again onto Carroll Street. Go down Carroll, crossing Jackson.

FRONTIER CEMETERY (8), on a slight rise shaded by moss-draped trees, is the final resting place of many early Fort Gaines settlers. John Dill is buried here, as well as John Brown, second president of Franklin College (now University of Georgia). The earliest legible date on a gravestone is 1830s.

Continue down Carroll to Troup and turn left. Go one block to Commerce Street and turn right, to the northeast corner of Commerce and Troup.

JOHN FOSTER HOUSE (9), built in the 1800s, presents the same facades on both Commerce and Troup Streets. It's built in an L shape; to go from one corner room to the other, you have to go through every room in the house or use an outside porch.

IRON HOUSE (10) was built by a young man who moved to Fort Gaines in the late 1800s and established a bar. Each afternoon, after sampling his product, he wove his way down the street to check on the progress of his house. Each day, it seemed to him the house was leaning, so he urged the carpenters to use more nails. When the house was finished it contained so many nails folks started calling it the Iron House.

In the early 1800s MILLER'S TAVERN (11) occupied this site where the Fort Gaines Police Department and City Hall now stand. When Fort Gaines was a rough-and-ready frontier town, a fight broke out one night at the tavern and one of the kerosene lamps fell over, starting a fire. The fire station, with water and a hand-pulled cart, was only a block away, but excited drunks don't make good firemen. They instead settled in across the street to watch the blaze. As the fire burned over to the whiskey barrels lined up behind the bar, they expected a humongous explosion. However, as the flames burned closer

"We're starting to look at the big picture instead of just putting things back the way they were," said Linda Adams, a staff member of the State Senate Committee on Agriculture and Water Resources, which has been holding hearings on the floods. "We've channeled the rivers into small spaces and they don't like it."

—New York Times *story on California floods, February 4, 1997* to the barrels, they flickered and died! The next morning, the fire marshal examined the scene, finding that proprietor Miller watered his whiskey so much it couldn't burn. Miller, it is said, was so humiliated he moved his business to another town.

Cross Hancock Street.

COLEMAN'S OPERA HOUSE (12) was built in 1880 when New York show troops spent summers in Fort Gaines fine-tuning performances to carry back to Broadway. Events held here included dances, concerts and cock fights. Later, the building became a movie theater. Today, it's an auto part store.

WAYSIDE INN (13), located immediately behind the Opera House, was established in 1863 by the city to care for sick and wounded soldiers.

Go to the end of the street and cross Washington Street.

THE BROWN HOUSE (14), to the left, was built around the 1830s as a private dwelling. It has served as a hotel and as an annex to the Dill House next door.

DILL HOUSE (15), the many-gabled pink house to the right, has a romantic history. In late November 1817, at the beginning of hostilities later called the First Seminole war, a boat carrying some 40 soldiers and wives and children of other soldiers was making its way from Mobile up the Apalachicola to Fort Scott, at the confluence of the Chattahoochee and Flint rivers, when it was attacked by a band of Seminoles. Everyone was killed, except two soldiers who escaped into the water, and a military wife named Elizabeth Stuart. The white woman was taken prisoner and made the servant of an Indian named Yellow Hair. Yellow Hair had been nursed through an illness by a white woman near St. Marys, so he felt it his duty to take the woman and treat her kindly. Five months later, she was rescued in Florida by Creek Indians under the Creek chief Gen. William McIntosh, who was fighting on the side of Gen. Andrew Jackson. According to legend, she noticed Indians returning from raids kept coins and threw paper money away, so she quietly gathered the bills and pinned them to her petticoats with briars and pine needles. Conducted to safety at Fort Gaines, where she learned her husband had been killed, Elizabeth married General John Dill, commander of the fort. The elaborate Dill House, with its carved cypress wainscotting and Italian mantels, is said to have been built with her petticoat money. At one time the house was a tavern and after the Civil War it was a hotel. Today, the 11,000-square-foot house has been painstakingly restored as a bed and breakfast inn.

Continue south on Washington, noting the Coca Cola sign on a corner building along the way, restored to its original condition by local residents.

The legend about GRIMSLEY HOUSE (16) begins with two young swains courting the same girl. The loser in this contest for love vowed to wait and marry the couple's first daughter, and that's what he did! Many years later, his widow came to Fort Gaines, ordered this house from Sears, Roebuck and lived there with her children.

SUTLIVE HOUSE (17), with its black iron fence, was built in 1820 by John Sutlive, a business partner of John Dill. Sutlive (called Chafee by his Indian friends, meaning "white rabbit") operated a ferry across the Chattahoochee until the first bridge was built in 1841.

CLAY COUNTY COURTHOUSE (18) has been in continuous use since its completion in 1873. Why isn't it on a square? Because Fort Gaines was already an old settlement by the time the courthouse was built, and there was no land available!

Continue to GA 37 and turn right (west). Just beyond the nursing home, turn left onto New Park Road.

Looking straight ahead from the entrance to the cemetery is a gazebo. It sits atop NEW PARK CEMETERY INDIAN MOUND (19) dating to 200 AD.

Return to GA 37. Go to GA 39 (Hancock Street) and proceed to the Fowler House on the left.

FOWLER HOUSE (20) was built early in the 19th century by an elderly one-legged sea captain. He ordered the high-pitched roof to prevent the accumulation of snow—betraying his New England roots and calling into question his knowledge of the local climate. Even a light snowfall is a rarity in Fort Gaines.

GRIST HOUSE (21) with its green roof, was constructed in the 1880s by Colonel Fredrick Grist, an internationally known game rooster breeder.

Turn right onto Jefferson Street.

B. C. BROWN HOUSE (22) is actually two houses pulled

"Shall we gather at the river, the beautiful, the beautiful river. Shall we gather at the river that flows by the throne of God."

—Methodist Hymn

River Equilibrium

Equilibrium in a river system can be affected by the results of dam construction. In the reservoir behind a dam, the gradient is reduced to zero. Hence, where the stream enters the reservoir, its sediment load is deposited as a delta and as layers of silt and mud over the reservoir floor. Because most sediment is trapped in the reservoir, the water released downstream has practically no sediment load. The clear water in the river downstream of the dam is therefore capable of much more erosion than the previous river, which carried a sediment load adjusted to its gradient. As a result, extensive scour and erosion commonly result downstream from a new dam.

Ken Hamblin, "River Systems," Earth's Dynamic Systems

together to make a single dwelling.

COLEMAN HOUSE (23), built in 1880 after a pond on the site was drained, remains occupied by fifth generation descendants of the original builder.

MCRAE HOUSE (24), a two-story structure on the right, served as barracks for Confederate officers stationed at Fort Gaines during the Civil War.

MCALISTER HOUSE (25), like many houses of its era, has a detached kitchen which protected the main house if the kitchen caught fire. The kitchen was the courthouse for this area before 1850. During the Civil War Union prisoners were brought here from Andersonville and placed under guard.

BROWN COTTAGE (26), across the street from the McAlister House, was the home of James Mason Brown, who left at the tender age of 14 to fight with the Confederacy. Five years later, he caught a train from Virginia to Atlanta, and from there walked 180 miles to Fort Gaines. Arriving exhausted late at night, he curled up on the porch and went to sleep. His excited family found him there the next morning, but he refused to let them touch him for fear of exposing them to lice. They put a wash pot of water on to boil in the back yard, constructed a screen of blankets, and gave him soap, clothes and a razor. He burned his discarded clothes, shaved all the hair from his body, bathed and dressed in his father's clothes. Only then was there a joyous family reunion.

Continue down Jefferson, crossing Troup Street.

WALTER RAY HOUSE (27). The first owner of this house was a man who refused to let minor problems interfere with life's pleasures. The house originally faced Commerce Street, a dusty, noisy thoroughfare between downtown Fort Gaines and the river steamboat landing. The commotion interfered with his relaxation, so he turned the house to face Jefferson.

GRIMSLEY HOUSE (28) served as a Presbyterian church from 1847 until 1904, when it was converted to a private dwelling.

Continue across Jackson Street, to tennis courts and historic marker on right.

Former site of FORT GAINES FEMALE COLLEGE (29). In 1857 the Georgia Legislature authorized a lottery to complete this college. But all the money was spent on construction, leaving nothing to pay off the winners. A fellow named William Cheshire drew a winning ticket and when he couldn't collect, two commissioners gave Cheshire their individual notes, hoping future sales would raise enough to retire their debt. However, the Fort Gaines citizenry grew disillusioned with the lottery and abolished it. A jury ordered the commissioners to pay $1,400, plus interest, to compensate Cheshire. During the Civil War, the building was used as a "tax-in-kind" depot for wool and food to support the war. At war's end, Confederate soldiers distributed the contents to local families before Union troops arrived. The school resumed operation but closed following a typhoid epidemic.

Turn back east on Jefferson and go to Hancock Street. Turn right and stop at the Clay County Library.

CLAY COUNTY LIBRARY (30) has, in its excellent genealogy department, a collection of artifacts from the area. Hours are Mon.-Fri., 9am-5pm.

Reprinted from Georgia Journal, *Sept/Oct 1996, "A Dot on the Map Full of History" by James Edgar Coleman.*

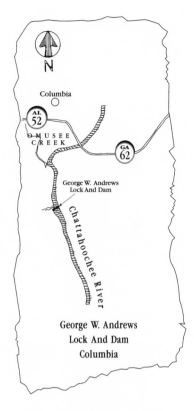

George W. Andrews
Lock And Dam
Columbia

FISHING

Gamefish on Walter F. George (Eufaula) and George W. Andrews include largemouth bass, white bass, hybrids, crappie, channel catfish and bream. Most of Walter F. George's original submerged vegetation has disappeared over the years, but since 1981 the Corps of Engineers, the Georgia Department of Natural Resources and the Alabama Department of Conservation and Natural Resources have maintained a series of fish attractors for better fishing.

Lake George W. Andrews is a 1,570-acre impoundment operated by the Corps of Engineers for navigation. The reservoir is actually a 29-mile long widened stretch of the Chattahoochee running from the Walter F. George Dam south to the George W. Andrews Dam, so the body of water is more like a large river than a lake, with the fish population and fishery more riverine in nature. For information on Water F. George water level, water temperature and generating schedule for the power plant, call 912/768-2424.

Fish Consumption Guidelines

Walter F. George Lake–Crappie under 16", no restrictions; catfish under 16", no restrictions; bass over 16", one per week; catfish over 16", one per month; hybrids over 12", one per month. As a general rule, eat smaller fish to be safe.

Source: Georgia Department of Natural Resources, 1997.

Aim your cast a foot or two in the air over the water so that it seems to hover before it settles. This will not alarm the waiting fish as much as a lure which goes bouncing over the water. Give interest to a lure by changing from fast to slow retrieves and visa versa. Give it a jerk for a bit then jerk it again.

A Tom Mann Fishing Lesson

Tom Mann has fished Lake Eufaula (Walter F. George) since it was impounded in 1963.

Question: I go to Wal-Mart and get outfitted. I buy some lures. I buy a spinning rod. Now, what do I do next? What's the number one thing to do?

Mann: Professional fishermen get a map and start looking for structure. Weekend fishermen don't. They look for pretty places. They know bridges is good because they see other folks tied up catching crappie there. Everybody goes to creeks where it's pretty and that's good fishing. Always the creeks is good. And they're fishin' shorelines where it's pretty.

Question: So that's the weekend fisherman's criteria, pretty?

Mann: That's right.

Question: The professional fisherman on the other hand does what?

Mann: You got to get a map. They learn to fish structure. They know where the ditches are. Where an old river runs, stumps.

Question: Would they look on the map and look for the change in depth?

Mann: They study that map.

Question: (Looking at one of Tom Mann's maps) Are these maps good for that? The hot spots marked on here are these good?

Mann: I've marked a 101 holes on that map. And everyone of 'em I've caught fish in them holes right now. I've got thirty years in that map. That's one of the best maps you can buy.

Question: They need a boat, obviously.

Mann: You can catch from the banks anywhere there's rocks. You can catch 'em walking around rocks. Over, up and down the dam. It's two miles on the dam that you can walk up

BEST ADVICE –Each lake, and every section of river, has its own particular bank topography, underwater structure, stream currents and fish population. Professional guides know all the peculiarities of their lake. The most experienced fishermen find that one or two days of guide fees are a good investment before launching out on their own. Inexperienced fishermen or families looking for a enjoyable day's outing will increase their pleasure ten-fold by taking advantage of the experience of a professional guide. The best guides not only make sure their customers catch fish but provide insights into the fishing habits of different species, lake ecology, weather lore and other aspects that will enhance your fishing experience. When booking a fishing guide, always check to make sure who is responsible for all tackle (rods, reels, lures), boats and gasoline, all live bait, life jackets, lunch, drinks, snacks and ice and rain gear. Understand exactly what is included in the guide fees

GUIDES –Eufaula Guide Service is operated with the endorsement of Tom Mann, one of the most well-known and respected fishermen in the Southeast. Services range from fishing basics for beginning fishermen to the most popular tournament techniques. Guides fish for bass, crappie and hybrids. Tackle is provided or bring your own. Eufaula Guide Service can also provide airport pickup and lodging arrangements. Day and half-day rates. Eufaula Guide Service, 515 North Orange Street, Eufaula, AL 36027; 334/687-5389.

BEST BOOKS AND MAPS –"Tom Mann's 101 Favorite Fishin' Holes on Lake Eufaula" is the best guide to fishing Eufaula. (To order see page 329). Mann, who knows the lake better than any man alive, has keyed his comments to numbers on the map. For example, number 48, Underwater Old Road Bed, on the map: "This is an underwater old road bed where the bridge was blown out. The concrete is still there. Fish the highest place. Some good Bass go here in May June and July. The rocks are great. On the new road bed, it's best to use Crank Baits, Spinner baits, worms, buzz baits." 53 Gator Hole: "This Gator Hole is a deep cove, and some big bass move in here in March, April and May, and back again in October and November. Lots of old tree tops are still here just under the water. A good place for crank bait and worms." This map also includes Tom Mann's tournament strategy and contains his personal approach to fishing Lake Eufaula on a month-by-month schedule with different baits for different months

Fishing Hot Spots' "Lake Eufaula Marked Fishing Map" is one in the series of excellent Fishing Hot Spots maps. This map provides information on specific fishing locations keyed to numbers on a detailed map. The map scale and the topographical information and road access information it contains are considerably more detailed than the Tom Mann map above. The map shows all boat ramp access points, fish attractors, mile markers, buoys, marinas and some structure and vegetation. (To order see page 325.)

U.S. Geological Survey 1:24,000 scale topographical maps covering this section of the river are Twin Springs, Eufaula North, Georgetown, Eufaula South, Hatcher, Fort Gaines NW, Fort Gaines NE, Fort Gaines, Columbia NE, Columbia, Gordon, Saffold, Donalsonville West, Bascom and Steam Mill. (To order see page 326.)

INSIDER TIPS AND HOT SPOTS –Here is Tom Mann's tip for fishing the rip rap on the west side of the Dam: "There have been more 12-pound bass caught here than anywhere on Lake Eufaula. Where all these big bass come from is a mystery. Some say they come up the river from Lake Seminole. They arrive in March and stay until June, with March, April and May being the best months. I've caught many big strings of bass here. All types of lures are good, crank baits, spinner baits, top water and worms. Worms are, by far, the best. For best results, the water must be running at the dam; that is the secret. You will always catch more fish when fishing against the current. Work from east to west. Keep your boat in 25 feet of water. Cast at an angle. Work your lures all the way back to the boat. Many big bass are caught in 7 to 15 feet of water. Learn to swim the worm over the rocks. I use 10-to-15-pound test line (1/4 ounce) with a Texas Rig Worm."

Good fishing opportunities are in the tailraces of the two dams. During late winter and spring, striped bass, hybrids and white bass are attracted to and concentrate in the tailraces. Both bank and boat fishermen using live shad, white jigs or shad imitations can do well.

and down and catch 'em. Caught a million and one like that. All the causeways. Anywhere's there's rocks, you can catch 'em.
Question: The rocks going out from the banks like that?
Mann: Uh huh. They hold forage fish and crawfish and stuff like that. So your bass will pile up on 'em.
Question: Algae grows on the rocks and the forage fish will...
Mann: The shads suck those algae and then your bream will get in there and hide in them rocks. They hide behind places and they feed in there some. So its got bream and bass and a little catfish and it's just hidden structure.
Question: And the bigger fish are feeding off those?
Mann: They're in there trying to catch 'em.

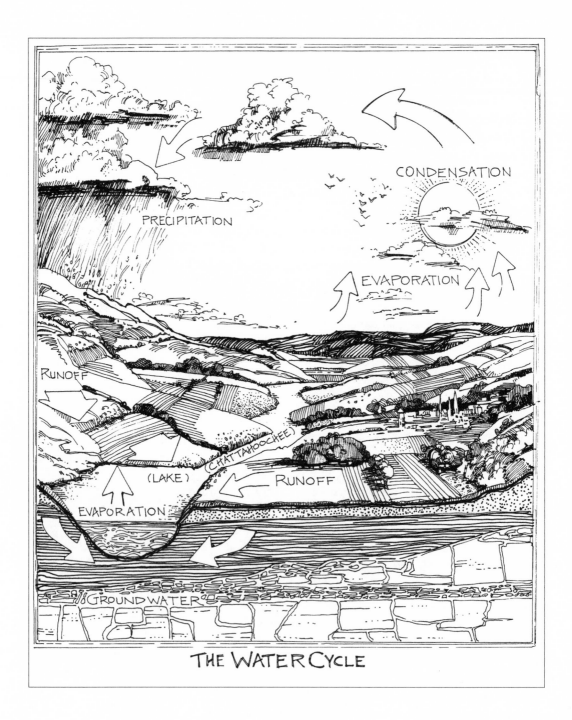

THE WATER CYCLE

BOATING

This portion of the river has two of the three locks on the river, the third being at Jim Woodruff Dam at the southern end of Lake Seminole. Locks transfer commercial barges and pleasure boats from one water level to another. Locks were primarily built for commercial use and, as a result, recreational boaters have lower priority during times of busy commercial traffic. Boaters who lock through with larger vessels should be particularly cautious.

Signal the lock master as you approach by calling on VHF radio Channel 16, by cell phone (Jim Woodruff Lock and Dam at 904/663-4692; George W. Andrews Lock and Dam at 912/723-3482; Walter F. George Lock and Dam at 912/768-2032) or by using the ropes at the upstream and downstream sides of the dam to sound a horn.

The lockmaster controls all movement of vessels through the lock by signaling with traffic lights or horn blasts. Wait for the lockmaster's signal before moving into the lock. A flashing red light means do not enter. A flashing amber light means approach slowly. A flashing green light means enter. If sound signals are used, one long blast means enter the lock, one short blast means leave the lock.

When entering the lock, pay attention to the lock attendants instructions and signals. If passengers are going to help in mooring, give them directions in handling lines before reaching the locks. Line handlers should wear PFDs. Passengers not involved should remain seated.

To avoid accidents, follow these guidelines: 1. Have at least one 150-foot mooring line ready. 2. Hang boat fenders on both sides of the boat. 3. On signal, enter the lock slowly. 4. Be ready to pass lines to the lock attendants to secure the craft safely to the lock wall or, where floating bits are available, secure the line to the bit. Be prepared to secure to another vessel if bits are taken. 5. Shut off the motor and do not smoke in the lock. 6. Follow the attendants instructions for paying out or taking in lines as the water level rises or falls. When the process is completed, release the lines on instruction from the lock attendant, wait for the signal to leave and proceed slowly.

Walter F. George Lock and Dam

This is the northernmost of the three locks and dams constructed on the Chattahoochee by the U.S. Army Corps of Engineers for the development of the A-C-F Waterway System and authorized for navigation, power generation and stream flow regulation. The total length of the dam is 13,585 feet with a maximum height of 132 feet. The massive navigational lock, built for transporting huge river barges carrying fuel and fertilizer, is 82 feet by 450 feet. It slowly drops, or lifts, its passengers the 88 feet between the Walter F. George lake level and the riverbed below the dam. The dam, operational since 1963, is open seven days a week from 8am to 4pm. The dam can be viewed from the Walter F. George Dam Area (see page 206). *Directions:* From Fort Gaines, take AL 46 and turn north onto the access road to the dam area.

The direction or point of the compass in which an object is seen is called the BEARING.

George W. Andrews Lock and Dam

Operational since 1963, this is the middle lock in the lock and dam system along the Chatta-hoochee. On a map, Lake George W. Andrews and the lock and dam are sometimes hard to spot because the dam is not very long, only 1,500 feet, and the lake above it merely looks like the Chattahoochee River. But the dam is 155 feet high and the drop through the lock is 25 feet. The lock is as large as Walter F. George, 82 feet by 450 feet; and, of course, carries the same barge traffic. The lock operates 24 hours a day, 7 days a week. The best place to view the dam is from the George W. Andrews Lock and Dam Area (see page 206). *Directions:* From Hilton, GA, take GA 62 west to Andrews Dam Road and follow the signs.

The Walter F. George Lock operates from 8am to 4pm EST 7 days a week; commercial lockages 24 hours a day. It has a lift of 88 feet and a pool elevation of 190 feet. The George W. Andrews Lock operates 24 hours a day. It has a lift of 25 feet and a pool elevation of 102 feet. The Jim Woodruff Lock at Lake Seminole operates 24 hours a day. It has a lift of 33 feet and a pool elevation of 77 feet.

Some Columbus residents dock their boats at Florence Marina State Park or other marinas on Walter F. George and travel this route to Apalachicola Bay and the Gulf of Mexico. Florence Marina State Park on the Georgia side of the river and Lakepoint State Park on the Alabama side of the river make good beginning points for the journey or stops along the way.

River Adventures Ltd. conducts guided river tours for charter groups. The grand tour begins in Columbus and goes to Apalachicola Bay, but custom tours are developed on request. *More Information:* River Adventures, P.O. Box 309, Kennesaw, GA 30144; 770/426-9302.

Boaters who wish to navigate this river section on their own have several good navigational tools at their disposal. The best one is the Navigation Chart published by the Corps of Engineers. This 14" x 21" soft-cover flip chart of aerial photographs overlaid with navigational aids such as boat ramps and distances provides a detailed guide to the river. It is available through the U.S. Army Corps of Engineers, Mobile District Office (see page 326). The Corps of Engineers recreation map for Lakes Walter F. George and George W. Andrews is available from the Mobile District Office or from the U.S. Army Corps of Engineers Lakes Walter F. George and George W. Andrews Resource Manager's Office (see page 326).

Fishing Hot Spots' "Lake Eufaula (Walter F. George Reservoir) Marked Fishing Map" is the best commercial map of Walter F. George. It points out fishing locations and shows access to waterside recreation sites and boat ramps (see page 325).

USGS topographical maps of the two lakes are listed in the fishing section on page 223.

Section 8
Seminole

Jack Wingate

"I saw five eagles diving in a school of coots out on the lake. Five bald eagles working on one raft of coots. It's a sight to behold. Made them coots a nervous wreck, I'm tellin' you. We got probably 200 osprey nests here, and I'll venture to say that in the Lake Seminole area there's 100 bald eagle nests. Unbelievable. There's an osprey to your left now. He's fishing. He's fixin' to catch him something. We got the great blue heron, just loads of them, and the little blue heron. I remember one time there was four photographers, each one loaded with cameras, got out of their cars and was about to jump over one another to get shots of the blue heron sittin' around the basin there. The white egret, the crooked beak ibis, the wood stork. Wood storks migrate but they have certain places they come back to every year. This lake probably is sitting in one of the best wild turkey areas there is in our part of the world. You could come into this basin we're sittin' in right here a month ago you would hear turkeys gobblin'. They were strutting and looking for mates. The great fox squirrel. He feeds on the seed of the pine tree. They're rare. Beautiful, too. You got deer. Bear is just about gone. A few wild hogs is left. We got the black panthers still here. The bobcat is here. The long tail cat is here–somewhat of a cougar. He's still here. Alligators. Some of the biggest alligators you've ever seen in your life. I've got a picture of one they killed back down here. Over ten feet long. Weighed 700 pounds. The lake is full of freshwater shrimp. I was seein' 'em pop the water there just then but I don't see 'em right now. In this big lime sink we're coming to you see the snails on the bottom. There, the little black pods there. That's what the shell cracker eats on. There's 250 islands in the lake. Wildlife everywhere on those islands. This is one of my favorite places. This is called Silver Lake Run. International Paper owns everything around us here. They raise pine trees. And what I was showing you a while ago on that island is government land and there's no reason for them to ever cut that on that island. If they let it grow 50 more years, you'll see a stand of timber very similar to what it was when the settlers first came into this country.

Jack Wingate is a fishing guide and owner of Wingate's Lunker Lodge on Lake Seminole.

THE LAKE

Lake Seminole, the junction of two Georgia rivers, the Chattahoochee and the Flint, sits at the border between Georgia, Alabama and Florida. This 37,500-acre lake has a 376-mile shoreline, which extends up the Chattahoochee 30 miles and up the Flint 35 miles. It is formed by the Jim Woodruff Lock and Dam, the 16th dam to impede the river and the last.

Since its completion in 1957, Seminole has been known nationally as one of the best places for sport fishing in the country. But in recent years, Seminole's reputation has been tarnished by events as varied as the growth of hydrilla, the flood of '94 and its own fine status as a hot bass lake.

In 1968 a lake resident went to a boat ramp on Spring Creek and dumped the contents of an aquarium into the water. Hydrilla, a common aquarium plant, took hold in the warm clear waters of Seminole and has been growing ever since. Thirty years after its introduction the spiny green plant that looks like a rifle bore brush is so abundant in over 80 percent of the lake that it clogs outboard motors and impedes boat traffic. It is also an extremely effective filter. It filters out plankton, which feeds the tiny shad which feed the bass. With hydrilla, there is no plankton; and therefore, there are no bass. Hydrilla's threat to the lake has been compared to Dutch elm disease, starlings and the English sparrow; but the best comparison is that hydrilla is analogous to an aquatic version of kudzu.

River gauges at boat ramps along the Chattahoochee and Flint Rivers are marked with the crests of three historic floods: the floods of 1875, 1929 and July 1994. The flood of '94 was a watershed, so to speak, in the lives of residents around the river and people who earn their living from it. It rearranged the lake bottom, sending sand and silt into free-flowing springs, clogging them. It washed the fish food supply downstream. Not everybody agrees on exactly what the flood of '94 did to the lake; but from university biologists to cane pole fishermen, they all agree that it did something, and that something was not good.

For years at Lake Seminole, big bass, the idyllic setting of

Tri-State Water Wars

While water appears to be an abundant resource in the Southeast, droughts in the 1980s revealed serious problems with supplying all desired uses in the Apalachicola-Chattahoochee-Flint and Alabama-Coosa-Tallapoosa River basins, particularly during low flow periods. Water supply for municipal and industrial uses, hydropower, wildlife, recreation, irrigation, flood control and navigation all vie for this finite resource. Explosive growth in metro Atlanta near the upper portion of both river basins has increased the population from one-half million people in 1950 to almost three million in 1990, and future growth projections reveal a continued upward spiral.

In 1989, when the U.S. Army Corps of Engineers presented its plans to distribute more water from the Chattahoochee to metro Atlanta's growing suburbs, the state of Alabama (downstream in the Chattahoochee basin) filed suit in federal court to stop the action and Florida subsequently joined in on Alabama's side. A truce was negotiated, the lawsuit put on hold, and the Corps and the governors of the three states signed an agreement in 1992 to conduct a comprehensive water study. From agriculture to hydropower to the environment, this study has attempted to determine how much water each user group needs in the future and how the users' demands might affect each other.

In 1997, the Georgia, Alabama and Florida legislatures passed a tri-state compact and began working towards a water allocation formula (i.e., a guarantee of a certain volume of water at state lines) to be determined by the end of 1998 based on information developed during the comprehensive water resources

skeleton cypress protruding from the dark clear water and the white blooms of lily pads that serve as a platform for leaping 8-pound bass have attracted fishermen from all over the world. Long a popular site for professional bass tournaments, the fishing pressure began taking its toll on Seminole in the late 1980s.

What is the answer to all of this? Auburn University fish biologists are experimenting with ways to eliminate hydrilla from the lake or at least reduce it. They have screened off a portion of the lake with a clever system of fences and gates that open with the bow pressure of motor boats and introduced carp into those sections. The carp eat the hydrilla. Cool overcast weather over the last few years have helped retard the plant's spread. It all seems to be having some positive effect

As far as the long term impact on the lake from the '94 flood, most people are taking a wait-and-see attitude. Great rivers like the Chattahoochee and Flint operate on a timetable that does not necessarily correspond to that of people. A year or two–or a decade or two–on the river timetable is relatively miniscule. The water and the river beds of the Chattahoochee and Flint will rearrange themselves in the way they see fit, and the bottom of Seminole will settle back into a configuration with which the rivers are comfortable. There is not much anybody can do about it.

The fishing pressure will take care of itself. As fishermen move on to another hot spot lake, the bass on Seminole will have a chance to grow.

PARKS AND RECREATION

Corps of Engineers campgrounds and day use areas as well as numerous city and county managed parks surround the banks of Lake Seminole. There are also two state parks on the lake. A third, Florida Caverns, is in Marianna, Florida, on the Chipola River which feeds into the Apalachicola south of the lake. The Corps campgrounds have attendants who live on-site and are available to help with registering and finding campsites. Due to the area's moderate climate, campgrounds and parks are open year-round. Boat ramps are open all hours while campgrounds are open from 8am-10pm. Fees for most parks are $2 for boat ramps, $1 per person for swimming with a $3 maximum per vehicle. For lake maps and additional information on the parks, contact the Resource Manager's Office, P.O. Box 96, Chattahoochee, FL 32324; 912/662-2001. For 24-hour lake information: 912/662-2814. Website: www.sam. usace.army.mil/sam/op/rec/. The following parks are listed counterclockwise around Lake Seminole, beginning with Neals Landing, the northernmost area on the Chattahoochee.

NEALS LANDING CAMPGROUND –This Corps of Engineers park is located far up the main channel of the west bank of the Chattahoochee between mile markers 21 and 22. *Facilities:* 12 campsites with no hookups, boat ramp, picnic area, bath houses, restrooms, dump station. *Fees:* $5 per night. *Directions:* From Florida state line, take FL 164 south about 1 mile and follow the signs.

NEALS LANDING PARK –This nicely wooded area lies adjacent to the campground. *Facilities:* Boat ramp, picnic area, restrooms. *Directions:* From Florida state line, take FL 164 south about 1 mile and follow the signs.

BUENA VISTA –This Jackson County operated park is located at mile marker 16 on a northwestern, woody, marshy arm of the lake that is still more Chattahoochee River than Lake Seminole. *Facilities:* Boat ramp, picnic area. *Directions:* From Sneads, FL, take FL 271 north for 15 miles and follow the signs.

PARRAMORE LANDING –Parramore Landing is first and foremost a catfish and seafood restaurant that also has a small campground. It is located on the west bank of the main channel of the Chattahoochee River at mile marker 13. The boat dock here is for restaurant patrons and overnight campers. A small bait and tackle shop adjoins the restaurant. There is no gas dock. *Facilities:* 10 covered boat slips; 8 campsites with electricity and water hookups, 5 with sewer; boat dock; restaurant; bait and tackle store; restrooms; drinking water. *Days/Hrs.:* Restaurant, Tue.-Thur., 4-8:30pm; Fri., 4-9:30pm; Sat., 11am-9:30pm; Sun., 11am-8:30pm. Bait shop, daily, 6am-6pm. *Fees:* User fees. *Directions:* From Sneads, FL, take FL 271 north to Parramore Road and turn right. *More Information:* Operators, Ralph and Diane Cox, Parramore Landing, 7768 Parramore Road, Sneads, FL 32460. Restaurant, 850/592-2091.

study. Environmentalists and others strongly support adequate instream flows that protect aquatic habitat and biodiversity and enhance recreational opportunities.

The water in the Chattahoochee River basin is shared by people and wildlife in three states–from burgeoning metro Atlanta to the seafood workers in Florida's Apalachicola Bay. It remains questionable, however, whether we will have collective wisdom to manage future growth to sustain these limited water resources.

Sally Bethea, Upper Chattahoochee Riverkeeper

May Flies

Harmless but abundant, may flies are native to the Lake Seminole area. Their presence is an indicator of good water quality. They appear in swarms. They do not bite, but swarms can be so thick they can impede breathing.

One night the Corps of Engineers got a call from a campground where may flies were clustering around an electric light. Campers complained that the odor from dead flies was bothersome. When Corps workers got to the site, they found a three-feet pile of expired flies that had to be hauled away with a front loader.

APALACHEE GAME MANAGEMENT AREA –This game management area operated by the State of Florida is open to hunting for ducks, deer, rabbit, squirrel, quail, snipe and woodcock. Public boat ramps provide easy access to the water for waterfowl hunters. Be sure to check on local regulations before hunting. Permits may be required in addition to state licenses and migratory waterfowl stamps. Fishing and hunting regulation booklets are available free of charge at the Resource Manager's Office and area stores. *Directions:* From Sneads, FL, take Fl 271 north and follow signs.

HOWELLS LANDING –This ramp near Sneads gets heavy use from fishermen as it is the first ramp on the west side with quick access to the main part of the lake. *Facilities:* Boat ramp. *Directions:* From Sneads, FL, take FL 271 north and follow signs.

THREE RIVERS STATE RECREATION AREA –This wooded, 800-acre Florida state park extends for four miles along the shore of Lake Seminole. Hardwood hammock and pine forests make up the area's hilly terrain which resembles the woods of the Appalachian Mountains. White-tailed deer, fox squirrels, grey fox and a host of birds make their home in the rolling hills and steep ravines of this area, which is very different from other parts of Florida. *Facilities:* Campsites with electricity and water hookups, boat ramp, picnic area, swimming beach, bath houses, playground, hiking trails, restrooms, drinking water, dump station. *Days/Hrs.:* Daily, year-round, 8am-sunset. *Fees:* $8 per night, $2 more with electricity. *Directions:* From Sneads, FL, take SR 271 north for 2 miles. *More Information:* Three Rivers State Recreation Area, 7908 Three Rivers Road, Sneads, FL 32460; 850/482-9006.

SNEADS PARK –This Corps of Engineers park is located in Sneads, FL, near the Jim Woodruff Dam and the Powerhouse for Lake Seminole. *Facilities:* Boat ramp, picnic area, an 150-person and an 100-person picnic shelters with grills and electrical outlets, swimming beach, bath houses, playground, restrooms, drinking water. *Fees:* $30 picnic shelter. *Directions:* Off US 90 in Sneads, FL.

WEST BANK OVERLOOK –This area is located on the west bank of the Apalachicola just below Jim Woodruff Dam. There are no facilities here, and the trees are so grown up that it is hard to get a good view of the lake and dam. *Directions:* Off US 90, just west of Victory Bridge in Sneads, FL.

JIM WOODRUFF DAM FISHING DECK AND POWERHOUSE –This day use area is located below the dam site on the east bank of the Apalachicola River. The Powerhouse and the Resource Manager's Office for Lake Seminole are both located here. The Resource Manager's Office has a nice relief map exhibit indicating parks, campgrounds, boat ramps and historic sites around the lake. There are also exhibits about the early history of the region and the building of Jim Woodruff Dam. *Facilities:* Fishing deck, restrooms, drinking water. *Directions:* Off US 90, just east of Victory Bridge in Chattahoochee, FL.

EAST BANK CAMPGROUND –This Corps area is on the south side of the lake near the dam and north of the Georgia-Florida border. Some campsites sit directly on the lake while others are in the mixed hardwood forest that covers the banks. *Facilities:* 69 campsites with electrical and water hookups; boat launch; picnic area, 30-person picnic shelter with grill and electrical outlet; nature trail; volleyball, tetherball, horseshoe pit, shuffleboard court; bath houses, restrooms, drinking water. *Days/Hrs.:* Daily, year-round. Gates locked between 10pm and 7am. *Fees:* $12 per night, full hookup; $8 per night, tent site; $2 per day, guest; $20 picnic shelter. *Directions:* From Chattahoochee, FL, take GA 192 north 3 miles and follow signs. *More Information:* East Bank Campground, 912/662-9273.

CHATTAHOOCHEE PARK –This Corps day use area is located on the Georgia side of Seminole's south shore. *Facilities:* Boat ramp; picnic area; 1 150-person and 2 100-person picnic shelters with grills, electrical outlets and lights; swimming beach; bath house; playground; restroom; drinking water. *Fees:* $30 picnic shelter. *Directions:* From Chattahoochee, FL, take GA 192 north and follow the signs.

RIVER JUNCTION LANDING CAMPGROUND –This Corps campground is located on the south shore of Lake Seminole about 4 miles east of the dam. *Facilities:* 10 primitive campsites, boat ramp, picnic area, bath houses, restrooms, drinking water. *Fees:* $8 per night, tent site. *Directions:* From Chattahoochee,

WATER MYTH: EGYPT

In Egyptian myth, Nun, the primordial ocean, contains the seeds to fertilize earth, animals and women.

FL, take GA 192 and follow the signs.

RIVER JUNCTION LANDING –This day use area lies adjacent to the River Junction Campground. *Facilities:* Boat ramp, picnic area, restrooms. *Directions:* From Chattahoochee, FL, take GA 192 and follow the signs.

FACEVILLE LANDING CAMPGROUND –This area is between mile markers 14 and 15 on the Flint River section of the lake. *Facilities:* Primitive campsites, boat ramp, picnic area, 100-person picnic shelter with grill and electrical outlet, pit toilets, drinking water. *Fees:* $30 picnic shelter. *Directions:* From Bainbridge, take GA 97 south and follow the signs.

FACEVILLE LANDING PARK –This Corps day use area lies adjacent to Faceville Landing Campground. *Facilities:* Boat ramp, picnic area, 100-person picnic shelter, pit toilets. *Fees:* $30 picnic shelter. *Directions:* From Bainbridge, take GA 97 south and follow the signs.

HORSESHOE BEND PARK –This boat launch area is located on the east side of the Flint River at mile marker 18. *Facilities:* Boat ramp, restrooms. *Directions:* From Bainbridge, take GA 97 south and follow the signs.

EARL MAY BOAT BASIN –This park, identified as the Bainbridge By-Pass Park on Corps of Engineers maps, is operated by the City of Bainbridge and is located on the south side of the city on the Flint River at mile marker 23. A dirt road connects this park with the Cheney Griffin Park just upstream (see below). *Facilities:* Campsites with water and electrical hookups, boat ramp, picnic area, swimming beach, playground, restrooms, drinking water. *Days/Hrs.:* Daily, 6am-11pm; beach closes at sunset. *Fees:* $9 per night with hookups. *Directions:* From Bainbridge, take College Street north to the Flint River. *More Information:* City of Bainbridge Parks and Recreation, 912/248-2010.

CHENEY GRIFFIN PARK –Picnic tables under Spanish moss-covered live oaks line the banks of the Flint River at this city park located in the heart of Bainbridge. It is identified as the Bainbridge Municipal Park on Corps maps. A dirt road connects this park with the Earl May Boat Basin Park just downstream (see above). *Facilities:* Boat ramp, picnic area, playground, restrooms, drinking water. *Days/Hrs.:* Daily, 6am-

"We're going up into some beautiful country now. We ain't seen nothin' yet, but we're fixin' to see some."

—Jack Wingate on a boat tour of Lake Seminole going from one gorgeous natural habitat to another.

11pm. *Directions:* From Bainbridge, take Water Street north to the Flint River. *More Information:* City of Bainbridge Parks and Recreation, 912/248-2010. For a driving tour including Earl May Boat Basin and Cheney Griffin Park see page 239.

BIG SLOUGH LANDING –This boat ramp is located at the mouth of Big Slough Creek above Bainbridge on the east side of the Flint River. *Facilities:* Boat ramp. *Directions:* From Bainbridge, take GA 311 north and follow the signs.

FLINT RIVER LANDING –This is the northernmost boat ramp on the Flint River portion of the lake. *Facilities:* Boat ramp. *Directions:* From Bainbridge, take GA 253 north and follow the signs.

HALES LANDING CAMPGROUND –This area is located on the west side of the Flint River at mile marker 18. *Facilities:* Primitive campsites; boat ramp; picnic area; 100-person picnic shelter with grill, electrical outlet and lights; restrooms, drinking water. *Fees:* $8 per night, tent site; $30 picnic shelter. *Directions:* From Bainbridge, take Ten Mile Still Road south and follow the signs.

HALES LANDING PARK –This Corps of Engineers day use facility lies adjacent to the Hales Landing Campground. *Facilities:* Boat ramp, picnic area, 100-person picnic shelter, restrooms. *Fees:* $30 picnic shelter. *Directions:* From Bainbridge, take Ten Mile Still Road south and follow the signs.

TEN MILE STILL LANDING –This boat ramp is located on the north side of the Flint River between mile markers 10 and 11. *Facilities:* Boat ramp. *Directions:* From Bainbridge, take Ten Mile Still Road south and follow the signs.

RALPH KING LANDING –This ramp is on the east side of the Spring Creek portion of Lake Seminole. *Facilities:* Boat ramp. *Directions:* From Bainbridge, take Ten Mile Still Road south to GA 253. Take GA 253 and follow the signs.

SMITHS LANDING –This is the northernmost boat ramp on the Spring Creek portion of Lake Seminole. *Facilities:* Boat ramp, picnic area, pit toilets. *Directions:* From Brinson, take GA 310 south and follow the signs.

DECATUR LANDING –This ramp is on Spring Lake on the west side of the GA 253 bridge. *Facilities:* Boat ramp. *Directions:* From Reynoldsville, take GA 253 north and follow the signs.

REYNOLDSVILLE PARK –This Corps day use area is located near Reynoldsville, GA, about halfway up the Spring Creek section of Lake Seminole. *Facilities:* Boat ramp, picnic area, pit toilets, drinking water. *Directions:* From Reynoldsville, take GA 253 south and follow the signs.

SPRING CREEK LANDING –This park is located at the mouth of Spring Creek next to Reynolds Landing fish camp (see page 245). *Facilities:* Boat ramp, picnic area, 100-person picnic shelter with grill and electrical outlet, restrooms, drinking water. *Fees:* $30 picnic shelter. *Directions:* From Donalsonville, take GA 39 south to GA 253. Turn left and follow the signs.

SEALY POINT –This park is located on an island on the large area of the lake between Fish Pond Drain and Spring Creek. *Facilities:* Boat ramp, picnic area, restrooms, drinking water. *Directions:* From Donalsonville, take GA 39 south to GA 374 south. Turn left and follow the signs.

HARVEL POND –This area is on Harvel Pond near the mouth of Fish Pond Drain. *Facilities:* Boat ramp, picnic area. *Directions:* From Donalsonville, take GA 39 south to GA 374 south. Turn left and follow the signs.

SEMINOLE STATE PARK –This 343-acre Georgia state park sits on the north side of Lake Seminole on the east side of Fish Pond Drain. It is surrounded by the Lake Seminole Waterfowl Management Area, one of the state's largest wildlife management areas. The gopher tortoise, the only tortoise native to Georgia, makes its home along a 2.2-mile nature trail specifically designed to interpret the wiregrass community habitat. *Facilities:* 10 rental cottages; 50 tent and trailer sites with electrical, water and sewage hookups; pioneer camping; picnic tables; 6 picnic shelters; 1 group shelter; 3 boat ramps; 2 fishing docks; canoe rentals; swimming beach; miniature golf; nature trail; restrooms. *Days/Hrs.:* Daily, park, 7am-10pm; park office, 8am-5pm. *Fees:* User fees. *Directions:* From Donalsonville, take GA 39 south to GA 253. Turn left and follow the signs. *More Information:* Seminole State Park, Route 2, Donalsonville, GA 31745; 912/861-3137.

CYPRESS POND PARK –This Corps day use area is in the wetlands area between Fish Pond Drain and Spring Creek. *Facilities:* Boat launch, picnic area, pit toilets, drinking water.

Directions: From Donalsonville, take GA 39 south to GA 374 south. Turn left and follow the signs.

RAY'S LAKE –This is the northernmost boat ramp on the Fish Pond Drain portion of the lake. *Facilities:* Boat ramp, picnic area, 100-person picnic shelter with grill, restrooms, drinking water. *Fees:* $20 picnic shelter. *Directions:* From Donalsonville, take GA 39 south to GA 374. Turn left and follow the signs.

CUMMINGS LANDING PARK –This park is located on the largest part of the lake between Fish Pond Drain and the main channel of the Chattahoochee. *Facilities:* Boat ramp, picnic area, restrooms, drinking water. *Directions:* From Donalsonville, take GA 39 south and follow the signs.

FAIRCHILD'S PARK –This day use area is at the 10 mile marker on the Chattahoochee channel of the lake. *Facilities:* Boat ramp, picnic area, pit toilets. *Directions:* From Donalsonville, take GA 91 south to GA 221. Turn left and follow the signs.

DESSER LANDING –This boat launch area is located between mile markers 14 and 15 on the east side of the Chattahoochee main channel. *Facilities:* Boat ramp, picnic area, pit toilets. *Directions:* From Donalsonville, take GA 91 south to GA 221. Turn left and follow the signs.

FLORIDA CAVERNS STATE PARK –Intricate cave formations, a magnolia-beech forest, a Florida floodplain swamp and a river which disappears and reappears are some of the unusual features found at this 1,800-acre Florida state park. The Spanish first mentioned this series of connecting caves containing limestone stalactites, stalagmites, columns, rimstone, flowstones and draperies in 1693. But the Indians knew of the caverns centuries before that. Millions of years ago when this area was under the sea, billions of sea creatures died, leaving their tiny shells to fuse and form the limestone rock which makes up Florida. This area is one of few in the state where dry caverns can be found; most are filled with water and some are channels for underground rivers which emerge as springs.

During the Depression, Civilian Conservation Corps workers dug out the passageways which go through the caves. Guided tours of the caves are now offered several times a day. One nature trail in the park travels beside a Florida floodplain swamp where the trees are specially adapted to alternating

"Wilderness holds the answers to questions man has not yet learned how to ask."

—Nancy New Hall quoted in Guale

periods of flood and drought. Another trail winds through the hilly terrain of a magnolia-beech forest. Here is the southern-most range of the forest of the Appalachian foothills. These large, tall hardwoods, surrounded by limestone outcroppings, have colorful fall foliage and mossy trunks.

The park borders the Chipola River (see page 277) which feeds into the Apalachicola River further south. The Chipola vanishes underground, then reappears a few hundred yards downstream, traveling through the same kind of underground cavities seen in the caverns, forming what is known as a "natural bridge." It is believed that General Andrew Jackson crossed this particular one with his troops in 1818. The Chipola River Canoe Trail begins in the park and runs for 52 miles. Because of a hazardous old log chute, canoeists are urged to put in two miles downstream of the park. *Facilities:* Campsites, boat ramp, picnic area, swimming area, caves, canoeing, hiking, horseback riding. *Days/Hrs.:* Daily, 8am-sundown; tours daily, 9am-4pm. No tours on Christmas and Thanksgiving. Tours have limited space; tickets are sold by 1pm on holidays and weekends. *Fees:* $12, campsites $2 more with electricity; $3.25 per vehicle for tour. *Directions:* From Marianna, FL, take SR 167 north 3 miles. *More Information:* Florida Cavern State Park, 3345 Caverns Road, Marianna, FL 32446; 850/482-9598 or 850/482-1228.

MARINAS

TRAILS INN MARINA AND CAMPGROUND –This site was once the landing for Butler's Ferry, which crossed the Chattahoochee River here. This privately operated marina, once called Embrey's Marina, is on property leased from the Corps. It is located on the east side of the main channel of the river at mile marker 8.2. *Facilities:* 23 covered, 15 uncovered boat slips; covered and uncovered dry storage on trailers; gas dock; ship store with bait, tackle, basic marine supplies and snack bar with some hot foods, such as hot dogs and chili, cold sandwiches and drinks; 7-acre picnic area; bank fishing; accommodations: 5-unit motel with fully-equipped kitchen, 13 full-service RV sites, 11 acres cleared primitive camping. *Maintenance/Repair:*

Will be glad to help anyone who needs boat repair assistance, but no service person on site. *Days/Hrs.:* Daily, 6am-6pm. *Directions:* From Donalsonville, take GA 39 south to GA 253. Turn right and follow the signs. *More Information:* Trails Inn Marina and Campground, Rt. 3, Box 188, Donalsonville, GA 31745; 912/861-2060 or 800/322-5916.

DRIVING TOUR

BAINBRIDGE –Near the confluence of the Chattahoochee and Flint rivers sits the town of Bainbridge. Seminole Indians once occupied the bluffs along this part of the Flint, and in 1765 it was the site of an Indian village called Pucknawhitla. By 1778 it became known as Burgess Town after trader James Burgess established a trading post here. From 1817 - 1824, it became a federal outpost called Fort Hughes, named after a U.S. Army bugler who Indians killed on the site in 1817. When the Seminoles were defeated in late 1824, Fort Hughes was re-named Bainbridge for Commodore William Bainbridge, Commander of "Old Ironsides" during the War of 1812. Land for a county seat was purchased in 1826, and the city was incorporated in 1829. The Flint, with its connection to the Chattahoochee and the Apalachicola, was part of a large ready-made water system; and Bainbridge from its earliest day was a river town, shipping products from surrounding farms and forests down the Flint to Apalachicola Bay. Indian villages, DeSoto explorations, Spanish missions, early trading, Andrew Jackson's Indian-fighting army–there was a lot going on up and down this valley. This is an area rich in American history, and Bainbridge is right in the heart of it.

The following tour begins at the Bainbridge town square, which was originally the Court House Square, but is now called Willis Park. This town square is characteristic of the south's personality and reveals more about its town than any other town square in the south. There are monuments to World Wars I and II and the Korean and Vietnam wars. There's a bell from the steamboat *John W. Callahan, Jr.* There are historical markers for El Cameo Real, an Indian trail which connected St. Augustine and Pensacola and crossed the Flint near present

---

Fish Consumption Guidelines

Lake Seminole–Bass over 16", one per week; channel catfish over 12", one per week; bullheads over 12", one per week. As a general rule, eat smaller fish to be safe.

Source: Georgia Department of Natural Resources, 1997.

"We are made to love the river and the meadow and the wind to ripple the water."

—Henry David Thoreau

Canoeing the Flint

About 200 yards south of I-285 below Hartsfield International Airport is a small brick structure that bears the name: "Flint River Pumping Station." This is where the feeder streams and rain culverts from College Park, Forest Park and the airport come together to form a stream. It's a drainage ditch around Riverdale, but by the time this stream flows east of Fayetteville, it's a river, on its way to becoming one of Georgia's most prominent, the Flint.

It was the river that ran between Tara and Twelve Oaks in Margaret Mitchell's *Gone with the Wind*. Scarlett could look out "across the endless acres of Gerald O'Hara's newly plowed cotton fields toward the red horizon" where the sun set "in a welter of crimson behind the hills across the Flint River."

As the Flint passes west of Griffin, it is a major river. When it enters Upson County and runs head on into the tail-end of Pine Mountain, it is one of Georgia's most scenic rivers and the reason all ages of outdoorsmen and women flock to it.

It is canoeable above GA 18 west of Thomaston. But be ready to do a lot of portaging and bushwhacking through deadfalls, dams and other obstructions. Below GA 18 the scenery changes dramatically, and the Flint becomes a mountain river full of Class I and Class II rapids. This kind of terrain continues for 20 miles or so and climaxes just below the GA 36 bridge with "Yellow Jacket Shoals," a boat-busting rapid that can easily jump to Class IV in high water. Fortunately, the GA 36 bridge just before the shoals is the usual takeout.

After the rapids and the Fall Line, the Flint becomes a big, strong flat water river, flowing south to create Lake Blackshear near Cordele, and finally, into Lake Seminole where it joins the Chattahoochee to form the Apalachicola in southwest Georgia.

CANOEING GA 18 BRIDGE TO POBIDDY (TALBOTON) ROAD —About three miles below GA 18 the country changes; Pine Mountain throws up a barricade to the river's edge, and resulting conflict between river and rock provides some of the most exciting scenic vistas along any Georgia river. The plants and animals of the mountains occur along this river valley, intermingled with coastal vegetation. As a result, Spanish moss hangs over mountain laurels and rhododendron, a strange but beautiful combination. The river has walled off, or more properly, carved off a sweeping bend in the Pine Mountain escarpment, leaving a cove protected on three sides by mountains and on the fourth by river. This river cove has provided isolation for plants, animals and people for thousands of years. Today, it offers the best recreation potential in the middle of the state if properly used. Just above Sprewell Bluff, a large ridge on the southwest side of the river, the Flint offers a series of shoaly rapids of no real consequence, but enough to pep up an otherwise placid run. A county park opposite Sprewell Bluff affords a takeout point for the upper trip, a place to enter the river for the lower stretch, or a picnicking and viewing point for the auto traveler. From Sprewell Bluff to GA 36, the river continues its good manners, with little gradient and no significant rapids. At the GA 36 bridge the river appears swift but smooth, a tempting place for an easy Sunday float. But don't believe it. Around the first bend, the canoeist will begin to encounter a building series of rapids, climaxing in the twisting drop at the bottom of Yellow Jacket Shoals. At high water (10 feet or greater on the GA 36 gauge), these rapids can build up some very heavy water, with large waves, big holes and a better than even chance to swamp an open canoe. At about 10 to 11 feet the river can be run by decked boats and rafts manned by competent, experienced paddlers. At high levels, even these paddlers would probably be endangered. At lower levels (8 feet) the river offers intricate maneuvering and long steep drops down narrow chutes. Minimum levels are around 7 feet. Take-out for this run is at Pobiddy (Talboton) Road. The Yellow Jacket Shoals stretch with medium flow requires about 3 hours running time, a comfortable afternoon run.

There are few other rivers in the world where tupelo trees form part of the obstacles in the rapid, where Spanish moss drips onto mountain laurel, where water and rock have combined to give such a beautiful sweep to the traveler's vision. *Put-Ins/Take-Outs:* This section of the river naturally divides itself into several different trips. From GA 18 to Sprewell Bluff (about 14 miles; 6 hours) is an easy trip with no significant rapids. From Sprewell Bluff to GA 36 (7 miles; 3 hours) is more of the same. From GA 36 to Pobiddy (Talboton) Road, it's a different story. Just around the bend is Yellow Jacket Shoals. Beginning boaters should remember that different water levels completely change the personality of a river. At 11 feet the sections above GA 36 will require more skill. *More Information:* For up-to-date information, maps, water levels, overnight camping, shuttle, history and the latest river conditions, stop at Jim McDaniel's Flint River Outdoor Center at the GA 36 bridge, 8 miles southwest of Thomaston. Born and reared near the river, Jim and his wife Margie have run this outpost since 1978; 706/647-2633.

day Bainbridge and DeSoto's discovery of the Flint. There are monuments to a local teacher, former mayors and former Georgia Governor Marvin Griffin. Magnolias, live oaks and crepe myrtles grace the lawn. Baskets of pink impatiens hang from the lightposts. The centerpiece of it all is a Confederate monument honoring the Bainbridge volunteers, later called the Bainbridge Independents. A white Victorian-style gazebo completes the setting. This square merits a leisurely walk, with time to read the inscriptions and reflect on the architecture as well as the very southernness of the setting.

From the square, go north on Broad Street and stop by the Bainbridge Hardware Company. Lofton Willis has assembled a large variety of products that reflect rural southwest Georgia life–catfish baskets, cotton baskets, iron skillets, tack for farm animals. His main line of business, however, is supplying big tools for the economic bedrock of this community–the farms, the peanut processing factories and the feed mills that line US 27. He's also got two mint-condition Model-T Fords in the store's attic.

Go back to Water Street and head west toward the Flint River. The first block of Water Street boasts some interesting historic structures. On the right corner is the Decatur County Courthouse, built in 1903. The original clock, weighing 1.5 tons, is still in use. There's a historical marker on the creation of Decatur County and a huge magnolia, being protected through a city ordinance to preserve landmark trees. Next is the courthouse annex, formerly the county jail. On the left side of the street is the Conger Building, built in the late 1800s by an old established Bainbridge family; the 1890 Mitchell Willis Building and the 1914 City Hall and Firehouse, reflecting the Mission-style architecture popular in the early 1900s. This building, now known as the Firehouse Center and Gallery, is home to the Bainbridge-Decatur County Council for the Arts and the Decatur County Historical Society Museum.

Continue on Water Street to Donalson Street and turn right. This street will curve to the right and turn into Jackson Street. At 330 Jackson is Chason Park, a very historic piece of property in Bainbridge. DeSoto and his men crossed the Flint at this site over four centuries ago. This site on the bluffs overlooking

Reece's Flint

On a Flint River canoeing trip, Reece Turrentine and friends Jim McDaniels and Guy Hutchinson left the river near Owens Island to look for the remnants of the Old Alabama Road, once a stagecoach route.

"We broke up and walked alone to search. It took a minute for it to soak in. In an instant we had stepped out of the river, and back hundreds of years, looking for the remnants of stagecoaches and wells. We found them, as well as some strange rock piles which Jim identified as Indian graves, or possible slave graves. Then we scattered again to see what else we could find. It was as if a time machine had transformed us to another world. Once again, I felt the old exhilaration, or maybe inspiration is a better term. Whatever, such feelings have swept over me many times. Through the years I've paddled rivers, camped by them, bathed in them, watched their moods and listened to their murmuring. I've been caressed by them and bruised by them...The plant life, and the amazing array of animal life that calls to you from a distance...it all makes you feel the energy and harmony of it all. It makes me want to reach out and claim kinship with the wholeness. But I can't do that. I can't ignore the fact that I'm an outsider. I'm more of an intruder than a kinsman...But I still get the old feeling. I knew Jim and Guy felt it. I could see them through the trees in the distance, walking slowly, looking at the ground and up in the trees... They were thinking it, or praying it in their own way, what every outdoorsman has felt: "O God, let it stay like this forever."

Reece Turrentine, "A River Makes Up Its Mind," Georgia Journal, Sept/Oct 1996.

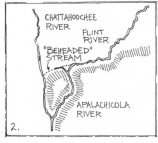

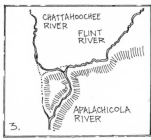

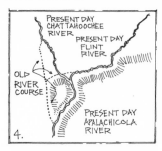

Stream Capture

Although the Chattahoochee and Flint rivers have probably flowed for millions of years, geologic evidence suggests that the Apalachicola River was once only a small tributary to the Chattahoochee. But over time, the Apalachicola actually "captured" the other two rivers.

the Flint is also the location of the 1817 Fort Hughes and the beginnings of Bainbridge.

Go back to Water Street and continue a little further until it ends at Cheney Griffin Park (see page 234). This park affords a wonderful view of the river as it flows under the Highway 84 Bridge upstream and an old railroad bridge downstream. Live oak adorned with Spanish moss, small cypress tress, sweetgum and hickory line the curves of the riverbank. Picnickers sit at tables under the trees, facing the river as boats cruise up and down. This is a particularly beautiful place to be at sunset. There's a wooden walkway for strolling along the river, and docks and boat ramps for boating. Smells from the Flint River Seafood Restaurant fill the air.

Continue left around the park to a dirt road that begins under the old railroad bridge and follows the curve of the river, providing one of the most scenic river experiences in Georgia. It compares to the Columbus Riverwalk (see page 182); but where Columbus is more urbanized with its lighted brick walkways, this is a more natural, rural riverbank environment. Moss-covered live oaks line both sides of the road right down to the riverbank. Motor boats cruise up and down the grey-green Flint, which is about 75 to 100 yards wide at this point. Locals fish and picnic under the trees in the evening. The west bank of the river is lined with wetlands and woods.

Cross under the new Highway 84 Bridge. The road continues along the riverbank and connects with the Earl May Boat Basin and its boat ramps, picnic areas, campsites and stocked fishing ponds (see page 234). There is a historic steam-powered train engine at the park, and it's worth the time to stop and take a look at this massive structure which overtook riverboats as a transportation preference. Also in the park is the Bainbridge-Decatur County Chamber of Commerce, located in the historic 1921 McKenzie-Reynolds Home. An interesting photo in the house shows it surrounded by water during the July 1994 flood. The chamber of commerce offers brochures for self-guided walking tours of historic structures in Bainbridge. *More Information:* Bainbridge-Decatur County Chamber of Commerce, P.O. Box 736, Bainbridge, GA 31717; 912/246-4774; fax 912/243-7633.

FISHING

Lake Seminole is a 37,500-acre impoundment, also called Jim Woodruff Reservoir, near Chattahoochee, Forida, with 8,000 acres in Florida and the remainder in Georgia. Easy access and popular bank fishing are available along FL 271 north of Sneads, Forida. Sunshine bass were first stocked here in 1975. Seminole is the former home of a Florida state record striped bass.

BEST ADVICE –Each lake has its own particular bank topography, underwater structure, stream currents and fish population. Professional guides know all the peculiarities of their lake. The most experienced fishermen find that one or two days of guide fees is a good investment before launching out on their own. Inexperienced fishermen or families looking for a enjoyable day's outing will increase their pleasure ten-fold by taking advantage of the experience of a professional guide. The best guides not only make sure their customers fish, but provide insights into the fishing habits of different species, lake ecology, weather lore and other aspects that will enhance a fishing experience.

When booking a fishing guide always check to make sure who is responsible for all tackle (rods, reels, lures); boats and gasoline; all live bait; life jackets; lunch, drinks, snacks and ice; and rain gear. Be sure to understand exactly what is included in the guide fees.

GUIDES –Jack Wingate has been operating Lunker Lodge (see page 244) on Lake Seminole since the lake opened, and he is the reigning expert on where and how to fish Lake Seminole. Any fishing expedition to Seminole should begin with a call to Wingate. Seminole fishing guides can be booked through the Lodge. Call 912/246-0658, fax 912/246-5518.

BEST BOOKS AND MAPS –Larry Larsen's "Guide to North Florida Bass Waters" is the most helpful guide to this section of the river. (To order see page 328.)

Atlantic Mapping's "Map of Lake Seminole" is the best fishing map for the lake, showing both the Chattahoochee and the Flint rivers from Bainbridge on south into the lake. It includes a wide variety of information, including access roads and boat

The most widely accepted theory about the evolution of the three rivers states that originally the Chattahoochee and Flint flowed around the west of the Tallahassee Tertiary Highlands as shown in the top illustration. At this point, the Apalachicola River was a small tributary of the Chattahoochee, just beginning to cut into the highlands.

Still a tributary of the Chattahoochee, the Apalachicola eventually cut through the highlands, capturing the Flint and diverting its waters southward along the newer channel as shown in the second illustration. Meanwhile, the beheaded section of the Flint became an inverted stream flowing back into the Apalachicola while slowly cutting headwaters to the west.

The third illustration shows the beheaded portion of the Flint itself becoming a "pirate," capturing the Chattahoochee and rapidly enlarging the Apalachicola River Valley.

The present courses of the three rivers is depicted in the last illustration.

Reece's River Food

"We'd usually get to the put-in late (after work), and paddle only down to "Dripping Rock" area for overnight camp. That gave us time to show off our "river-bank-special deluxe" supper. Already prepared, foil wrapped and frozen ahead of time were the required number of packages of hamburger steak, big slices of onion, potato slices, sliced carrots, cabbage, and anything else a culinary genius might devise. We'd dig a shallow pit, line it with charcoal and burn it until white, add a thin layer of dirt, lovingly place the packages in the pit, cover with dirt, build a charcoal fire on top, then go take a shower (or whatever) at Dripping Rock Falls. After two hours, as we served it up, the beasts of the fields and forest would all but do battle to capture our feast. Well, maybe that's a little exaggerated, but... it was good.

I tried it once on the grill on the back deck, and it was terrible. A package like that needs the river–and the dirt, the rocks, the waterfalls, the night critters–to make it work. River bank food is ethereal. As the day dies and a star or two appears, and the night sounds begin and friends gather around the campfire–the food is always good. But that's not the primary thing.

What's primary is who you are with, and where you are, and the sights and sounds you are seeing and hearing."

Reece Turrentine, "A River Makes Up Its Mind," Georgia Journal, Sept./Oct. 1996

ramps, contour lines, the river channel, mileage along the channel, boat launching ramps, submerged roads, boat roads, submerged ponds, submerged timber, depressions and channel markers, marinas and recreational facilities and lake and river depth. Maps are available at marinas, outdoor stores and bait shops in the area. (To order see page 325.)

U.S. Geological Survey 1:24,000 scale topographical maps covering the lake are Steam Mill, Dresser, Brinson, Bainbridge, Fairchild, Reynoldsville, Faceville, Fowlstown, Chattahoochee and Sneads. (To order see page 326.)

INSIDER TIPS AND HOT SPOTS –Seminole is shallow with a maximum depth of 35 feet and an average depth of 9 feet. The hot spots on Lake Seminole have adjacent deep water where the predators gather, waiting for the shad to swim around the point. Some of the better areas are Fort Scott, the Hutchinson Ferry Bank, Coot's Landing and Stone's Landing. The latter two are good locations to find hybrids, stripers and white bass.

Prime bass fishing is in the spring. Best baits include spinner-baits and plastic worms as the bass move into the shallows. Good topwater fishing for bass is later in the summer. Bluegill and shellcracker are caught in the spring using crickets and earthworms. Fly-fishing is excellent for bream when the mayflies hatch and fall into the lake. Some large strings of speckled perch are caught in January and February using live minnows.

FISH CAMPS

SEMINOLE LODGE –This lodge and marina are located on the Florida side of Lake Seminole, near Sneads at mile marker 2. *Facilities:* Lodge; campsites with water, electricity and some sewer; boat ramp; gas; boat dock; store with bait, tackle, groceries, ice; restrooms; drinking water. Going downstream, this is the last marina with gas for approximately 105 miles. *Days/Hrs.:* Daily, year-round. *Directions:* US 90 at Sneads on Legion Road. *More Information:* Operators, Monte and Becky Anderson, 2360 Legion Road, Sneads, FL 32460; 850/593-6886.

JACK WINGATE'S LUNKER LODGE –Their advertisement says, "not a marina, not a resort, just a fish camp." *Facilities:* 62 covered slips; gas dock; restaurant; store with bait, tackle and groceries; boat rentals. Accommodations: Lunker Lodge–air conditioned and heated motel rooms and a Stag Hangout sleeping 20 men; Bass Island Campground–48 campsites with combinations of electrical, water, sewer and cable TV hookups; 34 primitive campsites with electricity and water; recreation room; showers and restrooms; playground; 40-person covered pavilion; dump station. Fishing guide services available. *Days/Hrs.:* Daily, year-round. *Directions:* From Chattahoochee, FL, take GA 192 north and follow the signs. *More Information:* Jack Wingate, Lunker Lodge, Route 1, Bainbridge, GA 31717; 912/246-0658.

REYNOLDS LANDING –This fish camp is leased by Ducks Unlimited and is adjacent to Spring Creek Park. *Facilities:* Boat ramp; cabins; campsites with water and electricity; 8 slips for guests, 6 more for rent; picnic area; picnic shelter; showers; restrooms. Restaurant which serves breakfast and lunch. *Days/Hrs.:* Daily, year-round. Restaurant open daily, 6am-3pm. *More Information:* Reynolds Landing, Route 5, Box 1105D, Donalsonville, GA 31745; 912/861-3247.

SEMINOLE SPORTSMAN'S LODGE AND MARINA –This fish camp is located across from Seminole State Park (see page 236) on the main channel of Fish Pond Drain. *Facilities:* 47 covered slips; covered dry storage on trailer; open storage for RVs, campers and motor homes; gas dock; store with bait, batteries, fuses, basic camping needs, snacks and drinks. Accommodations: 12 fully-equipped motel units which sleep 3-10; 20 campsites with water and electricity, some with sewers. *Days/Hrs.:* Daily, year-round. Hours are flexible, depending on need; generally 6am-8pm. *Directions:* From Donalsonville, take GA 39 south for 18 miles and follow the signs. *More Information:* Seminole Sportsman's Lodge and Marina, GA 39 South, Rt. 3, Box 215-A, Donalsonville, GA 31745; 912/861-3862.

BOATING

Except for the inconvenience of hydrilla clogging boat props and choking off access to sections of the lake, the current fishing hiatus has not effected the lake for anyone

Jim Woodruff Lock and Dam

Completed in 1957, this southernmost lock and dam on the Chattahoochee, forming Lake Seminole, was built to improve navigation on the river and provide a source for the generation of electricity. The lock is 82 feet by 450 feet with a maximum lift of 33 feet and operates 24 hours a day, seven days a week.

Before construction of the project, the Chattahoochee and Flint rivers were only three feet deep. A channel nine feet deep and 100 feet wide is maintained to allow commercial traffic to Columbus on the Chattahoochee and Bainbridge on the Flint. Three power plant units, each with a capacity of 10,000 kilowatts, put out an average annual energy output of 220,000,000 kilowatts. The best places to view the dam are from the West Bank Overlook (see page 232) and the Jim Woodruff Dam Fishing Deck and Powerhouse Area (see page 233) on the east bank. Below the dam the mighty Chattahoochee becomes the mighty Apalachicola. *Directions:* The West Bank Overlook is off US 90, just west of Victory Bridge in Sneads, FL. To get to the east bank, continue east on US 90, crossing the river to Chattahoochee, FL.

*"Cuz, they bit yesterday.
They'll tare it up tomorrow."*

—*Entrance and exit signs at Jack Wingate's
Lunker Lodge on Lake Seminole*

interested in exploring a fascinating natural area for photography, bird watching, wild flower identification or any other type of waterborne naturalistic experience. Hydrilla, after all, is only one of 222 species of aquatic plants in Seminole; wetlands surrounding the lake add 600 or so more. Lake Seminole's only peer for such a wilderness experience in the North Florida-South Georgia region would be the Okefenokee Swamp. Yet many find Seminole preferable to the Okefenokee because the water is bigger and the terrain more open, allowing for better views and more photography opportunities.

Boaters should go by Jack Wingate's Lunker Lodge and ask him to mark a lake map, available at the lodge, with the best touring routes. Wingate has been guiding on Seminole ever since its creation and knows its natural areas and history as well as any man alive. Wingate will also take guests on tours of the lake on his boat or arrange for other guides to do so. He can accommodate small or large groups.

A LITTLE BLUE HERON
PERCHING ON THE EDGE OF THE RIVER

Section 9
Apalachicola River

"My folks were Huguenots, big-boned French. They tried to get to Louisiana, but got lost navigating the Apalachicola. In French my last name means female hawk.

The whole family has to sell the honey. It's a family operation: wife, daughter-in-law and son. I've been in it since I was born. I got out 15 years. I was an agricultural inspector in Georgia. I loved Georgia, but I wanted to be my own boss. I was tired of the government. Had too many bosses. When you make a mistake working for yourself, you've got no one to blame but yourself. So I came back to the river in '53.

There's always plenty to do in the bee business: peddle honey, take care of the bees, build boxes. You take the brood, the larvae, and make you a third hive out of two. That's called an increase. When you got more parts, it helps the genetics.

Beekeepers are always losing beehives, like cattle. Recently they're losing a lot across the nation because of mites. They're worse than the atom bomb. Alabama lost 60 percent. They're a mite so big you can see them. A lot of crops and flowers can't live three or four years without bees because of cross pollination. We have 800 or 900 colonies. Most beekeepers don't. Not that many. There's 30,000 to 50,000 in a top colony. It's hard work. Get stung. Can lose your shirt. One of the first big beekeepers we had was King Solomon.

Tupelo honey is the best there is. Doesn't granulate. Doesn't sour. It can be kept for years in a liquid state. I got a testimony about a diabetic using it on the jurisdiction of his doctor. It's a fruit sugar. If you can tolerate fruit sugar, you can tolerate tupelo.

This river is three different countries. The terrain by Owl Creek is like Africa. Where we are is a few palms, like the Panama Canal. And up river on the Apalachicola is farming country. The swamp is not that deep. The Apalachicola is called the Big River, the Chipola the Little River. I live on an island surrounded by an island, way out in the swamp, a mile from anyone else. My daddy built the road himself. I have 200 acres on the edges of the river swamp, full of tupelo, white tupelo, the honey tree. In the spring the flower is a little ball with little fur, green and pale white. The whole swamp smells like tupelo honey.

Lavernor Laveon Lanier, Jr.

My daddy started beekeeping in 1894, just a little ways above Owl Creek. There's no pollen in the deep swamp in the summertime, and he'd take his bees on the *John W. Callahan* to Bainbridge. The trip from Wewa was 25 cents. The *Callahan* hit a snag and went down in 1933. No more steamboats went up the river. The trucks put them out of business.

My daddy used to read the river, watch clouds going north from the Gulf of Mexico to get a preview of the weather. He'd figure if it was better to take his bees up there or skip it that year. During a flood in 1929 he drew a line in the house, two or three feet high. "That's where the water will crest." It did. There wasn't any dams to stop the flooding, but it seems like we were better off back then."

Lavernor Laveon Lanier is a beekeeper in Wewahitchka, Florida.

THE RIVER

From Lake Seminole on the border of Georgia and Florida, the Chattahoochee River changes names. It becomes the Apalachicola, a river that meanders through a winding, undammed path of 107 miles in the Florida Panhandle until it empties into the Gulf of Mexico at Apalachicola Bay. Florida's largest waterway in flow volume, the river releases 16 billion gallons of freshwater into the bay each day.

The Apalachicola begins where the Chattahoochee and Flint rivers meet, but that has not always been true. Today, its 20,000-square-mile drainage basin includes sections of Georgia and Alabama, but in the past its entire watershed was in what is now Florida. Once a small tributary of the Chattahoochee, the Apalachicola eroded a valley through the panhandle's northern hills until it captured the Flint (see page 242). Deprived of its major tributary, the Chattahoochee moved eastward until it rejoined the Flint to form the modern arrangement of the three rivers.

The channel of the dark, slow-moving river continues moving eastward, a fact dramatically illustrated along its banks for the first 25 miles. To the west is land the river has ground into submission eons ago, a vast expanse of flat, wet and low floodplains, covered in marshes and swamps. To the east is terrain

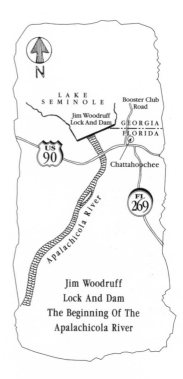

Jim Woodruff
Lock And Dam
The Beginning Of The
Apalachicola River

Jim Woodruff Lock and Dam

James Waldo Woodruff was born in Columbus, Georgia, in 1879. He was an engineer with a wide variety of business interests. He spent the greater part of his life working toward the goal of providing a navigable Apalachicola, Chattahoochee and Flint River system. In recognition of Woodruff's support for the project and distinguished public service, the project was named for him in 1957.

Apalachicola River History

The arrival of the Spanish in the 1500s transformed Native American society in the Florida Territory. As Franciscan friars opened missions across the panhandle, Indian populations plummeted, mostly due to exposure to European diseases. Armed conflict added to the disruption of Indian life for the next three centuries as Spain, England and the United States maneuvered for control of north Florida. Georgia Creeks in cooperation with the British raided the Spanish and their allies, the Apalachee tribe from Tallahassee and the smaller Apalachicola group, who lived in the Apalachicola River Valley. During this time, these tribes continued to visit the islands and coast for hunting, fishing and shellfish harvesting. In the early 1800s, the U. S. forcibly removed from northwest Florida most of the remaining Creeks, Apalachee, Apalachicola and related tribes, who together became known as the Seminoles. But the descendants of those who resisted populate several towns on the river, including, Blountstown, named after an Indian chief whose royal lineage has since continued for more than 100 years.

The only town on the Chattahoochee named Chattahoochee is on the Apalachicola.

the river is just beginning to work on, a series of steep bluffs which rise dramatically from the water's edge.

The Apalachicola Bluffs, 150-foot high walls of eroding, multi-colored limestone, sand and clay, do more than offer unrivaled vistas of the low swamplands of Florida, Alabama and Georgia. Along with some nearby ravines, uncharacteristically deep for Florida, they provide sanctuary to an incredible assortment of ancient and unusual plant species. Many are commonly found in the southern Appalachians, like mountain laurel, white baneberry, wild ginger, bay star vine and wild hydrangea—and understandably so. During the last ice age about 12,000 years ago, glacier-cooled waters pushed many plants and animals south along the Chattahoochee and Flint River corridors. Some plants died out in this region as the weather warmed and the ice receded, but other species remained in the bluffs and ravines, whose cool, moist climates resemble those found today in the higher elevations of Northeast Georgia.

In many places the river seems tame. Convoys of mammoth barges lumber along its banks. Schools of fishing and pleasure boats arrive in the warmer months, and river mileage and dredged channel markers make it seem like a highway. But there are other places where the river remains wild. Sometimes the river bends and twists so much the barges can barely pass. Many times they must stop, back up and steer furiously to one side to advance. Then there are the places where the river stretches out in great marshes and swamps, which only the alligators and snakes call home.

PARKS AND RECREATION

DEAD LAKES STATE RECREATION AREA —This 83-acre state recreation area has an interesting history before becoming a park in 1974. The Works Progress Administration, a New Deal agency, dug two ponds and two buildings for a fish hatchery, which the state Game Commission operated from 1936 to 1951. Both ponds and one of the structures, a house for the resident biologist, remain standing. Not far from the biologist's house, cedar shake shingles for roofing were once made. As late as 1944,

Spanish moss was collected from trees, hung to dry in the sun or sheds like tobacco and used for packing material and furniture stuffing. A still for turpentining, a major industry in the 1950s, was just outside the park's boundaries. Tupelos, one of the most common hardwoods in the park, once supported a thriving beekeeping industry. Bees in what is now the state park helped produce 1,000 barrels a year of tupelo honey. Other hardwoods in the park include sycamore, red maple, Southern magnolia, sweetgum, Southern red oak, sand post oak, turkey oat and sweetbay. *Facilities:* 10 campsites with electricity, 10 primitive campsites, boat ramp into the West Arm Creek section of the Dead Lakes, picnic area, hiking trails, restrooms, showers. *Days/Hrs.:* Daily, year-round, 8am-sunset. The gate is locked at sunset, but arrangements can be made ahead of time to enter the park after dark. *Fees:* Camping, $8 per night; with electricity, $2 more; day use, $2 per vehicle. The entrance station on the park brochure map does not exist; payment is on the honor system. *Directions:* From Wewahitchka, FL, take FL 71 2 miles north. *More Information:* Dead Lakes State Recreation Area, P.O. Box 989, Wewahitchka, FL 32465; 850/639-2702. The park has brochures with a map of the trails, campground and boat ramp.

TORREYA STATE PARK –Located within one of the most biologically diverse and topologically unusual areas in the state, this park has a long and distinguished natural history. The park is named after the Torreya tree, a nearly extinct species that clings to life in the steep ravines along the east bank of the first 20 miles of the Apalachicola River (see page 261). Visitors often remark that much of this park resembles the Appalachian Mountains, not only because of the steepness of the ravines but because of the many flora that migrated to this region during the Ice Age and remained here at its end, perfectly at home in the cool, shaded ravine climate. Further adding to the mountain illusion are several uncommonly clear creeks which bubble over tiny shoals of limestone rocks covered in moss. The creeks have shaped the ravines by cutting away the remains of ancient coastline dunes here. Similarly, the Apalachicola River is working furiously on the adjacent sand hills to create the most visually stunning vistas in the state, the Apalachicola

How the Apalachicola Got Its Name

Apalachicola, "meaning people of the ruling place," was an ancient Indian capital town located on the river about 30 miles below present day Columbus. The Spanish built a fort there in 1689 and referred to the whole river as Rio de Los Apalachicolas after the Indian town.

The English, however, called it the Chattahoochee. The name of the river at any one place and time depended on who controlled it militarily and who was drawing the maps.

Today, the river's name officially changes from Chattahoochee to Apalachicola at the Georgia-Florida state line, because that was the border established in 1781 between the English and Spanish territories.

"Let us cross over the river and rest under the shade of the trees."

—Stonewall Jackson

Dead Lakes

This giant swamp wound up with its eerie appearance and name thanks to both nature and man. Around 1860 an especially bad flood pushed a sandbar in the Apalachicola River to the mouth of the Chipola River, backing up the latter's water into a 12,000-acre expanse of five interconnected lakes. A logjam from beavers and lumberjacks at the mouth of the Chipola worsened the blockage.

Shortly thereafter, the Corps of Engineers, in digging a shortcut from the Apalachicola to the Chipola at the southeastern end of the lakes, inadvertently made the flood permanent. The cutoff shortened steamboat trips along the two rivers by a dozen miles or so, but allowed the faster Apalachicola a release to push water into the Chipola. The swamp cypresses, accustomed to seasonal dry periods, withered and died in droves. Their carcasses, still standing, inspired the area's name.

Apalachee is the name of a tribe of the Creek Indians who lived in today's southwestern Georgia and Northern Florida. The exact meaning is unknown but it may have been from the Choctaw word "apelachee" meaning "help" or "helper" or from "apeliche" meaning "the place in which to rule, preside or govern." Apalachicola has the same meaning but with the terminal element "okla" meaning "people" with an inferred meaning "people of the ruling place."

—Marion Hemperley, Indian Heritage of Georgia

Bluffs (see page 258). Several overlooks 125 feet or higher in the park illustrate the river's eastward migration over the ages. On the west bank is land the river has ground into submission eons ago, a vast expanse of wet and low floodplains covered in marshes and swamps. On the east bank is terrain the river is just beginning to sculpt, the high walls of multicolored sand, limestone and clay which rise straight up from the river's edge. From the surface of the river to the top of the bluffs and ravines, the floral scenery changes dramatically. Swamp forests of cypress, tupelo and willow tree grow in standing water along the river. Large watery hickory, swamp-chestnut oak and American oak trees rise above the flood plain, seasonally covered with nutrient-rich waters. Diminutive yews and Torreyas hide out in the steep bluffs and narrow ravines. Giant magnolias, beech and hickories rise majestically above the hilltops. In the ravines and bluffs, the deciduous trees put on one of the state's most dramatic displays of autumn leaves. In the floodplains on the opposite bank, vast stands of bald cypresses also offer a fine show of color changes from pale green in the spring to rusty brown in the fall. Amazed by the diversity, early botanists jested that this area was the original Garden of Eden and that Noah made his ark out of the Torreya tree. (Interestingly, many early church pulpits in the region were made of Torreya, also called gopherwood.) When humans first came to this area is uncertain, but a number of Indian sites have been discovered in the park. General Andrew Jackson crossed the river here with his army during the first war against the Seminoles in 1818. From 1840 to 1910, when the Apalachicola served as a commercial transportation corridor, more than 200 steamboats, loaded with cotton, timber or other goods traveled its channel. Planter James Gregory built a grand estate across the river from the park at Ocheesee Landing in 1849. During the Civil War six Confederate cannons stood guard over the highest bluff; the remains of the gun pit can be seen along the main bluff trail. In 1935 the Civilian Conservation Corps moved the Gregory House to its present location overlooking the river in the state park. *Facilities:* 30 campsites, primitive camping (no water), picnic area, picnic shelters, hiking trails, a youth camp, guided tours of the

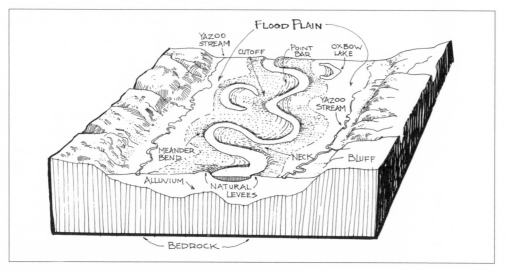

Features of a Floodplain

Most stream valleys are covered with large quantities of sediment that make up a flat surface over which the stream flows. This surface is called the floodplain, and during high floods it may be completely covered with water. Rivers that flow across floodplains are characterized by channels that either meander in sinuous loops or braid in interweaving multiple channels.

All rivers naturally tend to flow in a sinuous pattern, even if the slope is relatively steep. This is because water flow is turbulent, and any bend or irregularity in the channel deflects the flow of water to the opposite bank. The force of the water striking the stream bank causes erosion and undercutting, which initiate a small bend in the river channel. In time, as the current continues to impinge on the outside of the channel, the bend grows larger and is accentuated, and a small curve ultimately grows into a meander. On the inside of the meander, velocity is at a minimum, so some of the sediment load is deposited. This type of deposit occurs on the point of the meander bend and is known as a point bar. The two major processes around a meander bend–erosion on the outside and deposition on the inside–cause meander loops to migrate laterally.

Because the valley surface slopes downstream, erosion is more effective on the downstream side of the meander bend; thus, the meander also migrates slowly down the valley. As a meander bend becomes accentuated, it develops an almost complete circle. Eventually, the river channel cuts across the meander loop and follows a more direct course downslope. The meander cutoff forms a short but sharp increase in stream gradient, causing the river to completely abandon the old meander loop, which remains as a crescent-shaped lake known as an oxbow lake.

Another key process operating on a floodplain is the development of high embankments, called natural levees, on both sides of the river. Natural levees form when a river overflows its banks during flood stage and the water is no longer confined to a channel but flows over the land surface in a broad sheet. This unchanneled flow significantly reduces the water's velocity, and some of the suspended sediment settles out. The coarsest material is deposited close to the channel, where it builds up a high embankment. Natural levees grow with each flood. Some grow high enough so that the river channel is higher than the surrounding area.

As a result of the growth and development of natural levees, much of the floodplain may be lower than the river flowing across it. This area, known as the backswamp, is poorly drained and commonly is the site of marshes and swamps. Tributary streams in the backswamp are unable to flow up the slope of the natural levees, so they are forced either to empty into the backswamp or to flow as yazoo streams, streams that run parallel to the main stream for many kilometers.

Ken Hamblin, "River Systems," Earth's Dynamic Systems

Gregory House (see page 265). Anyone planning to camp must first register with a park ranger. *Days/Hrs.:* Daily, 8am-sunset, but arrangements can be made ahead of time to enter the park after dark. The park doesn't take reservations. *Fees:* Camping, $8 per night, $10 with electricity; primitive camping, $3 nightly per person; day use, $2 per vehicle. *Directions:* From Bristol, FL, go north on FL 12 for 4 miles. Turn left (west) on FL 270 and continue for about 7.5 miles. Turn left (northwest) on CR 1641, which soon enters Torreya State Park. *More Information:* Torreya State Park, HC 2 Box 70, Bristol, FL 32321; 850/643-2674.

WILDLIFE MANAGEMENT AREAS –WMAs are areas administered by the Florida Game and Fresh Water Fish Commission, mainly for hunting and fishing. Some are public lands, like the Apalachicola Wildlife Management Area, which has the same borders as the Apalachicola National Forest. More commonly, they are private lands, like the Edward Ball and Robert Brent Wildlife Management Areas, which are owned by timber companies. Besides hunting or fishing, there isn't too much recreational use. Ed Ball's 66,000 acres and Robert Brent's 89,000, for example, are basically industrial forests–single species pine crops in neat rows and various stages of harvest or growth. The public is allowed to access wildlife management areas on any of the roads which go through them. But roads and bridges in the private ones are subject to close on any given day with no prior notice for timber cutting. G.U. Parker, one privately owned wildlife management area near the Apalachicola River, was taken out of circulation a number of years ago and is no longer open to the public. Florida Game and Fish people say they are trying to increase traditional recreational activities like bird watching on their lands. They expect to implement day use fees in some areas within the next several years. *Directions to Ed Ball WMA:* From Apalachicola, FL, take US 98 west. Entrance is on the right. *Directions to Robert Brent WMA:* From Bristol, FL, take FL 20 east. Entrance is on the left. *More Information:* Florida Game and Fresh Water Fish Commission, Regional Office, RFD 7, Box 440, Lake City, FL 32055-8713; 850/758-0525.

APALACHICOLA NATIONAL FOREST –Water, trees and savannas

"This earth is something you protect every day of the year. A river is something you defend every inch of its course."

—James A. Michener

cover most of this 560,000-acre national forest, the largest in Florida. Six rivers flow through it, including the Apalachicola, which follows the western boundary of the forest, and the Ochlockonee, which divides the forest into two administrative sections, the Wakulla and Apalachicola Ranger Districts.

Historical evidence suggests few Indians lived in this forest, although the Apalachee Indians settled north and south of it. Creeks and Seminoles traveled to those areas in the 1700s and early 1800s. But after the United States gained control of Florida from Spain in 1821, most of the area went into private hands. After extensive turpentining and logging exhausted the pine and hardwood forests between 1880 and 1920, much of the land was abandoned and small towns along the Apalachicola Northern Railroad line disappeared. The federal government acquired most of the property during the Depression and established the national forest in 1936.

Several paved state highways pass through the national forest, as do dozens of forest service roads, virtually all graded, maintained and suitable for two-wheel drive vehicles. A few small towns are scattered throughout. Most along the Apalachicola Northern Railroad, like Vilas, Liberty, Bon Ami and Central City, remain on maps, but became ghost towns years ago with the decline of the turpentine industry. It's best to pick up supplies in the larger cities around the forest, like Bristol, Quincy, Sopchoppy or Tallahassee.

Camping is permitted throughout the forest, but limited to designated campgrounds or hunt camps during several hunting seasons, which begin in October and end in March. Contact a ranger office to find out the specific dates. Boat landings, campgrounds and primitive campsites are scattered throughout the forest, but most visitors don't stray far from either the Apalachicola or the Ochlockonee rivers. *More Information:* National Forests in Florida, Woodcrest Office Park, 325 John Knox Road, Suit F-100, Tallahassee, FL 32303; 850/942-9300. The Apalachicola Ranger District Office, P.O. Box 579, Bristol, FL 32321; 850/643-2282. Recreation Director, Apalachicola National Forest, c/o Wakulla Ranger District Office, 1773 Crawfordville Highway, Crawfordville, FL 32327; 850/926-3561. The ranger offices provide detailed maps of the national forest and know where the latest controlled burns have taken place if visitors are interested in exploring those areas.

The following recreational areas are all located in the Apalachicola Ranger District of the Apalachicola National Forest.

CAMEL LAKE CAMPGROUND –A pleasant, mostly pine-shaded place to pitch a tent or park an RV next to a 25-acre freshwater lake. *Facilities:* 6 campsites with tables and fire rings, boat ramp with 10hp motor limit, picnic area with tables and grills, unsupervised swimming beach, flush toilets, drinking water, trails suitable for hiking or off-road biking. Interpretive displays and trail maps are all but nonexistent. *Days/Hrs.:* Daily, year-round. There is no entrance station or gate. *Fees:* Camping, $4 per site; day use, $2 per vehicle. *Directions:* From Bristol, take CR 12 south for about 11 miles. Turn left (east) on FSR 105 and drive 2 miles.

BIG GULLY LANDING –This is a no-frills facility, used primarily by fishermen and hunters and located on the Equaloxic Creek, just downstream of where the Big Gully and Little Gully creeks meet. Unless visitors know the area and the many meandering creeks, they are better off putting-in elsewhere to reach the Apalachicola River. A lot of logs and roots clog the creek when it is low. *Facilities:* Primitive camping, boat ramp allows motorized crafts. There's no water, toilets or other public conveniences. *Days/Hrs.:* Daily, year-round. There is no entrance station or gate. *Directions:* From Bristol, go 12 miles south on CR 12, which then forks to the left. Bear right on CR 379 and 1 mile later go right (west) on FSR 133. The landing is at the end of the road, which is less than a mile long.

WHITE OAK LANDING –A primitive camp often used as a base for hunting or fishing, White Oak Landing is on the deep, slow-moving River Styx several miles upstream from where it joins with the Apalachicola River. *Facilities:* Primitive camping, a concrete boat ramp (one of the best in the national forest). *Days/Hrs.:* Daily, year-round. There is no entrance station or gate. *Directions:* From Sumatra, go north on CR 379 for about 7.5 miles. Turn left (west) on CR 115 and proceed 3.5 miles.

COTTON LANDING CAMPGROUND –This site, a designated hunt camp, is slightly more developed than Big Gully and offers

Nearly 200 sidewheel and stern wheel steamboats have traveled the Apalachicola River system as far north as Columbus since 1828.

primitive camping, fishing and boating along Kennedy Creek, about 4 miles upstream from where it meets the Apalachicola River. *Facilities:* 7 primitive campsites, boat ramp with no horsepower limits, chemical toilets. *Days/Hrs.:* Daily, year-round. There is no entrance station or gate. *Directions:* From Sumatra, take CR 379 northwest for 3.2 miles. Turn left (west) onto FSR 123 and follow it for 2.8 miles, then turn left (west) on FSR 123B and go 0.7 mile.

WRIGHT LAKE CAMPGROUND –This cypress-lined freshwater lake, much smaller than Camel Lake, is in a secluded pine forest and has some of the best camping facilities and interpretive trails in the national forest. It's home to some notable inhabitants such as the endangered red-cockaded woodpecker and the harper's beauty, a rare flower found nowhere else in the world. Hunters who used this campground in the past tend not to anymore since camping fees began in 1996. *Facilities:* 20 camp sites (no electricity), picnic tables and grills, small unsupervised swimming beach, two interpretive loop trails around the lake, handicap accessible bathhouse with flush toilets and warm showers, dump station, drinking water. *Days/Hrs.:* Daily, year-round. There is no entrance station or gate, only a self-service fee station. *Fees:* Camping, $6 nightly per site; day use, $2 per vehicle. *Directions:* From Sumatra, take FL 65 south for 2 miles. Turn right (west) on FSR 101 and drive for about 2 miles. Turn right (north) at the sign and go 0.25 mile.

SCREECH OWL

HICKORY LANDING CAMPGROUND –This flat area, shaded by thick pines next to Owl Creek, a deep, blackwater channel lined with cypress swamps, is one of the best places to access the Apalachicola River, little more than a mile downstream. Hickory Landing is a designated hunt camp. *Facilities:* 10 campsites with picnic tables and fire rings, boat ramp with no horsepower limit on motors, "vault" toilets which resemble outhouses, drinking water. *Days/Hrs.:* Daily, year-round. There is no entrance station or gate. *Directions:* From Sumatra, take FL 65 south for 2 miles. Turn right (west) on FSR 101 and go 1.5 miles, and then left (south) on FSR 101B for 1 mile.

STEAMBOAT TERMS

Roustabout–a man who worked on rivers
Mark Twain–a river depth of two (twain)
fathoms or 12 feet
Hitting a snag–a boat running into a fallen
tree in the river
Diper dredge–a steam shovel mounted on a
float and used to dig in the river.

WHITE-TAILED DEER

HIKING TRAILS

ALUM BLUFF HIKING TRAIL –This "paleorefugia," or sanctuary for ancient flora and fauna, is perhaps the best place to explore some of the Florida Panhandle's most breathtaking scenery and notable variety of rare and endangered species. The topography along the trail is similar to Torreya State Park, but the Nature Conservancy preserve generally offers a more peaceful setting because of less foot traffic. After going up and down several steep ravines, the trail abruptly halts on the sudden and sheer Alum Bluff. The view of the wide expanse of Florida, Alabama and Georgia offers evidence of the river's long history as a natural shaper of the land. As the river erodes the highlands to the east, it leaves behind a broad, low plain to the west. Of all the limestone and clay cliffs along the upper Apalachicola, Alum Bluff arguably offers the most dramatic view of the river and plains, and certainly exposes the oldest geological layers in the state–the bottom yellow to grey band at the bases dates back 17 millions years. The bluff also probably reaches the highest from the river's edge; height estimates for Alum Bluff from the river's surface range from 100 to 210 feet. Alum's true height is likely just about in the middle. As in Torreya State Park, Torreya trees and Florida Yews, two of the oldest and rarest species in the state, live in the bluffs and ravines in the preserve. Animals include bald eagles, kites, turkey, deer, gopher tortoise, indigo snakes, dusky salamanders, otters and alligators. *Distance:* 3.5 miles round-trip, including an optional 0.5 mile loop at Alum Bluff. The trail usually takes several hours because most of it covers steep terrain. *Trailhead Location:* From Bristol, take FL 12 north about 1.5 miles. Turn left (west) on Garden of Eden Road. A short distance later is a parking area for hikers. The trailhead, with an interpretive display and map, is a couple hundred yards further down the sandy road. *Features:* Evidence of Civil War gun pits remain on the edge of Alum Bluff. *Hazards:* The trail sometimes runs along the preserve border, and there is hunting in the winter on the surrounding private property. Insects and heat make summer a poor time to visit. *More Information:* The Nature Conservancy, 625 N. Adams St., Tallahassee, FL 32301; 850/222-0199. The preserve is open for self-guided tours during daylight hours only. There's no water, facilities or staff with regular hours on-site. The local preserve caretaker can be reached at 850/643-2756.

APALACHICOLA NATIONAL FOREST/FLORIDA NATIONAL SCENIC TRAIL –The Florida National Scenic Trail is a work in progress. Dreamed up by wildlife photographer and real estate broker James Kern in 1964 and added to the national trail system in 1983, the trail will one day extend 1,300 miles from Gulf Islands National Seashore in Florida's western panhandle to Big Cypress National Preserve in south Florida. Currently hundreds of miles in different parts of the state have become part of the Florida Trail, although many missing sections remain. A 55-mile section certified as part of the trail passes from west to east in the Apalachicola National Forest. The Apalachicola West section, 34 miles, goes through the Apalachicola Ranger District. One of the longest and most remote hikes in Florida, this level, mostly single track trail offers a true wilderness experience. *Distance:* 30 miles. *Trailhead Location:* Camel Lake Campground (see page 256). From Bristol, FL, take FL 12 south for about 11 miles. Turn left (east) on FSR 105 and drive 2 miles. Upon entering the campground area, park in the designated parking area on the left. The trail begins on the eastern edge of the lot. *End Point Location:* Porter Lake Campground. From Telogia, FL, take CR 67 for about 16 miles. Turn left (east) on FSR 13 and go about 3 miles. The campground will be on the right. Both Camel Lake and Porter Lake have drinking water. *Shuttle:* Private arrangements are necessary for travel between the two campgrounds. *Features:* There's abundant wildlife on the trail. Look for black bear, gopher tortoise, wild pig, otter, bobcat and the rare red-cockaded woodpecker. Rangers have marked with white bands the longleaf pines in which the woodpeckers live. *Hazards:* Some venomous snakes and alligators dwell in the area. Heat, humidity and biting insects make summer trips ill-advised. There are several hunting periods in the national forest from mid-October to mid-

"I thought in a panic; I shall never be happy on land again. I was afraid once more of all the painful circumstances of living. But when the dry ground was under us, the world no longer fluid, I found a forgotten loveliness in all the things that have nothing to do with men. Beauty is pervasive and fills, like perfume, more than the object that contains it. Because I had known intimately a river, the earth pulsed under me."

—*Marjorie Rawlings*

Sinkholes

The shopping malls and housing complexes mushrooming up all over Florida are literally built on shaky ground. At any moment the ground might collapse and give way to sinkholes, common yet sometimes disastrous occurrences throughout the state, often around Lake Seminole.

A sinkhole is a natural geological event. Underneath the sandy surface soil of Florida, caverns and channels form as acidic groundwater slowly eats into carbonic rock. Growing over centuries, a cavity eventually penetrates a protective layer of either limestone or clay, which can set off within weeks a dramatic collapse of the soil above into a large depression.

Sinkholes, which allow surface runoff to move quickly into the underlying aquifer, create some interesting waterscapes. Often clear, spring-fed lakes form in the depressions. In others, creeks run into them and disappear. At Florida Caverns State Park near Marianna, the Chipola goes underground in a river sink and resurfaces half a mile later. More dramatically 20 miles to the west at Falling Waters State Park, a creek drops into a 100 foot deep sink. Its final destination remains unknown.

Under natural circumstances, sinkholes form and grow slowly. But as humans divert, pump, dredge and otherwise manipulate surface and groundwater, they expand quickly with spectacular effect.

March. *More Information:* Apalachicola National Forest, Apalachicola Ranger District Office, P.O. Box 579, Bristol, FL 32321; 850/643-2282.

APALACHICOLA NATIONAL FOREST/CAMEL LAKE BIG LOOP TRAIL –Located in the northwest section of the Apalachicola National Forest, the trail mostly follows an easy, flat and narrow path. There are some wet spots and a few slight dips and rises. The trail passes through stands of longleaf pines, hardwoods and saw palmettos before going along the eastern edge of a large, wet savanna filled with pitcher plants and seasonal orchids. *Distance:* 9-mile loop. *Trailhead Location:* Camel Lake Campground (see page 256). From Bristol, FL, take FL 12 south for about 11 miles. Turn left (east) on FSR 105 and drive 2 miles. Upon entering the campground area, park in the designated parking area on the left. *Features:* Near Big Gully Creek are the most hilly areas. Some wet areas have narrow walking planks. *Hazards:* There are poisonous snakes, like diamondback rattlesnakes and copperheads, in the forest and alligators in the deep wetlands. Common sense should prevent any trouble. More common hazards are winter hunters and summer heat, humidity and biting insects. *More Information:* Apalachicola National Forest, Apalachicola Ranger District Office, P.O. Box 579, Bristol, FL 32321; 850/643-2282.

APALACHICOLA NATIONAL FOREST/CAMEL LAKE SMALL LOOP TRAIL –This easy walk begins at the Camel Lake Campground and goes along a wide, flat, single-track trail through clearings and pine and hardwood stands around the perimeter of the 25-acre body of water. *Distance:* 2-mile loop. *Trailhead Location:* Camel Lake Campground (see page 256). From Bristol, FL, take FL 12 south for about 11 miles. Turn left (east) on FSR 105 and drive 2 miles. Upon entering the campground, park in the designated parking area on the left. Head to the water's edge and begin this trail either at the eastern end of the camping area or western end of the picnic area. *Features:* The trail often passes close to the water, offering good vantage points to spot alligators sunbathing in the warmer months. *Hazards:* A few poisonous snakes live in the vicinity. Alligators are generally not a problem if visitors keep their distance and don't attempt to feed them. In the warmer months, biting insects are the most common nuisance. *More Information:* Apalachicola National Forest, Apalachicola Ranger District Office, P.O. Box 579, Bristol, FL 32321; 850/643-2282.

APALACHICOLA NATIONAL FOREST/WRIGHT LAKE LOOP TRAIL –This easy hike offers excellent viewing of diverse, undisturbed habitats: pine flatlands, sweet bay and gallberry forests, blackwater streams and several different kinds of swamps. There's also wet savannas covered in pitcher plants, sundews, butterworts and a wildflower found nowhere else in the world, the harper's beauty, a small, attractive yellow bloom that shows in May. Boardwalks cross some blackwater swamps, darkened by deep red tannins which seep from nearby cypress trees. Note: A 0.25-mile loop that follows the perimeter of Wright Lake, which also crosses a black swamp boardwalk, offers a view of most of the same flora and topography. *Distance:* 4.5 miles. *Trailhead Location:* From Sumatra, FL, take FL 65 south for 2 miles. Turn right (west) on FSR 101 and drive for about 2 miles. Turn right (north) at the sign and go 0.25 mile. An informative interpretive display marks the trailhead, to the left of the lake from the parking area. *Features:* Red-cockaded woodpeckers and alligators live in the vicinity. *Hazards:* There are venomous snakes, possibly alligators and biting insects in the summer. *More Information:* Apalachicola National Forest, Apalachicola Ranger District Office, P.O. Box 579, Bristol, FL 32321; 850/643-2282.

TORREYA STATE PARK/ORIGINAL LOOP TRAIL –Similar to the Alum Bluff trail, this hike crosses through many different natural features and habitats in the most ecologically unique part of Florida, the bluffs and ravines of the upper Apalachicola River. The view from the bluffs is not quite as spectacular as from Alum Bluff, but it does offer a descent to the river floodplain and passes close enough to Torreya trees to examine them. *Distance:* 7 miles. *Trailhead Location:* Torreya State Park (see page 251). From Bristol, FL, take FL 12 north for 4 miles. Turn left (west) on FL 270 and continue for about 7.5 miles. Turn left (northwest) on CR 1641, which soon enters the park. Park in front of the old Gregory House. Access to the loop trail begins at the south end of the parking lot. *Features:* Once plentiful, Torreyas are now on the brink of extinction. Formerly, trees 50

Torreyas

Nearly extinct, Torreya (Tor REY a) trees cling to life in the cool, shaded ravines and bluffs on the east bank of the upper Apalachicola River. Found elsewhere only in China, Japan and California, the widely scattered trees could be remnants of a once continuous forest across North America and East Asia when the two continents were part of the supercontinent Pangea millions of years ago.

The Torreyas share living quarters among the bluffs with their cousins, the rare Florida Yews.

Though once plentiful, Torreyas might not last much longer in the wild. In the past, trees commonly grew to 50 feet high and 8 feet around. Today, only a few tiny specimens remain in their natural environment, none more than a couple of feet high, and none of reproductive age. The tree does well as an ornamental; one of the largest such specimens in the world is in the gardens of the Biltmore Estate in Asheville, North Carolina.

Fungal epidemics have decimated the Torreya over the past 40 years. Traditionally, smoke from periodic wildfires swept down the river basin and acted as a natural fumigant to keep the Torreyas healthy. But human fire suppression to protect timber stands has allowed the blight to multiply unchecked.

The Spanish Moss Industry

As late as 1944, Spanish moss was collected from trees, hung to dry in the sun or sheds like tobacco and used for packing material and furniture stuffing. Moss gatherers would reach up with bamboo poles to take down from live oak trees strands of the moss, which is not a moss at all, but rather an air-growing plant related to the pineapple. For half a year the moss dried, often on wire fences in the yards of the collectors. After that they would take the moss to a nearby city where the strands would be ginned, or separated from their outer husks. Mostly poor rural farmers, both black and white, these moss collectors received pennies a pound for their labor. Sporadic moss collecting contin-ued for a number of years to supply the few upholsterers who still preferred moss to other filler.

feet in height and 8 feet in circumference were not uncommon. Today, only a few tiny specimens remain in the wild, none more than a couple of feet in height or of reproductive age. Some are by the trail near the river. They could die out before too long, some botanists believe. Smoke from once plentiful wildfires which traveled up the river corridor protected them from fungal epidemics. Modern human fire suppression to pro-tect timber stands, however, has inadvertently promoted unchecked epidemics for the past several decades. Many other rare species reside in the park as well, some found elsewhere only in the southern Appalachians, which is what the steep, cool and moist terrain resembles. Visitors don't have to hike the entire trail to see the Torreyas. A smaller, 45-minute loop along the river offers that opportunity. A good place to see Florida Yews is the trail near the Rock Creek stone bridge. Many rare wildflowers bloom in early spring, including Indian pink, white baneberry, rue-anemone, wild comphrey, eastern leatherwood, trout lily, mountain laurel, orange azalea and narrow-leaved trillium. Most also occur in the Alum Bluffs preserve. *Hazards:* Private property used for hunting borders some of the park, which also is a habitat for several venomous snake species. Biting insects make summer trips difficult. *More Information:* Torreya State Park, HC 2 Box 70, Bristol, FL 32321; 850/643-2674.

TORREYA STATE PARK/NEW LOOP TRAIL –Opened in 1985, this trail closely resembles the old loop trail as it passes through similar deep ravines along Rock Creek. Hardwoods make a canopy in the lower sections, pine trees in the higher. There are Torreyas, but not near the trail. Unlike the older loop, it doesn't go near the river. *Distance:* 8 miles. *Trailhead Location:* Torreya State Park (see page 251). From Bristol, FL, take FL 12 north for 4 miles. Turn left (west) on FL 270 and continue for about 7.5 miles. Turn left (northwest) on CR 1641, which soon enters Torreya State Park. Access the trail from the picnic area. Take the trail past the old youth camp restroom, turn left down service road to fork. Take right fork to Stone Bridge. The trail starts past the bridge on the left. From December to April, dur-ing eagle nesting season, the new hiking trail can only be accessed from the Torreya hiking loop, not the stone bridge trailhead. *Features:* The trail's remoteness and newness mean the terrain is less trampled underfoot than the other loop. *Hazards:* The new section is habitat to several kinds of venomous snakes. Biting insects make summer trips difficult. *More Information:* Torreya State Park, HC 2 Box 70, Bristol, FL 32321; 850/643-2674.

TORREYA STATE PARK/WEEPING RIDGE TRAIL –This trail leads to a ledge in a deep ravine where water seeps out of the ground and forms a small waterfall during the rainy season. *Distance:* One hour round-trip. *Trailhead Location:* Torreya State Park (see page 251). From Bristol, take FL 12 north for 4 miles. Turn left (west) on FL 270 and continue for about 7.5 miles. Turn left (northwest) on CR 1641, which soon enters Torreya State Park. Trailhead is at the entrance to the main campground. *Features:* Southern magnolia, white oak and spruce are common along the trail. *Hazards:* Biting insects in the summer. *More Information:* Torreya State Park, HC 2 Box 70, Bristol, FL 32321; 850/643-2674.

HISTORIC SITES

FORT GADSDEN STATE HISTORIC SITE –On Prospect Bluff, 18 miles upstream of Apalachicola on the east bank of the Apalachicola River, is one of the finest vantage points to view the river in the Apalachicola National Forest. Perhaps because of this view, it has been a strategic site for forts. In fact, four nations have occupied two forts on this overlook to fight enemies either up or down the river. The British constructed the first fortification at the beginning of the War of 1812 to recruit free blacks, ex-slaves and Seminoles to aid in their fight against the United States, whose territory extended to what is today the southern border of Georgia, about 50 miles due north.

Whether sympathizing with the former slaves, or relishing the trouble they might cause his former foes, the British post commander Lt. Col. Edward Nicholls at the end of the war in 1815 turned the fort over to a group of ex-slaves and free blacks under the leadership of a mulatto from Pensacola. Little is known about him except his name, Garçon. Along with the fort, the British handed over 9 cannons, 2,500 muskets, 500 car-

Turpentining

Tapping pine sap produced so many useful substances for wooden shipbuilding that the practice became known as the naval store industry. One substance in particular, turpentine, meant life for many in South Georgia and the Florida Panhandle.

Until the 1940s, armies of black turpentiners scratched a living from the pines, placing nails at the bottom of V-shaped cuts where gum dripped into waiting buckets. Making rounds between hundreds of trees, turpentiners collected the sap and distilled the rich ooze into turpentine, resin and pitch in their work camp stills. The trees, unless completely exhausted, were cut higher for new sap geysers the following year. Some survivors bear turpentine scars, called cat faces because the cuts resemble whiskers.

The turpentiners slept in windowless shacks, shared a pump house and bought on credit from camp bosses. The children worked the trees, too; labor laws did not apply to what the state declared an agricultural occupation. In recent times turpentiners sprayed sulfuric acid from flit guns to speed up the gum flow. Droplets of the potion sizzled through their clothes and blistered their skin.

The industry died as modern technology discovered how to extract turpentine from cut-over pine stumps. But as late as 1942, turpentining remained Florida's second largest employer.

bines, 500 pistols, 500 swords and 700 kegs of gunpowder.

Over the next year, runaway slaves, free blacks and Seminoles joined forces with those at the fort to create a quasi-independent state of about 1,000 settlers who farmed and traded along a 50-mile strip of the Apalachicola River Valley. The United States considered them a danger and threatened destruction of the fort. General Andrew Jackson ordered the construction of Fort Scott near present-day Chattahoochee, Florida, a border town between Spanish Territory and the United States on the Apalachicola River. Supplies for the new fort had to come from New Orleans up the Apalachicola River, meaning naval ships would pass under the guns of the Negro Fort, as it was called.

In early July 1816, the Americans, with two supply ships and two gunboats, dropped anchor in the Apalachicola Bay. From Fort Scott, Col. Duncan Clinch dispatched two companies of soldiers and a band of Seminole allies to rendezvous with the gunboats. On July 27, a Negro Fort cannon took aim at an American vessel but the 24-pound shot fell short, falling harmlessly in the water. The U.S. gunboats returned fire. After several near misses, a 12-pound "hot shot" heated by an onboard stove landed directly in the fort's magazine. Shaking the ground for miles and reportedly heard as far away as Pensacola, the explosion blew the Negro Fort to oblivion. Of the 300—many women and children—who took refuge at the fort, only 30 survived. "The scene...was horrible beyond description," recalled one U.S. soldier. "Hundreds of lifeless bodies were stretched on the plains, buried in sand and rubbish or suspended from the tops of pines."

Garçon and an Indian leader survived the blast, but the American-allied Seminoles burned them at the stake. The blacks along the river banks abandoned their settlements, many fleeing to the central Florida wilderness. Native Americans who lived in villages on the river soon suffered the same fate as the blacks. Two years later while leading a force down the river to destroy Seminole villages, Andrew Jackson instructed Lt. James Gadsden to build the fort which bears his name on the same site.

The United States maintained Fort Gadsden until Spain

ceded Florida to the United States in 1821. It remained unused until 1862 when the Confederate Army occupied the site to defend the Florida interior from Union ships running up the Apalachicola River. The troops abandoned the position a year later because of the threat of malaria, a common illness in the lowland swamps of Florida. Today, the King's Colors and the Twenty Star Stars and Stripes–the flags of 19th century England and the United States, respectively–fly over the graveyard near the museum. *Facilities:* Small outdoor museum with interpretive exhibits on its history, picnic area with grills, restrooms, drinking water. *Days/Hrs.:* Daily, year-round, 8am-8pm, but usually closes around sunset in the winter. *Fees:* None. *Directions:* From Sumatra, go south on FL 65 for about 4 miles, then turn right (west) on FSR 129 and drive about 2 miles. *More Information:* Apalachicola Ranger District, USDA Forest Service, P. O. Box 579 GA 20, Bristol, FL 32321; 850/643-2282.

GREGORY HOUSE –Planter James Gregory built this impressive home in 1849 on Ocheesee Landing, a short distance downstream from the house's current location on the opposite bank of the Apalachicola River. Gregory ran an extensive plantation where slaves produced a variety of crops, cotton in particular, on the fertile river flood plains. By 1851 the estate was well-established and included a steamboat landing, cotton gin, warehouse and many slave quarters.

After the Civil War, Gregory lost his estate but established another successful plantation in Gainesville, Florida, using freed slaves as sharecroppers. He never went back to Ocheesee; but his youngest daughter, Chaffa, after paying back taxes and repairing the house, returned to live in the home until her death in 1916. The house then fell into disrepair. Outlaws, tramps and river rats hid out on the property until 1935 when the Florida government acquired it from the Neal Lumber Company of Blountstown. Over the next three years, the state undertook an ambitious project to dismantle the house, float it across the river and reassemble it where it currently stands, on a high bluff in Torreya State Park overlooking the river.

The house looks the same as before the Civil War, except for the 5-foot high brick pillars to keep it above floodwaters. It

Mister Hoover

Mister Hoover, Mister Hoover,
can't you spare me a lousy
dime?
Mister Hoover, Mister Hoover,
can't you spare me a lousy
dime?
Bare-bone broke 'cause I work
in teppentime.

Got no home, Lord, Lord, but a
tintop hut;
Got no home, Lord, Lord, but a
tintop hut;
Saturday whiskey like to rot my
gut.

Mister Hoover, Mister Hoover,
can't you spare me a lousy
dime?
Mister Hoover, Mister Hoover,
can't you spare me one lousy
dime?
Starvin' broke cause I work in
the teppentime.

*Folk poem collected by Gloria
Jahoda,* The Other Florida,
Charles Scribner's Sons, 1967.

TEPPENTIME MAN

Teppentime man got a lonesome dollar,
Grits is cold and snaps is dry,
Freeze in winter and sweat in summer,
Burn in teppentime hell when he die.

—Folk poem collected by Gloria Jahoda,
The Other Florida, *Charles Scribner's Sons,
1967.*

Tupelo Honey

Some of Florida's major nectar plants are gallberry, citrus, saw palmetto, cabbage palm and black mangrove; but none compare in importance to the black, or ogeechee, tupelo blossom. The largest and densest stands of black tupelo trees grow in the swamps of the lower Apalachicola and Chipola rivers. Each spring beekeepers from all over the Florida Panhandle and South Georgia mine their unusually sweet blossoms. A constant buzz resounds for three weeks as bees work the flowers, little green marbles covered in tiny green and pale white petals. The entire river basin has the aroma of tupelo honey, one of the sweetest, purest varieties of honey in the world.

Tupelos grow elsewhere, like along the Altamaha River in Georgia, but nowhere so densely that honey made from them can be certified pure tupelo, a honey packed with fruit sugars that never hardens, granulates or sours. For this reason, it is used for some medicinal purposes. Doctors often recommend tupelo honey for their diabetic patients who can tolerate fruit sugars

To create pure tupelo honey, combs must be stripped of all stored honey before the tupelo blooms begin. The bees are given clear nesting boxes before being moved to a beeyard nearer the honey source. As soon as the bloom ends, beekeepers must harvest the product before it is mixed with different honey sources.

has authentic 1850s furnishings and the original lumber, complete with wooden pegs instead of nails.

Guided Tours: Park rangers lead regular, 45-minute tours, beginning at 10am every weekday and at 10am, 2pm and 4pm on weekends and holidays. Rangers dress in 19th century clothing and give candlelight tours of the home one evening each year, generally the second week of May. Confederate Civil War reenactors in uniform add to the atmosphere. *Days/Hrs.:* The Gregory House is in Torreya State Park (see page251), open daily, year-round, 8am-sunset. *Fees:* $1, adults; $0.50, children under 13. *Directions:* From Bristol, go north on FL 12 for 4 miles. Turn left (west) on FL 270 and continue for about 7.5 miles. Turn left (northwest) on CR 1641, which soon enters Torreya State Park. *More Information:* Torreya State Park, HC 2 Box 70, Bristol, FL 32321; 850/643-2674.

SIGNIFICANT URBAN EXPERIENCES

WEWAHITCHKA –Wewahitchka (we wa HITCH ka) is a Native American name for Water Eyes, a reference to two natural, round lakes which Indians reportedly thought looked like eyes gazing into the heavens for spiritual guidance. To see the water eyes, Lake Alice and Lake Julia, go west on FL 22 from downtown. Almost immediately, there's one on either side of the road.

Wewahitchka, or Wewa (WE wa) as locals say, traces its origins two miles south to Fort Place, founded in the early 1800s to fend off warring Indians. The first pioneers actually lived a few miles south of the fort in a small settlement called Dalkieth, a small patch of high ground whose surrounding swamps protected newly planted citrus groves from seasonal freezes. As the influx of new arrivals continued, many settled in Wewahitchka. The land around the lake eyes, uncommonly high, was especially suitable for farming. Besides citrus groves, livestock and beekeeping, Wewahitchka soon relied on timbering, being close to what seemed like an inexhaustible supply of hardwoods–the Dead Lakes (see page 252).

Wewahitchka today is a city of 1,800 residents with a non-descript downtown consisting of a library, a few banks and some small storefronts lining several blocks of FL 71. A new sandwich shop which opened in 1996 is still big news.

Beekeeping has remained one of the most important industries. Wewa is near the world's largest and densest stands of black tupelo trees, which grow along the banks of the Chipola River, the Apalachicola River and their tributaries in the lower half of the Apalachicola River Basin, producing tupelo honey. Wewahitchka celebrates the annual harvest during the Tupelo Honey Festival every April or May. *More Information:* The Gulf County Chamber of Commerce, P.O. Box 964. Port St. Joe, FL, 32457; 850/227-1223.

FISHING

Fishing on this section of river encompasses the Upper, Middle and Lower Apalachicola River; the Chipola River, Dead Lakes and Lake Wimico.

BEST ADVICE –The most experienced fishermen find that one or two days of guide fees is a good investment before launching out on their own. Inexperienced fishermen or families looking for a enjoyable day's outing will increase their pleasure ten-fold by taking advantage of a professional guide's experience. The best guides not only make sure their customers fish, but provide insights into the fishing habits of different species, ecology, weather lore and other aspects that will enhance a fishing experience.

When booking a guide always check to make sure who is responsible for all tackle (rods, reels, lures); boats and gasoline; all live bait; life jackets; lunch, drinks, snacks and ice; and rain gear. Understand exactly what is included in the guide fees.

GUIDES –Contact the fish camps listed in the section below for guides to this region.

BEST BOOKS AND MAPS –Larry Larsen's *Guide to North Florida Bass Waters,* Larsen's Outdoor Publishing, 2640 Elizabeth Place, Lakeland, FL 33813, is a the most helpful guide to this section of the river. (See page 328.)

U.S. Geological Survey 1:24,000 scale topographical maps covering the Apalachicola River are Chattahoochee, Sneads, Rock Bluff, Bristol, Blountstown, Estiffanulga, Orange, Dead

Fish Consumption Guidelines
Apalachicola River–No restrictions. As a general rule, eat smaller fish to be safe.

Source: Florida Department of Natural Resources, 1997.

When fishing in muddy waters, best results may be found under overhanging banks, around submerged stumps or trees and large boulders. Water is usually clearest in these spots, and this is where feeding fish can see your lure. Usually, fish don't move about much at this time so it is wise to know where they may be.

HONEY BEE

Ulee's Gold

Since opening in 1997, *Ulee's Gold,* a movie about a beekeeper in the tupelo swamps of the Apalachicola River, has won critical acclaim, playing the film festivals of Cannes, New York and Sundance, where it won Best Prize. A photo of a man and a young child gathering tupelo honey inspired Victor Nunez to write the script: "The image stayed with me for some reason. I wondered who these people might be, why they were out there, together, in that swamp."

Lavernor Laveon "L.L." Lanier, the elderly dean of tupelo beekeeping, jokes that "they made the movie about me." They did make it in his backyard, a wetland wilderness in the heart of tupelo country near Wewahitchka. "They even worked during the night in the swamp. When the tupelo season was ending, the flowers started dropping. They needed to shoot some pictures with them on the trees so they put some of the branches with flowers on them in a big freezer to use later."

Actor Peter Fonda considered the role of Ulee the beekeeper as one of the most rewarding of his career. "I've found a lot of

Lakes, Wewahitchka, Kennedy Creek, Forbes Island, Jackson River, West Pass and Apalachicola. Topographical maps covering the Chipola River are River Stills, Cottondale, Marianna, Oak Dale, Altha West, Clarkesville, Frink, Dead Lakes, Wewahitchka and Kennedy Creek. Dead Lakes topo maps are Wewahitchka and Dead Lake, and Lake Wimico topos are Lake Wimico and Jackson River. (To order see page 326.)

INSIDER TIPS AND HOT SPOTS, UPPER APALACHICOLA RIVER – The upper portion of the Apalachicola extends from Lake Seminole to Blountstown and includes the tailwaters below the reservoir at Chattahoochee, FL. This section can be reached via US 90 at Chattahoochee, FL 20 at Blountstown and off FL 69, over sand roads to the river.

There is tremendous sunshine bass fishing in the spring and fall months. Many state record sunshine bass have been taken in the tailrace below Jim Woodruff Dam. Best baits include jigs, spoons and live shad. Sunshine bass often school on the surface in the fall, and limits can be caught in minutes on spoons. White bass fishing is good primarily in March using small crawfish and grass shrimp while bottom fishing. Bluegill and redbreast fishing is best during the spring on crickets, earthworms and catalpa worms. Best strings of shellcrackers are caught around the race shoal area using red worms. Good bass fishing occurs in the spring and early summer using plastic worms and crankbaits. Striped bass fishing is fair in the fall and spring. Best baits in the fall include small live eels fished off the Jim Woodruff Dam catwalk and deep-diving minnow-type lures.

INSIDER TIPS AND HOT SPOTS, MIDDLE APALACHICOLA RIVER – This portion of the river takes in Blountstown and includes the tributaries of Old River, Outside Lakes, Equaloxic Creek, Larkin Slough, River Styx, Kennedy Creek and numerous other sloughs and streams. This section can be reached from FL 20 at Blountstown.

Bluegill and shellcracker fishing is excellent in spring around river treetops and in sloughs off the river. Best baits are crickets, earthworms, catalpa worms and oak worms. Superb river bass fishing occurs in spring and summer. Anglers should use plastic worms and crankbaits. White and sunshine bass can be caught in the spring and fall by fishing off sandbars. Best baits are jugs, spoons and live shad. Catch speckled perch from January through March around treetops using live minnows.

INSIDER TIPS AND HOT SPOTS, LOWER APALACHICOLA RIVER, OR DELTA –This lower section of the river takes in numerous sloughs and streams, including Brothers River, Howards Creek, Brickyard Cutoff, Owl Creek and East River. It can be reached off FL 71 at Honeyville, from FL 381 to Willis Landing on Brothers River and from US 98 and FL 319 at Apalachicola.

Sunshine bass may be caught during the spring and fall, primarily off sandbars. Best baits include live shad and spoons. Largemouth bass fishing is excellent in the spring, using plastic worms and crankbait. Strings of bass can be caught using live shrimp fished around grass flats and canals. Bluegill and shellcracker can be caught primarily in the spring using earthworms and crickets. Fly-fishing for bream is also recommended in the early morning and late afternoon. Nice channel catfish can be caught in the river channel using earthworms and catalpa worms.

INSIDER TIPS AND HOT SPOTS, CHIPOLA RIVER –The Chipola River, a very scenic spring-fed, cold water river with fast water shoals, is home to the rare coosa bass. It can be reached at Marianna, FL, by US 90, at Clarksville by FL 20 and FL 274 west of Altha.

The Chipola offers excellent bream fishing in the spring, depending on the water level. Bream, including redbreast and bluegill, are taken on beetle spins, redworms and crickets. Some bass are taken in the spring on plastic worms.

INSIDER TIPS AND HOT SPOTS, DEAD LAKES –This 6,700-acre lake, on the Chipola River near the town of Wewahitchka, is located in both Gulf and Calhoun counties. The strangely beautiful, dark water of Dead Lakes is filled with cypress snags and stumps.

The lake enjoys a fine reputation for springtime bluegill and shellcracker fishing. Best baits for bluegills are crickets and earth worms fished among the cypress trees. Earthworms catch shellcrackers. Bass fishing is good in the spring and fall on artificial worms and broken-back minnow lures.

INSIDER TIPS AND HOT SPOTS, LAKE WIMICO –Lake Wimico is a

Ulee in my father. He kept a couple of hives and I can see him hop-footing it across the lawn, thinking he had a bee up his pant leg."

"Three things a man should do in life; Trust God, love a woman, catch fish."

—*Sign in Tom Mann's Fish World, Eufaula*

4,055-acre natural lake accessible only by boat via intracoastal waterways from Apalachicola or White City. Fresh and saltwater species are intermixed.

This wide, shallow lake has good bluegill and shellcracker fishing in the spring and early summer. Best baits include crickets and earthworms. Some bass are caught during this time on artificial worms and crankbaits.

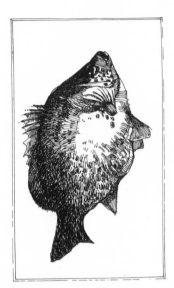

The sunfish has a deep compressed body with a metallic luster.

FISH CAMPS

TUCKER'S BAIT AND GROCERY –Private ramp, bait, tackle, ice and groceries. Scott's Ferry on FL 71. Operator Joseph Tucker, Route 1, Box 99, Blountstown, FL 32424; 850/674-8290.

BRYANT'S LANDING AND STORE –Rental boats, boat launching facilities, groceries, ice, beverages, RV facilities, bait. FL 381, 3.3 miles east of FL 71. Travel FL 381 until you see the sign. Operator Bob and Frances Gurganus, Route 1, P.O. Box 848, Wewahitchka, FL 32465; 850/639-2853.

CYPRESS LODGE – Private ramp, boats, licenses, motors, bait, tackle, cabins and restaurant. Off FL 71, 4 miles north of Wewahitchka. Operator Wanita Deal, Route 3, P.O. Box 172-A, Wewahithcka, FL 32465; 850/639-5414.

DOUGLAS LANDING –Boats, beverages, ice, groceries, gas and oil, licenses, full RV facilities, campgrounds, hot showers and private boat ramps. FL 71 south from Wewahitchka, left on C-381, 4.5 miles east of FL 71. Operator Kenneth Clemmons, P.O. Box 821, Wewahitchka, FL 32465; 850/639-5481.

FISHERS BAIT AND TACKLE –Private ramps on Dead Lakes and on Chipola Cutoff, camping facilities, cottages with cooking facilities, boats, licenses, groceries, bait, tackle and hunting supplies. At Dead Lakes Dam. Operator Milton Fisher, Route 2, P.O. Box 2095, Wewahitchka, FL 32465; 850/639-5051.

GATE'S FISH CAMP –Licenses, tackle, bait, boats, motors, camping facilities and modern-equipped cabins. 4 miles north of Wewahitchka on FL 71. Operator Leland Taylor, Route 3, P.O. Box 279, Wewahitchka, FL 32465; 850/639-2768.

LAKE SIDE LODGE –Private ramp, boats, motors, bait, tackle, guides, licenses, campsites and overnight living units for rent by the day, week or month. One mile north of Wewahitchka on FL 71. Operator Jack McCoy, P.O. Box 1069, Wewahitchka, FL 32465; 850/639-2681.

LANDS LANDING –Public ramp. 1.5 miles south of Wewahitchka. Turn east on Lands Road (across from C-386 intersection) and go to end of road.

WHITFIELD LANDING (UPPER LANDING) –Private launch facilities, motel, RV hook-ups, houseboats for rent, restrooms, groceries. Operator Ed Hill, Route 1, P.O. Box 181, Wewahitchka, FL 32465; 850/229-6587.

HOWARD'S CREEK BOAT LANDING –Private launching facilities, camping facilities for tent and RV. Operator Gene Boddye, 91 Duval, Port St. Joe, FL 32456; 850/229-8389.

PUBLIC RAMP –Public boat ramp to Depot Creek and access to Lake Wimico. 7.5 miles east of Port St. Joe on US 98. Turn north at Odena Fire Tower.

BREAKAWAY MARINA –Private ramp, boats, gas, bait, tackle, ice, groceries, guides and licenses. Restaurant and lounge, motel units and campsites. Operator Gina Irving, 200 Waddell Road, Apalachicola, FL 32320; 850/653-8897. (See page 310.)

BAY CITY LODGE –Boat ramp, gas, boat rental, motel, cottages, restaurant, bait-and-tackle store. FL 384 at Apalachicola. Operator Tom Gordon, P.O. Box 172, Apalachicola, FL 32320; 850/653-9294. (See page 310.)

SPORTSMAN'S LODGE –Private ramp, gas, bait, tackle, ice, guide service, living units, public ramp available nearby. 400 yards north of US 98 on Apalachicola Bay, east of the bridge. Operator Bob Allen, P.O. Box 606, East Point, FL 32328; 850/670-8423. (See page 311.)

BOATING

To some boaters' tastes, this is the most interesting and varied section of the river, surpassing even the rugged and scenic North Georgia mountains. Here, serene explorations of swampy creeks or the discovery of an oxbow lake replaces the thrill of Upper Hooch rapids. Alligators take the place of beavers. Tupelos and the rare Torreya trees line the banks instead of mountain laurel, hemlock and pine.

"The wilderness is one of the few places where our sense of control is in doubt, where we are vulnerable to storm and flood and encounters with wild things."

—Alan S. Kesseim, Big Sky Journal, Fall 1996

Above Seminole the Chattahoochee is one water ribbon interspersed by dam-tied bows at the lakes. Below Seminole the river is a pompon with the streamers pointing north. Tributaries, like the Chipola, St. Marks River, Brothers River, Jackson River and the River Styx, are sisters, each related but with a slightly different personality. Some of those tributaries, as well as smaller creeks flowing into the main channel, provide interesting boating experiences.

What follows here is an overview trip on the Apalachicola from Chattahoochee, Florida–the little town just below the Jim Woodruff Lock and Dam which holds back the waters of Seminole–to the boat ramp at Bay City Marina at Apalachicola Bay, a total distance of 107 miles. Following the overview are recommended short trips on the Apalachicola and Chipola rivers, Owl Creek, Kennedy Creek and River Styx. The adventurous boater will want to order topographical maps and create his or her own boating experience on this remarkable section of river.

THE APALACHICOLA BELOW LAKE SEMINOLE TO APALACHICOLA BAY –The river here is big and wide. An occasional cabin dots the wooded banks. Boat ramps and campgrounds are generally plain to primitive. At some boat ramps unofficial campgrounds have been set up; some campers appear to be permanent residents. Float houses, the Coastal Plain's equivalent of Piedmont hunting cabins and deer stands, punctuate the river, particularly further south. Some of these are inhabited year-round by picturesque–and not so picturesque–Mark Twain characters who sustain themselves largely from what they take from the river. Many of these structures are illegal and are slowly being removed from the waterway. The river flows through Jackson, Gadsden, Calhoun, Liberty, Franklin and Gulf counties which are among the most rural and poorest in the state of Florida. (It is one of the ironies of the river that it bestows its richest blessings on the poor and the rural.) Red and green buoys mark the channel for barges carrying gravel, liquid fertilizer or soybeans up and down the river. Mile markers show the distance to the coast. Boaters in all types of boats, from canoes to large power boats, can enjoy this section of river. Even pleasure boaters from Columbus use it as their water highway to Apalachicola

Bay. The ideal form of transportation on this section of river would be a power boat for covering long distances with an inflatable or small kayak or canoe for exploring streams along the route. *Put-In:* The boat ramp at Chattahoochee just below Lake Seminole. There is a campground here as well as a bait-and-tackle shop and a Hardee's. *Take-Out:* The southernmost take-out for the trip is the boat ramp at Bay City Lodge in Apalachicola Bay (see page 310). To shorten the trip, take-out at boat ramps between Chattahoochee and Apalachicola. Some recommended takes-outs include: Bristol, where there is a campground with trailer hookups, is about 1 walkable mile from the boat ramp to the town where there are modest motel and restaurant accommodations and a bait-and-tackle shop; Estiffanulga (which the locals refer to as "Stiff 'n Ugly") whose boat landing is closed for repairs but worth checking out (a house sits on the bluff of the river bank next to the ramp poised to tumble into the water); and Ocheesee Landing boat ramp, the old steamboat landing for the Gregory House (see page 265). *Distance:* 107 miles. *High Points:* Many alligators inhabit this section of river. A particularly large congregation of them live in the 4-to-5-mile segment of river below the Jim Woodruff Dam. Apparently some fish get mangled in the dam and provide a partially chewed dinner for lazy waiting reptiles; even humans can discern the strong fishy odor here. Below the dam is a popular fishing spot for locals who fish from the banks and from boats. Just below US 90 is the wreck of an old river barge which met an untimely fate. The section of the river from Seminole downstream for about 30 or 40 miles into Florida is known as the Apalachicola Steep Head Ravine. It is characterized by small clear cold streams which undercut the bluffs, forming picturesque ravines. The effect is surprising for those who expect the Florida Panhandle to be entirely flat. Blue Spring is a freshwater spring with a sand bar and a pond just off the river, making it an attractive area. A 2-3-foot waterfall provides hot sweaty boaters a scenic opportunity for a splash bath. Torreya State Park (see page 251) has a boat ramp. Boaters can dock here and walk the park's hiking trails where indigenous plants and trees are marked with small identification signs. Rock Bluff is a pretty bluff featuring beautiful sand-

Navigation Window

In the drier months of the summer, the Apalachicola River dribbles down in some places to a depth of four feet, too low for large barge traffic. During such droughts the U.S. Army Corps of Engineers periodically unleashes an extra measure of water from its dams to boost the water level to eight or nine feet so commercial vessels can steam up the river. The release is coordinated among all the Corps dams from Buford on Lake Lanier to Jim Woodruff on Lake Seminole. The releases happen about four times a year and take place according to a schedule set in advance by the Corps. For two days the river slowly rises, remains navigable for up to 14 days, then goes down to its former level within a day or two after the water is shut off. Commercial towing boats, having gathered near the mouth of the Apalachicola River, race up the temporarily invigorated river during the two-week period, better known as a navigation window. According to the Corps, barges haul 33,000 tons of cargo up the river during each window and 637,000 tons each year.

bars, some as large as a football field, that give boaters places to sun, picnic or camp. The sandbars are easily accessible in summer months when the water is low. In winter's high water months they may be smaller or totally underwater. Alum Bluff (see page 258) is a spectacular site on a beautiful bend in the river. There is a camping spot across the river with a view of the bluff. The endangered Torreya tree grows on this section of river. On the curve at mile marker 71 is an oxbow lake (see page 253). If the water is high enough, boaters can explore it. Near Wewahitchka the character of the river begins to change to that of a swampy, coastal river. Cypress and tupelo trees become more prevalent, and other flora and fauna of the swamp is apparent. Yellow crown night herons perch on the bank. The tupelo trees from this section of river produce the legendary tupelo honey (see page 266). Sand bars still rise up out of the water but with less frequency. *Low Points:* The large dredge site between mile markers 36 and 37 is typical of how the Corps of Engineers once disposed of dredge material taken from the river. These mounds interrupted the flow of water in the river and adversely affected the fisheries in the Apalachicola estuary. The Corps has modified its practices and now hauls the dredge away or spreads it along the river bank. *Hazards:* Boaters share this section with large river barges hauling gravel, soybeans and liquid fertilizer up and down the river. If boaters are alert and exercise reasonable caution, these barges do not present a serious hazard; they cause some wake, but most of the impact is dispersed over the wide river. Wooden pylons about 1.5 feet apart extending in a perpendicular line from the river bank control bank erosion; exercise caution near them. The Corps of Engineers provides controlled water releases from Lake Seminole to provide "navigation windows" for barge traffic in times of low water. During these windows the water level in the river is increased significantly and may adversely effect boating. It is a good idea to check with the Corps of Engineers for water release information (850/663-2291). Water levels vary from season to season. In winter months the water level rises and the velocity of the current increases. Boating may be unsafe or impossible. It is always wise to check with local marinas or the Corps of

"It seems that every human being is born knowing how to use a canoe. The canoe itself inspires such attitudes, because in form it is the most beautifully simple of all vehicles."

—John McPhee, The Survival of the Bark Canoe

Engineers when planning a boating trip. A listing of local phone numbers is provided in the Resource Section of this book. *USGS Topos:* Chattahoochee, Sneads, Rock Bluff, Bristol, Blountstown, Estiffanulga, Orange, Dead Lakes, Wewahitchka, Kennedy Creek, Forbes Island, Jackson River, West Pass and Apalachicola.

Boating explorations of the water world are almost unlimited. Here are several recommended trips on this section. The adventurous boater will order topographical maps to create his or her own river adventures.

CHATTAHOOCHEE TO BRISTOL –This makes a good two-or-three-day canoe trip which includes Torreya State Park, the scenic Alum Bluff and many good sandbars for sunning, picnicking or camping. *Put-In:* Boat landing at Chattahoochee, FL. *Take-Out:* Boat landing at Bristol. *Distance:* About 25 miles. *USGS Topos:* Chattahoochee, Rock Bluff, Blountstown and Bristol.

OWL CREEK –Hickory Landing, where a welcoming party of small alligators await with their snouts protruding from the water, is a good put-in for a trip on Owl Creek. About 2 miles upstream from the Apalachicola River, Hickory Landing (see page 257) provides camping, restrooms and water free of charge. There is a small boat dock but no boat ramp. Boaters will have to portage their boats to their cars. Below Hickory Landing, Owl Creek is wide and deep and is lined by the beautiful river swamp habitat that extends from the banks of the Apalachicola River. Like most waterways in the area, Owl Creek was clear cut up to the banks in the 1920s and '30s. A couple of the historic barges, fastened with wooden pins instead of nails, remain in Owl Creek. One is within a mile of Hickory Landing going upstream. *Put-In/Take-Out:* Hickory Landing (see page 257). From Sumatra, take FL 65 south for 2 miles. Turn right (west) on FSR 101 and go 1.5 miles, and then left (south) on FSR 101B for 1 mile. *Distance:* Downstream to the Apalachicola River is about 2 miles. Boaters can work their way upstream for several miles until the creek becomes impassible. *USGS Topos:* Sumatra, Fort Gadsden, Kennedy Creek and Forbes Island. *More Information:* Apalachicola National Forest, Apalachicola Ranger District Office, P.O. Box 579 Bristol, FL 32321; 850/643-2282.

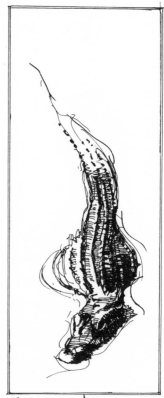

AMERICAN ALLIGATOR BASKS IN SUN ALONG THE RIVER.

"The movement of a canoe is like a reed in the wind. Silence is part of it, and the sounds of lapping water, bird songs, and wind in the trees. It is part of the medium through which it floats, the sky, the water and the shores. A man is part of his canoe and therefore part of all it knows. The instant he dips his paddle, he flows as it flows, the canoe yielding to his slightest touch and responsive to his every whim and thought."

—Sigurd F. Olson

Florida Springs

Natural water oozes, bubbles or gushes into pools, creeks and rivers all over Florida, the state with the largest collection of springs in the nation. Their clear, mild waters attract swimmers, cave divers and paddlers, should they be large enough. They vary greatly in size and duration–small ones seep into the soil only once in awhile; large ones issue forth millions of gallons a day, forming the head-waters of major rivers.

The state's largest springs concentrate in east central Florida, but there are a few of note on the Chipola River, a tributary of the Apalachicola almost entirely spring fed. Some run into the river on the west bank just below I-10. Countless minor ones originate just upstream of the city of Marianna. One large exception, Bozell Springs, with rocky limestone ledges and a crystal clear bottom 25 feet deep, is popular with cave divers. It feeds a creek that quickly empties into the Chipola.

There are two springs associated with the upper Apalachicola River, the first about 100 yards below the Jim Woodruff Lock and Dam on Lake Seminole. It's invisible in the muddy waters of the Apalachicola, but state fish and game officials have cleared out its path to enhance the flow because sport fish such as striped and hybrid bass like the spring water. The other spring, about a mile further downstream, originates in the woods.

WEWAHITCHKA TO OWL CREEK –This paddle is from Wewahitchka down the Apalachicola then up Owl Creek to Hickory Landing. *Put-In:* Gaskin Wayside Park. *Take-Out:* Hickory Landing or Owl Creek. *Distance:* About 21 miles. *USGS Topos:* Dead Lakes, Wewahitchka, Kennedy Creek, Forbes Island and Sumatra.

OWL CREEK TO APALACHICOLA –Another Owl Creek option is to paddle from Hickory Landing downriver on the Apalachicola. Stop at Fort Gadsden State Park (see page 263), about 2 miles from the creek, to study interpretive material. Take-out at Bay City Lodge in Apalachicola where there is a marina, restaurant and motel. *Put-In:* Hickory Landing. *Take-Out:* Bay City Lodge (see page 310). *Distance:* About 23 miles. *USGS Topos:* Apalachicola, West Pass, Jackson River and Forbes Island.

KENNEDY CREEK –Kennedy Creek is a short tributary off the Apalachicola River. The creek offers beautiful scenery on a lazy, winding current. The banks are lined with cypress, tupelo and other swamp trees. Like most tributaries of the Apalachicola, Kennedy Creek is heavily steeped in the deep red tannin of the swamp trees. In shallow sections where white sand bottoms are exposed, such streams appear like brewed tea. As most of Kennedy Creek is deep, the water appears black. Water levels fluctuate but the deep channel allows passage year-round. Hunters and fishermen often run motorized craft in the creek. *Put-In/Take-Out:* Cotton Landing (see page 256). From Sumatra, take CR 379 northwest for 3.2 miles. Turn left (west) onto FSR 123 and follow it for 2.8 miles, then turn left (west) on FSR 123B and go 0.7 mile to Cotton Landing. There are signs along the way. *Distance:* From Cotton Landing, paddlers can go upstream 2 miles or downstream 4 miles to the Apalachicola River. *Hazards:* Snakes, alligators and biting insects are common sights in the summer. *USGS Topos:* Sumatra and Kennedy Creek. *More Information:* Apalachicola National Forest, Apalachicola Ranger District Office, P.O. Box 579 Bristol, FL 32321; 850/643-2282.

RIVER STYX –This river offers a comfortable day trip most easily reached from White Oak Landing where boaters can go either up or downstream. Throughout the year, the slow-moving creek is fairly deep and is not affected much by fluctuations in the water level. White Oak is popular with fishermen and hunters in winter. *Put-In/Take-Out:* White Oak Landing (see page 256). From Sumatra, go north on CR 379 for about 7.5 miles. Turn left (west) on CR 115 and proceed 3.5 miles. *Distance:* Upstream, the river quickly becomes a confusing mix of channels and swamps. The Apalachicola River is a short 2-to 3-mile trip downstream. *Hazards:* This is snake and alligator habitat. Biting insects are a major nuisance in summer. *USGS Topos:* Sumatra, Kennedy Creek and Wewahitchka. *More Information:* Apalachicola National Forest, Apalachicola Ranger District Office, P.O. Box 579 Bristol, FL 32321; 850/643-2282.

CHIPOLA RIVER –Lush hardwood hammocks and limestone outcroppings characterize the Chipola, which means "clear water." Some parts of the river look emerald green with no precipitation, smoky green with light rain, and muddy tan with heavy agricultural soil runoff. Occasional springs issue forth pockets of extra clear water. Sometimes it runs along tree-lined banks. Other times it slows the pace with marshes, swamps and the occasional bluff on either side. The Chipola begins in southeast Alabama, becomes navigable a few miles north of the city of Marianna, but soon goes underground for 0.5 mile underneath Florida Caverns State Park (see page 237) where the Chipola River Canoe Trail begins. This beautiful trail flows through river swamp and hardwood forests of beech, magnolia, oak and dogwood. Beaver, alligator and turtles are sometimes seen on the river, and the pileated woodpecker can be heard drumming in the forest. Limestone bluffs and caves are also seen along the river. Several shoals are found in this pale-colored stream, especially in low water. Six-to-eight-foot-limestone banks line the river on the 5-mile stretch below the rapid. After that, the banks are lower with only a few high bluffs. *Put-Ins/Take-Outs and Distances In Between:* (1) Florida Caverns State Park, 3 miles north of Marianna on FL 167. (2) FL 167 Bridge, 1 mile north of Marianna (1 mile). (3) FL 280A bridge, 1 mile west of FL 71, just south of I-10 (10 miles). Remote section with steep sloping banks and good runs around a few islands where the river splits. (4) FL 278 bridge, 1 mile west of

Chipola River

The main tributary of the Apalachicola River, the Chipola, begins in southeast Alabama. Sometimes it runs swiftly along tree-lined banks with a limestone bottom. Other times it slows the pace, and marshes and swamps with occasional bluffs take up either horizon. The name is Indian for "clear water," and much of the river has a clear emerald color. A little rain turns it smoky green; a lot makes it tan. Springs bubble forth along the way. The Chipola becomes navigable a few miles north of Marianna, but soon goes underground for one-half mile underneath Florida Caverns State Park. Most trees native to the panhandle grow along some part of its path. Wild azalea, daisies and cardinal flowers bloom in the spring. Turtles and alligators sun in the river. Bird-life is abundant, especially in the lower section. Catfish, bream and bass are the most common catches. Near the end of its 80-mile journey, a sandbar transformed the increasingly swampy river into the Dead Lakes, five connected bodies of water littered with the standing remains of thousands of dead trees.

"A canoe trip has become simply a rite of oneness with a certain terrain, a diversion of the field, an act performed not because it is necessary but because there is value in the act itself."

—*John McPhee,* The Survival of the Bark Canoe

Chipola Cutoff

In the late 1800s, the U.S. Army Corps of Engineers dug a two-mile shortcut from the Apalachicola River to the Chipola River near the eastern edge of the town of Wewahitchka, Florida. The Chipola Cutoff saved steamboats dozens of miles going from the Chipola River to the Apalachicola, but also allowed the faster flowing Apalachicola a release valve to push large volumes of water into the slower moving Chipola. In fact, the Apalachicola sends more water into the cutoff than into its natural channel, dramatically illustrated as the muddy waters of the Apalachicola boil into the clear waters of the Chipola.

The Apalachicola had in the past pushed a natural sand bar to the mouth of the Chipola, which backed up and flooded thousands of acres of river swamp that became known as the Dead Lakes because of all the standing, drowned trees. The cutoff ensured the flooded condition would remain permanent by constantly dumping in Apalachicola water.

The Corps has informally talked about putting in a dike to redirect more water flow down the Apalachicola, but opposition by locals and state officials precludes that action, as well as closing the cutoff altogether. Taking away the cutoff might seriously affect the Dead Lakes, a favorite hangout for fishermen, and dry up the nearby swamps, one of the richest sources of tupelo honey nectar.

FL 71, 6 miles south of I-10. (10 miles). Similar to the previous section. Soft limestone bottom is quite noticeable. (5) FL 274 bridge, about 3 miles west of Altha (FL 71) 11 miles south of I-10. (8 miles). Look and Tremble Rapid, a limestone shoal that spans the river makes this run one of the river's most popular. Tubers and picnickers gather here in warmer months. Locals call Look and Tremble, Glance and Giggle. It's nothing above a mild Class II on its best day. (6) FL 20 bridge, 1 mile east of Clarksville at Wayside Park (10 miles). After passing the mouth of Fox Creek a few miles into the trip, the Chipola begins to dramatically change its appearance. High banks give way to much lower ones. Oak and pines give way to tupelos and cypresses. The limestone bottom is no longer apparent, and lily pads begin to appear along with large patches of sawgrass, a tan stalk of up to 18 inches with rough edges like a saw blade. The river becomes increasingly swampy, especially after passing Juniper Creek at mile 5, and spreads out into a swamp area called Ward Lake around mile 10. (7) FL 71 bridge, at Scott's Ferry (13 miles). Downstream of FL 71 the Chipola River becomes Dead Lakes and then a swamp. Both are difficult to navigate without a guide. There may be access points (both public and private) in addition to those listed here. Please remember that some sites may require a fee for launching and/or parking. *Hazards:* Canoeists may wish to begin their trip at the FL 167 bridge. The trail downstream from the state park is dangerous and requires technical paddling skills. The trail here is an old log chute with little water and very low hanging trees. An optional ending for the trail is at Dead Lakes State Recreation Area (see page 250). The thousands of dead trees still standing in the lake were killed when the area was impounded. Do not attempt this portion in bad weather. During low water, log jams and submerged rocks may require portage. Not all of the bridges along the Chipola have boat ramps. Put-ins and take-outs may require complicated maneuvering in fairly swift currents and carries up steep banks. Scout put-ins and take-outs. *USGS Topos:* Marianna, Oakdale, Altha West, Clarksville, Frink, Dead Lakes and Wewahitchka. *Other Maps:* County highway maps for this section of the Chipola River are Jackson, Calhoun and Gulf. *More Information:* Rickie and Anna McAlpin, Bear Paw Canoe Trails, P.O. Box 621, Marianna, FL 32446; 850/382-2200. Florida Caverns State Park, 3345 Caverns Road, Marianna, FL 32446; 850/482-1228. Note that canoes provided by rental services in state parks are generally for use on the water body at the location of the individual park. *Emergency Phone Numbers:* Jackson County Sheriff, 850/482-3132; Marianna Police Department, 850/526-3125; Calhoun County Sheriff, 850/674-5049; Gulf County Sheriff, 850/227-1115.

MUD SWAMP/NEW RIVER WILDERNESS: CARR BRIDGE TO MAGNOLIA LANDING –This trip is definitely worth the effort because it offers a firsthand look at the 8,090-acre Mud Swamp-New River Wilderness. Canoeists pass through an area that is off limits to motorized boat travel and encounter some of the prettiest and most remote canoeing in north Florida. Canoeists share the swamp with alligators, black bear, eastern diamondback and pygmy rattlesnakes and biting insects. Every season produces its own wild flowers and plants. The best season to explore here is winter when heat, humidity and insects are at a minimum. New River is challenging because of the many downed trees and logs that require canoeists to pull over or portage. The water level in New River fluctuates considerably and, while stream gauge readings are not available, visual inspection should provide a reasonable clue of what to expect. Interested adventurers might also want to call the ranger district office in Bristol, Florida, before making the trip. Drought conditions in the region create almost impassible conditions on the New River. Few, if any people have made it all the way through Mud Swamp because the main channel starts to break up into numerous branches before coming back together on the southeast corner of the wilderness. Most maps of the area show the New River as having a channel through the swamp; there isn't one. It's just like the name: mud and swamps. *Put-In:* From Sumatra, go north on FL 65 10 miles. Turn right (east) on FSR 13 and go 5 miles to Carr Bridge. Access to the river is on the south side of the bridge before you cross the river. *Take-Out:* From Carr Bridge, continue east on FSR 13 about 4.5 miles. Turn right (south) on FSR 170 and continue 3 miles. Turn right (west) on FSR 182 and continue 5 miles to Magnolia

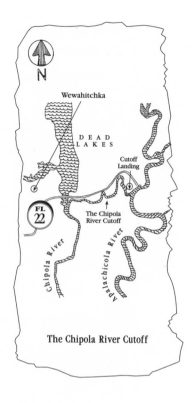

The Chipola River Cutoff

A river with waters dyed a reddish color by tannic acid from tree roots and rotting vegetation is called a BLACKWATER STREAM.

www.chattahoochee.org

⑥ We welcome your comments, suggestions, recommendations and input regarding this book and the river, via the Internet at the Riverkeeper's website: www.chattahoochee.org.

You can also access the website for additional information regarding the Chattahoochee and the many issues that affect the river.

ALL IS BORN OF WATER;
ALL IS SUSTAINED BY WATER.

Landing, a primitive campsite by the river with a parking area and a few picnic tables. Most canoeists park their cars at Magnolia Landing, except for the shuttle vehicle which takes everyone to Carr Bridge. *USGS Topos:* Wilma, Queens Bay, Sumatra and Owens Bridge. *More Information:* Apalachicola Ranger District, Apalachicola National Forest, FL 20, P.O. Box 579, Bristol, FL 32321; 850/643-2282.

WOODY MILEY'S FAVORITE RIVER SWAMP BOAT TRIPS –Woody Miley spends a lot of time roaming the Apalachicola River and Bay in his role as environmental administrator for the Apalachicola National Estuarine Research Reserve. When Miley wants to introduce friends to the Apalachicola River Swamp, there are two boat trips he takes them on. Trips can be taken in a canoe or kayak or a jon boat with a small outboard; Woody uses his 13-foot Whaler. Boaters interested in these trips should obtain topographical maps and study them when planning. One trip is to go up the Apalachicola, then down the St. Marks to the East River Cutoff. Then go up the East River back to the Apalachicola and back to the starting point.

Miley's other favorite route is to go up the Apalachicola then down the St. Marks to the first big left which is East River Cutoff, "crooked as a snake track," in Miley's words, but still big water. Go down the East River to Montgomery Ferry Slough. The slough entrance is not shown on some maps and is no wider than a door frame until the boater passes through it. It can be identified by a burnt-out hunt camp on the east bank which is just past the cutoff. Then come out on Blounts Bay. Exploring up Saltwater Creek will extend the trip. *USGS Topos:* Apalachicola, West Pass, Beverly and Jackson River.

Section 10
Apalachicola Bay

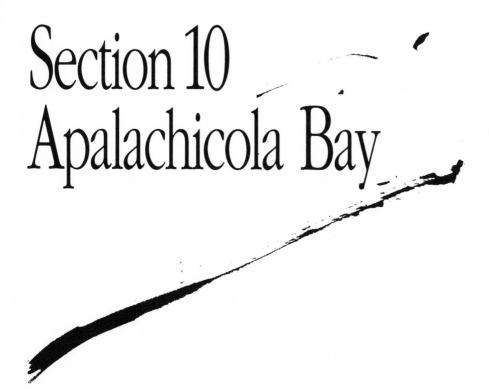

"palachicola Bay is the most productive estuary in the northern hemisphere on a production per acre basis. We even blow Chesapeake away. We harvest from two-to-six million pounds of oyster meat a year out of our bay. That's over 90 percent of the oysters harvested in Florida and over ten percent of the oysters harvested in the nation. Shrimping, economically, is more important than the oyster industry; but it employs fewer people so it's really tough to say which is king. Shrimping, we harvest four-to-seven million pounds of shrimp a year. Locally grown shrimp. Totally renewable–almost no overhead. In the open Gulf of Mexico, 95 percent of all species harvested commercially and 85 percent of all species harvested recreationally have to spend a portion of their life cycle in an estuary system like the Apalachicola. The coastal marshes along here are up to seven times as productive as cultivated wheat fields complete with irrigation and fertilizer. Nature does it seven times better. Economic evaluation of these marshes show that from a production value they are worth $89,000 dollars an acre. Again, a totally renewable resource with no overhead.

We can't protect Apalachicola Bay–or any other estuary– just as *that* system because of the functional relationship with flood plains, rivers, marshes, the bay, barrier islands. An estuary by *definition* is nothing more than where fresh water and salt water mix and meet. From a *functional* standpoint it goes 80 miles north of Atlanta to the headwaters of the Chattahoochee. Eighty-eight percent of the 19,800 square mile drainage basin that feeds or pollutes Apalachicola Bay is in Georgia and Alabama. Only 2,400 of that's in Florida. Based on average flow, 84 percent of the fresh water that feeds or pollutes Apalachicola Bay originates out of the state. We change the name of the river at man's political boundaries, but the river doesn't know it's changed. If you stand in Georgia and look down, there's the 'Hooch, there's the Flint and somewhere down there, there's the Apalachicola. If you stand in Apalachicola and look up, you get a better picture. Functional. From here, you see there's only one river.

Woody Miley is the Environmental Administrator for the Apalachicola National Estuarine Research Reserve.

Woody Miley

THE BAY

The Apalachicola Bay on the Florida Panhandle coast in the Gulf of Mexico is large, long and shallow. From west to east it spans 55 miles; from north to south 6 miles at the widest. Eighty-six percent of the surface is open water. The remaining 21,860 acres is marshes, spread out along the Apalachicola River mouth, the coast and the northern edge of a series of barrier islands.

Located on the bay's southern perimeter, the long barrier island chain runs toward the northeast. Dog Island, the smallest, is furthest east. To its west is St. George Island, the longest island. A man-made channel was cut into St. George in the 1950s, creating Little St. George Island to its southwest. The triangular-shaped St. Vincent Island is the furthest west and the largest of the barriers.

The bay averages 9 feet deep, with sand, clay and silt the primary sediments. Because of a concentration of oyster reefs, the bay is shallowest toward St. George Sound in the east. Three-quarters of the bay's fresh water originates more than 107 miles upstream at the junction of the Chattahoochee and Flint rivers where they form the Apalachicola. The Apalachicola releases 16 billion gallons of fresh water a day and 1 million tons of sediment a year into the bay.

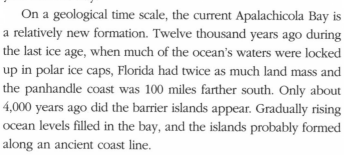

On a geological time scale, the current Apalachicola Bay is a relatively new formation. Twelve thousand years ago during the last ice age, when much of the ocean's waters were locked up in polar ice caps, Florida had twice as much land mass and the panhandle coast was 100 miles farther south. Only about 4,000 years ago did the barrier islands appear. Gradually rising ocean levels filled in the bay, and the islands probably formed along an ancient coast line.

The scarcity of fresh water on the islands and the inhospitableness of the swamps around the Apalachicola River floodplain and delta prevented much habitation by early Indians.

Oystermen

A fiercely independent breed, oysterfolk keep irregular hours, work for themselves and hate being cooped up indoors. They usually go out into the bay in the morning in simple boats around 22 feet long and congregate in oyster beds east of the St. George Island Bridge. Most work in crews of two. One attacks the oysters with 12-foot poles, or tongs, connected like pliers with rakes on both ends. He tongs up oyster clumps known as burrs. His partner on the other end of the boat splits the burrs into single oysters on a culling board, a thick, strong length of wood attached to the boat, with an iron rod that resembles a giant ice pick.

They work in shallows, usually four or five feet deep. And after they've cleaned out an oyster bed, they move into the next one, dragging along the bottom a mini-anchor, usually an automobile crankshaft. Cramming every inch of the boat with oysters, they can collect ten or more bushels on a good day.

Many boats have small cabins to protect the crews from rain.

However, peoples associated with the Mississippian culture of 1000 to 1500 AD left their mark. They mostly lived upriver in settled communities growing corn but occasionally made forays to the coast, where they harvested oysters and fish. The barrier islands and neighboring mainland shore are dotted with middens, or mounds of discarded oyster shells and pottery perhaps left by these groups.

American settlements sprang up along the coast soon after Spain ceded Florida to the United States in 1821. Apalachicola, founded in 1831, soon became the third largest port on the Gulf of Mexico.

The Apalachicola Bay is part of the largest estuary sanctuary in the nation. The 193,758-acre Apalachicola National Estuarine Research Reserve encompasses the bay, much of the barrier islands and a section of the Apalachicola River and adjoining floodplains. In contrast to the majority of estuaries in Florida, which have been closed to commercial fishing because of pollution, the Apalachicola Bay remains relatively clean because there is comparatively little land development around the bay or along the Apalachicola River. The total haul of all seafood from the bay nets about $100 million retail a year. Yet, the local industry has weathered its share of storms in past years. A government ban on many commercial fishing nets sunk much of the fleet in the early 1990s. About the same time, national media attention focusing on isolated illnesses from consuming raw bay oysters didn't help matters. The pounding has taken its toll. While there were 60 seafood processing houses on the bay ten years ago, today there are 12; and much of the catch they sort and package comes from foreign waters. Nevertheless, the seafood industry remains by far the most important in the region. A major concern of those who rely on it is protecting the Apalachicola Bay and the three rivers which feed it: the Apalachicola, Chattahoochee and Flint.

Although one of the richest biologically, the Apalachicola Bay region is one of the state's poorest economically. But the times could be changing. People are snapping up properties along the coast, turning them into condos and hotels. Many locals who live off the bay's bounty worry that a development boom could threaten the bay's health.

THE BARRIER ISLANDS

DOG ISLAND –The smallest inhabited and easternmost island of the barrier chain, Dog Island remains mostly undeveloped but has about a dozen permanent residents. A sandy road from the dock in Tyson Harbor meanders through the length of the island, passing by a small private airstrip, 100 homes and the Pelican Inn, a rustic, 8-room hamlet made of cinder block and cypress, right on the gulf. Visitors must bring their own food and drink. There's no public store on the island, and the inn does not serve meals. The 400-square foot rooms do have fully-equipped kitchens and room to sleep four. Two-thirds of the 1,800-acre island is a Nature Conservancy preserve. The low number of visitors to the island make its beach a good place to find shells. A former beachfront dune line has migrated into the interior of the long, narrow island. Gnarled sand pine and live oak live on either side. There is no bridge to the island. The dock is available for day use. There is regular ferry service between Dog Island and Carrabelle on the *Ruby B*, captained by Raymond Williams. The round-trip cost is $18 for non-property owners and $14 for property owners. Visitors can catch it at the end of Marine Street in downtown Carrabelle. *More Information:* Pelican Inn, 800/451-5294 or 850/697-4728; Ruby B Ferry Service, 850/697-3434.

ST. GEORGE ISLAND –The longest barrier island is a place of many contrasts. It's 27 miles in length, but no greater than 1 mile in width. In some places a rock can be thrown from the bay to the gulf. The eastern third is a state park with pristine wilderness, primitive trails and nesting bald eagles. But the remainder of St. George has the largest concentration of houses and businesses in all the barrier islands. It also has the only island bridge to the mainland.

A handful of eccentric wanderers, artists and ex-hippies who migrated to the then-quiet St. George decades ago remain on the island. But well-heeled beach lovers increasingly are crowding them out. Right along the gulf, there's a strip of rental rowhouses that obliterate the view and would look to be more at home in Baltimore or Washington, D.C.

Wild dreams and big money have long been part of the

Inside each there will likely be a packed lunch, radio and cell phone.

Most of the bay is state-controlled and open to all oystermen, although a few beds are privately owned and harvested. Oystermen say times were better in the old days when they could work three or four half days a week and make a decent living. Government controls–a favorite topic of discussion–and some bad press following some well-publicized illnesses from oyster consumption have hurt the industry. They maintain it's not the oysters getting sicker, but the people. Everyone can enjoy oysters cooked, but no one with serious health problems or chronic diseases should eat them raw. Of most concern is *e. coli* infections. To help prevent oysters from getting contaminated with this dangerous bacteria, the bay is closed immediately following heavy rains of a day or longer.

Those so desiring can launch a boat and work the same oyster bars as the pros. But others hunting more convenient mollusks can go oyster hogging, picking over with a culling iron the oyster bars exposed near the shoreline during low tides. Generally, oysters from coon bars, as they are called, have skinnier and longer shells than those further out in the bay. The latter grow better as they are always underwater. Oyster season is year-round, but the best months are those with an R in them, especially the winter ones. The bag limit is one bushel (60 pounds or two five-gallon buckets) per person, and the oysters must be three inches in their greatest dimension. Out-of-staters must have at least a temporary license for recreational saltwater fishing.

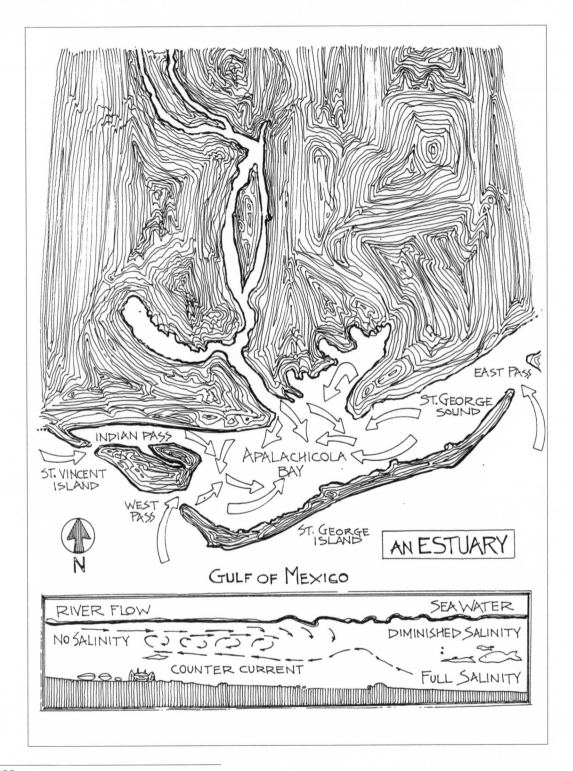

EAST PASS

ST. GEORGE SOUND

INDIAN PASS

APALACHICOLA BAY

ST. VINCENT ISLAND

WEST PASS

ST. GEORGE ISLAND

AN ESTUARY

N

GULF OF MEXICO

RIVER FLOW   SEA WATER

NO SALINITY   DIMINISHED SALINITY

COUNTER CURRENT   FULL SALINITY

local history. Pirate captain Billy Bowlegs in the late 1700s reportedly buried a treasure somewhere on the island. And in the early 1900s land speculator William Lee Popham came up with an ambitious real estate scheme–he sold over and over again to different buyers and all of the plots underwater.

The island now has more than 600 full-time residents and 2,000 dwellings. Several motels, convenience stores, real estate businesses, churches, art galleries, a kayak rental store, a video rental shop and a small water tower are located in the central section of the island, along with a number of decent seafood restaurants and watering holes, including Harry A's. "If something fun happens, it happens at Harry A's," boasts one ad for the casual local hangout. It delivers. Order a cold drink and a dozen oysters and before too long there's a chance of getting into a deep philosophical discussion with an islander on where to find the best sunrises and sunsets.

St. George has numerous boat landings. Public access is available by the bridge or in the state park. *More Information:* St. George Island Business Owners' Association, 128 Market Street, Apalachicola, FL 32320; 850/653-9419.

LITTLE ST. GEORGE ISLAND –Until the Corps of Engineers cut a permanent pass in 1952, Little St. George Island was the western extension of St. George Island. Now it's a narrow, 10-mile-long strip of publicly owned land. Locally known as Little St. George, it's officially called the Cape St. George State Reserve, and managed by the Apalachicola National Estuarine Research Reserve in Eastpoint. There is no bridge to the island. Like the other barrier islands, this one is mostly salt marshes and ponds on the bay side, white sandy beaches on the gulf side, with dune lines running parallel to the length of the island in the interior. On the gulf, sea oats anchor low, newly forming dune ridges. In the interior, scrub oaks grow along taller, older dune ridges, with slash pines and savannas scattered with cabbage palms in the low, flat areas. Small mammals and rare animals like bald eagles, peregrine falcons, snowy plovers and loggerhead sea turtles have been spotted here.

Although protected since the state purchased the bulk of the island in 1977, Little St. George suffered from much human use before then. Some dune ridges continue to heal from when

Estuary

A constantly changing mix of fresh and saltwater at the junction of rivers and oceans, estuaries are home to a tremendous abundance of life. River currents send freshwater downstream and ocean currents push saltwater upstream. When the two meet, they form a wedge; the lighter freshwater continues flowing on top toward the ocean, and the heavier saltwater is driven downward and up the channel. If the freshwater river is clear, the wedge can easily be seen. Clear water flows downstream on the surface; but underneath, dark muddy water flows in the opposite direction. The location of the wedge within an estuary zone changes often–sometimes within a matter of minutes–depending on tides, seasons and weather conditions. Strong incoming tides and storms can push it far up the channel. So can low river flows during summer and winter. Conversely, outgoing tides or spring river floods send it far into the bay. Temperatures in the wedge vary as well. In summer and autumn, incoming freshwater is warmer than the ocean. In the winter and spring, the opposite is true. Life is extremely difficult in the estuary because of rapidly changing water levels, currents, salinity content and temperatures. Despite the harsh conditions, there is plenty of food for estuary life. Much of the nutrient load that comes with rivers is slowed or stopped by the incoming ocean current. The settling organic matter feeds marsh grasses, algae and microscopic plants and continues up the food chain.

Estuaries support more life than any other natural environment. They serve as spawning ground for over 75 percent of all commercially harvested shrimp, crabs, oysters and fishes.

Apalachicola Bay Facts

Between 65 and 85 percent of local residents make a living directly from fishing.

The retail value of the bay's seafood is about $100 million a year.

The bay yield of four-to-six million tons of oyster meat a year provides 90 percent of Florida's, and ten percent of the country's, oyster harvest.

The bay is 55 miles long and, at most, 6 miles long. The bay averages only 9 feet in depth.

Fourteen percent, or 21,860 acres, of the total water area in the bay is covered in estuary marshes.

Almost 84 percent of the bay's freshwater originates in Georgia; a much smaller percentage comes from Alabama

One million tons of river sediments wash into the bay every year.

Daily average flow into the bay is 16 billion gallons.

Maximum flow is more than 200 billion gallons.

When tides go out, 700 billion gallons leave the bay.

"What people have to realize is that everything that happens upstream affects us down here."

—*Woody Miley, Apalachicola, quoted in* Living Waters

the military flattened them during amphibious training up through the 1960s. Many island pines bear V-shaped scars from when they were tapped for turpentine in the 1910s and again in the 1950s. The old turpentine camp buildings remain near the government dock. There is one sign from the past, however, that many are trying to save–the lighthouse. When the lighthouse was built in 1852 on the cape in the middle of Little St. George on the gulf, there was over 1,000 feet of sand between it and the sea. Yet, since Hurricane Kate hit in 1985, it has teetered on the brink of collapse on the edge of the beach. The Coast Guard hadn't planned to save the lighthouse when it took it out of service three years ago. But people in the bay area have raised private funds to construct a new foundation and sea wall and hope to get the green light from the Coast Guard to begin building in 1997. *More Information:* Apalachicola National Estuarine Research Reserve, 350 Carroll Street, Eastpoint, FL 32328; 850/670-4783.

St. Vincent National Wildlife Refuge –Of all the barrier islands, St. Vincent has the most intriguing history, richest biodiversity and fewest signs of civilization. The westernmost and largest of the barrier islands at 12,538 acres, it is triangular-shaped, 9 miles long from east to west and 4 miles at its widest.

St. Vincent has some of the oldest Native American settlements in the region. Small pottery shards, many dating back 2,000 years, cover a sizable section of the western beach on the bay side. Spanish Franciscan monks named the island in the 17th century, just passing through on the way to visit nearby Creeks and Seminoles, some of who lived at least temporarily on the island the following century.

In 1868 a former mayor of Cincinnati, George Hatch, bought the island for $3,000 to get away from it all–and did so permanently; his is the only marked grave on St. Vincent. During the early part of the 20 century, limited cattle grazing and timber removal took place. Dr. Ray Pierce and brothers Alfred and Henry Loomis bought the island in 1908 and 1948, respectively. Both owners imported exotic game animals to make it a private hunting reserve, complete with zebras, elands, black bucks, ringnecked pheasants and oriental jungle fowl. Of all the foreign species, only the Southeast Asian sambar deer remain. In 1968, the federal government bought the island from the Nature Conservancy with proceeds from "Duck" stamp sales and turned St. Vincent into a wildlife refuge. The other exotic animals had become tame and were easily corralled, but the sambar remained wild and could not be caught. The paddled-eared Southeast Asian deer, who tip the scales at 600 lbs–much larger than their native cousins–prefer the low wetlands.

St. Vincent has an abundance of habitats: rolling sand dunes, oak ridges, pine flatwoods, cabbage palm, magnolia hammocks, tidal marsh, swamps and 20 freshwater lakes. There are many unique or endangered species that live naturally on the island: giant alligators, eastern indigo snakes, diamondback rattlers, bobcats, foxes, coyotes, wild pigs, freshwater fish, loggerhead sea turtles, peregrine falcons, a peak population of waterfowl. Two hundred and fifty different bird species have been identified on the island. In 1990 St. Vincent became one of several coastal islands where endangered red wolves are bred for reintroduction into the wild. After the pups are weaned, they're taken to other federally protected lands in the Southeast like the Great Smoky Mountain National Park and Alligator River National Wildlife Refuge in North Carolina.

Limited fishing is allowed on the island. About 130 acres of the refuge are actually scattered elsewhere in the Apalachicola Bay region, including 46-acre Pig Island in St. Joseph Bay. *Facilities:* There's virtually nothing to remind visitors of modern man, except for 80 miles of old sandy logging roads, some densely covered by trees, that crisscross the interior and make good hiking or biking trails (see page 295). *Days/Hrs.:* For day use only, daily, year-round, except during several brief hunt sessions with bows and arrows or muzzle loading guns for both kinds of island deer, wild pig or raccoon each November, December and January. Camping is prohibited, except by the hunters in designated primitive sites. However, there's a campground next to Indian Pass (see page 291) on the mainland and a primitive camping site on the western tip of Little St. George (see page 292). Access might be restricted in areas with nesting bald eagles near the freshwater lakes. A government dock on the western tip and a ranger cabin on the eastern tip are

WATER RELIGION:
BABYLONIA

In the Babylonian creation story, Apsu and Tiamat, representing fresh and saltwater in the primeval ocean, mix chaotically and give life to all other living things.

closed to the public. *Directions:* The Refuge is about 9 miles offshore from Apalachicola, 0.33 mile west of Little St. George Island, and 0.2 mile from Indian Peninsula on the mainland. Access is by boat only. The shortest crossing is at Indian Pass, 0.2 mile west of the island's easternmost tip. There's a public boat ramp there. Make sure weather conditions are calm. It's best not to cross if the tide is rushing in or out, especially the latter when boaters could easily wind up in the gulf where paddling is much more difficult if not dangerous. Consult local newspapers and fishing lodges for tide tables and weather forecasts. *More Information:* St. Vincent National Wildlife Refuge, P.O. Box 447, Apalachicola, FL 32329; 850/653-8808. The refuge office is in downtown Apalachicola at the northern end of Market Street and has knowledgeable rangers and interpretive displays.

PARKS AND RECREATION

APALACHICOLA BAY CAMPGROUND –This former KOA campground has little shade, looks desolate, and is not within walking distance of the bay. *Facilities:* 59 campsites with water, electricity and cable hook-ups, 50 of those with sewer; pool in the summer; laundry; showers; dump station. Indoor pets allowed. *Days/Hrs.:* Daily, year-round. Office, 10am-12pm and 2-6pm. Self-registration during night is permitted. *Fees:* $15 a night or $65 a week for 2 people. *Directions:* In Eastpoint on the south side of US 98. *More Information:* Manager Chuck Jacks, P.O. Box 621, Eastpoint, FL 32328; 850/670-8307.

CAPE SAN BLAS CAMPING RESORT –A cozy, remote location with sites nestled among small sandhills and coastal canopy, some almost next to the beach. *Facilities:* 40 campsites, 6 rental cottages, swimming pool, canoe rentals, volleyball and horseshoes, hot showers, camp store, dump station, pets allowed, private access to 2 miles of undeveloped beach. *Days/Hrs.:* Daily, year-round. Office, 8:30am-8:30pm. Self-registration at night permitted. *Fees:* Basic camping rate based on 2 people per site is $12 in beach area, $10 in the pool area. Cottage rentals begin at $40-55 daily and $240-330 weekly. There is a 20 percent discount from Nov. 1 to Feb. 29. *Directions:* From

Port St. Joe, take 30A about 8.5 miles, then turn right (west) on 30E. Go about 1.5 miles and the campground is on the right. *More Information:* Don and Rhonda Thiel, P.O. Box 645, Port St. Joe, FL 32457; 850/229-6800. Website: www.homtown.com/capecamp.

GULF VIEW CAMPGROUND –RV and tent campsites here are on a grassy, pine shaded field with a nice view of the gulf. *Facilities:* 45 campsites with hookups, laundry, heated bath-house. *Days/Hrs.:* Daily, year-round. Office, 8:30am-8pm. Self registration at night allowed. *Fees:* $10 a night without hookups; $13 a night or $75 weekly with hookups. *Directions:* 2 miles east of Eastpoint on US 98. *More Information:* John Enloe, Gulf View Campground, 897 US 98, Eastpoint, FL 32328; 850/670-8970.

INDIAN PASS CAMPGROUND –This unassuming, slightly junky campground with plenty of shade is the nearest launching ramp to St. Vincent Island. *Facilities:* 40 sites with hookups, pool, bathhouse. *Fees:* $10 a night and $60 a week for 2 people. *Days/Hrs.:* Daily, year-round. Office, 8am-6pm. Self-registration at night allowed. *Directions:* From Apalachicola, go 8 miles west on US 98, then left (west) on 30A. About 9 miles later turn left (east) on 30B. Two miles at the end of the road is the campground. *More Information:* Manager Mike Moree, SR 1 Box 905, Port St. Joe, FL 32456; 850/227-7203.

LAFAYETTE PARK –This picturesque Apalachicola city park features two acres of thick grass and moss-covered oaks. When it opened in 1832, the park was out in the country. The original city grew along the riverside, not the bay shore. Stately homes on the park perimeter came later beginning in the 1890s timber boom. Marsh grass runs along the water now, but there was a sandy beach here before the 1935 causeway for the bay bridge altered the bay current. *Facilities:* Gazebo, children's playground, picnic tables, 100-foot pier for cast net fishing. *Days/Hrs.:* Daily, year-round for day use only. *Directions:* In the Apalachicola Historic District at the intersection of 14th Street and Bay Avenue. *More Information:* Apalachicola City Hall, 1 Avenue E, Apalachicola, FL 32320; 850/653-9319.

CARRABELLE WAYSIDE PARK –Called New Beach by the locals, this no-frills, modern day use area is a 100-yard strip of

William Augustus Bowles

One of the most colorful characters on the river, William Augustus Bowles rose to power in a way reminiscent of Joseph Conrad's *Heart of Darkness*. Abandoning his life as a British officer after the American Revolution, the Maryland native took an Indian wife from a village on the lower Chattahoochee and led a revolt of Creeks and Seminoles that threatened to drive the Spanish out of Florida. In 1797 when the schooner *Fox* ran aground on St. George Island, most passengers waited for a passing ship to rescue them, but Bowles paddled up the Apalachicola River in a makeshift raft, carrying salvaged guns, powder and bullets. He planned to reunite with his Creek family and create an independent Creek state under British protection. Declaring himself general director of the Creek confederacy, Bowles and his followers captured and held for a month the Spanish fort at St. Marks in 1800. Losing control of its only fortification between St. Augustine and Pensacola embarrassed Spain and signaled its fragile hold on Florida. As much as Spain detested Bowles, so did Panton, Leslie & Company, a powerful British firm that monopolized Florida trade. Bowles' unpredictable actions threatened their pocketbooks, especially since he was supplying the Creeks with arms and ammunition. Panton and Spain put a $4,500 price on Bowles's head. American agents and Creek allies conspired to collect. In 1803 a summit of Creek chiefs took place. Arriving with a band of his Seminoles, Bowles expected to be chosen king of the nation. Instead, he left in chains on his way to a Cuban prison, where he later died.

Beach Sand

"A river system is best thought of as a system of moving water and sediment because an enormous volume of sediment is constantly being transported to the ocean by running water. The sediment is moved in suspension, by traction and in solution. It is visible in most rivers, especially where it is being deposited as a delta near the river's mouth." *Earth's Dynamic Systems, p. 296.*

"Since the ancient separation of the land from the water, exposed rocks have been splitting and crumbling, forming smaller and smaller pieces and finally cobbles, pebbles, sand and mud. Some of this debris becomes a vital part of life-giving soil. Sooner or later most of it reaches the edge of the continent." *The Beaches Are Moving, p. 27.*

"As the pebbles and cobbles are carried by flowing water, they themselves are worn down by striking one another and the channel bottom. Their corners and edges are chipped off, and the particles become smaller, smoother and more rounded. Large boulders that have fallen into a stream and are transported only during a flood are thus slowly broken and worn down to smaller fragments. Ultimately, they are washed away as grains of sand." *Earth's Dynamic Systems, p. 272.*

"To say that beaches are made of sand does not tell us how to make a beach. The recipes for beach materials are often simple, but there is no national cuisine. Each beach has its own special materials, its own provincial recipe. Nature relentlessly reminds us of this even in relatively quiet inland waters." *The Beaches Are Moving, p. 46.*

"Immediately west of the

concrete next to a swimming beach right off the highway. Locals hang out at Old Beach, one block east and two blocks south of here. The older swimming area has no facilities and is not maintained. There's not a boat launch at Old Beach, but people use it to put in sail boats or kayaks. *Facilities:* Picnic tables, restrooms, unsupervised swimming beach. *Days/Hrs.:* Daily, year-round for day use only. *Directions:* On US 98, 1 mile west of downtown Carrabelle in Carrabelle Beach. *More Information:* Florida Department of Transportation, Maintenance Department Yard, Route 1, Box 2860, Havana, FL 32333; 850/488-9872.

SALINAS PARK –This is an attractive, public day use gulf swimming area with overhanging oaks, dunes and access to miles of undeveloped beaches. Thatched roofs over the picnic tables give it a tropical look. Cape San Blas is about a 2-mile walk along the beach. *Facilities:* Picnic area with tables and grills, trails to beach. *Days/Hrs.:* Daily, year-round. *More Information:* Board of Commissioners, Gulf County Courthouse, 1000 5th Street, Port St. Joe, FL 32456; 850/229-6106.

CAPE ST. GEORGE STATE PRESERVE –Known as Little Saint George, this narrow, 10-mile-long island (see page 287) is an excellent locale for exploring widely different habitats in a natural barrier island landscape. Many birds, including peregrine falcons and bald eagles, and a few kinds of small mammals can be seen in the dune ridges, marshes, cabbage palm savannas and sea oat beaches which cover the island. Among the few signs of human presence on the island are a dock, scientific field station, shelter and old turpentining camp on the bay side in the middle of the island, a few old turpentining roads and a teetering antebellum lighthouse on the edge of the gulf near the cape. *Facilities:* Overnight stays are limited to primitive campsites with no facilities on the western and eastern tips of the island. Access is only by boat, which must be beached. The government dock and shelter are off-limits, except to special tours arranged with the Apalachicola National Estuarine Research Reserve, which manages the preserve. *Days/Hrs.:* Daily, year-round, but overnighters must notify the research reserve in advance. *Location:* East of St. Vincent and west of St.

George islands. *More Information:* St. George Island State Park, HCR Box 62, St. George Island, FL 32328; 904/927-2111.

DR. JULIAN G. BRUCE ST. GEORGE ISLAND STATE PARK —One of the best examples of Florida's barriers islands, St. George is also one of the most fragile (see page 285). The state park's 9-mile stretch of undeveloped, fine-grained sugar sand is considered one of the best beaches in the country. Its 1,962 acres of wind sculpted dunes, sandy coves, salt marshes and bayous and pine and oak forests offer some rewarding sights and hiking. Yet, because the island in some places is so narrow the bay and gulf practically touch, it is especially vulnerable to the heavy storms which occasionally pass through and do some major earth engineering. For example, migrating dunes have in recent years permanently obliterated two boardwalk trails. Loads of shore birds, marsh snakes, raccoons and ghost crabs populate the park. Currently the last 1.5 miles of the main park road that leads to the eastern tip of the island is closed due to extensive storm damage, but could be reopened sometime in the future for 4-wheel drive vehicles. *Facilities:* 60 campsites, 30 with RV hookups, picnic tables, fire rings, showers, restrooms; a 2.5-mile trail (see page 300) with primitive camping allowed at the end; bath houses on the beach; 2 boat ramps on the bay; youth camp and interpretive amphitheater. There are no lifeguards. Saltwater fishing is permitted with a required fishing license. *Days/Hrs.:* Daily, year-round, 8am until sunset. Make arrangements ahead of time if arriving late. *Fees:* Day use entrance fee, $3.25 for a carload of up to 8 people; camping, $12 without electricity and $14 with electricity for up to 4 people February through August; and $8 and $10, respectively, September through January. *Directions:* Located on the eastern end of St. George Island, 10 miles southeast of Eastpoint. From there, follow the signs. *More Information:* St. George Island State Park, HCR Box 62, St. George Island, FL 32328; 850/927-2111.

T. H. STONE MEMORIAL ST. JOSEPH PENINSULA STATE PARK —A 2,516-acre park surrounded by the gulf and St. Joseph Bay, this park has perhaps the most spectacular dunes and migratory bird watching in the region. Towering 40-foot sand dunes stand as close as 25 yards to the gulf. In between the dunes

bend, the Apalachicola River dramatizes the special dependence of the Gulf Coast on inland sediment. The river does not carry the clear water from Florida's limestone and peat-bottomed swamps. It originates in Georgia at the union of the Flint and the Chattahoochee rivers, and from them it takes tons of red Georgia clay and soil. The red-brown fan of new materials colors the gulf three miles from shore. The river's delivery system is seen in the sandy beaches and the long straight barrier islands formed from its burden."
The Beaches Are Moving, p. 46.

"The Chattahoochee is coming down here and the Flint is coming down here and they come together right at the bottom of the state to form the Apalachicola which then drains straight out and forms a little delta. Now if you trace those rivers back to where they come from, they come from the Piedmont and Blue Ridge. The Piedmont and Blue Ridge are made out of silica rich rocks, things like granites and schists and gneiss and things like that. If you get rain falling on the granite, which is made of mica, feldspar and quartz, the mica and feldspar start to deteriorate and turn into clay and so they wash away. Then all you have left is little grains of quartz. Quartz is very stable and tends not to break down chemically, partly because it's such a simple chemical composition—the silicon oxygen bond that holds quartz being one of the strongest bonds in nature. Now these little grains are loose. They are no longer part of a rock and so they'll be transported by a stream as sand and they'll end up on a beach somewhere."

Timothy LaTour, Georgia State University Geology Professor.

and gulf is eight miles of unbroken soft, white sandy beaches. The unique geography of this narrow peninsula in relation to the mainland contributes to the densest regional concentration of migratory hawks in the autumn over its interior of thick forests and dune ridges (see page 298). Monarch butterflies also come through in large numbers at the same time on an annual trek to Mexico.

SMALL MARSH RABBITS FEEDING ON GRASS.

The underwater turtle grass jungle in shallow St. Joseph Bay provides a haven for many underwater creatures, including horseshoe crabs, octopus and tasty scallops, which visitors can harvest during the summer. Low tide is best because the water is clearer. When you see their eyes twinkling, take a breath and scoop them up. Unpleasant odors from a paper mill in Port St. Joe are usually not a problem during the summer, but commonly blow across the bay in the winter. *Facilities:* 8 furnished cabins, 119 campsites with water and electricity, primitive camping, picnic table and grill, restrooms, showers, a youth camp tenting area, boat ramp, picnic area, canoe rentals, summer marina with store, beach, interpretive loop trail along the bay's edge, 7-mile primitive trail (see page 299). Saltwater fishing is permitted with required fishing license. *Days/Hrs.:* Daily, year-round, 8am until sunset. Make arrangements if arriving late. *Fees:* Camping, Mar.-Oct., for up to 4 persons, $15; Nov.-Feb., $8; electricity, an extra $2 per night. Cabin rentals, Mar.-Sept. 15, $70 a night for 4 people; remainder of year, $55. Primitive camping, $3 a night. Day use entrance fee, $3.25 per vehicle. *Directions:* Take C30 off US 98 and follow the signs, either 20 miles from Port St. Joe or 25 miles from Apalachicola. *More Information:* St. Joseph Peninsula State Park, Star Route 1, Box 200, Port St. Joe, FL 32456; 850/227-1327.

MARINAS

BATTERY PARK MARINA –Not much to look at. This Apalachicola city park has a tiny shack and two beat up old cannons with no interpretive explanation on an acre of scruffy grass and sand. But these aren't the main attraction, the marina is. The docks are the home of local floating luminaries like the river cruising *Apalachicola Belle* and the 1880s schooner the *Governor Stone* (see page 337), a national historic landmark and the South's oldest active sailing vessel. Sometime within the next several years, the city plans to renovate the park and include an interpretive display with the cannons, whose broad arrow stamps identify them as British guns from the 1820s. *Facilities:* Slips, public boat ramp, cast net fishing pier, playground, community center. The shack is home to local boy and girl scout troops. *Days/Hrs.:* Daily, year-round for day use only. The new community center is only open for private functions and summer children's activities. *Fees:* None for the park; transient wet slips, $12 per night. *Directions:* In downtown Apalachicola, beneath the US 98 bridge at the intersection of 4th Street and Bay Avenue. *More Information:* Apalachicola City Hall, 1 Avenue E, Apalachicola, FL 32320; 850/653-9319. For information on the *Governor Stone's* cruise schedule, visit the Apalachicola Maritime Museum at the corner of Market Street and Avenue D downtown, 850/653-8708.

RAINBOW INN AND MARINA –Popular with locals and tourists, the Rainbow provides great views of the bay and river, especially at sunrise. *Facilities:* 30 transient wet slips, gas and fishing guides available with advance reservations, 30-room hotel, fine dining restaurant, oyster bar, cocktail lounge. *Days/Hrs.:* Daily, year-round. Caroline's Restaurant is open for lunch, dinner and weekend brunch; Boss Oyster Raw Bar for breakfast, lunch and dinner. *Fees:* Rooms start at $64. For charter fishing, half-day bay trips run about $185 for up to 4 people. Half-day offshore excursions begin at $385 for up to 6. *Directions:* In Apalachicola on Water Street, right on the river. *More Information:* Owners Larry Maddren and Caroline Chovstic, 123 Water Street, Apalachicola, FL 32320; 850/653-8139.

HIKING TRAILS

ST. VINCENT ISLAND –St. Vincent Island easily surpasses all other barrier islands in natural wonders and outdoor delights. The island, protected as a national wildlife refuge (see page 288), is a textbook case of habitat diversity. Mostly east-west running ridges covered in oak scrub forests cover the island.

"Whoever coined the term 'mouth' for the terminal end of the river needs a lesson in anatomy."

—Woody Miley, Apalachicola

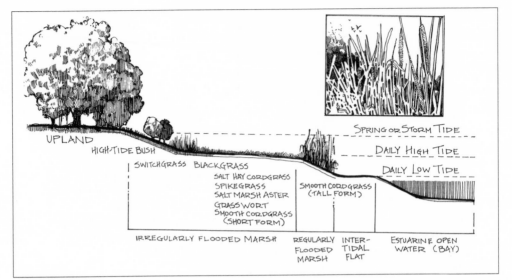

UPLAND
HIGH-TIDE BUSH
SWITCHGRASS BLACKGRASS
SALT HAY CORDGRASS
SPIKEGRASS
SALT MARSH ASTER
GRASS WORT
SMOOTH CORDGRASS
(SHORT FORM)
SMOOTH CORDGRASS
(TALL FORM)
SPRING or STORM TIDE
DAILY HIGH TIDE
DAILY LOW TIDE

IRREGULARLY FLOODED MARSH REGULARLY FLOODED MARSH INTER-TIDAL FLAT ESTUARINE OPEN WATER (BAY)

Marsh Walk

Seemingly barren expanses of grass and mud, salt marshes on first glance appear like wastelands. Look again. The grass fields like those ringing the Apalachicola Bay give untold benefits to nature and man. Each acre can produce 20 tons of plant matter annually, far more prolific than any agricultural rival. This biological factory feeds and shelters young shrimp, mollusks, crustaceans and fish; 75 percent of commercial seafood species spend part of their lives here. Marshes do much for humans, purifying sewage better and cheaper than any man-made facility and generating 20 percent of the world's oxygen.

Besides utility, marshes exhibit considerable natural elegance. Black needle rush, a highly adaptable short grass with sharp tube-like leaves, dominates in the bay marshes. Smooth cordgrass, a broad-bladed plant up to three-feet high, cling to the outer, drier edges of the bay. And ripcord, a common grass in Georgia coast marshes, lives only on the inner, wetter edge here.

Underfoot, rich black mud gasps and pulls at the boots of the unwary. The odor announces anaerobic bacteria, which emit hydrogen sulfide when they digest organic material. No one sinks much further than a knee. Firm ground is several feet below.

Birds feed and nest. Oysters proliferate, as do hermit crabs and periwinkle snails, which slide up and down cordgrass stalks feeding on microscopic protozoa. Stuffing themselves with nutrient rich mud, herds of fiddler crabs race to tiny burrows if threatened, their collective stampede sounding like soda pop fizz. The males linger, waving their dominant claw in displays of bravado.

It is best to visit marshes at low tide when more is exposed. Access is difficult to impossible, but here are three reasonably accessible locations:

ST. VINCENT SOUND—On US 98 about 8 miles west of Apalachicola, bear left (west) on C30. Between 13 and 14 miles west of Apalachicola, on the southside of the road, are a few small signs on trees marking St. Vincent National

Wildlife Refuge property. Their headquarters were here until a hurricane blew it down in the mid-1980s. On the left (south) is a dirt road, usually gated. Refuge rangers say it's okay to park by the gate and walk the 200 yards to the short-grass marsh. There aren't too many oysters in this section of the bay.

INDIAN LAGOON—Continue from the above location on C30A several miles to C30B. Turn left (east) and almost immediately on the left (north) side of the road is an extensive marsh in Indian Lagoon. Park along the shoulder. There are more tidal creeks here than the previous marsh. The oysters begin to appear near the edge of the lagoon.

EAST COVE, ST. GEORGE ISLAND—Enter St. George Island State Park and 1 mile later (east), take a left (north) into the driveway for the youth camp and boat ramp where parking is usually available. The East Cove marsh, which has high grass and many oysters, runs all along the shore to the east.

Pine woods and marshy wetlands fill up the lowlands in between the ridges, each of which was once on the shoreline of the island; as sediment deposited by gulf and river currents accumulated, the island grew progressively larger. The shallow freshwater ponds and inlets are inhabited by alligators. Saltwater bayous, marshes and ponds, filled with oysters, fish, snakes and water fowl, make up much of the northeastern part of the island. The elusive 600-pound sambar deer, with large paddle-shaped ears, likes to forage here. Five freshwater lakes, some a mile long, are found in the southeastern section and cater to alligators, large game fish and more birds. Fourteen miles of white beaches with high sand dunes covered in sea oats border mostly the southern and eastern faces of the island. Birds like migrating Canada geese, gulls, herons, egrets and terns are often spotted here. The beach along the bay face on the western side contains many prehistoric pottery fragments. Federal law prohibits removal of artifacts on the island. *Directions:* The island is only accessible by boat and for day use except during brief primitive weapons hunting seasons. Paddling a canoe or kayak over early in the morning from Indian Pass on the mainland is the easiest way to cross without a motor boat. A public boat ramp is located at the terminus of FL C30B at Indian Pass. (See page 291).

Eighty miles of old timber roads, some so densely canopied the midday sun cannot penetrate, crisscross St. Vincent Island and make fine hiking trails. The ones running north-south are numbered, the ones east-west are lettered. Selected hikes on the island are as follows:

TRAIL ONE: INDIAN PASS THROUGH PICALINE AREA –The trail heads eastward through pine flatlands and along sand ridges with scrub oaks, reindeer moss and sage and rosemary shrubs. After 0.8 mile it heads north to St. Vincent Sound, skirts the coast for a short distance, and once again heads east. *Distance:* 3.5 miles. *Features:* All along the beach are thousands of pottery fragments bearing intricate designs. They are the remains of prehistoric Indian feasts that have leaked out of middens (mounds of pottery shards, discarded oyster shells and sediments deposited by water currents). Some middens have become long ridges on the island. *Trailhead Location:* Ranger

Station on western end of island at Indian Pass.

TRAIL TWO: ST. VINCENT SOUND, PICALINE AREA TO THE GULF OF MEXICO –This trail picks up where trail one ends, and offers a good view of some of the island's more striking natural features. It crosses several of the sand dune ridges which run the length of the island. *Distance:* 2 miles. *Features:* Good view of bay beaches, saltwater marsh, scrub oak forest, wet savannas, and sand dunes on the gulf.

TRAIL THREE: WESTERN TIP NEAR INDIAN PASS TO WEST PASS –This route is along white sandy gulf beaches. Just inland are large sand dunes and areas of sea oats. There are lots of shells on the beach. Pelicans search the surf for food, and other sea birds line the tidal pools, their faces turned toward the breeze. Along this stretch of usually deserted beach, porpoises sometimes play offshore, occasionally escorting small boats. *Distance:* 9 miles, one way. *Features:* Near the end at about 8.5 miles and to the left was Ft. Mallory, a Confederate Navy fortification that protected the Florida coast from Union attacks. More than 100 men were stationed here during the Civil War, but the 1985 Hurricane Kate covered up all of the small depression marking the outline of the wall. *Trailhead Location:* Ranger Station on western end of island at Indian Pass.

TRAIL FOUR: RANGER STATION NEAR WEST PASS TO VINCENT POINT –Trail begins at the ranger station near the government barn and shop. The narrow trail heads northeastward through salt marshes and a thick forest of cedar and cabbage palms. Because the palms trees are thick and reminiscent of the South Pacific, rangers call the area "Tahiti." The trail travels over a long midden. Wild boar take refuge in the surrounding marshes. *Distance:* 3.3 miles. *Features:* Ranger station is cabin once used by staff of wealthy island owners. Other cabins and the main house were removed by the wildlife refuge. The grave of George Hatch, the island's first owner, is near the cabin, which was built by Dr. Raymond Pierce, a later owner. *Trailhead Location*: Ranger station on the eastern edge of the island next to West Pass.

ST. JOSEPH PENINSULA HAWKS AND HIKE –For bird watchers, hiking St. Joseph Peninsula (see page 293) is hard to beat. In the autumn, it becomes a heavily trafficked international air space, as large numbers of hawks flap, glide and soar their way from as far away as Canada to Mexico and South America for the winter. It's a prime viewing spot because of the unique topography of the peninsula, formed when two barrier islands connected with each other and the mainland a thousand years ago. Hawks generally fly a wide corridor, but avoid flying over water. Because they funnel into the air over the peninsula, only 0.33 mile wide, they can be easily seen in great numbers. Typically, a hundred or more can be spotted in a single day, but the sighting record is 600 in one hour. The most common wayfarers on the wing are sharp-shinned hawks, followed by Cooper's and broad-winged hawks. The peninsula is the only place in northwest Florida where the rare peregrine falcon is spotted with some regularity, although their number is limited to a handful each season. Sightings are common from late September through October, particularly a few days after the first autumn cold front. The best places to watch is from Eagle Harbor and the peninsula tip during the early morning.

ST. JOSEPH PENINSULA PRIMITIVE TRAIL HIKE: FROM EAGLE HARBOR TO PENINSULA TIP –Following an old sandy logging road that runs the length of the peninsula, this primitive trail through the wilderness area offers a chance to examine pine scrub forest, pine flatwoods and dune ridges. Toward the peninsula's northern tip, the trail bends right, conforming with the curving of the increasingly smaller dune ridges. The trail ends on the bay, a little south of the peninsula tip. Visitors can hike back the same way or go around the tip to the gulf side and walk back along the beach. *Distance:* 7 miles, one way. *Features:* Often on either side of the sand dune ridges which parallel the length of the peninsula are shallow ponds, swamps and meadows. These wetland depressions are ideal places to observe bird life. There are usually lots of shells at the end of the peninsula because few people get out this far. *Trailhead Location:* St. Joseph Peninsula State Park. (See page 293.) Park at the picnic area north of Eagle Harbor. Walk north on the paved road to the rental cabins for about 0.5 mile to the trailhead. Note: The number of day hikers is unrestricted, but that of overnight campers is limited to 25. Campers must hike in a mile from the trailhead before setting up camp.

ST. GEORGE ISLAND PARK BEACHES –St. George Island has what some consider one of the finest beaches in the country. The sand is comfortably soft and white; the water is blue-green and clear. There are many kinds of shells, particularly at the eastern tip of the island, and also sand dollars, jellyfish, sea cucumbers, sponges, sea plants and other odd life forms that wash up on shore. Like other gulf barrier islands, St. George is a prime birding area in the autumn when numerous migratory species pass through. Nesting birds are also common on the beach and grass flats. Keep an eye out for black skimmers, snowy plovers and least terns. Dunes are low or absent along much of the beach thanks to recent hurricanes. In some places, 20-foot sand dunes dotted with sea oats and pine trees are about 100 yards to the north of the beach. In others, the island is flat, covered only in grass and narrow enough to throw a rock to the other side. *Distance:* 9 miles of uninterrupted beach from the park entrance to the eastern tip of the island. *Features:* Two miles east of the second day use area is the eastern tip of the island; here the lack of human traffic and sea currents have produced perhaps the island's densest concentration of shells, including occasional giant conchs. East Pass, between St. George Island and Dog Island to the east, is a popular fishing spot for birds. Walking on the bay side beach–which continues for several miles until it runs into marsh–provides a good chance of finding numerous intact skeletons of the sailcat fish. Its sun-bleached remains have an uncanny resemblance to a bearded man on a cross, earning it the name of the crucifix fish. *Trailhead Location:* St. George State Park. Five and seven miles east of the St. George State Park entrance, to the right of the main road, are 2 nicely landscaped day use beach facilities with parking lots, picnic pavilions, water and bathrooms. Both have short boardwalks with access to the beach.

ST. GEORGE PRIMITIVE TRAIL –This easy hike from the designated campground to Gap Point along an old, sandy logging road offers some interesting sites. Most of the trail is flat and shaded by slash pine forest. There are some signs that many of the trees were tapped for turpentine, an industry which flourished here in the early part of the 20th century. There's frequent scrub oak stands, migrating dunes on the northern side and plenty of tiny one-segmented prickly pear cacti underfoot. *Distance:* 2.5 miles one way. *Features:* Look for bald eagles. One or two nesting pairs are on the Gap's Point peninsula roughly halfway down the trail. Rangers are mum on their exact whereabouts. Near the end of the hike on the right is a good illustration of the deadly effects of dune erosion. As several dunes migrate straight into the bay, they're taking with them dozens of pine trees, whose dead trunks drop from sand cliffs into the water. More are perched on the edge of oblivion, their roots searching for soil no longer there, 10 feet above the water line. There's a primitive campsite at the end of the trail at Gap Point with a few picnic tables and a fire ring. Pelicans, gulls, egrets, herons and other coastal birds frequently fish in the cove southeast of Gap Point. *Trailhead Location:* At the end of the designated campground in the park, there's a marked trailhead by a split rail fence where you can park.

SIGNIFICANT URBAN EXPERIENCES

APALACHICOLA –Nestled between the Apalachicola River to the east and the Apalachicola Bay to the south, this town took its name from the Apalachicola Indians, a small tribe related to the Creeks that were living in small villages along the river when the first Europeans–Spanish missionaries–arrived in the 1500s. Apalachicola has been translated to "land of the friendly people" and "the people who live on the other side" by authorities. The second reference might have come from the much larger Apalachee tribe, centered around present-day Tallahassee. They were in close contact with the Spanish friars, who explored and mapped the area.

The city was first settled in 1821 by Americans when cotton grown in the Chattahoochee and Flint River valleys needed to find a way to world markets. In that year a port custom house was built. And soon after incorporating in 1832, Apalachicola became the third largest port city on the gulf and the third largest cotton port in the United States. For decades steamboats chugged up and down the Apalachicola River, bringing cotton down to the port and manufactured goods to upriver cities and plantations. A growing sponge industry, which became the third largest in the state, gave the economy a boost as well. By 1840, about $17 million worth of goods passed through Apalachicola, more than the rest of the ports in the state combined. The city boasted an opera house, a racetrack, two banks and plenty of mansions, one the residence of a Dr. John Gorrie. Gorrie, the city's most honored son, served as bank director, postmaster, city treasurer, city councilman and as a physician. Gorrie was not fully recognized for his greatest contribution until after his death; while trying to cool the rooms of patients with yellow fever, he invented the first ice-making machine. Gorrie entertained guests during the summer by putting ice in their drinks, but was unable to market the invention. In part, he had no success because the contraption produced ice so slowly. But another reason was opposition from the powerful Northeast ice industry. Storing and shipping giant blocks of ice as far down the coast as the Caribbean was big, profitable business. After Gorrie's death in 1855, however, the novelty caught on, making possible modern refrigeration and air conditioning.

But Apalachicola's good times didn't last. In the 1850s, the city took a hit when cotton began to ride the rails. During the Civil War, the economy collapsed when Union ships blockaded the port. After the war, the town rode the crest of a lumber boom, but by the late 1920s, the vast swampy plains to the north had been completely stripped of cypress. Since then, Apalachicola has turned to harvesting and processing seafood to make a living, which can easily be seen by a stroll down Water Street. Shrimp boats and deep sea charters crowd the docks. Large tin buildings that process seafood line the street, spitting out mounds of shell from their sides. Amid the standing remains of several, crumbling brick cotton and sponge warehouses, there have sprung up trendy art galleries, antique stores, coffee shops and restaurants, serving seafood right off the boat.

A distant–but growing–second industry is tourism, increasingly playing an important role to the local economy. Apalachicola, a town of 3,000, has all the charm of historic coastal cities like Savannah or Mobile, but none of the urban blight. There's plenty of historical landmarks, antebellum homes and oyster bars, but no shopping malls, few convenience stores and only one traffic signal. (Actually it's a caution light.)

In the historic district, about 200 19th century homes remain, many shaded by oaks and magnolias and spread out along wide streets and historic parks. The city was built with plans from Philadelphia, which in turn was based on the old grid streets of ancient Rome. The square block streets in the historic district are broken up with a number of open squares, originally serving as fire breaks and animal grazing areas.

Most of the historic homes and buildings are within a 2-square mile area, offering an opportunity to take an easy stroll back through time. The Chamber of Commerce downtown on Market Street has self-guided walking tour maps. Some notable stops include:

Cotton Warehouse–This is one of the original 42 cotton warehouses built in 1838. Around the first-story front door are some of the original granite posts and lintels which earned Apalachicola the name "the city of granite fronts." Nearby City Hall is housed in the other remaining cotton warehouse.

Sponge Warehouse–Built around 1840, this is one of the original sponge trade warehouses. When fast-talking auctioneers sold the stuff by the crateload in the late 1800s, thousands of sponges spilled out from the door and clear across the street. In 1895 the sponge trade employed 100 men.

Raney House–David Raney, a wealthy commission merchant, built this Greek Revival home in 1838. The city owns and restored the house, which contains many original furnishings. The site of the local historical society, Raney House is on the National Register of Historic Places and open to the public on Sat., 1am-5 pm or by appointment.

Orman House–Planter and merchant Thomas Orman sometimes put a keg of nails on the roof during the Civil War, but not for home repairs. If Union Troops came through town, Confederate sympathizers hiding upriver would see the keg and stay in the woods. The restored house is now the Magnolia Hall Bed and Breakfast.

Marks-Bruce House–Built in 1804 in St. Joe, the cottage house was abandoned during a Yellow Fever epidemic and in 1854, like many of its neighbors, was relocated by barge to Apalachicola.

Chapman House–Dr. Alvin W. Chapman, renowned 19th

century botanist who wrote the "Flora of the Southern United States," built the house in the 1840s. He was a secret Union sympathizer and reportedly helped federal prisoners escape from a nearby prison.

Chestnut Street Cemetery–Dating from 1832, the cemetery has brought together in eternal peace a rainbow of peoples: Confederate and Union soldiers, blacks, whites, Jews, Irish, Italians and yellow fever victims. The rundown condition, along with wrought iron gates and moss-covered trees add to the eerie charm.

John Gorrie Museum and Grave–His original ice-making machine is in the Smithsonian, but a replica resides in the museum. *Days/Hrs.:* Daily except Tues., Wed. and holidays, 9am-5pm. *More Information:* 850/653-9347.

Trinity Episcopal Church–The circa 1838 Greek Revival building was shipped in sections from New York and assembled with wooden pegs. It's on the National Registry of Historic Places. Drs. Chapman and Gorrie were active in the parish.

The Coombs House Inn–This 1905 Victorian mansion has been restored into a bed and breakfast.

Wefing House–The Queen Anne style of this circa 1896 home was popular with many timber barons who built near the town's bayshore from the 1890s to 1920s.

The Gibson Hotel–This 1907 Victorian hotel is one of few inns on the Federal Register of Historic Places still operating. This local landmark has good seafood, a full bar, 31 luxurious rooms and a 2-story, 3-sided porch with bay and river views.

More Information: Apalachicola Area Historical Society, 128 Market Street, Apalachicola, FL 32320. Apalachicola Bay Chamber of Commerce, 84 Market Street, Apalachicola, FL 32320; 850/653-9419.

THE APALACHICOLA FLORIDA SEAFOOD FESTIVAL –This is the oldest and largest maritime spectacle in the state. Some of the most popular draws include the oyster shucking and oyster eating contests. For the second event, spectators avoid sitting in the first row or two because some of the contestants are unable to abide by the prime directive–keeping down the oysters. There is also a contest to select a festival queen and king, the second dubbed King Retsyo (oyster backwards) in honor of the mythological son of Neptune who protects the Apalachicola Bay. There are arts and crafts, musical acts and, of course, plenty of seafood to sample. Held the first weekend of each November in the city's Battery Park Marina, the 33rd annual celebration in 1996 brought over 10,000 visitors. The proceeds go to selected civic causes in the community. *More Information:* Apalachicola Bay Chamber of Commerce, 84 Market Street, Apalachicola, FL 32320; 850/653-9419.

CARRABELLE –About 20 miles east of Apalachicola at the mouth of the Carrabelle River, this tiny, unassuming fishing village is all about the sea and it shows. Giant shrimp and deep sea fishing boats crowd the docks. Their weatherworn crews far outnumber the few tourists in the handful of modest bars, restaurants and motels. Rundown shacks ring the outskirts of town, a 3-minute drive from end to end.

The fur trade brought early Indian and European settlers, but after the Civil War the timber industry and naval supply trade really brought Carrabelle its first boom times. Cypress and pine cut from inland swamps came down the Carrabelle River. Ocean schooners, after anchoring behind Dog Island, sailed back and forth to pick up cargo. When Carrabelle incorporated in 1893, it bustled with lumber mills, wharves, stevedores, a railroad station and hotels, including the Lanark Village Hotel, a popular luxury resort. A disastrous hurricane in 1897 nearly destroyed the town, which also weathered hard economic times between the two world wars.

During the Depression money came from under the table. Prohibition bootleggers smuggled contraband from the Caribbean and hid it in the woods north of Carrabelle, and local fishermen bartered for agricultural goods from farmers further north. It also came from the federal government when the Roosevelt Work Relief Project built US 98 and some of Carrabelle's larger buildings. Camp Gordon Johnston opened near Carrabelle right before World War II. Many U.S. soldiers came to the military base for training during the war. Some German troops came to the area, too, as prisoners of war. After the war the camp closed. Part of it now is the Lanark Village retirement community.

Today, the town has become a center of commercial and

Carrabelle Police Station

The "world's smallest police station" in the heart of the one-block downtown of Carrabelle has an intriguing history. In the past the cops answered the phone on the outside of a building. To keep its two officers out of the rain, the city installed an old phone booth in 1963 and the name soon followed, as did the national media in search of an interesting story. In the beginning, Carrabelle lost a bundle when people, mistaking the station for a phone booth, discovered free, unlimited long distance calls. One officer was so large he couldn't fit in the police station. (He still lives in town, but has since switched professions.) A man from Tennessee tried to take the booth home on a truck, and a hurricane once knocked it over. But the booth remains and the police still wait for calls in their car next to the phone.

Oysters

The oyster's life isn't an easy one. Most are swallowed up as small free-swimming larvae. If they survive that two-week ordeal, they sink to the bottom and attach themselves to rocks and other hard surfaces. They start out life as males, but later become females. As adults, they feed on tiny organisms filtered in from the water in tissue that doubles as breathing gills. Their hard shells usually provide secure quarters, but don't always work against the snails, starfish and birds that have evolved ways to bore, suck or pick their ways in. Oysters average an inch of growth a year, although the ones in the Apalachicola Bay tend to increase in size faster because of ideal growing conditions. Ninety percent of Florida's, and ten percent of the country's, oysters come from the bay.

Those oysters from the Apalachicola Bay are considered some of the finest tasting in the world. The blend of salt-and freshwater in the bay gives them their ideal slightly salty or iodine flavor. "Fresh" oysters are not desirable; locally that means too much freshwater.

In the 1800s the prized mollusks were fed cornmeal in barrels as they were taken by steamboat up the Apalachicola and Chattahoochee rivers. Today fine restaurants as far away as Hawaii fly them in on ice.

There's no single place to eat the best oysters. Many restaurants along the Gulf Coast take them right out of the bay. However in Apalachicola, the Boss Oyster Raw Bar, where tables are right on the Apalachicola River, and the Hut, with patio seating overlooking the gulf, are popular eating spots, along with the Grill, the Magnolia Inn and the Gibson Hotel.

Small oyster shacks lining the

sports fishing. Carrabelle has the Moorings, an international marina resort, and the Big Bend Saltwater Classic fishing tournament every Father's Day weekend. East of the city in Carrabelle Beach is Julia Mae's, a popular seafood joint. *More Information:* Carrabelle Area Chamber of Commerce, P.O. Drawer DD, Carrabelle, FL 32322; 850/697-2585.

EASTPOINT –Six miles east of Apalachicola, on the eastern edge of the Apalachicola Bay, Eastpoint is the heart of the local oyster industry. Most of the oysters commercially harvested from the bay come from St. George Sound just south of the city, explaining why so much of it is covered in oyster houses, plywood and corrugated metal shacks. Inside oysters are shucked and processed. Underneath, shells accumulate in heaps, carried away later by high tides. Commercial oyster, shrimp and fish businesses pack the town's waterfront on US 98, along with a modest marina, a few hotels, restaurants and grocery stores. Much of the business comes from people going to St. George Island, the only barrier island to have a bridge to the mainland. Access is south off US 98 in the middle of town.

Near the bridge entrance is the former site of the home of Captain S. E. Rice, one of the original citizens who in 1898 came down the Chattahoochee River by barge with five families. They brought all their belongings and livestock and lived temporarily in palm tree shelters. The group was led by David H. Brown, a Virginia-born Quaker and member of the Commonwealth Colony, an experimental religious and economic cooperative inspired by the Populists. In the new frontier, his wife established the first post office in the family home, built in 1901. One son brought mail to Carrabelle each morning until roads were cut between the towns in 1915. A handful of Browns remain, some in the original Brown home.

Travel between Eastpoint and Apalachicola did not become common until free ferry service began in 1932. The bay bridge was built three years later. *More Information:* Apalachicola Bay Chamber of Commerce, 84 Market Street, Apalachicola, FL 32320; 850/653-9419.

PORT ST. JOE –The largest city near the Apalachicola Bay, Port St. Joe has little of the seaside atmosphere of neighboring towns. A quiet, prosperous community, Port St. Joe's primary source of income is not the gulf waters, but a giant paper mill and nearby chemical factory, downtown right by the coast. Perhaps the city wanted to make sure it was doing something completely different than Apalachicola, 20 miles to the southeast. An earlier town, St. Joseph, was founded here in 1835 for the sole purpose of taking business away from Apalachicola. St. Joseph built a railroad and canal to the Apalachicola River to siphon off Apalachicola's lucrative cotton and river trades, and convinced Florida leaders to host the first state constitutional convention in 1838. It didn't work. A yellow fever epidemic and hurricane in 1841 convinced the last of St. Joseph's residents to abandon the town. Ironically, many homes were dismantled and put back together in Apalachicola. Only a cemetery offers evidence of the former town, and the site remained uninhabited until the new town was established about 100 years ago. During the Civil War Confederate troops removed some of the few remaining bricks from home foundations and chimneys to build a saltworks on St. Joseph Bay.

Twenty-five miles from shore is evidence of another conflict, World War II. One hundred feet down rests the *Empire Mica*, a British oil tanker torpedoed by a German submarine in 1942. Several vessels from Apalachicola rushed out and saved 14 members of the 50 man crew. The Axis power sunk 50 vessels in the Gulf of Mexico during the summer of 1942, but the general public had no idea. The U.S. Government figured it was best not to let the Nazis know how well they'd done, or the Americans know how close the war was.

Clear visibility and an abundance of fish, turtles and rays make the 450-foot long war relic popular with divers. Captain Black's Dive Center in Port St. Joe regularly takes boats out there, 850/229-6332.

Port St. Joe doesn't cater to tourists. There are hardly any hotels or seafood restaurants, only a strip of traffic lights, fast food restaurants and nondescript industrial buildings off US 98. The warm, shallow water of St. Joseph Bay, protected by St. Joseph Peninsula, produce some notably sweet scallops. Across the bay is St. Joseph Peninsula State Park, an undeveloped area with striking dunes, soft beaches and pine forests. *More Information:* Port St. Joe/Gulf County Chamber of

coast can be worth visiting, particularly the Indian Pass Trading Post Raw Bar, 18 miles west of Apalachicola at the intersection of C30 and C30B. A small building covered with old peeling white paint, it doesn't mess too much with minor details like decor, appetizers or entrees. It just serves up heaps of the tastiest and biggest oysters year-round. People stop from miles around to take them home by the bagload for dinner–if they can resist eating them immediately at the countertop.

More important than where an oyster is eaten, however, is *when* an oyster is eaten. Winter months are the best. That's the season they store fat and are plumpest.

Also important is what is put on an oyster. Right out of the bay with a drop or two of Tabasco on a saltine cracker is the preferred eating method by the natives.

Best Oyster Fritters

If the oysters come from Indian Pass Trading Post and Oyster Bar at Indian Pass just west of Apalachicola, this receipe just might cook up the best oysters ever eaten.

1/2 cup flour
1 tbs baking powder
1/2 tsp ground black pepper
1 egg, slightly beaten
1 pint oysters
1 to 1 1/2 tbs oil

Sift flour, baking powder and pepper into a bowl. Add egg and oysters. Stir together. Add more flour if batter needs thickening. Put oil into a frying pan and heat. Drop large spoonfuls of flour mixture into pan. Fry each fritter until golden brown on both sides.

Commerce, P. O. Box 964, Port St. Joe, FL 32456; 850/227-1223.

ST. JOSEPH PENINSULA –A long finger of land that arcs northward back toward the mainland, St. Joseph Peninsula offers some of the finest outdoor recreation in the region. The beaches in 2,516-acre St. Joseph Peninsula State Park (see page 293), are arguably more breathtaking than those on the barrier islands, with dunes as high as 40 feet coming as close as 25 yards to the gulf. St. Joseph Bay offers excellent snorkeling and wading because so many different kinds of sea creatures thrive in the turtle grass shallows, including, octopus, crabs and sweet bay scallops.

Many vacation homes, several private campgrounds and convenience stores dot the peninsula south or west of the state park and closer to the mainland. Cape San Blas, a small southerly outcrop at the base of the peninsula, has a public beach with sandy beaches and a military radar installation with a lighthouse. A 0.25-mile road to the cape off C30E has at its entrance a gate, an air force sign and a warning that the area is closed. Actually, if the gate is open, the road can be used by the public to access the beach. Visitors can drive down, park and walk 100 yards to reach the cape, which is noted for the variety of seashells that wash up on its shores; but they cannot walk over by the buildings, or to the lighthouse, whose metal rod base makes it looks like a short, squat radio tower. It went up on its present site in 1917 and was retired by the Coast Guard in 1996.

Just east of Cape San Blas are the remains of a Confederate saltworks, which made salt for rebel troops through evaporation of bay waters. With a daily capacity of 150 bushels, the saltwork's destruction in 1862 by the *U.S.S. Kingfisher's* guns and a Union landing party was a serious blow to the Southern cause. The bricks for the saltworks came from the ruins of the old city of St. Joseph, abandoned in 1841 following a yellow fever epidemic and hurricane. Only a few bricks remain on the grounds of a private rental cottage village next to a historic marker on C30.

Autumn brings migratory hawks and monarch butterflies in large numbers over St. Joseph Peninsula. Forty-two acre Pig Island, just off the peninsula in St. Joseph Bay, is part of the St.

Vincent National Wildlife Refuge. *More Information:* Port St. Joe/Gulf County Chamber of Commerce, P. O. Box 964, Port St. Joe, FL 32456; 850/227-1223.

FISHING

Apalachicola Bay and its fingers, St. Vincent Sound, St. George Sound and East Bay, include more than 175 square miles of protected saltwater fishing.

BEST ADVICE –The most experienced fishermen find that one or two days of guide fees is a good investment before launching out on their own. Inexperienced fishermen or families looking for an enjoyable day's outing will increase their pleasure ten-fold by taking advantage of the experience of a professional guide. The best guides not only make sure their customers fish, but provide insights into the fishing habits of different species, bay ecology, weather lore and other aspects that will enhance a fishing experience.

When booking a fishing guide, always check to make sure who is responsible for all tackle (rods, reels, lures); boats and gasoline; all live bait; life jackets; lunch, drinks, snacks and ice; and rain gear. Be sure to understand exactly what is included in the guide fees.

GUIDES –These are sources of information on guides and guide services. Breakaway Marina, 850/653-8897; Cool Change Charters (offshore charters), 850/927-2604; Sportsman's Lodge, 850/670-8423; Captain Tommy Robinson, 850/653-9669; Survivor's Island Bait and Tackle, 850/927-3113; Willis Charters (offshore charters), 850/653-9847; Cypress Lodge, 850/639-5414; Lakeside Lodge, 850/639-2681; Magnolia Lodge, 850/639-5212; Sign of the Shinner, 850/639-5272; Fred Kimbrough, 850/653-8875.

BEST BOOKS AND MAPS –U.S. Geological Survey 1:24,000 scale topographical maps covering the Bay are Apalachicola, Sugar Hill, Goose Island, West Pass, Indian Pass, Cape San Blas, St. Joseph Peninsula, St. Joseph Point and Port St. Joe. (To order see page 326.)

OTHER SOURCES OF INFORMATION –Fish camps are good sources of information. (See page 310.)

Shrimping

Many commercial shrimp harvesters comb the waters in the region, but as the mouth of the Apalachicola River is rather shallow, most anchor in nearby Carrabelle, which has one of the deepest ports in the gulf. Small bay boats usually stay within the island perimeter on short daily trips, but offshore shrimp boats, 65 feet in length or longer with refrigerated cargo holds, roam the gulf for up to a month at a time. Their lights crisscross the horizon at night, when shrimp, generally nocturnal creatures, leave the sand or mud burrows that protect them in the day. Most of the big boats are from Alabama, Texas or Louisiana where shrimp harvests are generally much larger. Yet, mild gulf waters in the Apalachicola area allow at least limited shrimping year-round.

Recreational harvesting is not common given the cheapness and abundance of commercial shrimp in the region, but some Floridians are hooked on the hobby. From the middle of December until early May, the shrimp are often near the surface of the water. During their nightly runs, they can be caught from bridges, piers, bulkheads or boats along salt marshes of the Apalachicola Bay by dipping a shrimp net–21 feet is a good size– as they swim or float through an area lighted by flashlight.

It's a game of chance trying to figure out where the shrimp will run, but hit a mother lode that fills up a 5-gallon bucket and supermarket shrimp won't taste the same again.

Mullet Fishing

The lowly mullet gets no respect, but it should. It's the lowest-priced fish in the market, not surprising considering that it teems everywhere near the Apalachicola Bay, in saltwater and fresh. Although common, mullet is tasty. Just ask the locals who like to catch them out of the bay, particularly with a cast net.

Whether from a dock, pier, boat or while wading in the water, anyone can catch a mullet. Look for schools of mullet running near the surface, their heads poking out of the water. Take a net and with as much skill and technique as possible–sort of like a lasso–fling it out to make it spread out fully.

Casting the perfect net has been described as a zen-like pleasure. It almost doesn't matter if the fish are hauled in, it's how the net spreads, some say. Want to give it a spin? Most local hardware and bait-and-tackle stores sell the nets.

INSIDER TIPS AND HOT SPOTS –St. Vincent Refuge is a 12,350-acre island located about 5 miles offshore from Apalachicola, accessible only by boat. Primitive freshwater fishing areas may be reached from the island's east shoreline. Fishermen will need to carry a small boat since occasional portaging is necessary. Bream and bass fishing is excellent in spring, but ponds are open to fishing only during certain months according to U.S. Fish and Wildlife Service regulations. Best bream baits are crickets and earthworms. Bass are caught most easily using plastic worms and live shiners. More fishing information and maps available on request from St. Vincent National Wildlife Refuge, P.O. Box 447, Apalachicola, FL 32320; 850/653-8808.

FISH CAMPS

BAY CITY LODGE –This fishing lodge sits on a picturesque, swamp-canopied canal leading into the river at mile marker 3.5. It's a prime starting point for salt and freshwater fishing excursions or barrier island sightseeing tours. *Facilities:* 35 transient wet slips, dry dock storage, gas, charter guides and guide boats, 10 motel rooms, 6 cottages, boat ramp, restaurant, tennis court, bait-and-tackle store. *Days/Hrs.:* The restaurant is generally open all year but winter and serves breakfast and dinner only. Inshore fishing guides are available in spring, summer and autumn. *Fees:* Motel rooms, $45; cottages $55 a night. Guides, including 22-ft boat rentals, run $275 for 4 people for a full day. *Directions:* From Apalachicola, go north on 12th Street for 2 miles. Turn right (east) on Bay City Road and continue for 1 mile. *More Information:* Manager Tom Gordon, P.O. Box 172, Apalachicola, FL 32329; 850/653-9294.

BREAKAWAY MARINA, MOTEL & RESTAURANT –Light brown cinder blocks make up many of the buildings at this fishing lodge, about 4 miles upstream of Apalachicola Bay. It caters to salt and freshwater fishers alike. *Facilities:* 15 transient wet slips; boat ramp; gas; guided boats for rent; 15 motel rooms; 4 open RV spaces with complete hookups, restrooms and showers; restaurant; bait-and-tackle shop. *Days/Hrs.:* Lodge and restaurant, daily, year-round except two weeks at Christmas; restaurant serves breakfast and dinner all seasons and lunch in summer. *Fees:* Rooms, $39 a night for double occupancy; RV spaces, $10 a night; the lodge doesn't directly book guides, but generally, they run $300 a day for inshore fishing for up to three people and $450 a day for offshore trips for up to 4. *Directions:* From Apalachicola, go north 3 miles on 12th Street. Turn right (east) on Waddell Road and go about 1 mile. *More Information:* Manager Jerry Cathen or owner Gorrie Wilson, 200 Waddell Road, Apalachicola, FL 32320; 850/653-8897.

SPORTSMAN'S LODGE –Cluttered, but relaxed and tranquil, this motel and marina is in Eastpoint right on the bay. It has a charming German hostess and a nice view of sunset from Magnolia Bluff. The lodge is close to the bayous to the north and St. George Sound to the south. *Facilities:* 10 transient wet slips; 20 campsites with hookups; 30 motel units, 10 with kitchenettes; gas; boat ramp; charter boats for deep sea and bay fishing. *Days/Hrs.:* Daily, year-round. *Fees:* Motel units daily, $36 for bay view, $46 for bay front kitchenettes and $56 for large family units; RV spaces $15 daily. The prices are the same all year. Offshore fishing, $600 for 6 people per day. Bay fishing, $275 for 4 people per day. *Directions:* In Eastpoint, one block north off US 98 on North Bay Shore Drive. *More Information:* Owners Bob and Edda Allen, Sportsman's Lodge, 99 North Bay Shore Drive, Eastpoint, FL 32328; 850/670-8423.

BOATING

DOG ISLAND SEA KAYAK TRIP –Paddle across St. George Sound, part of the Apalachicola Bay, to Dog Island, a small, mostly undeveloped barrier island in the Gulf of Mexico. A trip to Dog Island is worth the effort. The beaches here are mostly uncluttered and unchanged from times past. *Put-In:* Go to Lanark Village, a small retirement community 4 miles east of Carrabelle on US 98. This is the mainland point closest to Dog Island, about 3 miles due south. Boaters can launch from the private Lanark Village Boat Club, but must park off premises. An alternate location would be from Old Beach in Carrabelle (see page 292). *Take-Out:* Many parts of the island are accessible, but Tyson Harbor near the eastern end of the island on St. George Sound is a common stopping place. *Distance:* 3 miles. Usually

How to Catch Blue Crabs

Ever since a giant one pinched Hercules as he fought the many-headed Hydra, crabs have gotten a bad rap. The Latin word for crab, "cancer," means terrible disease. But blue crabs, scattered across the world from the Egyptian to the Argentinean coasts, are an exception. Their scientific name, *Callinectes sapidus Rathbun*, refers to them as swimmers that are beautiful– and savory.

Blue crabs are abundant in the Gulf of Mexico. Males prefer to stay in upper bays and river mouths, but females usually migrate into the open gulf waters as their eggs require a lot of saltwater to develop. The eggs, which appear as an orange sponge mass on the belly of the mother crab, hatch into zoeas, bizarre-looking creatures with big black eyes, long cylindrical bodies and tails like shrimp, which they snap to swim backwards.

There are several ways to catch the savory swimmers. Fold-up traps lay flat on the water bottom until a crab goes for the bait inside–chicken necks are ideal. The line is then drawn to enclose the catch within the trap's walls. Regular baited traps made of galvanized wire with funnel-shaped entries to trap crabs inside are also popular. State law permits recreational fisherman to use up to five crab traps, during daylight hours only. Many people use baited lines to catch dinner. After a crab takes the bait, the line is slowly pulled in. A crab generally won't let go until it's near the surface, where a dip net is used to scoop it up to a boat, a pier or a bucket. Nighttime with a light is the best way to catch blue crabs with just a dip net.

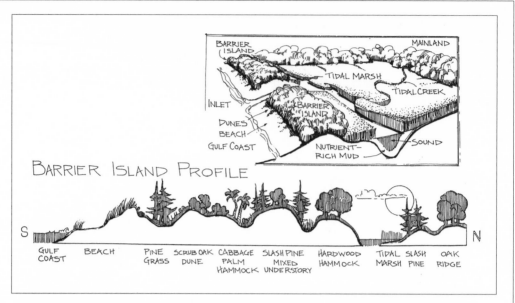

BARRIER ISLAND PROFILE

| GULF COAST | BEACH | PINE GRASS | SCRUB OAK DUNE | CABBAGE PALM HAMMOCK | SLASH PINE MIXED UNDERSTORY | HARDWOOD HAMMOCK | TIDAL MARSH | SLASH PINE | OAK RIDGE |

Profile of a Barrier Island

Barrier islands are elongated structures parallel to the shoreline and usually made up of sand. They may be tens of miles long and are almost always less than a few miles wide. Estuaries and wetlands, which may vary in size from narrow lagoons to extensive sounds almost 30 miles wide, separate them from the mainland. Generally located in areas with low sloping coastal plains and moderate tidal range, the barrier islands are in a constant state of rearranging themselves or being rearranged by the forces of tides, waves and winds. In fact, the coastal zone is probably the most dynamic natural system on the surface of the earth.

Barrier island beaches offer little resistance to storm waves and efficiently absorb and dissipate the tremendous forces that confront them. They enclose and protect priceless estuarine resources from the battering of storms and ocean currents. At the same time, the islands provide living places and food for hundreds of species of coastal birds, fish, shellfish, reptiles and mammals.

Of the 283 barrier islands that adorn the coast of the United States, four of them lie along the Apalachicola Bay area. During the last ice age 12,000 years ago, the Florida Panhandle coast was 100 miles south of its present location. The barrier islands around the bay formed only 4,000 years ago along an old coastline after rising water levels covered the bay.

Sand from offshore bars wash on these beaches to form dunes on the gulf, which slowly migrate to the bay. Generally about 40 years and from 50 to 150 feet separate each dune line. The long, mostly east-west lines of the dune ridges, which run the length of the islands, are visible from the air.

Sometimes barrier islands get closer to the mainland due to island migration or river sediments that fill in a bay. But as sea levels gradually rise in the present age, the Apalachicola Bay barrier islands are getting longer, skinnier and rapidly eroding.

Besides gradual natural forces, cataclysmic storms can alter barrier islands in a flash. For example, those around the Apalachicola Bay were once connected in a chain until hurricanes broke them up.

takes 1 to 1.5 hours. *High Points:* Observations of sea life in the sound, much of which is made up of shallow oyster beds, prime and other aquatic animals like fish, crabs, other mollusks and rays; observations of bird life in the bay and along the coast of Dog Island; and human life, with the oystermen fleets. *Hazards:* Weather and wind conditions are the biggest factors to consider on a kayak trip across St. George Sound. The wind is normally calm in the morning and picks up to maybe 10 mph in the afternoon. Any sign of white caps on the sound means that it will be very rough to paddle. Make sure to check the forecast. Tides are not much of a factor because of their general mildness along the panhandle. Only experienced kayakers should attempt this crossing, making every effort to follow all safety procedures: wear life jackets, use flotation, travel in groups and dress to avoid hypothermia in cooler weather. Winter can be a good time to kayak, because in the summer, thunderstorms kick up in a couple of hours. *Other Trip Options:* Boaters looking for a different kind of trip might consider loading their kayak on the Carrabelle Ferry (see page 305) to go to Dog Island and spending a day or two paddling around it. The island's perimeter is 22 miles, although three separate portages could significantly reduce the trip length; at Shipping Cove, Ballast Cove and Tyson Harbor, the distance from the bay to the gulf is a hundred yards or less. The bay side usually offers easy paddling while the gulf side can prove extremely challenging, depending on weather conditions. *USGS Topos:* Dog Island and Carrabelle.

ST. GEORGE ISLAND KAYAK TRIP –From two launching points in St. George Island State Park, boaters can spend from one hour to more than a day exploring several miles of pristine salt marshes, oyster islands, pine-covered peninsulas and protected coves found on the eastern bay side of the island. Make sure to pick up a map at the entrance station. *Put-In/Take-Out:* St. George Island State Park (see page 293). Put-in and take-out at one of two boat ramps in the park, both within the first mile or 2 from the main entrance. The first is in the youth camp area and the second is off the main road on the left. *Distance:* Varies. *High Points:* Ideal for less experienced paddlers because of its relative ease, this trip nonetheless offers a good cross-sec-

How to Cook Crayfish

Crayfish, crawfish, crawdaddies, land lobsters. Whatever their name, they're everywhere. More than 225 species live in freshwater streams, ponds and lakes all across North America. Close relatives of the American lobster, most crayfish grow only a few inches long, although one in Tasmania shoots up to the size of a 16-inch lobster. Their thin hard exoskeletons are usually brownish green, but red crayfish live in streams of the Apalachicola River Basin. After hiding under stones all day, they come out and feed during the night, mostly on small animals or decaying things. Some live partly on land, mounds of dirt piled above their burrows. Like their saltwater cousins, crayfish sometimes find themselves in boiling pots of water.

Crayfish Etouffee:
4 tsp Louisiana-type hot sauce
1 small bell pepper, diced
1/3 cup chili oil
1/4 cup flour
1 medium onion, chopped
2 cloves garlic, minced
2 stalks celery, diced
2 medium tomatoes, peeled and chopped
1 can minced clams
1/2 tsp basil
1/4 tsp thyme
1 bay leaf
1/2 tsp filé
1/2 cup shallots, diced
freshly ground black pepper to taste
1 lb crayfish meat (about 4 lbs prior to shelling)
Heat the oil in a heavy skillet until hot. Gradually stir in the flour and stir constantly until the mixture turns brown. Be very careful that it does not burn. Sauté the onions, garlic, celery and bell pepper in it for 5 minutes. Add the tomatoes, clams,

tion of habitats to observe up close. East Cove is an excellent laboratory of crustaceans, oysters, skates, rays, fish and water fowl. Tiny cliffs of oyster dot the waters. Goose Island, a 10-acre land form about a mile northwest of the cove, offers fine marsh grass and marsh inlet exploration. It's a good place to have a lunch, rest and work out cramped legs. Hermit crabs, crucifix fish bones and the oyster colonies ring the island. The best place to land is the north side of the island which is mostly sandy beach. Avoid the areas between the many oyster reefs on the southeastern side of the island that make the water extremely shallow. Grass marshes cover much of the south side of the island. Much of the open bay has a smooth, flat and sandy bottom which seems like a tiny Martian landscape riddled with circular craters and volcanoes, the work of small burrowing bay creatures. Alien looking skates and rays might zip underneath a kayak to give the full effect. Little of this underwater laboratory exceeds 4 feet in depth. Boaters can paddle around the cove for hours and return to the starting point, or camp at Gap Point, where primitive camping is allowed near the beach. There's a fire ring and a few picnic tables. Near Gap Point on small dune cliffs bordering the bay, the roots of many dead pines now hang oddly out into the air, a testament to how quickly the land shifts shape because of the winds, waves and rains. Because of severe dune erosion, many trees have fallen into the bay while others teeter on the edge of the dune cliffs. A 2.5 mile primitive trail runs from Gap Point back to the park campground (see page 300), offering some interesting sights of migrating dunes, slash pine forests and scrub oak trees. Many winged hunters gravitate toward the East Cove. Pelicans fly inches above the water seeking their quarry, climb to a couple of dozen feet and dive bomb their targets, scooping up fish in long beaks and gulping them down in elastic throats as they crash into the water. Egrets, herons and other birds also hunt here. Some bald eagles live in the vicinity. *Hazards:* Not many, but check weather, wind and tide conditions to make there will be peaceful paddling. Low tide is best for water clarity and underwater viewing. Sharp shells on oyster beds can scratch a kayak bottom. *USGS Topos:* Carrabelle, Sugar Hill, Goose Island, Apalachicola, New Inlet, Cape St. George and West Pass.

ST. GEORGE ISLAND TO LITTLE ST. GEORGE –This paddle in the bay along the coast of St. George Island and Little St. George offers a close-up view of many pristine marshes, tidal coves, oyster reefs and a chance to explore some undeveloped land areas in the barrier islands. It'll probably last longer than a day. Primitive camping is allowed on either the western or eastern tip of Little St. George. It's recommended to experienced kayakers only. It's a minimum of 15 miles round trip to the eastern tip of Little St. George. *Put-In/Take-Out:* St. George Island (see page 293). Because so much of the island is privately owned, the nearest point to Little St. George for put-in is the old marina on Bay Shore Drive, just west of the bridge to the mainland. There's parking there. A private luxury marina is planned for the property sometime in the future. If it is developed, parking on country property should remain available on Bay Shore Drive just on the other side of the bridge. *Distance:* Variable, but probably an overnight trip. *High Points:* Near mile 5, right after Cedar Point, is Nick's Hole, the largest and what some consider the most biologically rich cove along the coast of St. George Island. Boaters can explore it by portaging or maneuvering around the shallow oyster reefs there. Many islanders are fighting to protect the land around it, which the owner is considering turning into a residential development. On St. George Island, much of the bay coast is heavily forested with pines, with houses and docks sometimes coming into view. But across the Bob Sikes Channel, Little St. George, a state preserve managed by the Apalachicola National Estuarine Research Reserve (see page 292), remains almost completely undisturbed. Continue west along the bay coast to mile 5 where there is a government dock. From here an island trail runs south through the interior a little less than a mile to Cape St. George on the gulf where a leaning, circa 1852 lighthouse clings to the edge of the island. From the dock, 5 miles further northwest is the western end of the island, a long, narrow sandy extension where primitive camping is allowed. *Hazards:* Because of the trip length, it is extremely important to know the predicted weather as far in advance as possible. Another concern is crossing the Bob Sikes Channel between St. George Island and Little St. George. A strong funnel effect can

basil, thyme and bay leaf. Bring to a boil, stirring constantly. Reduce the heat and simmer for 15 minutes or until it thickens to a sauce. Add the hot sauce, crayfish, filé and shallots and simmer for an additional 5 minutes or until the crayfish are done. Remove the bay leaf and serve over rice.

Darn Good Boil:
4 gallons water
2 packets of seafood boil seasoning
1 tbs of fresh minced garlic
1 tsp of cayenne
2 lemons, squeezed
1 sweet medium onion, chopped
1 lb of andouille or kielbasa sausage, cut up
5 ears of corn
1 1/2 lb red jacket potatoes
5 lbs crayfish prior to shelling
Add spices, lemon, onions and garlic to boiling water, then the sausage, corn and potatoes. When potatoes are tender, add the crawfish and cook for 2 or 3 minutes longer. Serves as an appetizer for one real Cajun or four non-Cajuns.

Compliments of Crawdaddies Cajun Cafe in Carrollton (ten miles from the Chattahoochee River).

Fish Consumption Guidelines
Apalachicola Bay–Oysters, do not eat when there are local shellfish bans related to rain, river level and bacteria counts. As a general rule, eat smaller fish to be safe.

Source: Florida Department of Natural Resources, 1997.

occur through the narrow, 100-yard pass during incoming and outgoing tides. Check a tide table, available at local fish lodges and convenience stores, for crossing at relatively calm times, like slack tides or days when the difference between high and low tide water levels is not too great. It's particularly a good idea not to cross when the tide is going out. It can sweep boats into the gulf. *USGS Topos:* New Inlet, Cape St. George and West Pass.

St. Joseph Bay Canoe or Kayak –A paddle around the shallow flats, marshes and peninsulas of St. Joseph Bay can last as little as an hour or as long as all day, depending on an boaters interest. Make sure to pick up a map at the park entrance. Exploring St. Joseph Bay by kayak or canoe is in some ways more rewarding than the Apalachicola Bay. It's well protected waters are usually much clearer and the unusual abundance of turtle grass, a brownish-green foot-high plant, provides safe haven to many different sea creatures. It looks like a giant aquarium filled with spider crabs, horseshoe crabs, rays and skates, octopus, fish and scallops. Viewing is best at low tide when much of the bay is only 3 or 4 feet deep. *Put-In/Take-Out:* St. Joseph Peninsula State Park (see page 293). Enter the park and about a mile north on the main road is Eagle Harbor. There is a boat ramp, and a park boat rental. Canoes can be rented year-round for $3 an hour or $15 a day. *Distance:* Variable. *High Points:* During July and August visitors can harvest the scallops out of the bay. Look for the twinkling blue eyes which line their shell mouths. There are salt marshes on the peninsula coast a little north and south of Eagle Harbor where the trip begins, but the second one, about 0.75 mile south, has a channel and bayou large enough to explore in a kayak. *Hazards:* Not really so much a hazard as a nuisance, unpleasant odors from a mainland paper mill sometimes waft across the bay in the winter. *USGS Topos:* Cape San Blas, St. Joseph Peninsula, Port St. Joe and St. Joseph Point.

Cash Bayou, Doyle Creek and Whiskey George Creek –Three paddles around the bayous, marshes and creeks on the perimeter of the bay offer excellent close-up views of wildlife in freshwater and estuarine ecosystems. Generally, the marsh edges offer good viewing of all kinds of wildlife, like alligators and turtles or wading birds such as egrets and herons. Most of the long, flat freshwater marsh areas consists of sawgrass, which grows higher than six feet. Upon entering the estuary or mixed fresh and salt water in the bay, fresh water remains on the surface, but underneath is much denser saltwater. *Put-In/Take-Out:* Cash Bayou—from the intersection of US 98, go north on FL 65 for about 5 miles to the Cash Bayou bridge. Boaters can park and put-in from an unimproved ramp on a small dirt road on the west side of the road and south bank of the bayou. Whiskey George or Doyle Creek—continue north from Cash Bayou and about 2.5 miles later the road crosses the Whiskey George Creek. Immediately following on the left is a fire tower, and then 0.25 mile later on the same side is the dirt entrance to a boat ramp on the Whiskey George. Note: Boaters can follow all three channels upstream for a 0.5 mile or longer. The Whiskey George is wide enough to continue for several miles, but from the put-in point mentioned above, it meanders so much boaters can easily get lost. To go up the Whiskey George, it might be wiser to go back 0.5 mile on FL 65 to the Whiskey George Bridge. Park and put-in from an unimproved boat launch next to the bridge. The creek doesn't meander quite so much from there. *Distance:* Variable. *High Points for Cash Bayou:* It's a narrow creek at the put-in, but gradually widens to about 0.33 mile across when it enters East Bayou 2 miles south of the bridge. *High Points for Whiskey George and Doyle Creek:* About 0.25 mile downstream from the put-in point, the Whiskey George meets Doyle Creek. The combined creek snakes down about 2 miles before dumping into West Bayou, which soon widens to 0.33 mile across. *Hazards:* Check tide conditions. Low tide makes the channels more shallow and portages might be necessary. If possible, time a trip to go in the same direction as the incoming and outgoing tide to prevent too much exertion. Check weather conditions. If going into the open bay, consider that even if the water looks calm, a passing storm or strong winds could quickly make it very choppy. Topo maps are a must and a compass strongly recommended to prevent getting lost in side creeks or pools all along the three meandering waterways. Biting insects are common in the summer. And fishermen in motor boats frequently

www.chattahoochee.org

We welcome your comments, suggestions, recommendations and input regarding this book and the river, via the Internet at the Riverkeeper's website: www.chattahoochee.org.

You can also access the website for additional information regarding the Chattahoochee and the many issues that affect the river.

ALL IS BORN OF WATER;
ALL IS SUSTAINED BY WATER.

use all three channels during the warmer months. *USGS Topos:* Beverly and Green Point.

GUIDED WATER TRIPS IN AND AROUND APALACHICOLA BAY –Captain Tom's "Adventures in Paradise," owned and operated by Tom Gray, provides a variety of ways for individuals to explore the Apalachicola Bay area. Gray, a U.S. Coast Guard licensed boat captain has made his home in Apalachicola since 1984. He has had experience on a variety of vessels, taught biology and been a commercial fisherman. Explorations include: Little St. George Island–Cruise to the bayside, landing near the old Marshall house and stroll to the historic old lighthouse. St Vincent Island–Hiking and trail biking on St. Vincent Island or canoeing to the island from Indian Pass. St. George Island–Paddle East Cove and around Goose Island to Rattlesnake Cove to see salt marshes, wildlife, live oyster bars, and the conchs, horseshoes, hermits and other residents of the bay shallows. Harbor and Estuary Tour–Cruise Apalachicola's riverfront for a close-up look at the fishing fleet, docks, buildings and marina; go up river to see marsh sloughs and forest with myriad plants and wildlife. Net Casting–Learn to select and throw a cast net. Bay Shallows by Night–Wade the bay shallows by night to see flounder, crabs. Other Captain Tom adventures include photo tours, sailing lessons, sunset sails, canoe shuttle service and boat rental, he will also custom design an adventure. *More Information:* Captain Tom's Adventures in Paradise, 64 Avenue C, Apalachicola, FL 32320; 850/653-8463.

"That's when we change the world...when we change our own back yard."

—John Cronin, Hudson River Riverkeeper

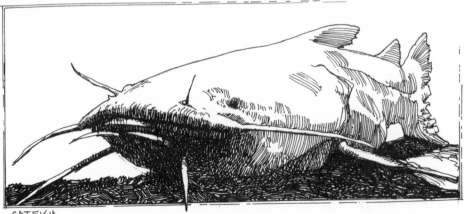

CATFISH

AFTERWORD by Fred Brown

fter 18 months of working on this book one thing is clear to me: The river is doing fine. But *we* are in trouble. The problems that occupy our conversations and newspaper articles about the river: pollution caused by Atlanta's R. M. Clayton Sewage Treatment Plant; how should water be allocated among Georgia, Alabama and Florida; should we or should we not dredge the lower part of the river…this list is a long one. These are big problems for us, but to the river they are no more than gnats on an elephant's back.

Take Morgan Falls Dam for instance, a 65-foot dam built on the Chattahoochee near Atlanta in 1904. Less than 100 years after its construction, the upstream side of the dam has silted up so much that today you can stand on the bottom of Bull Sluice Lake and put your hands on top of the dam. Is this a concern to us? Of course it is. There is increased siltation causing changes at the Chattahoochee Nature Center. The lake may have to eventually be dredged. But is Morgan Falls Dam a concern to the river? Hardly. One hundred years is a mere blink of an eye in River Time. The Chattahoochee River is millions of years old. Over time it has carved off almost a mile of rock and dirt from the surface of the Appalachian mountains and sent it downstream to form floodplains and beaches on the Gulf Coast. This river, like other rivers, is the most powerful force on earth. Rivers are the number one determiner of the earth's shape. A watershed, like the Chattahoochee watershed, is nature's primary organizing principle. It is like a pocket folder in the file cabinet called Earth.

We are totally preoccupied with and blinded by our own sense of self importance and the importance of artifacts like dams, lakes and sewage treatment plants that we have created over the past few hundred years. The river does not have a problem. We do. And the problem is this: if we continue to mistreat the river, it is going to punish us. It is not going to allow us to drink from it. It will decide not to water our crops. It will decide we cannot eat the fish and oysters and shrimp we take from it.

The Indians had it right. The river is a Great Spirit and we are making it angry.

It is amusing, instructive and embarrassing to look back just 30 years and see how our limited human perceptions and aspirations for one of nature's great forces have changed. For example, 30 years ago the idea of making the Chattahoochee navigable all the way to Atlanta was a hot topic. Joel Smith, the publisher of the *Eufaula Tribune*, attended the dedication of Buford Dam in 1968 and wrote, "One of the highlights of the dedication ceremony at the Buford Dam on the upper stretch of the long meandering Chattahoochee was the breaking of a large bottle containing Gulf of Mexico water." The dignitaries taking part in that historic event envisioned the day when ocean going tugs and barges would ply between the Gulf and Atlanta. Ralph McGill, publisher of the *Atlanta Constitution*, was a big proponent of river navigation and wrote as if it were an accomplished fact. It is, he opined, just a matter of time and money. Today, river navigation is a non-issue. Downstream effects of Chattahoochee dams were of little concern during their design and construction. We just considered them good for the river and a boon for economic progress. Changes in fish populations or riparian vegetation were unanticipated or not taken seriously.

During the course of researching this book, I talked to a boat manufacturer whose number one goal is to increase weekday business on Lake Lanier so that it more closely resembles the traffic on Lake of the Ozarks where, "they have a jillion different cottages and hotels and motels and so forth on the lake, and it's developed much greater than here." He feels this way despite the recent research that shows that pleasure boats account for about 420 million gallons of oil and hydrocarbon pollution per year–the equivalent of about 40 Exxon *Valdez* oil spills.

One of my favorite quotes in this book came from Joe Cook, who along with his wife, Monica, canoed the entire length of the Chattahoochee in 1995. I asked Joe for some of his special memories of the trip. "We were paddling south of Atlanta", he recalled. "It was late in the afternoon. The wind was blowing the cottonseed. The sun was backlighting it, and it looked like snow. It was very peaceful and beautiful land. We were right there south of Atlanta and that to me just kinda said something about, you know, it's a beautiful river. But while we were seeing this, we were smelling this stench coming from the wastewater treatment plants. Smelly, but it was so beautiful and peaceful. The experience we got from the river was, oh gosh, what a beautiful place, but *gosh."* I can identify with that. So many of the truly exhilarating experiences I had on the river during this 18 months were tempered with, "but *gosh.*" I wrote in the introduction that one of the most inspiring sites on the river is the overlook on Sweetwater Creek where a dozen miles from Atlanta's Five Points dramatic whitewater rapids tumble over the Brevard Fault. But that is darkened by the knowledge that just downstream the creek flows into the most abused urban section of the entire 540-mile river. That kind of this-is-beautiful-but-gosh experience occurred again and again. During 18 months of exploring the river, there were few times when I was out of sight of a styrofoam cup.

The Chattahoochee is a rare, rare treasure. This book is filled with memorable sites and river experiences available to everyone. But if we continue along the same course of development and abuse we have followed in the past, the river will not permit the author of the 2025 Chattahoochee Guide to write this kind of book.

Peggy Theus, a friend in Columbus who has preached Chattahoochee to a small congregation for a dozen years or more, has a favorite line: "Only God can make a river. And he is not making any more." She is right. We had better be careful.

RESOURCES

Organizations can provide us with a way to get involved with the river. Through programs, seminars, outdoor activities and newsletters, each organization, in its own way, gives us a structure in which to participate in protecting the river and the environment in general. Listed below are some organizations and government agencies that advocate river preservation and related topics.

UPPER CHATTAHOOCHEE RIVERKEEPER. Sally Bethea, Executive Director, 1900 Emery Street, Suite 450, Atlanta, GA 30318; 404/352-9828; fax: 404/352-8676; e-mail: rivrkeep@mindspring.com; website: www.chattahoochee. org. Established in 1994, the Upper Chattahoochee Riverkeeper Fund, Inc. is an independent environmental advocacy organization dedicated solely to protecting the Chattahoochee River. The group's primary geographic focus begins at the river's headwaters in the north Georgia mountains and continues downstream to West Point Lake, encompassing more than 200 miles of the Chattahoochee.

From its headwaters to West Point Lake, the Chattahoochee is severely impacted by urban development, industrial discharges and agricultural runoff. While significant improvements have been made in the river since the 1960s, much remains to be accomplished. One or more state water quality standards are violated along the entire stretch of the upper Chattahoochee. Development in Atlanta and the continued discharge of untreated sewage in the river during storms are significant problems for communities downstream.

The Riverkeeper mission is to advocate and secure the protection and stewardship of the Chattahoochee River, its tributaries and watershed in order to improve and maintain its environmental integrity and to preserve the natural, scenic and recreational character of the river corridor. The Riverkeeper actively uses advocacy, education, research, communication, cooperation, monitoring and legal actions to protect and preserve the Chattahoochee and its watershed.

The Riverkeeper quarterly publication, *River Chat,* keeps members informed of all issues involving the Chattahoochee River. Articles include updates on the Riverkeeper's legal action program, Adopt-A-Stream Network, headwaters project and membership activities.

AMERICAN RIVERS. 1025 Vermont Avenue, NW, Suite 720, Washington, DC 20005; 202/347-7550; fax: 202/347-9240; e-mail: amrivers@amrivers.org; website: www. amrivers.org. Northwest Regional Office, 400 East Pine Street, #225, Seattle, WA 98122; 206/323-8186. Southwest Regional Office, 3601 North 7th Avenue, Suite D, Phoenix, AZ 85015; 602/234-3946. Founded in 1973, American Rivers is dedicated to protecting and restoring America's river systems and fostering a river stewardship ethic. The organization focuses on three river conservation goals: protecting the nation's last wild rivers, restoring hometown rivers that run through urban areas and rural communities and repairing the big rivers that are the arteries of the continent. Within five years, they hope to protect the headwater, flows and riparian areas of wild rivers by reforming land and water development policies and practices; restore riparian areas and flows of hometown rivers by reforming land and water management practices and by creating incentives for community-based action; and provide more natural flows by changing the design and operation of dams, reservoirs and other river-control structures.

ATLANTA REGIONAL COMMISSION. 3715 Northside Parkway, Building 200, Suite 300, Atlanta, GA 30327; 404/364-2500; fax: 404/364-2599. Established in 1947, the ARC is the oldest and largest publicly supported, multi-county planning agency in the U.S. Funded through a number of sources from local, state and federal governments, it is the official planning agency for the 10-county Atlanta region. One of the many focus areas of this government agency is planning for an adequate water supply for the Atlanta region's future, proper waste water and storm water management and protection of key environmental resources, including the region's main water supply, the Chattahoochee River. To do this, the ARC assists local governments in implementing the Metropolitan River Protection Act (see page 80), which seeks to protect the quality of the Chattahoochee. A 1988 ARC map of the Chattahoochee River Corridor, showing the corridor, national park land and city/county park land, can be obtained from the agency.

GEORGIA ADOPT-A-STREAM. 7 Martin Luther King Drive, SW, Suite 643, Atlanta, GA 30334; 404/656-0099 or 0069; fax: 404/657-7031; e-mail: michele_droszez@mail.dnr.state.

ga.us. This organization, under the auspices of the Water Protection Branch of the Georgia Environmental Protection Division, strives to increase community awareness on the issues of water quality and nonpoint source pollution by educating individuals about what they can do to improve water quality in their communities and encouraging local solutions to nonpoint source pollution problems (see page 122). Sixteen Community/ Watershed Programs, funded by counties, cities and nonprofit organizations, are set up to organize Adopt-A-Stream groups within their watershed, county or city. Five Adopt-A-Stream Regional Training Centers, providing training, technical and organizational support to groups in their area, are located at state universities.

GEORGIA CANOEING ASSOCIATION. P.O. Box 7023, Atlanta, GA 30357; 770/421-9729; e-mail: gacanoe@mind spring.com; website: www.mindspring.com/~gacanoe. This 30-year-old canoe and kayak club promotes recreational paddling, river courtesy, skill development and river safety. It sponsors about 200 paddling trips a year, including trips on the Chattahoochee north and south of Lake Lanier; organizes annual paddling and camping events; and offers canoe, kayak and safety instructional clinics. Its monthly newsletter, *The Eddy Line*, keeps members informed of activities. The GCA is active in all aspects of river protection, including environmental impacts, river management issues and protecting paddlers' access to rivers. One of its activities is monitoring the Chattahoochee above Lake Lanier for the Upper Chattahoochee Riverkeeper.

GEORGIA COUNCIL OF TROUT UNLIMITED. Bobby Bell, Regional Director, 108 Sycamore Street, Rome, GA 30165; 706/234-5310 or 706/234-8006. This nonprofit organization is part of the 100,000-member national Trout Unlimited organization, organized for the purpose of conserving, protecting and restoring North America's trout and salmon fisheries and their watersheds. National issues pursued by the organization include point and nonpoint pollution, habitat protection and restoration, acid rain, hydro dams and Pacific and Atlantic salmon recovery. Chapters in the Chattahoochee watershed include: Chattahoochee, Upper Chattahoochee, Tailwater, Kanooka, Georgia Foothills and Cohutta. Chapter members participate in monthly meetings, fundraisers, kid's fishing days, environmental education, stream improvement projects with the U.S. Forest Service, float stocking with the Georgia Department of Natural Resources and fishing trips.

GEORGIA WILDLIFE FEDERATION. 1930 Iris Drive, Conyers, GA 30207; 770/929-3350; fax: 770/929-3534. The oldest and largest private citizen's conservation organization in Georgia and the official state affiliate of the National Wildlife Federation, this organization speaks out on issues ranging from clean air and water to wetlands preservation and wildlife management. The organization has set up Schoolyard Wildlife Habitats, certified by the national organization, in schools across Georgia and has a goal to establish outdoor classrooms in every school in the state. Each year the Federation hosts the Buck-arama, Fisharama, Turkeyrama and Duckarama to raise money for conservation work and to raise conservation awareness among sports enthusiasts. Members receive a newsletter, *The Call*, which keeps them updated on events and current environmental issues and a quarterly magazine, *Georgia Wildlife*, which features articles on conservation issues across Georgia.

HISTORIC CHATTAHOOCHEE COMMISSION. Doug Purcell, Executive Director, P.O. Box 33, Eufaula, AL 36072-0033; 334/687-9755. The commission, which is dedicated to the preservation and promotion of tourism throughout the lower Chattahoochee River Valley, is a joint effort between the states of Alabama and Georgia and is the first and only tourism/preservation agency in the nation officially sanctioned to cross state lines to pursue goals common to all member counties. Projects of the commission include sponsoring or supporting the publication of numerous books and manuscripts about the Chattahoochee River Valley, assisting local organizations with the funding of historical markers, conducting rural architectural surveys of historic residential buildings, producing an audiovisual educational program on the evolution of domestic architectural styles and distributing thousands of brochures and purchasing magazine ads promoting the Chattahoochee Trace region of Alabama and Georgia. A quarterly newsletter, *Chattahoochee Tracings*, is free to interested citizens.

LAKE LANIER ASSOCIATION, INC. 393 Green Street, NW, Gainesville, GA 30501; 770/503-7330; fax: 770/503-7329. Over 30 years old, this organization is dedicated to the preservation of Lake Lanier. The organization has more than 2,000 members, representing families, homeowners, boaters, businesses and environmentally concerned citizens. Membership dues are $30. The association publishes a quarterly publication, *Lanier Outlook*.

OFFICE OF GREENWAYS AND TRAILS. Florida Department of Environmental Protection, 325 John Knox Road,

Building 500, Tallahassee, FL 32303-4124; 850/488-3701. Field Office: 8282 SE Highway 314, Ocala, FL 34470; 352/236-2464. Recognizing the appeal of Florida to outdoor enthusiasts of all kinds, the Florida Recreational Trails Act of 1979 authorized the establishment of a network of recreation, scenic and historic trails. The Office of Greenways and Trails, a division of the Florida Department of Environmental Protection, is dedicated to designating, establishing and maintaining this connected system of greenways and trails throughout Florida. They have acquired abandoned railway corridors for developing linear parks for hiking, biking, jogging and horseback riding. Thirty-six canoe trails are also designated under the Act. The Office of Greenways and Trails sends out information on all of these. They have put together a marvelous package of canoeing information, including individual brochures on the 36 canoe trails, a listing of canoe outfitters in the state, a map of canoe trails in the National Forests in Florida and other helpful information. Included in the package are several canoe trails on rivers and creeks that feed into the Apalachicola, including the Chipola River and the River Styx, Kennedy Creek, Owl Creek and New River.

RIVER NETWORK. National Office, P.O. Box 8787, Portland, OR, 97207; 503/241-3506; e-mail: rivernet@igc. apc.org. Founded in 1988, this organization, which believes solutions to river degradation are primarily local and must be created by citizen action–watershed by watershed, is dedicated to building citizen groups to speak out for rivers in every watershed across the country. River Network's mission is to help people organize to protect and restore rivers and watersheds by supporting river and watershed advocates at the local, state and regional levels, helping them build effective organizations and promoting a nationwide movement for rivers and watersheds. The organization also acquires and conserves riverlands that are critical to the services that rivers perform for human communities; drinking water supply, floodplain management, fish and wildlife habitat, recreation and open space. River Network's longterm vision is to establish vigilant and effective citizen organizations in each of the 2,000 major watersheds in the United States.

SIERRA CLUB. 85 Second Street, Second Floor, San Francisco, CA 94105-3441; 415/977-5500; fax: 415/977-5799; website: www.sierraclub.org. Founded in 1892 by John Muir, the Sierra Club immediately set about protecting America's forests and wild lands and has since played a key role in safeguarding more than 132 million acres in the nation's national park and wilderness systems. The club's goal is "to secure respect for the rights of all living things and for the integrity of the natural environment upon which we all depend" as it promotes conservation of the natural environment by influencing public policy decisions–legislative, administrative, legal and electoral. The nonprofit member-supported organization has more than 550,000 members in 65 chapters in both the U.S. and Canada. The club offers hundreds of recreational outings, such as paddling and pedaling, all over the world as well as service trips where members build trails, preserve archaeological sites and help clean up the environment. There are numerous chapters of the Sierra Club in Alabama, Georgia and Florida. To locate a chapter in your area contact the national organization. State chapters are also linked to the national website or can be accessed individually: www.sierraclub.org/chapters/al/ (Alabama); www.sierraclub.org/chapters/ga/ (Georgia) and www.sierraclub.org/chapters/fl/ (Florida).

THE CHATTAHOOCHEE RIVERKEEPER, INC. P.O. Box 1492, Columbus, GA 31902; 706/317-4837. This sister River-keeper organization monitors the Lower Chattahoochee River from West Point Lake downstream to Columbus.

THE CONSERVATION FUND. 1800 N. Kent Street, Suite 1120, Arlington, VA 22209-2156; 703/525-6300; fax: 703/525-4610; e-mail: mail@conservationfund.org; website: www.conservationfund.org. Southeastern Regional Office, P.O. Box 1362, Tucker, GA 30085-1362; 770/414-0211; fax: 770/938-0585. Florida Office, 4400 PGA Boulevard, Suite 900, Palm Beach Gardens, FL 33410; 561/624-4925; fax: 561/624-4948. This national nonprofit organization is dedicated to protecting America's legacy of land and water by working in partnership with different groups, businesses, agencies and individuals. The Fund's mission is to seek sustainable conservation solutions for the future, emphasizing the integration of economic and environmental goals. Through land acquisi-

tion, demonstration projects, education and community based activities, the Fund looks for innovative long-term measures to conserve land and water.

THE GEORGIA CONSERVANCY. State Office, 1776 Peachtree Street, NW, Suite 400 South, Atlanta, GA 30309; 404/876-2900; fax: 404/872-9229; e-mail: tgc@ mindspring.com; website: www. gaconservancy.org. This nonprofit organization established in 1967 is dedicated to the responsible stewardship of Georgia's vital natural resources. Striving to balance the demands of social and economic progress with a commitment to protect the environment, the Conservancy has three main focus areas: water, natural areas and air. Past accomplishments include securing protection for special natural areas, including the Chattahoochee River National Recreation Area (see page 80); achieving protective statues for freshwater wetlands and the Chattahoochee National Forest (see page 10); and strengthening standards for water quality, air quality and hazardous and solid waste management. Its newsletter, *Panorama*, is published bimonthly.

THE NATURE CONSERVANCY OF GEORGIA. 1330 West Peachtree Street, Suite 410, Atlanta, GA 30309-2904; 404/ 873-6946; fax: 404/873-6984; website: www.tnc.org/ Georgia/index.html. This state chapter of an international conservation organization dedicated solely to preserving natural diversity uses scientific information to identify rare species and natural communities and then provides for the long-term protection of these vital habitats. As of 1997, the 15,000-member organization, advocating conservation through private action, has preserved more than 57 natural areas–some 157,000 acres, including the

Chattahoochee National Forest (see page 10), the Chattahoochee River National Recreation Area (see page 80) and Smithgall Woods-Dukes Creek (see page 14). Members receive *Nature Conservancy*, a bimonthly magazine that focuses on the organization's national and international projects and *Chapter News*, the state's quarterly newsletter.

THE TRUST FOR PUBLIC LAND. Atlanta Field Office, 1447 Peachtree Street, NE, Atlanta, GA 30309; 404/873-7306; fax: 404/875-9099. This national organization conserves land for people to improve the quality of life in communities and to protect natural and historic resources for future generations. Founded in 1972, the Trust specializes in conservation real estate, applying its expertise in negotiation, public finance and law to protect land for public use. Nationwide the Trust has helped protect more than 1 million acres of land for people to enjoy as parks, greenways, playgrounds, historic landmarks and wilderness areas. In Georgia the Trust's top priority is to save the last remaining lands along the Chattahoochee River from the north Georgia mountains to Columbus. The organization believes that this will help restore the river's water quality while creating a vibrant center for community life. To date the Trust has acquired 12 properties along the river, including the historic Hyde Farm and Powers Homestead in Cobb County, a 3-mile greenway from Lake Lanier to GA 20 in Gwinnett County and 1 mile of river frontage at Bowman's Island near Lake Lanier in Forsyth County.

THE UPPER CHATTAHOOCHEE RIVERKEEPER ADOPT-A-STREAM NETWORK. Dana Poole, Upper Chattahoochee Riverkeeper, 1900 Emery Street, Suite 450, Atlanta, GA 30318; 404/352-9828; fax: 404/352-8676; e-mail: rivrkeep @mindspring.com. The Riverkeeper Network works cooperatively with and promotes the Georgia Adopt-A-Stream program in the Chattahoochee Watershed. The Network was formed in 1995 to bind together the existing Chattahoochee Watershed Adopt-A-Stream groups. Since then more groups have formed and become a part of the Network. Beyond the benefits of Georgia Adopt-A-Stream, the Network offers a quarterly newsletter, internet stream information, resources for students and teachers, technical assistance for long-term trend analysis and assistance in solving local pollution problems.

MAPS, BOOKS AND PUBLICATIONS

Maps

Of all the research tools that we have–and this includes books, files and the internet–maps are our single most important tool in researching guidebooks. We also believe they are the single most important tool in enjoying any trip. We taped together state highway maps and hung them on the wall to get a better perspective of the Chattahoochee River. We acquired all the topo maps for the river and laid them out on a local gymnasium floor so we could "walk" the entire river. We ordered all the county highway maps for the river, taped them together, cut them into the 10 sections we developed for the book and colored the river and lakes blue. These county maps–taped, torn, written on and wrinkled–went wherever we went and were our best friends when recounting a day's adventures. And still there were more maps–Forest Service maps, lake recreation maps, trail maps, fishing maps, maps for the boat, maps for the car–the list goes on and on. The following are the major maps we used and places to get them.

ATLANTIC MAPPING RECREATION AND FISHING GUIDE MAPS. Atlantic Mapping, Inc., P.O. Box 739, Marietta, GA 30065; 770/426-5768. These waterproof recreation and fishing maps with topography are a must when exploring the river or lakes by boat, but we also keep copies in our files because they contain an enormous amount of information. These maps depict all recreation areas along the water with a graph indicating the facilities at each. They also indicate normal pool levels and all mile markers and list the geographic coordinates for selected fish shelters and structure sites. Maps we used for this book were the Chattahoochee River from Helen to Atlanta, Lake Lanier, West Point Lake, Lakes Oliver and Goat Rock, Lake Walter F. George (which includes the river and all three lakes from Columbus to the Jim Woodruff Lock and Dam at Lake Seminole) and Lake Seminole.

CHATTAHOOCHEE RIVER NATIONAL RECREATION AREA MAP. National Park Service, U.S. Department of the Interior, Superintendent, 1978 Island Ford Parkway, Atlanta, GA 30350-3400; 770/399-8070. This free map is a must for exploring the CRNRA. It shows all the park lands that sit along the 48-mile stretch of river from Buford Dam to Peachtree Creek, their facilities and the

Atlanta streets and highways that surround them. More detailed maps of the parks can be found in the Buford Dam to Peachtree Creek section of this guidebook as well as at the individual parks.

COUNTY ROAD MAPS AND OFFICIAL STATE HIGHWAY MAPS. Most of us have used or at least seen an Official State Highway Map. Published annually in color and distributed free by each state's highway department, they make a good glove-compartment map for travelers. But to us, no one can truly explore an area without County Road Maps. These maps include every paved and dirt road in a county and identify a wealth of other man-made and natural landmarks useful to travelers and explorers who want highly detailed information. County road maps can be ordered by mail or purchased over the counter at the individual state's Department of Transportation office. Prices vary so call for a price list. Alabama Highway Department, 1409 Coliseum Boulevard, Room R-103, Montgomery, AL 36130; 205/261-6071. Georgia Department of Transportation, Map Sales Division, 2 Capitol Square, Atlanta, GA 30334; 404/656-5336. Florida Department of Commerce, Collins Building, Tallahassee, FL 32399-2000; 850/263-3510.

FISHING HOT SPOTS. Fishing Hot Spots, Inc., P.O. Box 1167, Rhinelander, WI 54501; 800/255-6277; fax: 715/365-5575. These are serious fishing maps–they're waterproof, tearproof and they claim to float. These hydrographic contour maps feature plenty of fishing holes marked by local experts and guides, and each map includes boat landing locations, stocking reports, fishery survey results, migration patterns and fishing tips and techniques. We used the Lake Eufaula (Walter F. George Reservoir) and West Point Lake maps for our research. Map prices range from about $6 to $9. Call the toll free number for a free list of the more than 500 maps available, prices and ordering information.

FOREST SERVICE MAPS. U.S. Department of Agriculture, Forest Service, Visitor's Center, Room 154, 1720 Peachtree Street, NW, Atlanta, GA 30367-9102; 404/347-2384. These large Forest Service maps show the individual national forest in detail with recreation sites, paved and unpaved roads, trails, trail shelters, creeks and other points of interest marked. One interesting feature of these maps is an index to the topographical maps that cover the particular forest. We used the Apalachicola National Forest and the Chattahoochee National Forest maps in researching this guidebook.

TROUT STREAMS OF GEORGIA. Georgia Department of Natural Resources, Wildlife Resources Division, 2123 US 278, SE, Social Circle, GA 30279; 404/656-4863. This free map was produced to guide trout anglers in locating trout streams. One side is a map of northwest Georgia, the other side is northeast Georgia. Due to scale limitations, not all streams are named and only enough roads to give the angler access to streams, particularly those on public land, are included. A Trout Index, indicating heavily stocked, infrequently stocked and wild streams and stocked lakes, provides information on where to fish for trout.

U. S. ARMY CORPS OF ENGINEERS LAKE MAPS. These maps are a must when exploring or recreating on any Corps of Engineers lake. There is text explaining the different types of recreation found at the lake; boating, swimming and skiing rules; lake and dam statistics; and a map of the lake with campgrounds, day use parks and marinas keyed to a graph listing each recreation area's facilities. Maps are free and can be obtained at each lake's management office. Lake Seminole, Resource Management Office, P.O. Box 96, Chattahoochee, FL 32324; 912/662-2001. Lake Sidney Lanier, Resource Manager's Office, P.O. Box 567, Buford, GA 30518; 770/945-9531. Lakes Walter F. George and George W. Andrews, Resource Manager's Office, Route 1, Box 176, Fort Gaines, GA 31751-9722; 912/768-2516. West Point Lake, Resource Management Office, 500 Resource Management Drive, West Point, GA 31833-9517; 706/645-2937.

U. S. ARMY CORPS OF ENGINEERS NAVIGATION CHARTS - APALACHICOLA, CHATTAHOOCHEE AND FLINT RIVERS. DISTRICT ENGINEER, U.S. Army Corps of Engineers District, Mobile, Map Sales, LM-SR, P.O. Box 2288, Mobile, AL 36628; 334/441-5631. This bound series of 67 14" x 21" black-and-white aerial navigation charts gave us a real bird's-eye view of the river from Columbus to Apalachicola Bay. Although photographed in 1985, the maps are amazingly accurate. Each tenth of a mile is marked, and broken lines indicate the best water to navigate. Symbols approximate the location of mile marker signs, buoys and daymarks located on the river. The maps, in order and numbered from 1 to 58 going upstream, begin at the mouth of the river at Apalachicola Bay and end at Columbus. Following these are another set of 9 navigation charts that map the course of the Flint River from Bainbridge to the Jim Woodruff Dam. Noted on these maps is a caution that they are furnished for infor-

mation only and should not be used for navigational purposes; but navigating the river, particularly from Jim Woodruff Dam to Apalachicola Bay, would have been less enjoyable without them. Maps can be purchased from the Mobile District Office for $29.50, plus $5 shipping and handling.

U.S.G.S. TOPOGRAPHICAL MAPS. Topographical maps are fun maps to look at and use and add immeasurably to the experience of exploring. They distinguish terrain features–cliffs and hills, rivers and streams, watersheds and flood plains–plus some man-made landmarks such as churches, cemeteries and firetowers. The detail with which these are depicted depends on the scale of the maps. As the ratio of the scale numbers decreases, the map's detail increases. The U.S. Geological Survey produces topo maps in scales of 1:250,000, which requires only 14 maps to cover the state; 1:100,000; and 1:24,000, which divides Georgia into 1016 quadrangles. We prefer the smaller scale which shows local terrain features in great detail. Topos can be purchased at several places, but we think the best and easiest way to buy a topo is to order it from Powers Elevation. Powers always have all topos in stock, they are just a phone call away, they take credit cards and they will overnight topos if you need them to do so. Powers charges $6, plus postage and handling, for each map; and they will send you a free index of maps for any state. Powers Elevation Co., Inc., P.O. Box 440889, Aurora, CO 80044-0889; 303/321-2217 or 800/824-2550; fax: 303/321-2218.

WHITEWATER RIVER MAPS BY WILLIAM NEALY. These 18" x 35" black-and-white, hand-drawn river map posters are by artist William Nealy, who has written and illustrated several books on kayaking. The maps, not-to-scale and "intended for off-river use only," are fun to look at and interesting to read with cartoon-type illustrations and text covering every inch. The text is humorously written and accurate–Nealy has paddled each of the southeastern rivers he has mapped. The two Nealy maps we have that pertain to this book are the Upper Chattahoochee (Helen to Duncan Bridge) and the Lower Chattahoochee (Morgan Falls Dam to Paces Mill Take-Out). Maps, $4.95 each, can be purchased from most large outfitters or ordered from Menasha Ridge Press, 700 South 28th Street, Suite 206, Birmingham, AL 35233-3417; 800/247-9437; website: www.menasharidge.com.

Books

During 18 months of research, we accumulated a vast number of books on the Chattahoochee River, rivers and river-related topics. History, canoeing, hiking, fishing, the environment–we found books on all these topics and others not only helpful, but necessary, in writing this guidebook. Some books provided specific resource material while others were read just to broaden our base of knowledge. The following books from our library are those which we used in our research and which we would recommend to anyone interested in pursuing more information on rivers.

52 Weeks on Lanier by Ken Sturdivant. Professional angler and instructor Ken Sturdivant has filled a 3-ring binder with information on how, when and where to fish Lake Lanier. For a copy, send $24.95, which includes postage and handling, to 106 Hickory Ridge, Cumming, GA 30130.

A Canoeing and Kayaking Guide to the Streams of Florida, Vol. 1, North Central Peninsula and Panhandle by Elizabeth F. Carter and John L. Pearce. Birmingham: Menasha Ridge Press, 1985. One or both authors paddled every mile of every waterway in this guidebook. Information on each trail includes how to get to the river, distance, difficulty and description of run and scenery.

Archaeological Salvage in the Walter F. George Basin of the Chattahoochee River in Alabama by David L. DeJarnette. Tuscaloosa: University of Alabama Press, 1975. This book records the findings of a 1947 preliminary archaeological survey of the Chattahoochee Valley covering the area from the Florida border to Phenix City, Alabama, as well as the minor excavations conducted at later times on several sites. The purpose of the survey, which located 124 Indian village sites and 20 mounds and mound groups in the basin area, was to locate only those sites which would be submerged by proposed dams on the Chattahoochee River. Only a few sites which lay outside a 4-mile wide area west of the river were investigated. We found this study particularly interesting as the number of sites found truly emphasizes the concentration of Indian culture in the area. The book's publication was sponsored by the Historic Chattahoochee Commission.

A Storybook Site by David Coughlin. This is a detailed account of the early history and construction of Buford Dam and Lake Lanier. Nearly 400 pages of text, over 700 historical and contemporary photographs, official documents and letters, newspaper articles, maps, interviews and statistical data. Price is $75. Books can be ordered by contacting Coughlin at 770/932-2614.

Cemochechobee: Archaeology of a Mississippian Ceremonial Center on the Chattahoochee River by Frank T. Schnell, Vernon J. Knight, Jr. and Gail S. Schnell. Gainesville: University Presses of Florida, 1981. This is an archaeological study of a large prehistoric community that existed from AD 900 to 1400 on the Chattahoochee River in Clay County, Georgia. The construction of Walter F. George Dam destroyed approximately two-thirds of the Cemochechobee village site. The remainder is known today as the Rood Creek Indian Mounds (see page 210). We have been fortunate not only in obtaining this book for our library but in being among several groups that have toured Rood Mounds with Frank Schnell (see page 162), one of the book's authors.

Dams and Rivers, A Primer on the Downstream Effects of Dams by Michael Collier, Robert H. Webb and John C. Schmidt. Denver: U.S. Geological Survey, 1996. This is a study that explores the changes to rivers–such as changes to river beds and banks and to riparian habitats and animal communities–downstream from dams. Several pages are dedicated to the Chattahoochee River.

Earth's Dynamic Systems by W. Kenneth Hamblin and Eric H. Christiansen. Englewood Cliffs: Prentice Hall, 1995. The "River Systems" section of the book's 7th edition was one of our favorite resources in writing this book and is quoted extensively throughout this guidebook (see page 3). The book contains well-explained information for anyone studying any of the earth's dynamic systems.

Fair to Middlin' by Lynn Willoughby. Tuscaloosa: The University of Alabama Press, 1993. This is a detailed but very readable account of the antebellum economy, which depended heavily on cotton trade, within the Apalachicola/Chattahoochee River Valley. The terms "fair" and "middlin'" were two of the 13 distinct grades of cotton with "middlin'" being the basic grade from which all other classifications were figured and "fair" being the lowest on the scale.

From Mount Vernon to Chattahoochee by Grady Turnage. Chattahoochee, Fla., 1986. Turnage, who worked in the Chattahoochee Post Office for 36 years, is known in the area as being someone who has been around for a long time and knows all the stories. This self-published history of Mount Vernon, River Junction, Chattahoochee and vicinity has numerous historical photographs, drawings and maps. The paperback 39-page booklet can be purchased at the Chattahoochee Post Office in Chattahoochee, Florida.

Georgia's Rivers edited by George Hatcher. Athens: University of Georgia Press, 1962. This is a collection of articles written about Georgia rivers by writers of the *Atlanta Journal and Constitution Magazine*. We have quoted a Ralph McGill article about the Chattahoochee headwaters in a sidebar on page 10.

Guide to North Florida Bass Waters by Larry Larsen. Lakeland, Fla.: Larsen's Outdoor Publishing, 1991. This is one book in a series that fishing expert Larsen has written after fishing more than 1,000 of Florida's lakes and rivers. We used this book in gathering information on

bass fishing on both Lake Seminole and the Apalachi-cola River. It includes specific areas to fish, best techniques, lures and baits, maps and launch ramps.

LARGE-MOUTH BASS

Indian Trails of Georgia by Marion R. Hemperley. Garden Club of Georgia, 1994. This is an excellent collection of Indian culture, Indian towns, roads, trails, place names and myths. Selections have been used extensively throughout this book, particularly as page turners.

Living on the Unicoi Road: Helen's Pioneer Century and Tales from the Georgia Gold Rush by Matt Gedney. Marietta, Ga.: Little Star Press, 1966. This interesting history is woven from the stories of the white families who pioneered settlement of the Chattahoochee River's headwaters in the Helen Valley.

Northern Georgia Canoeing by Bob Sehlinger and Don Otey. Birmingham: Menasha Ridge Press, 1980. This is a comprehensive guide to the streams of the Cumberland Plateau, Blue Ridge Mountains and eastern Piedmont regions of northern Georgia. We referred to it often when selecting canoe trips for the headwaters section.

Perilous Journeys: A History of Steamboating on the Chattahoochee, Apalachicola and Flint Rivers, 1828-1928 by Ed Mueller. Eufaula, Al.: Historic Chattahoochee Commission, 1990. Filled with interesting illustrations, maps and photographs, this book traces the history of vessel traffic on the Chattahoochee, Apalachicola and Flint rivers from the late 1700s up to the last days of steamboats on the rivers in the 1920s. It provided us with invaluable information when researching the history of the Lower Chattahoochee River Valley.

Southern Georgia Canoeing by Bob Sehlinger and Don Otey. Birmingham: Menasha Ridge Press, 1980. A companion volume to *Northern Georgia Canoeing* (see above), this guide explores the streams of Georgia's western Piedmont and Coastal Plain, with special chapters on the Okeefenokee Swamp and the Georgia seacoast.

Tailwater Trout in the South: An Angler's Guide by Jimmy Jacobs. Woodstock, Vt.: Backcountry Publishers, 1996. Jacobs is the authority on fishing the tailwater sections of rivers. This guide is a tailwater trout fishing tour through 9 states and 38 fisheries. It includes maps, tactics, techniques, secret spots and regulations. The book helped us understand why fishing is so good directly below Buford Dam.

The Beaches Are Moving: The Drowning of America's Shoreline by Wallace Kaufman and Orrin H. Pilkey, Jr. Durham, N. C.: Duke University Press, 1983. This book about why shorelines must migrate and why man is foolish to try and stop it has provided us with good information when researching numerous other projects. This time we focused on its information on barrier islands.

The Bluff at Fort Gaines, Georgia by James Edgar Coleman. Fort Gaines, Ga. 1997. We received this little self-published history from Mr. Coleman, a lifetime citizen of Fort Gaines, after our guidebook research was complete, but we wish we had acquired it sooner. There are chapters on botany, Indians, bridges, river traffic and Steam Boat Road to name a few.

The Federal Road Through Georgia, The Creek Nation and Alabama, 1806-1836 by Henry DeLeon Southerland, Jr and Jerry Elijah Brown. Tuscaloosa: The University of Alabama Press, 1989. Throughout our travels while researching this guidebook, we came upon historical markers about the Federal Road–a road that began as a horse path for mail carriers who traveled from middle Georgia to lower Alabama through Creek Indian territory. This is an account of the settlement of the region through travel experienced along that road. This is yet another book sponsored by the Historic Chattahoochee Commission in Eufaula, Alabama.

The Georgia Conservancy's Guide to the North Georgia Mountains edited by Fred Brown and Nell Jones. Atlanta: The Georgia Conservancy and Longstreet Press, 1990. We are a little partial to this detailed guidebook, organized by natural boundaries, that contains hiking and canoe trails, historic sites and natural history of the area. For this guidebook, we referred to information

from the Eastern Blue Ridge Mountain Section.

The Hiker's Guide to Florida by M. Timothy O'Keefe. Helena and Billings, Mont.: Falcon Press Publishing Co., 1993. This guide describes more than 130 hikes and walks throughout Florida from the Panhandle to the Keys. It contains trail information and detailed maps as well as tips on hiking with children and backcountry safety.

The Historical Markers of North Georgia by Kenneth W. Boyd. Atlanta: Cherokee Publishing Company, 1993. This book relates the complete text and the location of various state and non-state historical markers throughout 44 north Georgia counties.

The Natural Environments of Georgia by Charles H. Wharton. Atlanta: Georgia Department of Natural Resources, 1978. This is the definitive work on Georgia's natural environments. Though sometimes difficult to interpret, it contains invaluable information on everything from flora to fauna to underground aquifers, mountain rivers, river marshes and estuaries.

The Official Boy Scout Handbook by William Hillcourt. The Boy Scouts of America, 1979. We find there is always something worthwhile to learn or re-learn from this handbook. Tying knots, rowing techniques, fishing, tracking, the water cycle, how a compass works, orienting a map and camping are just a few of the many topics of instruction found here.

The Old Beloved Path: Daily Life Among the Indians of the Chattahoochee River Valley by William W. Winn. Eufaula, Ala.: The Historic Chattahoochee Commission, and Columbus, Ga.: The Columbus Museum, 1992. This very readable account of the Indians who inhabited the Chattahoochee River Valley for at least 12,000 years focuses on their daily life: food gathering and preparing, religion, social organization, education, family life and government. Winn, who is editorial page editor of the *Columbus Ledger Enquirer,* is a veritable wealth of knowledge not only on the Indians of this Valley but also the history of it in general (see page 138).

The Other Florida by Gloria Jahoda. Port Salerno, Fla.: Florida Classics Library, 1967. This personal exploration, mainly on unpaved back roads, tells the story of Florida's panhandle area through its history, natural beauty, wildlife, people and events. Of particular interest when researching this guidebook were the chapters, "The Garden of Eden," and "Dr. Gorrie's Wonderful Ice Machine."

The Story of Helen and Thereabouts by Matt Gedney.
Marietta, Ga.: Little Star Press, 1998. Gedney's second
book about the Chattahoochee headwaters area tells the
story of how Helen, a rather down-at-the-heels small
mountain town, became "Georgia's Alpine Village" and
the tourist mecca it is today. Most of the book, however,
is dedicated to the history and sights in the Helen area.

The Survival of the Bark Canoe by John McPhee.
Toronto: McGraw-Hill Ryerson, Ltd., 1975. Anyone who
has paddled a canoe will enjoy this McPhee classic,
which is a personal narrative about his 150-mile trip
through the Maine woods in a birch-bark canoe.

*This So Remote Frontier: The Chattahoochee Country of
Alabama and Georgia* by Mark Fretwell. Eufaula, Ala.:
Historic Chattahoochee Commission, 1990. This very
readable history relates the story of the area from
ancient Indian times through the Civil War period
through the men who explored it, settled it, farmed it
and fought on it. Reading this book emphasized to us
how important the Chattahoochee River was in the lives
of these people and, in general, how important rivers
were to the people who settled around them.

Tom Mann's 101 Favorite Fishin' Holes on Lake Eufaula
by Tom Mann. The title says what it is–favorite fishing
holes of an expert fisherman. This book is not widely
distributed, but it is available from ProMaps, P.O. Box
4008, Huntsville, AL 35815.

Travels by William Bartram. New York: Penguin Books,
1988. It seems no matter what project we are researching in the Southeast, we find inspiration in Bartram's
travelogue. First published in the United States in 1791,
it is still an interesting and valuable look at the
Chattahoochee Valley as well as other areas.

Water by Paola Jarvis. New York: Barnes and Noble,
Inc., by arrangement with DoGi, srl. 1997. Part of a
series of books called "How Science Works," this is a
wonderfully illustrated picture book for adults and children alike that was first produced in Italy. Each 2-page
spread covers a specific topic such as the water cycle,
shaping the landscape, springs, canals, water supply and
waste disposal and pollution.

Water, A Natural History by Alice Outwater. New York:
Basic Books, 1996. We loved this book. It is a highly
readable look at how the complex ecological system that

once kept American water clean has been randomly
broken down through the centuries to the point where
it can no longer do its job. The book is filled with wonderful and truly amazing facts–for instance, "a family of
beavers can build a 35-foot-long dam in a week."

Water, Water Everywhere by Melvin and Gilda Berger.
Nashville, Tenn.: Ideals Children's Books, 1995. Through
simple text and full-color illustrations, this children's
book about the water cycle traces the journey of water
as it travels from the oceans to the skies to rivers to our
homes. It explains things such as clouds, fog,
snowflakes, oceans, reservoirs and sewage treatment.

Publications

During our research we came across publications about
the Chattahoochee, rivers in general or the Chattahoochee
River Valley region. Pamphlets, posters, handbooks and
tabloid-sized weekly and monthly newspapers are just a
few of the publications we collected and added to our files.

Everyone Lives Downstream. U.S. Geological Survey,
Georgia District Office, Peachtree Business Center, 3039
Amwiler Road, Suite 130, Atlanta, GA 30360; 770/903-
9100; fax: 770/903-9199; website: www.ga.usgs.gov/
nawqa. This U.S. Geological Survey color poster depicts
water quality issues related to the urban development of
the upper Chattahoochee River watershed. There is
information on population growth, erosion and sedi-
mentation, urban runoff, phosphorus, sewage overflows,
waterborne pathogens, toxic metals, pesticides and PCBs
and chlordane in fish as well as a timeline showing
waste treatment, federal drinking-water legislation, federal stream-quality legislation, state and local legislation,
land use, resource management, population and dams
and water supply. Copies can be obtained by calling the
U.S.G.S. Georgia District Office.

Florida Sport Fishing Regulations Summary and the
Florida Hunting Handbook and Regulations Summary.
Florida Game and Fresh Water Fish Commission, 620
South Meridian Street, Farris Bryant Building,
Tallahassee, FL 32399-1600; 800/488-4676. Updated regularly, these free publications are distributed by the
Florida Game and Fresh Water Fish Commission. They
include such information as new regulations and
changes in laws, license fees, limited and unrestricted
fish consumption guidelines, hunting season dates, daily
and season bag limits, possession limits, open and

closed areas and legal methods of taking resident game birds and resident game mammals.

Florida State Parks ... the Real Florida. Department of Environmental Protection, Dept. - GS, 9225 West Fishbowl Drive, Homosassa, FL 34448; 904/628-5343. This free Florida State Park Guide was created to inform the public about the Florida park system and its resources. The detailed booklet features information on biking, hiking, camping, fishing, birding, canoeing, swimming and exploring in each one of Florida's numerous state parks.

Georgia Better Boating Handbook. Department of Natural Resources, Wildlife Resources Division, Law Enforcement Section, 2070 US 278, SE, Social Circle, GA 30279; 770/918-6408. This 84-page handbook is an excellent resource for boat operators and can be obtained at Corps of Engineers Resource Manger's Offices as well as through area Wildlife Resources Division offices. It contains information on types of boats, trailering boats, motors, life saving, navigational aids, locks and dams, mooring and knotting, what to do in an emergency and boating maintenance.

Georgia's Freshwater and Saltwater Sport Fishing Regulations. Department of Natural Resources, Wildlife Resources Division and Coastal Resources Division. Wildlife Resources Division, 2123 US 278, SE, Social Circle, GA 30279; 770/918-6418. Coastal Resources Division, One Conservation Way, Suite 300, Brunswick, GA 31520-8687; 912/264-7218. Georgia's fishing regulations are set by the Board of Natural Resources acting on the recommendations of DNR's fishery biologists and other field personnel. Laws are set by the General Assembly. This free publication has loads of information, including length limits, reciprocal agreements with bordering states, special trout stream regulations, consumption guidelines, license fees and requirements and seasons for freshwater fishing, shrimping, crabbing and shellfishing. The booklet is available at most bait-and-tack shops, marinas and Corps of Engineers Resource Manager's offices along the river. Call 800/ASK-FISH for licensing and fishing information.

Groundwater and Land Use in the Water Cycle. Geological and Natural History Survey, Wisconsin Department of Natural Resources, 1984. In this illustrated color poster, artist Jim McEvoy depicts the various ways water is used as it moves through its cycle. A lower half cutaway of the soil layers shows the direction of groundwater movement while an upper half illustration of farm, city and hilly landscape displays the human-induced impacts on groundwater as well as the natural process of the cycle.

How to Save a River: A Handbook for Citizen Action by David M. Bolling. This handbook gives precise information on what individuals and communities can do to save their rivers from being polluted. The publication can be ordered for about $18 from River Network, P.O. Box 8787, Portland, OR 97207-8787; 800/423-6746.

Influences of Environmental Settings on Aquatic Ecosystems in the Apalachicola-Chattahoochee-Flint River Basin. U.S. Geological Survey, Georgia District Office, Peachtree Business Center, 3039 Amwiler Road, Suite 130, Atlanta, GA 30360; 770/903-9100; fax: 770/903-9199; website: www.ga.usgs.gov/nawqa. This U.S.G.S. booklet is Water Resources Investigations Report 95-4278. Copies may be obtained by calling the U.S.G.S. Georgia District Office.

Lake Ecosystem. Department of Natural Resources, Wildlife Resources Division, Aquatic Education Program, 2070 US 278, SE, Social Circle, GA 30279; 770/918-6408. One side of this colorful poster-sized foldout is a cutaway illustration of a lake and the animals, plants and fish that live in it. The other side contains a key to the animals and plants as well as procedures for activities that middle school teachers can use when using the poster in their classroom.

LakeSide on Lanier. Alan Hope, Publisher/Editor, 1101 G2, Washington Street, #200, Gainesville, GA 30501; 770/287-1444. This friendly, small town-style newspaper contains articles on boating topics, events on Lanier and Lanier's history; Lanier fishing reports; profiles on people and places on Lanier; an outdoor cooking column and a dining guide among other things. It is distributed in more than 220 locations around the lake or can be delivered to homes and offices with a $12 subscription.

River Chat. Upper Chattahoochee Riverkeeper, 1900 Emery Street, Suite 450, Atlanta, GA 30318; 404/352-9828. This quarterly newsletter, published by the Upper Chattahoochee Riverkeeper, keeps members informed of all environmental issues involving the Chattahoochee River. Articles include updates on the Riverkeeper's legal action program, Adopt-A-Stream Network, headwaters project, membership activities and action alerts.

Southern Appalachia Fly Fishing Guide for the Chattahoochee River Tailwater. Dave Teffeteller, Ol'Fart Trading Company, Inc., P.O. Box 22, Decatur, GA 30031. This handy little fold-out pocket-size pamphlet is loaded with information about the tailwater: primary species found, recommended flies to use, mean water temperature, regulations and a map showing the river from Buford Dam to Peachtree Creek. Available through outfitters for $4.95.

The Chattooga Quarterly. Chattooga River Watershed Coalition, P.O. Box 2006, Clayton, GA 30525; 706/782-6097; fax: 706/782-6098; e-mail: crwc@iga.apc.org. This is a wonderful publication which truly reflects the purpose and goals of the Chattooga River Watershed Coalition, a nonprofit organization. Each issue is filled with well-written articles and photographs, written specifically for the publication or reprinted from others, which have a specific focus–for example, the many roles of the private sector in natural resource conservation, or public land acquisition.

The Shouter. Bill Lane, Publisher, P.O. Box 7194, Bainbridge GA 31718; 912/243-8617. This small, free tabloid-sized newspaper, geared to residents and visitors in Southwest Georgia, calls itself a "collection of encouraging news for and about Southwest Georgia." For instance, one issue included articles on the history of

Donalsonville and Seminole County, the Environmental Quality Incentives Program and the U.S. Department of Agriculture.

The St. George Island Times. A. William Irvine, Publisher, 312 Gander Street, St. George Island, FL 32328; 904/927-3225. This 25 cent monthly home-town publication is great for residents and tourists alike. It's filled with classifieds and feature-type material about the island, including nature, fishing and cooking columns, a listing of island activities, a service directory and a downtown directory. Subscriptions are $12 per year.

Wetlands for Clean Water: How Wetlands Protect Rivers, Lakes and Coastal Waters from Pollution. Clean Water Network and Natural Resources Defense Council, April 1997. This educational booklet explains how wetlands filter out pollutants from contaminated runoff through natural processes that improve the quality of water downstream and how conserving out nation's remaining wetlands provides one of the best means of defense against polluted runoff. The booklet was produced by the Clean Water Network, a national coalition of 900 organizations representing environmentalists, commercial and recreational fishermen, surfers, environmental justice advocates, faith communities, civic associations, boaters, labor unions and recreational enthusiasts, and the Natural Resources Defense Council, a nonprofit environmental membership organization of scientists and lawyers that works to protect the world's natural resources and improve the quality of the human environment. Copies of the report are $5. Contact the Clean Water Network, 1200 New York Avenue, N.W., Suite 400, Washington, DC 20005.

Woods 'n Water. Patricia O. Pillow, 1110 West Main Street, Perry, FL 32347; 904/584-3824; fax: 904/584-4217. This tabloid-sized monthly newspaper, published for about 20 years, is loaded with fishing and hunting information. It includes articles by professional fishing guides (including Lake Seminole's Jack Wingate and Carabelle's Bruce Johnson) and wildlife educators, fishing reports, classifieds and numerous photographs of proud hunters and fishermen with their big catch. Yearly subscriptions are $9.

OUTFITTERS AND FISHING GUIDES

Outfitters

An outfitter is not just someone who will sell you a new pair of hiking boots or rent you a canoe. An outfitter is someone who will get you into the out-of-doors with as little hassle as possible. Outfitters can set up your entire outdoor experience–equip you with the latest in gear, cater your meals, arrange your accommodations and personally guide you on your trip. They are skilled outdoorsmen who know about wildlife, plants, weather and what to do in an emergency. And they are environmentalists who care about the mountains, woods, rivers and streams that they work in and enjoy. Many outfitters are family-owned and operated–have been for years– and operate their businesses in a family-oriented atmosphere. We have found the following outfitters in the Chattahoochee River Valley to be ones who will help you get the most from a day in the out-of-doors.

APPALACHIAN OUTFITTERS. Ben and Dana LaChance, owners, P.O. Box 793, Hwy. 60 South, Dahlonega, GA 30533; 706/864-7117; reservations: 800/426-7117; fax: 706/864-4370; e-mail: appoutga@aol.com. Listed under "open" hours on their brochure is a line in capital letters which reads "ANY OTHER TIME WE CAN ACCOMMODATE YOU!" That pretty much sums up the philosophy of Ben and Dana LaChance who have owned and operated Appalachian Outfitters on the Chestatee River for nearly 20 years. Canoe, kayak and tubing trips down the Chestatee. Overnight camping available. Rates include all equipment, a return shuttle, and basic skills and safety instructions. Monthly canoe clinics teach and critique basic and whitewater canoeing skills, river dynamics and river safety.

BEAR PAW CANOE TRAILS. Rickie and Anna McAlpin, owners, 2100 Bear Paw Lane, Marianna, FL 32448; 850/482-4948; fax: 850/482-3141. The McAlpins believe that "you deserve an adventure," so they provide full-service float trips on the Chipola River that can include fresh water spring swimming, dry cave exploring and artifact hunting. Varying lengths of canoe and tubing trips with transportation included in rates. Overnight and 3-day camping trips available.

CANOE THE HOOCH OUTPOST & LODGING. Larry and Becky Portwood, owners, 46 Portwood Drive, Cleveland GA 30528; 706/865-5751; e-mail: rgport@stc.net. The Portwoods have just recently added lodging to their outpost services on the Upper Chattahoochee River just south of Helen. Varying lengths of canoe and rafting trips offered with all equipment, tax, parking and shuttle included in rates. Fully-equipped outpost cabin sleeps 2 to 6; nightly and weekly rental; swimming and fishing on premises.

HIGH COUNTRY OUTFITTERS, INC. Gerald Marshall and Bubba Sloan, owners. Three locations: 3906 Roswell Road, Atlanta, 404/814-0999; Perimeter Mall, Atlanta, 770/391-9657; Riverchase Galleria, Birmingham, 205/985-3215. Gerald and Bubba have been operating High Country for over 23 years and are an especially good source of information on canoeing, kayaking and sea kayaking. High Country Adventures offers whitewater rafting, mountain biking and caving trips; ropes courses, kayaking and rock climbing instruction and wilderness schools. Retail stores carry equipment for hiking, backpacking, rock and ice climbing, whitewater and ocean kayaking.

JEANNI'S JOURNEYS, INC. Jeanni McMillan, owner, 139 E. Gorrie, St. George Island, FL 32328; 850/927-3259; fax: 850/927-3831; e-mail: jjinc@digitalexp.com. Having camped in and explored the Panhandle area for nearly 25 years, McMillan is knowledgeable of its history and wildlife. Her guided trips are set up to share that knowledge with visitors. Kayak and canoe trips on Black Creek and Owl Creek near the Apalachicola River, St. Vincent Island and Little St. George Island. Boat trips, kids-only trips, fishing trips and seasonal marine experiences. Kayak, canoe, sailboat, fishing tackle, snorkel gear, boogie board and surfboard rentals. Reservations recommended.

MOUNTAIN SOUTH OUTFITTERS. Across from Brasstown Valley Resort. 706/379-2096; fax: 706/379-1258; e-mail: lanecom@stc.net. Not a small operation, Mountain South is a division of Wildwater, Ltd., one of the nation's largest outdoor outfitters. Guided services include whitewater rafting trips on the Ocoee, Nantahala and Chattooga rivers; trout and fly-fishing trips; hiking trips; pontoon cruises and mountain bike trips. Mountain bikes, fishing poles, waders and boots, fly rods and camping equipment rentals. Outdoor store with clothing, gear, fishing licenses, guidebooks and maps.

REI. Location #1: 1800 NE Expressway, Atlanta, GA 30329; 404/633-6508. Location #2: 1165 Perimeter Center West, Suite 200, Atlanta, GA 30346; 770/901-9200.

Loaded with paddling, cycling, backpacking, camping and climbing equipment, this consumer cooperative is Atlanta's largest and most complete outfitter retail store. Good inventory of rock climbing gear and a 12' 3" practice wall. Best selection of maps and outdoor books in town. Tents, backpacks and sleeping bags for rent.

WILDEWOOD OUTFITTERS. Ann Gale, owner. Outpost: Located on the Chattahoochee River at Duncan Bridge Road, P.O. Box 999, Helen, GA 30545; 706/865-4451 or 800/553-2715. Retail shop: Located 0.4 mile south of Helen on GA 75; 706/878-1700; fax: 706/878-1949. Anyone who has canoed the headwaters of the Chattahoochee River knows Ann Gale and Wildewood Outfitters. Opened in 1974, the outfitter was one of the first on the Upper Chattahoochee and is still one of the most respected. Guided kayak, canoe and raft trips. Kayak, canoe, raft and sit-on-top rentals. Rates include all equipment, shuttle and parking. Lunches offered with reservations; reservations recommended. Canoe and kayak instruction. Retail shop with paddling, hiking, climbing and biking gear.

Fishing Guides

The first time we fished West Point Lake, we went with Tommy Mike–and we were hooked on the fishing guide experience. Guides add immeasurable enjoyment to a first-time fishing trip or a first-time trip on a particular lake or river. They know where to go to catch the fish, they instruct, they provide the gear–and they tell great stories. They are also environmentalists who care about the out-of-doors and the quality of our rivers and lakes. Here are some top regional guides and guide services. For others, contact local marinas and bait shops.

EUFAULA GUIDE SERVICE. 515 N. Orange Street, Eufaula, AL 36027; 334/687-5389. This guide service on Lake Eufaula (Lake Walter F. George) specializes in fishing trips for Bass, Crappie and Hybrids. Guides provide instruction from fishing basics for beginning fishermen to tournament techniques.

DOWNRIVER FLY FISHING. Phil Sharpe, guide, Marietta, GA; 770/319-7012. Phil, who works at the Fish Hawk, is a part-time fishing guide, permitted by the National Park Service to guide on the Chattahoochee River through the CRNRA. Specializes in wade and float tube trips.

GLENN MORRISON'S LAKE LANIER GUIDE SERVICE.
Glenn Morrison, guide, 588 Woodland Lane, Lawrence-
ville, GA 30043; 770/962-8738; e-mail: HGMFish@aol.com;
website: www.georgiafishing.com. A diver as well as a
professional guide, Morrison knows Lake Lanier "from
the bottom up." Specializes in on-the-water fishing
instruction for Kentucky spotted bass and striper. Rates
include bait, tackle and gas.

HARLAN TRAMMELL. We logged a lot of river miles with
Harlan in his 16-foot jet-propelled jon boat while
researching this book. Harlan, the Upper Chattahoochee
Riverkeeper boat captain and a professional fishing
guide, knows where all the fish hide from the Chattahoochee headwaters to West Point Lake. Harlan can be
reached through the Upper Chattahoochee Riverkeeper
Office at 404/352-9828.

JACK WINGATE. Wingate's Lunker Lodge, 139 Wingate
Road, Bainbridge, GA 31717; 912/246-0658. One of the
most enjoyable days spent researching this guidebook
was exploring Lake Seminole with Jack Wingate. He knows
everything there is to know about the area– Indian history,
Civil War history, wildlife, flora, fishing–you name it. If
you can't get Wingate personally, book a fishing guide
through his Lunker Lodge–but it just won't be the same.

LAKE EUFAULA GUIDE SERVICE. 334/687-9595. This
guide service on Lake Eufaula (Lake Walter F. George)
has 3 full time fishing guides with over 100 years of
combined fishing experience. Fishing instruction, using
different techniques and a variety of baits. Full and half-
day trips for Largemouth Bass, Crappie and Hybrid.
Reservations recommended.

RIVER THROUGH ATLANTA GUIDES. Christopher Scalley,
guide, 710 Riverside Road, Roswell, GA 30075; 770/650-
8630; e-mail: ChatGhille@aol.com. The Orvis ad of fishing guides, Chris is a familiar sight on the Chattahoochee Tailrace where he specializes in fly-fishing for
trout. Full-day river trips and mountains stream trips
include equipment, photographs and refreshments. All
levels of fishing skills.

RON SAVAGE PROFESSIONAL GUIDE SERVICE. Ron
Savage, guide, P.O. Box 2602, LaGrange, GA 30241;
706/884-6232. After 17 years on West Point Lake, Savage
says he has a "Master's Degree in Experience." Rates
include baits, gas, oil, snacks, ice and drinks. Tackle
available.

SOUTHERN TROPHY SEEKERS. 770/929-1376. This trout
guide service, specializing in float tube fishing, claims to
have brought guided float fishing to the Chattahoochee
River. Full and half-day rates available for professionally
guided wade, boat and float tube fishing trips. Rates
include guide, tackle, deli lunch and soft drinks.

THE FISH HAWK. 279 Buckhead Avenue, NE, Atlanta,
GA 30305; 404/237-3473. Gary Merriman, owner of this
top Atlanta fishing store, is an excellent source of information on local fishing, including Lake Lanier and the
Chattahoochee River. He and his staff will be happy to
give you their recommendations on professional guides
for the area.

TOMMY MIKE GUIDE SERVICE. 4006 White Oak Lane,
LaGrange, GA 30240; 706/882-8187. Ask for West Point
Lake fishing guide Tommy Mike specifically. He's the
one you want to fish with. Rates include all tackle, bait,
life jackets, rain gear, lunch, drinks and snacks. Special
services include fishing
clinics, mini-tourna-
ments, fish cleaning and
packaging.

**TROUT, SHAW GUIDE
SERVICE.** Ralph F. Shaw,
232 Goshen Creek
Crossing, Clarkesville,
GA 30523; 706/947-1403
or 706/947-3434.
Trophy trout, private
streams, float trips
by canoe.

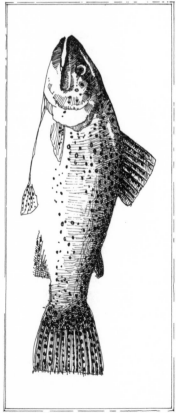

TROUT

MARINAS, BOAT RENTALS AND TOURS

Marinas

We define a marina as any facility on the water that has boat slips and fuel. We discovered that knowing a marina's location is particularly important when navigating the river between Columbus and Apalachicola Bay because there are few places a river traveler can pull up and get gas. In fact, there is no gas between Bagby State Park on Lake Walter F. George and Trails End Marina on Lake Seminole–that's nearly 70 miles. And there is no gas between Seminole Lodge, 2 miles north of the Jim Woodruff Dam, and Breakaway Marina, 4 miles north of Apalachicola–that's about 105 miles. We learned the hard way that a 2-mile walk to the nearest gas station in Blountstown, Florida, carrying a five-gallon gas tank is not a lot of fun.

The following are the marinas in order from Bagby State Park to Apalachicola Bay identified by their river mile marker number.

MILE MARKER 77 - George T. Bagby State Park (see page 205) located on the east bank of Lake Walter F. George about 0.5 mile up Sandy Creek on the south side of the creek.

MILE MARKER 8.2 - Trails End Marina and Campground (see page 238) on the east bank of the river on Lake Seminole.

MILE MARKER 2.5 - Seminole Lodge (see page 244) on the west bank of the main body of Lake Seminole.

Jim Woodruff Lock and Dam is Mile Marker 0 on the Chattahoochee River. Once you lock through and enter the Apalachicola River, the mile markers begin with Mile Marker 107.

JUST BELOW MILE MARKER 4 - Breakaway Marina, Motel and Restaurant (see page 310) on the west bank of the Apalachicola River.

BETWEEN MILE MARKER 3 AND 4 - Bay City Lodge (see page 310) on the west bank of the Apalachicola River.

Boat Rentals and Tours

We discovered that the best type of boat to use on the river depends on where you are and what you want to do. We've canoed and kayaked the upper portions of the river, traveled in motor boats from Columbus to Apalachicola, cruised along in large pontoons and sailed in Apalachicola Bay. Outfitters will rent you a canoe or kayak; but the following businesses give you another choice in enjoying the river–be it tubes, pontoons or guided cruises.

ALPINE TUBING. Located on US 75 just north of Helen at Robertstown. 707/878-TUBE; 800/882-4649. Tubing and rafting are a great way for young children to take their first trip down the Chattahoochee. Alpine Tubing offers a 3-mile float down the river through Helen. Free parking. Life vests, shuttle, changing rooms, snack bar, game room and group rates available.

APALACHICOLA ESTUARY TOURS. EcoVentures, Inc., P.O. Box 578, Apalachicola, FL 32329; 850/653-2593. These tours are a good way to cruise along the river and learn something about its ecology as well. Tours explore the shallow rivers, marshes and swamps of the Apalachicola estuary reserve or head across the bay to the barrier islands. Osprey: a 40-foot, all-weather, 32-person tour boat; 2-hour cruise. Pelican: a 24-foot, 6-passenger open skiff; charters only; 2 hour minimum. Boarding at dock on Water Street at Avenue G.

BENIGN BOAT WORKS, INC. 317 Water Street, Apalachicola, FL 32320; 850/653-8214. This company offers boaters numerous ways to travel up the Apalachicola. Canopied electric boats for tranquil exploring, Carolina Skiffs, creek boats, houseboats and pedal boats. Captains available for guided touring. Coolers, ice, binoculars and cell phones available.

CHATTAHOOCHEE OUTDOOR CENTER. 1990 Island Ford Parkway, Dunwoody, GA 30350; 770/395-6851. This is the place to go for a float down the Atlanta Hooch from Johnson Ferry to Paces Mill. Canoe and raft rentals and shuttle services. Rates are for 1 trip down the river and include life jackets, paddles and shuttles. Group rates available.

COOL RIVER TUBING COMPANY. Located at Edelweiss Drive on the river in Helen. 706/878-COOL; 800/896-4595. This tube rental for a 3.5 mile float down the

Chattahoochee River advertises as the longest tube ride in Helen. Free shuttle, parking and picnic tables. Changing rooms and restrooms available.

FLEA MARKET TUBING. Located on US 75, 1 mile north of Helen. 706/878-1082. This is where you get the hot pink tubes that float on the river through Helen. Tube rental for a short run and long run float trip. Free parking, changing rooms, shuttle bus, restrooms and picnic tables.

FOREVER RESORTS. Lake Lanier Houseboat Rentals, Holiday Marina, 6900 Holiday Road, Buford, GA 30518; 770/271-5705; reservations: 800/255-5561; fax: 602/968-5449. This is houseboat rental–only with the amenities of home. Four queen-size beds and queen-size sofa sleeper; linens, towels, pillows and blankets; cooking utensils and dishes; TV, VCR and stereo; waterslide.

GRASS SHACK BOAT RENTALS, INC. 6002 Holiday Road, Buford, GA 30518; 770/271-PLAY (7529). In business since 1991, Grass Shack introduced waverunners to Lake Lanier. These days they specialize in pontoons for family and small corporate outings. Rentals include waverunners, pontoons with gas grills, ski, deck and fishing boats, runabouts, skis, tubes and knee boards.

GOVERNOR STONE. Apalachicola Maritime Museum, Inc., P.O. Box 625, Apalachicola, FL 32329-0625; 850/653-8700. Sunk twice and beached twice by hurricanes, this beautiful 63-foot Gulf Coast Schooner built in 1877 is a National Historic Landmark and is considered the oldest operating sailing vessel of the American South. Operated and maintained by the nonprofit Apalachicola Maritime Museum, the historic vessel serves as a working museum and as the primary training vessel for a sail training program for youths, ages 12-18. Daily 2-hour sails (1pm,

4pm, 7pm) out of Apalachicola with reservations; group charters, special occasion arrangements such as weddings and reunions, extended excursions, sunset and moonlight cruises also available.

HARBOR LANDING. KSL Lake Lanier, 6950 Holiday Road, Lane Lanier Islands, GA 30518; 770/932-7255; fax: 770/932-7372. Located on Lake Lanier Islands, Harbor Landing has about any type of boat you would want for getting around the lake. Group boats for 35, 45 and 65 passengers with catering available; 10-person houseboats; island skimmers; 8-person pontoons, ski boats, sport boats and wave runners.

JEANNI'S JOURNEYS, INC. 139 E. Gorrie, St. George Island, FL 32328; 850/927-3259; fax: 850/927-3831; e-mail: jjinc@digitalexp.com. Besides kayaks and canoes, outfitter Jeanni McMillan (see page 333) also rents sailboats, snorkel gear, boogie boards and surfboards. Reservations recommended.

JUBILEE PADDLEWHEEL RIVERBOAT TOURS. Apalachicola, FL; 850/653-9502. This replica of a 50-foot turn-of-the-century paddlewheeler tours the Apalachicola waterfront as well as the upriver sloughs and channels. Reservations required for 1.5-hour tour. Departs from the Apalachicola River docks at 329 Water Street.

THE CHATTAHOOCHEE PRINCESS RIVERBOAT. 1000 Bay Street, Columbus, GA 31901; 706/324-4499 or 800/934-2628. This authentic 1880s-era riverboat paddles along the river below the Dillingham Street Bridge. Friday and Saturday night dinner and party cruises; Saturday and Sunday afternoon river rides. Catering available. Reservations required for cruises.

DAMS, LOCKS AND BRIDGES

Dams

Sixteen dams harness the power of the Chattahoochee as it rolls towards Apalachicola Bay–9 of those in the Columbus area alone. If you are navigating down the river, you must portage around the first 13 dams and lock through the last 3. Once through the last lock, the Chattahoochee turns into the Apalachicola and runs free for 107 miles to the Bay.

NORA MILL DAM. Built in 1824, the privately owned Nora Mill Dam (see page 26) continues to power an operating gristmill. It crosses the Chattahoochee 1 mile below Helen.

BUFORD DAM. Completed in 1956, Buford Dam (see page 52) is operated by the U.S. Army Corps of Engineers. It impounds Lake Lanier and produces hydroelectric power. The dam is located on Lanier's downstream end.

MORGAN FALLS DAM. Completed in 1904 and built to produce Atlanta's first hydroelectric power, Morgan Falls Dam (see page 87) played an important role in the city's industrial growth. Owned by Georgia Power, it impounds Bull Sluice Lake. The dam crosses the Chattahoochee between Mile Marker 313 and 312.

WEST POINT DAM. Completed in 1974, the U.S. Army Corps of Engineers designed West Point Dam (see page 149) to permit construction of a navigation lock for the day vessels would navigate the Chattahoochee all the way to Atlanta. The dam impounds West Point Lake and produces hydroelectric power. It is located on the downstream end of West Point Lake.

LANGDALE DAM. Built by the West Point Manufacturing Company in 1908, Langdale Dam (see page 185) provided power for the company's textile plant. Today, it is owned by Georgia Power and produces hydroelectric power. The dam is located 4 miles south of West Point, Georgia.

CROW HOP DAM. Constructed sometime after the completion of Riverview Dam (below), Crow Hop Dam (see page 186) was built to push the Chattahoochee's water toward the western side of the channel to provide more water for Riverview Dam generators. The small dam,

owned by Georgia Power, is located right above Riverview Dam.

RIVERVIEW DAM. Built in 1918, Riverview Dam (see page 187) originally powered several West Point textile mills. Today, it produces hydroelectric power for Georgia Power. It is located one river mile downstream of Langdale Dam, directly behind Riverview Mill.

BARTLETTS FERRY DAM. This 1926 dam (see page 188) was built to provide hydroelectric power for the City of Columbus. Owned by Georgia Power, it impounds Lake Harding. The dam is located on the downstream end of Lake Harding, about 17 miles north of Columbus.

GOAT ROCK DAM. Completed in 1912, Goat Rock Dam (see page 189) has changed very little since it was first constructed. Owned by Georgia Power, it produces hydroelectric power and impounds Goat Rock Lake. It is located on the downstream end of Goat Rock Lake, about 9 miles north of Columbus.

OLIVER DAM. Completed in 1959 by Georgia Power, Oliver Dam (see page 190) produces hydroelectric power and impounds Lake Oliver. It is located on the downstream end of Lake Oliver in north Columbus on the site of a 19th-century textile mill.

NORTH HIGHLANDS DAM. Built in 1899, North Highlands Dam (see page 191) was the first large dam in the South and powered the Bibb Cotton Mill in Columbus. Today, owned by Georgia Power, it produces hydroelectric power and impounds Bibb Pond. The dam crosses the river in the Bibb City area of Columbus, 1 mile south of Oliver Dam.

CITY MILLS AND DAM. Built by the City Mills Company in 1907, City Mills and Dam (see page 192), a once prosperous gristmill, now lies abandoned. The dam crosses the river at 18th Street in downtown Columbus.

EAGLE & PHENIX MILLS AND DAM. This 1866 dam (see page 193), the second oldest in this area, once powered a textile mill but is now abandoned. It crosses the river right above the Dillingham Street Bridge in downtown Columbus.

LAKE WALTER F. GEORGE LOCK AND DAM. The most northern lock and dam constructed on the Chattahoochee by the U.S. Army Corps of Engineers,

Walter F. George Lock and Dam (see page 225) was completed in 1963 and impounds Lake Walter F. George, produces hydroelectric power and allows navigation of the river. It is located on the downstream end of Lake Walter F. George.

GEORGE W. ANDREWS LOCK AND DAM. Operational since 1963, George W. Andrews Lock and Dam (see page 226) impounds Lake Andrews, produces hydroelectric power and allows navigation of the Chattahoochee. It is operated by the U.S. Army Corps of Engineers and is located on the downstream end of Lake Andrews.

JIM WOODRUFF LOCK AND DAM. Completed in 1957 by the U.S. Army Corps of Engineers, Jim Woodruff Lock and Dam (see page 245) impounds Lake Seminole, produces hydroelectric power and allows navigation of the Chatta-hoochee. It is the southernmost dam on the river and is located on the downstream end of Lake Seminole.

Locks

One of the most interesting and anticipated experiences traveling up or down the lower Chattahoochee is that of going through the locks. Three dams on the Chattahoochee River–Walter F. George, George W. Andrews and Jim Woodruff–have navigation locks that allow recreational as well as commercial boats to travel both upstream and downstream. The locks are necessary to transfer boats from one water level to another. "Locking through" can cause anxiety the first time you do it, but it is relatively easy if you are prepared and follow the proper procedure.

1. Signal the lockmaster as you approach by calling on VHF radio Channel 16 or by cell phone (lockmaster numbers listed below) or by using the ropes at the upstream or downstream sides of the dam to sound a horn. A VHF radio or cell phone is good to have when going through the locks. We had neither the first time we locked through the Woodruff Dam on Lake Seminole. Most approach ropes are on the end of the approach corridor farthest away from the dam gate, but this one is extremely close to the gate, and we could not reach it in the choppy water. We had to go back two miles to Seminole Lodge to call the lockmaster to tell him we wanted to come through.

2. The lockmaster will signal you through the lock via traffic lights or horn blasts. A flashing red light means

"do not enter," a flashing amber light means "approach slowly" and a flashing green light means "enter." A long horn blast means "enter the lock" and a short horn blast means "leave the lock."

3. Pay attention to instructions and signals from lock attendants as you enter the lock; they will direct you to one of the floating locks. Be particularly cautious if you are entering with a lot of other boats or a very large vessel.

4. Have at least one 150-foot mooring line ready. On all three Chattahoochee River locks, boat passengers do the mooring. These passengers should wear PFDs. Tie the line to the floating lock and shut off the motor.

5. The lowering and lifting process is fairly slow. Sometimes you will not even feel it. But the noises of the floating locks as they do their job is eerie–especially in the Walter F. George Lock, which is the largest and very hollow.

6. When the process is completed, the lock gates will open. You are now on the same level as the river. Release your lines and proceed slowly from the lock.

WALTER F. GEORGE LOCK AND DAM. This 82' x 450' lock on Lake Walter F. George drops, or lifts, passengers 88 feet between the lake level and the riverbed below the dam (see page 225). Open 7 days a week, 8am-4pm. 912/768-2032.

GEORGE W. ANDREWS LOCK AND DAM. This lock on Lake George W. Andrews is the same size as the Walter F. George Lock (82' x 450'), but the lift/drop through the lock is only 25 feet (see page 226). Open 7 days a week, 24 hours a day. 912/723-3482.

JIM WOODRUFF LOCK AND DAM. This lock on Lake Seminole is also 82' x 450' but it has a lift/drop of 33 feet (see page 245). Open 7 days a week, 24 hours a day. 904/663-4692.

Bridges

Bridging the Chattahoochee has always been a part of the river's history.

For thousands of years, shoals or slow-moving, wadable water were the choice of animals and Indians for fording the river. Much later, during the Civil War, crossing the river was part of the strategic game played by Union and Confederate troops as they tried to outmaneuver each other in the bloody battles for Atlanta (see page 105). Slave Horace King (see page 182) earned his freedom by building a bridge across the Chattahoochee River in a given amount of time. He went on to become a master builder of covered bridges throughout the South.

Several bridges stare hauntingly at the river, long past their heyday–the rusted half-structure of Jones Bridge in the Chattahoochee River National Recreation Area (see page 104), and the old abandoned railroad bridge, just upriver from the GA 208 Bridge, where teenagers have daringly jumped into the waters below for generations– to name a few.

Other bridges have long since disappeared–burned, or torn down in the name of progress.

Today, more than 75 bridges span the Chattahoochee River from its headwaters to Apalachicola Bay. We have traveled over most of them and looked up from the river at all of them. The most northern bridge to span the river is actually a wooden foot bridge that crosses the narrow Chattahoochee stream right before it joins Little Horse Trough Creek directly below Horse Trough Falls (see page 20). The most southern bridge is the beautiful John Gorrie Memorial Bridge which symbolizes the end of the river and the beginning of Apalachicola Bay.

The following is a list of the major highway and railroad bridges that cross the river with their distance in river miles from ground zero, the Headwaters at Chattahoochee Gap, as well as the distance from one bridge to the next.

	Total River Miles	Approx. Distance To Next Bridge
HEADWATERS AT CHATTAHOOCHEE GAP	0.00	2.6
FS 44	2.6	7.56
BRIDGE AT ROBERTSTOWN	9.16	1.0
HAMBY STREET BRIDGE AT HELEN	10.16	0.47
CHATTAHOOCHEE [1] RIVER BRIDGE	10.63	1.89
BRIDGE AT NACOOCHEE [2]	12.52	0.378
GA 75 BRIDGE [3]	12.89	1.51
NEWS BRIDGE [4]	14.4	6.8
GA 255 BRIDGE	21.2	4.15
SIDNEY LANIER BRIDGE	25.35	3.78
DUNCAN BRIDGE [5]	29.13	9.82
BELTON BRIDGE	38.95	3.0
LULA BRIDGE	41.95	8.5
CLARK BRIDGE	50.45	4.34
LONGSTREET BRIDGE	54.79	2.64
THOMPSON BRIDGE	57.43	3.0
LANIER BRIDGE	60.43	7.84
BROWNS BRIDGE	68.27	12.75
BUFORD DAM AND BRIDGE	81.02	2.74
GA 20 BRIDGE	83.76	2.26
SETTLES BRIDGE	86.02	3.78

[1] Chattahoochee River Bridge in Helen
The town of Helen and White County dedicated the bridge to Georgia Governor E. D. Rivers in 1938.

[2] Bridge at Nacoochee
This bridge is located just north of GA 385 and south of Nora Mill. A plaque on the bridge is inscribed, "In memory of Lamartine Griffin Hardman M.D., LLD, Governor of Georgia, 1927-1931. Beautiful Nacoochee Valley visited by Hernando DeSoto 1540," and carries this verse: "Child of the Chattahoochee / Hid in the hills afar! / Beautiful Nacoochee / Vale of the evening star. / Hushed in the mountain shadows / with the May dew on her breasts, / Her breath is the breath of meadows / and her very name sighs 'rest!' / The voice of a loved one calling / The feet that have wandered far; / Come, for the night is falling! / Rest with the evening star." 1941

[3] GA 75 Bridge
This bridge has a plaque with the same inscription as the Nacoochee Bridge just north.

[4] News Bridge
Locals leap into a swimming hole from this wood-and-metal girder bridge located on Bottoms Road in Nacoochee Valley.

[5] Duncan Bridge
This old iron bridge spans the river 50 yards upstream from Duncan Bridge.

	Total River Miles	Approx. Distance To Next Bridge
LITTLES FERRY BRIDGE	89.80	4.72
ABBOTTS BRIDGE	94.52	1.32
MCCLURE BRIDGE	95.84	3.0
MEDLOCK BRIDGE	98.84	5.29
HOLCOMB BRIDGE	104.13	6.99
GA 400 BRIDGE	111.12	1.13
ROSWELL ROAD BRIDGE	112.25	6.8
JOHNSON FERRY BRIDGE	119.05	4.06
I-285 BRIDGE	123.11	1.98
I-75 BRIDGE	125.09	7.56
COBB PARKWAY BRIDGE	132.65	0.567
PACES FERRY ROAD BRIDGE	133.21	2.64
MARIETTA BOULEVARD BRIDGE	135.85	0.378
SEABOARD RAILROAD BRIDGE	136.23	1.22
SOUTH COBB DRIVE BRIDGE	137.45	0.567
RAILROAD BRIDGE	138.02	0.378
I-285 BRIDGE	138.40	1.13
BANKHEAD HWY BRIDGE	139.53	1.89
BARRETTS BRIDGE	141.42	0.756
I-20 BRIDGE	142.176	3.40
CAMP CREEK PARKWAY BRIDGE	145.57	4.53

6 US 29 Bridge in West Point
This is the John C. Barrow Bridge built in 1977. The old metal bridge visible upstream was built by the Virginia Bridge and Iron Company of Roanoke, Virginia, in 1914.

7 US 80 Bridge
From this bridge, built in 1985, you can look upstream at the Oliver Dam and downstream to the North Highland Dam, built in 1899 to power the Bibb Cotton Mill.

8 Dillingham Street Bridge in Columbus
A plaque tells us that this bridge was erected between 1910 and 1912; it's 790 feet long and 44 feet wide, made of concrete with steel arches in 128 foot spans. Rhodes Browne was mayor when the bridge was built; W. E. Margru was chairman of the bridge committee and B. H. Hardaway was contractor.

9 GA 208 Bridge
Located near the town of Omaha, Georgia, this bridge was built in 1987 and named for Joseph Wilson Smith.

	Total River Miles	Approx. Distance To Next Bridge
GA 166 Bridge	150.10	4.53
Campbellton Rd Bridge	154.63	20.97
Old Metal Bridge	175.60	0.945
GA 16 Bridge	176.54	24.94
US 27 Bridge At Franklin	201.48	14.83
GA 219 Bridge	216.31	8.97
Railroad Bridge	225.28	1.51
GA 109 Bridge At La Grange	226.79	11.62
US 29 Bridge [6] In West Point	238.41	1.60
I-85 Bridge In The Valley	240.01	32.13
US 80 Bridge [7]	272.14	2.17
Railroad Bridge	274.31	0.378
14th Street Bridge In Columbus	274.68	0.661
Dillingham Street [8] Bridge	275.34	0.661
James Oglethorpe Bridge, US 27	276.01	14.4
General Eddy Hwy Bridge, Ft. Benning	290.41	23.9
Seaboard Coastline Bridge	314.31	0.5
GA 208 Bridge [9]	314.81	21.8
Richard Russell [10] Bridge	336.61	0.6

[10] Richard Russell Bridge

Built in 1961, this bridge, part of US 82, crosses the river between Eufaula, Alabama, and Georgetown, Georgia. It bears the name of Richard Russell who was speaker of the Georgia House of Representatives, Governor of Georgia and United States Senator.

[11] US 90 Bridge

Known as the "Victory Bridge," this is the first bridge on the Apalachicola. It crosses the river at Chattahoochee, Florida. The old Works Progress Administration Bridge, built in the 1930s during the Roosevelt administration, is visible just downstream.

	Total River Miles	Approx. Distance To Next Bridge
CENTRAL OF GEORGIA RAILROAD BRIDGE	337.21	20.8
GA 37 BRIDGE IN FORT GAINES	358.01	24.2
CENTRAL OF GEORGIA RAILROAD BRIDGE	382.21	0.3
GA 62 BRIDGE	382.51	13.4
SEABOARD COASTLINE RAILROAD BRIDGE	395.91	0.1
US 84 BRIDGE	396.01	11.5
HERMAN TALMADGE BRIDGE	407.51	24.2
US 90 BRIDGE [11]	431.71	0.8
LOUISVILLE & NASHVILLE RAILROAD BRIDGE	432.51	4.9
I-10 BRIDGE	437.41	20.6
CALHOUN BRIDGE	458.01	74.9
APALACHICOLA NORTHERN RAILROAD BRIDGE	532.91	4.5
JOHN GORRIE MEMORIAL BRIDGE, US 98	537.41	0.0

THE COMMON SNAPPING TURTLE

INDEX